DATE DUE

MAR 9 1994			

DEMCO 38-297

SCANDINAVIAN MODERN DESIGN 1880-1980

SCANDINAVIAN MODERN DESIGN 1880-1980

COOPER-HEWITT MUSEUM
The Smithsonian Institution's National Museum of Design, New York

DAVID REVERE McFADDEN, GENERAL EDITOR
Curator of Decorative Arts

HARRY N. ABRAMS, INC., PUBLISHERS, NEW YORK

This catalogue was made possible by a grant from the National Endowment for the Arts in association with the "Scandinavian Modern: 1880–1980" exhibition, a project of SCANDINAVIA TODAY, at Cooper-Hewitt Museum, The Smithsonian Institution's National Museum of Design.

Presentation of this exhibition was made possible in part by Helsingin Sanomat, Finland; Wartsila/Arabia, Finland; Kansallis-Osake-Pankki Bank, Finland; Union Bank of Finland, Ltd.; Pohjola Group of Insurance Companies, Finland; CITIBANK/CITICORP; and the New York Chapter of The American-Scandinavian Foundation.

SCANDINAVIA TODAY, an American celebration of contemporary Scandinavian culture, is sponsored and administered by The American-Scandinavian Foundation, and made possible by support from Volvo, Atlantic Richfield Company, the National Endowment for the Humanities, and the National Endowment for the Arts.

SCANDINAVIA TODAY is organized with the cooperation of the Governments of Denmark, Finland, Iceland, Norway, and Sweden through the Secretariat for Nordic Cultural Cooperation and with the aid of a grant from the Nordic Council of Ministers.

SAS, Finnair, and Icelandair are the official carriers for SCANDINAVIA TODAY.

Editor: Margaret Donovan

Designers: Patrick Cunningham, Steven Schoenfelder

Library of Congress Cataloging in Publication Data
Main entry under title:
Scandinavian modern design, 1880–1980.
  Catalogue of an exhibition at Cooper-Hewitt Museum,
New York, Sept. 14, 1982–Jan. 2, 1983; Minnesota
Museum of Art, Landmark Center, St. Paul, Feb. 27–Apr. 24,
1983; Renwick Gallery, Washington, D.C., July 8–Oct. 10,
1983.
  Bibliography: p.274
  Includes index.
  1. Design—Scandinavia—History—19th century—
Exhibitions. 2. Design—Scandinavia—History—20th
century—Exhibitions. I. McFadden, David Revere.
II. Cooper-Hewitt Museum. III. Minnesota Museum of Art.
IV. Renwick Gallery.
NK1457.S35 1982   745.4'4948   82-8899
ISBN 0-8109-1643-6

CONTENTS

FOREWORDS 7
Lisa Taylor, Brooke Lappin, Pehr G. Gyllenhammar and
Robert O. Anderson

SCANDINAVIAN MODERN: A CENTURY IN PROFILE 11
David Revere McFadden

UNITY AND DIVERSITY IN SCANDINAVIAN DESIGN 25
Ulf Hård af Segerstad

NORDIC DESIGN: A MULTITUDE OF VOICES 37
Helena Dählbeck Lutteman

VIKING REVIVAL AND ART NOUVEAU:
TRADITIONS OF EXCELLENCE 47
Elisabet Stavenow-Hidemark

THE EARLY 20TH CENTURY: DESIGN IN TRANSITION 87
Erik Lassen

THE 1930S: A NEW FUNCTION FOR DESIGN 107
Jarno Peltonen

MID-CENTURY: YEARS OF INTERNATIONAL TRIUMPH 131
Peter Anker

CONTEMPORARY DESIGN: CHALLENGE AND RENEWAL 209
Jan-Lauritz Opstad

DESIGN TODAY: NATIONAL POINTS OF VIEW 253
Jens Bernsen (Denmark), Tapio Periäinen (Finland),
Stefán Snaebjörnsson (Iceland), Rolf Himberg-Larsen (Norway),
Lennart Lindkvist (Sweden)

BIOGRAPHICAL NOTES 261
SELECTED BIBLIOGRAPHY 274
ACKNOWLEDGMENTS 279
INDEX 281
PHOTO CREDITS 287

FOREWORDS

In its role as The Smithsonian Institution's National Museum of Design, the Cooper-Hewitt Museum is committed to documenting and interpreting design on a global basis and to fostering appreciation of the challenges that have confronted designers through the ages. Thus, it is appropriate that the Museum participate in the international SCANDINAVIA TODAY program by organizing a major exhibition tracing the history of modern design in Denmark, Finland, Iceland, Norway, and Sweden.

In the course of the past century, geographical and cultural barriers, which previously had limited the influence of design, have virtually disappeared, and innovative ideas now spawn design traditions in an astonishingly short period of time. The international influence of Scandinavian design is a reflection of these changes. With dedication and determination, the Scandinavian countries have created designs that speak with eloquence and sensitivity to the concerns of modern man. "Scandinavian Modern: 1880–1980" is an opportunity to acknowledge these contributions and to reassess current ideas about design.

This exhibition could not have become a reality without the spirit of cooperation we have enjoyed in our negotiations with the museum directors and their staff members in each of the five Scandinavian countries. They have extended us every courtesy in this major international effort. We acknowledge a great debt to the Nordic Council of Ministers and the Secretariat for Nordic Cultural Cooperation. Their facilitation of international contacts was of critical importance in the realization of this exhibition. The American-Scandinavian Foundation, the sponsor and administrator of the SCANDINAVIA TODAY program, has conscientiously given of its expertise, advice, and guidance. We trust that this exhibition will realize the program's goals—to nurture the cultural, social, and intellectual ties that exist between the United States and the Scandinavian countries. American museums and lenders have also become a part of this exhibition; to them and to the many individuals who have contributed to the planning and implementation of this exhibition, we offer our sincere appreciation.

It is deeply gratifying to welcome "Scandinavian Modern: 1880–1980" to the Cooper-Hewitt Museum, and in so doing to embrace the spirit of international cooperation that is the basis of our Museum's mandate.

Lisa Taylor
Director, Cooper-Hewitt Museum,
The Smithsonian Institution's
National Museum of Design

Nils Landberg. *Glasses from the* Tulip *series*, 1957 (no. 169)

In 1976 the National Endowment for the Humanities endorsed the concept of a six-part series of TODAY programs designed to explore and pay tribute to the cultural and intellectual achievements of foreign neighbors. The series opened in 1977 with CANADA TODAY and, with the assistance of the National Endowment for the Arts, continued over the next four years to honor Mexico, Japan, Belgium, and Egypt. SCANDINAVIA TODAY, celebrating an entire region of the world, is the most ambitious and challenging of the TODAY programs, requiring the full cooperation of the Governments and private and public institutions of six sovereign nations—Denmark, Finland, Iceland, Norway, Sweden, and the United States.

SCANDINAVIA TODAY is an enthusiastic confirmation of the spirit of international cooperation, requiring the combined energies of hundreds of cultural and governmental leaders. The American sponsor for SCANDINAVIA TODAY is The American-Scandinavian Foundation, a private institution founded in 1910 to advance cultural and intellectual relations between the United States and the Scandinavian countries. On the Nordic side, the Nordic Council of Ministers, a supranational organization, administered this collaborative effort through its Secretariat for Nordic Cultural Cooperation.

It is impossible to thank all who contributed to this extraordinary effort, but several deserve special recognition. Dr. Patricia McFate, who counseled all six of the TODAY programs as Deputy Chairman for the National Endowment for the Humanities, joined The American-Scandinavian Foundation in 1981 and provided policy leadership for all aspects of the SCANDINAVIA TODAY program; Carl Tomas Edam, Secretary General, SCANDINAVIA TODAY, Nordic Council of Ministers, administered the program on the Nordic side with wit, wisdom, and diplomacy; and the national staff of SCANDINAVIA TODAY—Bruce Kellerhouse, Albina De Meio, Kathleen Madden, and Larry Clark—shared talents and expertise that were invaluable in the day-to-day coordination of the program.

To all the others who gave so generously of their time and talent, we extend our profound gratitude. The validity of SCANDINAVIA TODAY speaks through the exceptional quality of its multifaceted programs, of which "Scandinavian Modern: 1880–1980" is an excellent example.

The American-Scandinavian Foundation, the five Nordic Governments, the Nordic Council of Ministers, and more than two hundred American cultural institutions welcome the American public to this in-depth investigation and celebration of contemporary Scandinavian culture.

Brooke Lappin
National Program Director, SCANDINAVIA TODAY

As national corporate sponsors of SCANDINAVIA TODAY, Volvo and Atlantic Richfield Company are pleased to represent the corporate community, which plays such an active part in cultural relations between the Nordic countries and the United States. Through our sponsorship of SCANDINAVIA TODAY, which brings an outstanding variety of Scandinavian art exhibitions, music, film, theater and dance programs, lectures and symposia to the United States, we confirm the vital links that join our nations. The publication *Scandinavian Modern Design 1880–1980,* which has resulted from this ambitious and successful program, treats many issues with which we feel great affinity.

Design issues affect not only the individual artists, whose work embodies their own perception and understanding, but also the audience for whom the designs are ultimately intended. Thus, the creative process is of interest to consumer and producer alike, united in a quest for quality in their lives and their environment. Scandinavian design over the past century, as documented in the exhibition "Scandinavian Modern: 1880–1980," eloquently addresses mutual concerns that transcend national boundaries. The de-

signs themselves serve as pertinent reminders of our needs, our aspirations, and our willing acceptance of change.

SCANDINAVIA TODAY provides a unique opportunity for Volvo and Atlantic Richfield Company to enhance international communication on cultural, social, and intellectual levels. The effort to create a new forum of mutual understanding between nations lies at the foundation of the SCANDINAVIA TODAY program.

We share our pride in this project with all who participate in SCANDINAVIA TODAY. We at Volvo and Atlantic Richfield Company consider such programs a vital and necessary part of our corporate life and a special contribution to our own international audience.

Pehr G. Gyllenhammar
Managing Director and Chief Executive Officer of the Volvo Group

Robert O. Anderson
Chairman, Atlantic Richfield Company

SCANDINAVIAN MODERN:
A CENTURY IN PROFILE

DAVID REVERE McFADDEN
Curator of Decorative Arts, Cooper-Hewitt Museum

Poul Henningsen. *Lamp*, 1958 (no. 202)

In these remote countries a powerful art movement is forcing its way into the general art development of Europe and . . . will undoubtedly, ere long, claim greater public attention.

—*The Studio*, London, 1901

A new spirit of confidence in the future of Scandinavian design was expressed in these words from a review of the decorative arts shown at the Exposition Universelle of 1900 in Paris. The exhibition was an international arena of design that presented the arts and industries of the emerging century to a large audience of visitors, critics, and artists. Scandinavian designs—textiles and ceramics, furniture and metalwork—received particular notice there; among the most outstanding were the bold narrative textiles of Gerhard Munthe of Norway, the brilliant porcelains from the Rörstrand factory in Sweden, and the dramatic, virile architecture of the Finnish pavilion by Herman Gesellius, Armas Lindgren, and Eliel Saarinen. The designs embodied a recent revitalization of the arts in Scandinavia as well as the challenge of the coming decades. In addition, they reflected significant changes in the public posture of Scandinavian design, particularly the radical shift from provincial isolation to self-assertiveness in an international design setting.

A century of intense design activity had commenced about 1880 in the vast and diverse geographic region encompassing   11

Denmark, Finland, Iceland, Norway, and Sweden. From Scandinavia's variegated matrix of cultures, languages, traditions, and politics there emerged a multifaceted design philosophy that became a major international influence. Each country within Scandinavia played a significant role in the formation of a modern tradition, and each responded to the challenges of the modern world in a distinctive manner. All the countries recognized social equality, industrialization, and urbanization as major factors of modern life. Yet, these factors and their impact on the arts and crafts were encountered differently in each country, giving a special identity to the design traditions of each. A dilemma thus confronts attempts to survey the design history of Scandinavia as a whole: the separate identities of the nations proceed along separate lines of development.

By the middle of the twentieth century, however, the design traditions of Scandinavia had become known as a "style." And, furthermore, the impact on international design of this style was such that it cannot be undervalued. Thus, the history of Scandinavian design suggests that there are unifying features within the tradition that allowed such a generalization. These common characteristics can be charted externally, by referring to the designs themselves, as well as internally, by examining the way the designs were regarded. "Scandinavian Modern: 1880–1980" is an effort to provide a chronological survey of both internal and external developments in the history of Scandinavian design. It ranges from early "modern" ideas of the arts and crafts through the decades of international ascendancy in the field and concludes with a look at design principles and practices in the last twenty years.

Twenty-five years ago a large number of Americans could claim familiarity with the term "Scandinavian Design" and, to exemplify the term, could point to at least one of the domestic furnishings—ceramics, glass, textiles, furniture—that were then prominently featured in department stores and popular magazines. Scandinavian Design defined a unity comprising a variety of products, artists, factories, and materials. During the 1950s, the "style" attracted an almost unprecedented following of critics and consumers. The primary virtue ascribed to Scandinavian objects was an overall design excellence, aesthetically and functionally. Although many could recognize the Scandinavian Design style, few could connect the image of the 1950s with developments in Scandinavia prior

Danish designs at the Milan Triennale of 1960

to that date. An even smaller segment of the American population could today claim familiarity with developments in Scandinavian design subsequent to midcentury. In particular, the period from 1960 to the present, because of our proximity in time, appears even more diversified than the early twentieth century.

To review this century of Scandinavian design requires the distillation of a vast amount of historical information about each country. The complexities of each tradition cannot be simplified without limiting the field to major issues, individuals, factories, trends, and effects. Following these introductory essays is a chronological overview of design in Scandinavia in which design aesthetics are compared and contrasted. In this approach, common directions lend unity to the design profile, while the variety of Scandinavian responses to the challenges and requirements of history is also acknowledged. Design in each period speaks of ideals and realities; thus, the way in which history is shaped by objects is confirmed.

Scandinavian design is also a story of continuity over time. Basic and inherent characteristics shared among countries appear and reappear throughout this chronology. Isolation of these "internal" factors defining a tradition is a formidable challenge. A substantial literature of design history and criticism has treated the artistic and social context of Scandinavian design, but most of this material has been published only within Scandinavia. Other works, particularly those in English, have conscientiously attempted to reduce a multitude of ideas, individuals, and movements to a series of comprehensible, generalized principles: over the past century, Scandinavian design has been acclaimed both for its sophisticated grace and its unmannered charm, for its socially determined philosophy and its celebration of purely visual beauty, for its innovative boldness and its conservative traditions. The apparent contradictions in these attributes—each of which can be supported by actual objects—indicate the richness and variety of the tradition. Yet, despite previous efforts, principles of design that may be shared by all of the countries at one time or another remain only partially revealed. How then to approach questions of "Scandinavian" aesthetics?

During the past century, Scandinavian designers have participated in a number of important exhibitions, some international in scope and effect and others of importance as national manifestations. Stereotypes of Scandinavian design—restraint in form and decoration, embodiment of traditional values, unity of form and function, and reliance on natural materials—may be tested against the history of exhibitions in which Scandinavians participated. Issues raised in exhibitions include: how each individual country achieved a national identity while remaining part of a larger geographic and cultural unit; how design in Scandinavia reflects attitudes toward the natural environment and the social environment; how design may incorporate tradition within contemporary concerns; how design may contribute to the amelioration of social ills in general; and how design in Scandinavia reflects changes within society.

The renaissance of Scandinavian design activity at the Paris Exposition of 1900 drew its strength both from traditional sources—native spirit, ethnic character, and valued techniques—and from a modern and nationalistic aesthetic. By 1880 issues of nationalism had galvanized Scandinavian social and artistic theorists, and the effects of their reevaluation of national history were made known to the world at large in the 1900 exhibition. From Helsinki to Oslo, designers zealously pursued an original synthesis of past and present that enhanced the self-identity of each country. Their aim was to counter the stylistic tropism that had guided design in Scandinavia for well over a century (Continental eighteenth- and nineteenth-century models had long predominated in the field of decorative arts).

The intellectual, literary, and artistic stirrings in the Nordic countries during the second half of the nineteenth century were paralleled by a newfound self-assertiveness in social and political spheres. Thus, the way was prepared for a new view of national history and for an equally new view of the future. Ethnic traditions and ancient Nordic history began to be considered more than simple romantic antiquarianism. In fact, underlying both were two basic tenets of modernism: that, to be significant, design must be an outgrowth of the fundamental values of a society; and that the role of the artist/craftsman is to manifest such values through the creative process.

The Norwegian painter Gerhard Munthe (whose tapestry designs at the Paris exhibition were based on Nordic legend) defended the new role of tradition. His teleological arguments held that tradition is "not what many believe it to be—viz., ancient romance or history. The first condition demanded of a nation by tradition is that it can be . . . absorbed by it, and tradition, therefore, depends largely upon the developing power of the nation itself." (Quoted in *The Studio*, vol. 8, pp. 221–23.)

Room for King Oscar II, designed by Ferdinand Boberg, Swedish Pavilion, Paris Exhibition of 1900

Munthe's philosophy demanded an ethical basis for nationalism in the arts and called for a dynamic interaction between the past and present so that works of art and design would be suffused with the spirit of a people. Pride in the past, shared among the Scandinavian countries, clearly shone forth at the Paris exhibition and remained a vital thread in the development of modern design in the five countries. The brilliant Viking revival silver from Norway shown in Paris was only one example of the designs that reflected this new intensity of purpose. So, too, was the architecture of the Finnish pavilion, viewed as the symbolic voice of Finland's independence and true national spirit.

Although certain of the Nordic, Viking, or Karelian revival designs were of less serious intent than others, a further awareness of native Scandinavian strength was acknowledged in the growing respect for the crafts tradition. Crafts had been conscientiously nurtured within Scandinavia by a number of guilds and societies formed during the nineteenth century, but heretofore their work had focused on internal preservation efforts. In Paris, the fine craftsmanship of Scandinavian designs could not be ignored; although they were shown in an intensely competitive atmosphere, the inherent quality of the tradition was obvious. The status of crafts and craftsmen in Scandinavia was enhanced during this period of renewed energy, and craftsmanship has remained an undercurrent of concern within the modern movement. National pride in tradition and respect for quality craftsmanship—today almost trite generalizations concerning Scandinavian design—take on an increased validity in this historical context.

It would be inaccurate to see the Paris 1900 exhibition as the setting for new nationalism alone, for this exhibition also marked an important public recognition of Scandinavia's emerging organic style, one related to the Art Nouveau movement, which was having a strong impact in Europe. Simultaneously, there was a perpetuation in the Nordic lands of neoclassicism, and a curious parallel existed between the two styles. Thus, Scandinavian Art Nouveau designs embody a distinctive clarity, discipline, and restraint, while neoclassical designs (which flourished with particular strength during the 1920s) were gentler, more lyrical, and intimate than those of the previous century.

Art Nouveau designs had emerged in Scandinavia considerably earlier than 1900—significantly, at the 1897 Exhibition of 15

Art and Industry in Stockholm—but the Paris 1900 exhibition brought such designs to the attention of an international audience. Porcelains on exhibit from the Swedish firms of Rörstrand and Gustavsberg, with virtuoso designs by Alf Wallander and Gunnar Wennerberg, respectively, bore the salient characteristics of the Art Nouveau style in Scandinavia —sensitive and delicate modeling, native flora and fauna used as forms and decoration, and a soft palette of muted and pastel shades ranging from a satiny pink to an atmospheric gray-green. The Art Nouveau textiles, ceramics, and metalwork produced in Sweden, Denmark, and Norway gave an impression of ordered and rational nature rather than organic turmoil, of poetic restraint rather than passionate choreography. Finland's distinctive variation of the style is best exemplified by the Iris Room, which featured designs by Akseli Gallen-Kallela. More stylized and geometric than designs from the other Scandinavian countries, the Finnish style emphasized abstract patterns, a hallmark of that nation's design that continued into the next century.

Other issues not as clearly indicated at the Paris exhibition must be noted in passing. In certain countries, particularly Denmark, the late nineteenth century was also a time of dedicated interest in the Orient; there is probably no better single example of the undercurrent of orientalism than the work of Thorvald Bindesbøll of Denmark, whose bold ceramics, metalwork, and textiles evoke the opulence and strength of Chinese designs. Oriental ceramics have inspired several generations of Danish potters, and the work of Patrick Nordström and Axel Salto in the twentieth century documents this fascination, but so too does the serene pottery of Berndt Friberg of Sweden. The perennial fascination with rare woods in Danish furniture design, while showing an appreciation of natural materials, also hints at a fully absorbed exoticism.

Between 1900 and 1920, Scandinavian designers participated in several exhibitions that successfully exploited their triumphs in Paris and in others that reflected their growing awareness of other modernist strains. In 1904 the Louisiana Purchase Exposition in St. Louis, Missouri, brought examples of virtuoso craftsmanship from Scandinavia to receptive audiences in America. Norwegian enamels, including those by Gustav Gaudernack, won acclaim, as did the innovative crystalline-glazed ceramics by Valdemar Engelhardt from the Royal Copenhagen factory. Engelhardt's jewel-like porcelains were avidly acquired by collectors such as J. Lionberger Davis, whose ceramics from the 1904 exhibition were later given to the Cooper-Hewitt Museum.

Other early-twentieth-century exhibitions had greater significance to developments within the Scandinavian countries themselves. In 1906, an exhibition at Norrköping in Sweden featured furniture by Carl Bergsten that reflected a strong Viennese influence. The 1909 Århus Exhibition in Denmark was a final salute to the Art Nouveau style; in the same year an exhibition in Stockholm organized by the Swedish Society of Industrial Design recognized increased problems of urbanization and economics by presenting designs for furnishing dwellings of limited space. However, works by Wennerberg and Wallander, the acknowledged leaders of Art Nouveau design, were still prominently featured at Stockholm, as were the textiles of Märta Måås-Fjetterström. There was severe criticism of the elitism of most of the designs shown at the Baltic Exhibition held in Malmö in 1914. Protesters called for revision in the fields of art and industry and affirmed the designer's responsibility to create good design for all of society.

Ceramics from Gustavsberg displayed at the Liljevalchs Art Gallery, Stockholm, 1917, including the Liljeblå *service by Wilhelm Kåge*

Social responsibility in design was thus an underlying theme of an exhibition held in Stockholm in 1917 at the Liljevalchs Art Gallery. Twenty-three interiors were displayed, complete with furnishings that included tableware and other necessary objects of daily use. The exhibition featured the innovative but highly unsuccessful *Liljeblå* service designed by Wilhelm Kåge. Although intended for the average working-class family and combining good design with inexpensiveness, the service was rejected by its intended customers in favor of more traditional and heavily decorated wares. Brought into focus at the exhibition were important issues concerning the integration of social and democratic values in the design industry in order to create objects that were not only aesthetically meaningful but also available to a wide non-elite market. It was strongly urged that artists be placed within the manufacturing industries to guide and shape the course of production. Three underlying features of Scandinavian aesthetics were thus expounded: that good design is a serious responsibility; that design has an impact on the quality of life in all aspects of society; and that the arts can be a vehicle for social improvement. Artists, designers, and craftsmen were encouraged to consider their roles as one, combining in the process of design both the social mandate and the human aesthetic need.

Many reverberations of this principle can be traced throughout the history of Scandinavian design. Kaare Klint's furniture studies from 1910 to 1920, Aino Aalto's pressed glass of the 1930s, and, in the 1970s, the Ergonomi Design Group's *Eat and Drink* service for the handicapped all perpetuate this basic principle. The polemics of design arising from this philosophy range from the 1919 publication of Gregor Paulsson's *Vackrare vardagsvara*, a plea for better design in everyday goods, to these vehement words by Poul Henningsen:

Interior designed by Gunnar Asplund, Paris Exposition, 1925

> Dear craftsmen friends! How can you expect us to go on respecting you, while this swindle continues in the name of art, and while you ignore all your obligations to the modern world? We have no proper tumblers, plates, water-sets, spoons, knives, or forks, while richer homes are flooded with trash and rubbish at fantastic prices! Think a little, and consider your obligations to make things for the delight of your fellow-men in their daily life! Throw away your artists' berets and bow-ties and get into overalls. Down with artistic pretentiousness! Simply make things which are fit for use: that is enough to keep you busy, and you will sell vast quantities and make lots of money. (Quoted in *A Treasury of Scandinavian Design*, Erik Zahle, ed., New York, 1961, p. 10.)

It is important to bear in mind that, at first, social-design theory did not achieve its desired effect with any uniformity. While services for the tables of the working classes were being introduced with limited success, other design developments were occurring which had less to do with social responsibilities than with artistic excellence. Certain fields, such as silver and jewelry, had always remained somewhat outside the mainstream of social-design theory for the obvious reason that they were first and foremost "luxury" goods. Particularly in Denmark, the art of the silversmith has rarely retreated in importance as an active field of design, except in periods of severe economic depression. Art glass was likewise a field of vigorous aesthetic pursuit, and it was in the area of luxury goods that Scandinavian designers stunned the world at the "Exposition des Arts Décoratifs et Industriels Modernes" of 1925 in Paris. While ideals of social responsibility were not totally ignored in Scandinavia during the 1920s, they certainly took a back seat in the activities surrounding Scandinavia's participation in this international event. Henningsen of Denmark did show lighting devices that derived their form by fulfilling a necessary function with an economy of means and materials that made them ideal for mass production. Yet it was the unabashedly neoclassical elegance of the Swedish furniture by Gunnar Asplund, the ceramics from Gustavsberg and Royal Copenhagen, and the spectacular glass from Orrefors that really captured the attention of visitors and critics alike. Although the neoclassical designs of the 1920s were relatively short-lived, it cannot be denied that the principles behind these elite designs—their coherence and clarity of form and decoration, their reduction of extraneous elements, their emphasis on surface, materials, and craftsmanship—were traits entirely consistent with a traditional pattern of design in Scandinavia. Their overall effect was one of exuberant joy in virtuoso design and technique.

Popular reaction to the works shown in Paris was overwhelming. A new term, "Swedish Grace," was coined by the English critic Morton Shand to express the refined self-assurance of the designs, and the response to the designs in other countries can be clearly documented. Within two years of the Paris showing, the first major Scandinavian design exhibition was organized in the United States. "Swedish Contemporary Decorative Arts" opened at the Metropolitan Museum of Art in New York in January, 1927, with more than eighty examples of furniture, ceramics, glass, textiles, and other decorative arts. Within the first six weeks of the show, attendance totaled 54,970, and over 4,000 copies of the catalogue had been sold. After the exhibition, thirteen pieces of Swedish glass acquired by the museum were published as new acquisitions. The attention this landmark exhibition focused on Scandinavian design, and on Swedish design in particular, is crucial, since the modern design traditions of Scandinavia were now formally acknowledged by an American museum. Although this exhibition was to receive a tremendous amount of publicity, it should be noted that another American museum—The Newark Museum in New Jersey—had begun to acquire Scandinavian decorative arts as early as 1912 and Swedish art glass by Simon Gate and Edward Hald in 1925.

In spite of the successes of the 1920s in an international setting, Scandinavian design was still wrestling with internal problems involving both social issues and growing industrialization within the countries. Attitudes at the beginning of the 1930s found their most eloquent expression in the Stockholm Exhibition of 1930. Often termed a "breakthrough" for functionalism in Scandinavia, this exhibition showed designs that could be readily mass-produced inexpensively and efficiently

A view of the Stockholm Exhibition of 1930

19

and displayed them in interiors of radical modernity. While the ideals of this exhibition created a furor inside Scandinavia, its effects remained mostly internal since by this date critics in both Europe and the United States had become familiar with the furniture designs from the Bauhaus. The style of the European avant-garde had already been broadcast internationally through exhibitions such as "Die Wohnung" in Stuttgart in 1927, where functionalist designs by Le Corbusier, Behrens, Gropius, and Mies van der Rohe had set forth new standards for the twentieth century.

Interior designed by Herman Munthe-Kaas, Norway, 1930s

Although less radical in an international setting, the 1930 exhibition did, nevertheless, pose fundamental questions about Scandinavian design that were to resolve themselves into a new attitude that had a subsequent impact on the world at large. Classic functionalism had already demanded that industrial materials and processes provide the basic equation in achieving an aesthetic and functional end. In Stockholm in 1930, however, principles of construction, clarity, and modesty combined with a traditional attitude toward craftsmanship and materials to produce a functionalism that was humanized. And it was this ethic of design that was to have such a dramatic ascendancy during the decade following World War II. The rise in international awareness of Scandinavian design can be documented by examining the Triennale exhibitions in Milan and the first comprehensive design exhibition to tour the United States.

Music room designed by Arne Jacobsen, Denmark, 1930s

In 1933, only three years after the Stockholm exhibition, the most impressive Scandinavian contributions to the Triennale were the furniture designs of Alvar Aalto. By the late 1920s, Aalto had already resolved the issues of function and aesthetics in a series of designs which are exceptions to the rule that design reflects its own times. Also in the exhibition were glasswares by Aino Aalto and an extensive display of domestic and art glass from Sweden's Orrefors with designs that were, in the main, less than revolutionary. During the 1940s, Sweden was able to continue to participate in the Triennale exhibitions, while those countries directly affected by the war were restricted in such activities. In 1948 both Berndt Friberg and Stig Lindberg, working at the Gustavsberg factory in Sweden, were awarded gold medals for their ceramics. A return to the design mainstream by the other Scandinavian countries was quick in coming after the war, and the 1951 Triennale presented a much different picture. Grand prizes in that year were

Living room designed by Axel Larsson, Swedish Pavilion, New York World's Fair, 1939

Living room designed by Josef Frank, 1930s

awarded to Hans Wegner of Denmark for his furniture; to Tapio Wirkkala of Finland for glass design, sculpture, and the installation of the Finnish exhibition; to Kay Bojesen of Denmark for silver; and to Dora Jung of Finland for textiles— only a few of the more than two dozen Scandinavian winners of various prizes. Among the entries that especially indicated the widespread health and vigor of the pan-Nordic tradition were the textiles of Juliana Sveinsdottir of Iceland, which were also awarded a gold medal that year.

Recognition at the Triennale exhibitions of the superior qualities of Scandinavian designs necessarily meant that an affluent design market could be generated for exports, and during the 1950s an international economic structure was created that assured even Americans in the Midwest a supply of these satisfying designs. The popular appeal of Scandinavian design during the period can now be viewed as a validation of many of the principles so assiduously followed since the beginning of the modern tradition. The products, whether furniture, ceramics, glass, metalwork, or textiles, were aesthetically appropriate and exciting; they were competently and conscientiously designed and fabricated; they were functional but humanized; and, whether seen in a public auditorium or the smallest apartment, they carried an obvious mantle of quality. They were both art and craft, and distinctions between the two were nonessential to their appreciation.

American awareness of Scandinavian design, if not already assured by the publicity gained at the Triennale exhibitions and by wide coverage in the media, was enriched by the appearance of the most extensive exhibition of contemporary Scandinavian design ever to be shown there. This landmark exhibition, "Design in Scandinavia," circulated to a great many American and Canadian museums from 1954 to 1957. The impressive promotion effort behind the exhibition involved most major factories in Scandinavia, the heads of the crafts and design organizations in each participating country (Iceland was regrettably not represented), and patrons that included the presidents of the United States and Finland and the kings of Norway, Sweden, and Denmark. Never before had such a monumental effort been made to survey the current design situation in the Scandinavian countries, and the effect in America was dramatic. The independent outlets that had sold Scandinavian design, such as Frederik Lunning, Inc., and George Tanier, Inc., of New York, were joined in the market by department stores ranging from Bloomingdale Brothers to Pacific Overseas, Inc., of San Francisco.

A series of embodied design principles had become a style, at least as perceived in the public eye. With historical distance we might now be tempted to view the designs of the 1950s with a revised meaning, appreciating them more for their aesthetic quality than for their social implications. To do this would be to lose sight of a factor important to the appreciation of the history of Scandinavian design, since its inherent humanism cannot be divorced from its aesthetics.

The decade of the 1950s gave Scandinavian design the most visibility it had ever enjoyed, for in addition to the Triennale success were an astonishing number of international exhibitions. Many of these were organized by Finland: in 1952 the Finnish Society of Crafts and Design toured an exhibition of industrial and fine arts to thirteen cities in North America and to Glasgow, London, Leeds, Brighton, and Dublin; an exhibition of rugs mounted by the Finnish Society of Crafts and Design in 1956 toured Norway and then traveled to New York, Faenza, and Augsburg; twelve West German cities were host to a Finnish-organized industrial art exhibition in 1956–57. Tremendous interest was generated at the international "H 55" exhibition in Hälsingborg, Sweden, and Swedish designs later appeared in exhibitions in Berlin and Zurich in 1957. Designs from various Scandinavian countries were exhibited in Brussels (1958), Syracuse, New York (1958), Paris ("Formes Scandinaves," 1958–59), Amsterdam (1959), and Boston (1959), to mention only the most prominent. Finland even sponsored a South American exhibition which brought the designer Timo Sarpaneva and his work to four cities in Brazil, Argentina, and Uruguay.

In the early 1960s, this strong showing in exhibitions continued to be promoted, with the important "Finlandia" exhibition of 1961 in Zurich, "The Arts of Denmark" which toured the United States during 1960–61, and the Cooper Union Museum's "Creative Craft in Denmark" in 1962. Nevertheless, by mid-decade, a change had occurred which indicated that the force of Scandinavian design was dissipating and that the international audience for design was looking toward new developments in other creative centers, and with particular favor toward Italy. Although national manifestations of design from Scandinavia continued to appear, the climate of world opinion had shifted radically. Within the Nordic countries

"Design in Scandinavia," traveling exhibition, United States and Canada, 1954–57

themselves, coordinated design activities fell victim to a series of debates that centered on a new direction for the arts, crafts, and industrial design. It is this recent period of Scandinavian design history, which has witnessed tremendous upheaval and reorganization, not unlike the early decades of the modern design movement, that is unfamiliar to an American audience.

Within the past decade, a new generation of craftsmen, artists, and designers has arisen in Scandinavia; many of these new contributors to the history of modern design have actively participated in exhibitions, but the majority of these have occurred within Scandinavia itself and in other European countries. There has been little information available in the United States regarding these artists, particularly those now working outside of industry, and the designs of a considerable number are being shown in the United States for the first time in the course of this exhibition.

Above all other considerations is one feature of the current design situation that cannot be overlooked: within the various traditional mediums—ceramics, glass, metalwork, woodwork, and textiles—there has been a noticeable and emphatic reassertion of the aesthetic potential of the materials and of the craftsman/designer as a creative and synthesizing force within society. Although industrial designers have grown into a separate field of expertise, developing their own methodology, techniques, goals, and philosophy, the new design tradition in Scandinavia is now broad enough to accommodate such a variety of approaches. Both industrial design and design in the crafts have achieved a new validity within Scandinavia, a fact which indicates a healthy and active future.

Design in Scandinavia has always been a combination of highly diverse influences and activities, and in our eagerness to look for similarities, we may have lost sight of many critical differences between artists, countries, and ideas. Current revolutions in Scandinavian design promise to hold for the future the same potential for creative development as did earlier decades. Seen against the backdrop of the 1950s, the current design milieu in Scandinavia takes on new meaning; seeing the 1950s themselves against their own historical context gives an important shift in emphasis away from a "style" and toward an aesthetic. "Scandinavian Modern: 1880–1980," it is hoped, will establish a context for the present design traditions of Scandinavia and open new areas for future consideration.

Ilmari Tapiovaara (Finland). Lukki Chair, *c. 1957*

UNITY AND DIVERSITY
IN SCANDINAVIAN DESIGN

ULF HÅRD AF SEGERSTAD
Author, critic, and professor, Stockholm

Henning Koppel. *Ewer,* 1952 (no. 192)

When you look at Scandinavian design, you see that it scatters flowers before your feet and lays the pale colors and mild beauty of the Nordic summer before your eyes. Less apparent is the truth that this sunny effect is achieved against a background of darkness, cold, ice, and snow. Scandinavian design is perhaps, at heart, winter design, its most characteristic products snowplows and icebreakers. I mean this paradoxical contrast seriously and will try to clarify it and to sketch a quick outline of the phenomenon "Scandinavian Design" in a larger, broader context. What are its characteristic features? How have they emerged in the special conditions prevailing in the constellation Denmark, Finland, Iceland, Norway, and Sweden?

But first let me clarify some terminology. Not everything that is commonly called "Scandinavian" design is really "Scandinavian Design." It may, of course, seem legitimate to call all products from the five countries Scandinavian, considering their geographic origin. But Scandinavian Design in a more specific sense is a term popularized in the early 1950s, within the context of an exhibition touring the United States and Canada. The objects for this exhibition were chosen on the basis of a philosophy or ideology which, while admittedly vague, resulted in a unified presentation that gave the exhibition its character. Today, it is easier to see both the strengths and the weaknesses of this ideology more clearly and, equally, to understand its significance. It dealt with a mode of design that evolved in a somewhat tentative way during the years

25

before World War I and that flowered during the two decades after World War II. This, to me, is Scandinavian Design in a somewhat more precise sense. This essay will describe its characteristics and, above all, the conditions that produced it.

Another exceptionally vague term is "design." In the present context, the term refers to domestic objects and furnishings, particularly those that combine practical and functional features with aesthetic qualities in a distinctive manner. Let me begin by listing, completely unsystematically but with a particular reason in mind, a handful of well-known pioneers in Scandinavian Design.

Finland's great architect Alvar Aalto commonly referred to his colleague Gunnar Asplund from Sweden as his first important model. Aalto respectfully called his friend, twelve years his senior, "Father Asplund." And Asplund, in turn, often acknowledged his affection for Danish architects and architecture, especially the wonderful little eighteenth-century Liselund castle, which was long his ideal. Hannah Ryggen was born in Sweden and lived there for thirty years before she moved to Norway and became its leading modern designer of monumental textiles. Sweden's foremost artist in the same field, Alf Munthe, was influenced early by his Norwegian uncle, the national romantic painter and textile artist Gerhard Munthe. The Finnish textile artist Viola Gråsten made her major contribution in Sweden with industrially printed fabrics. Patrick Nordström, a ceramist and pioneer in stoneware, left his native Sweden for Denmark. His work was carried on by Denmark's Nathalie Krebs, who for a time worked with Finland's Gunnar Nylund. Nylund himself later became artistic director of a porcelain company in Sweden.

And furthermore: Asplund's internationally acclaimed functionalist exhibition in Stockholm in 1930 was an important source of inspiration for innumerable architects and designers throughout Scandinavia. In a similar way, the Snedkerlauget's legendary exhibitions in Copenhagen, especially after World War II, influenced and stimulated a large number of furniture designers from the other Scandinavian countries. Even during the paralyzing war years, neutral Sweden served as a shelter for many architects and designers from its war-torn sister countries. Sweden is where they met, exchanged ideas and experiences, and planned more or less together the work they would do when peace finally came. Almost all of Iceland's design-

A view of the Stockholm Exhibition of 1930

26

ers, who joined the community only a score of years ago, have been trained in one of the other Scandinavian countries.

We could easily expand the list of inter-Scandinavian migration, personal interchange, and other areas, such as exhibitions, which offer unlimited potential for strengthening common frames of reference. But a glimpse certainly suffices to illustrate the unique fact that professionals from five separate countries—three kingdoms and two republics, each with a long history—have made and are still making spontaneous and natural efforts to create an essentially common form of design. If we were to illustrate these moves with a diagram, however, it would not be symmetrical. The magnetic pole in the Scandinavian force field has shifted at different times, depending among other things on which material was undergoing the most vital period of development, toward a center of gravity in one particular country. In general we might, however, venture to say that Copenhagen—for reasons I will explain later—has repeatedly drawn the magnetic needle to its pole, while Stockholm provides the center further north. With all the characteristics the five Scandinavian countries share in common, each has its own special features, which occasionally are so marked as to form sharp contrasts. It is the tension between unity and diversity that gives excitement and at times a certain drama to Scandinavian design.

Scandinavian design should be considered a special province within the countries' larger cultural context. Design, in other words, is one manifestation of "things Scandinavian." Here I have touched upon the perennial problem of art as an independent activity. Is art created and judged independently of a society's politics, economics, and mores? The issue is problematical, but it is reasonable to presume that design, in its different forms, is linked to other currents in society. Even more: Scandinavian design is significantly dependent on specific external factors. This is not to underestimate the internal, creative contributions; studying the influence of one designer upon another—the "comparative" method usually employed in presenting Scandinavian design—undoubtedly has value. It is also fully legitimate, following Kant's example, to try to enjoy the formal characteristics of the objects shown here with "disinterested pleasure," but I believe that our experience may be enriched by understanding an object in a more hermeneutic way, as a reflection of external conditions.

Who, for example, can deny that it is important to be aware of the following facts in order to understand these objects? Designs in the latter half of the century-long cavalcade were made in what are now among the world's richest countries, while the earlier objects were made in five very poor countries with an average standard of living that can be compared to Indonesia's today. They were also produced at a time when the largest number of people in the history of the five countries was emigrating, and when a flood of Scandinavia's best workers was still trying to get across the ocean into the enticing United States.

It might not seem particularly relevant to people today to point out a country's geographic location in a discussion of design. It is true that the unprecedented improvement in communications over the last two decades has brought all countries closer together (attenuating the distinctive character of Scandinavian design in the process). We should remember, however, that Scandinavian design emerged during a period of relative isolation. In fact, the position of these five countries on "the top of Europe" provides the foundation for their special features. In the past, impulses from the leading cultural nations on the Continent passed only very slowly through the filters of geographic distance and poverty, and a great deal of time elapsed before they were adapted to the harsher conditions of the north. As a result, no Scandinavian country could match the brilliant cultures of the Continent. It cannot be denied that Denmark and Sweden, during economically favorable epochs, tried to live up to the example of their Continental models, but with limited success.

Scandinavian design has fused the waning peasant and craft culture of the late nineteenth century (with its simplification and utilitarian ideas resulting from harsh conditions) with industrial efficiency and more or less socially oriented functionalism. Or, in other words: the sturdy and practical character of the Scandinavian crafts tradition harmonized with the new industrial rationalism. In a unique way they merged—not without difficulty but fairly smoothly compared with the course of events in the large industrial countries. We can hardly speak of an industrial revolution in Scandinavia, but we can speak of an evolution. Even today, Scandinavian industrialism, with all its efficiency, seems fairly Utopian in comparison with conditions elsewhere.

28 A look at the map shows that the countries on the top of

DENMARK

1 Copenhagen
2 Fredericia
3 Holmegaard
4 Bornholm

SWEDEN

5 Malmö
6 Hälsingborg
7 Båstad
8 Boda
9 Kosta
10 Orrefors
11 Rejmyra
12 Göteborg
13 Lidköping
14 Gustavsberg
15 Stockholm
16 Gävle
17 Lapland

NORWAY

18 Oslo
19 Porsgrunn
20 Egersund
21 Bergen
22 Jevnaker
23 Vatne
24 Trondheim

FINLAND

25 Lapland
26 Jyväskylä
27 Nuutajärvi
28 Iittala
29 Riihimäki
30 Kerava
31 Porvoo
32 Helsinki
33 Turku

ICELAND

34 Reykjavik
35 Hafnarfjördhur

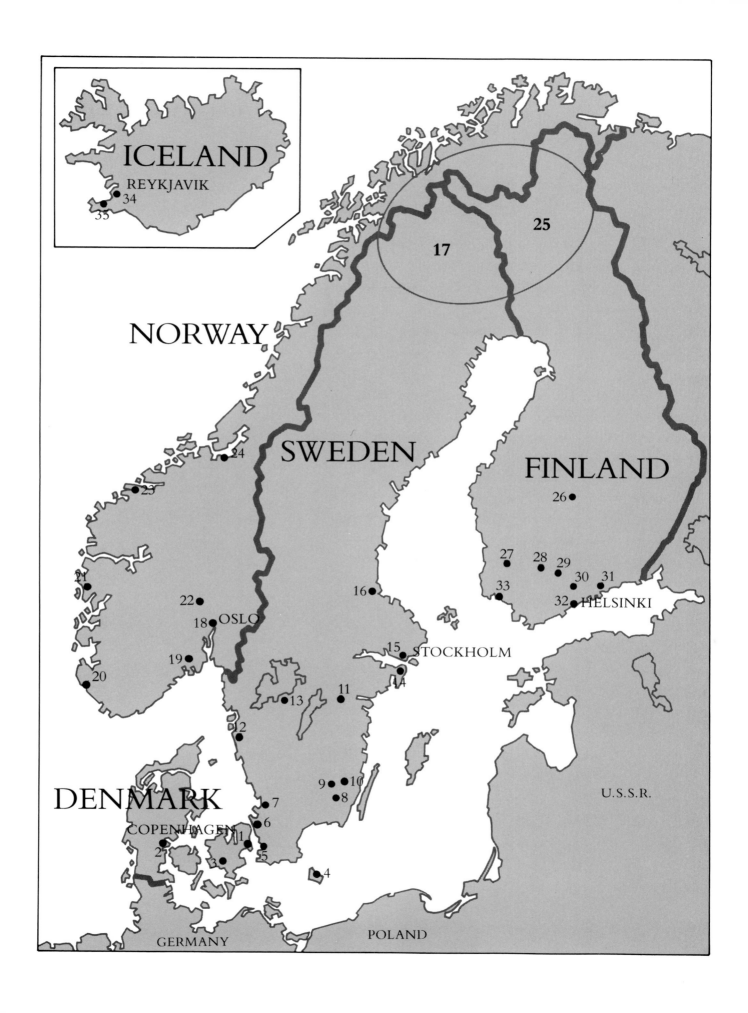

ICELAND

REYKJAVIK
34
35

NORWAY

SWEDEN

FINLAND

17

25

DENMARK

COPENHAGEN

OSLO

STOCKHOLM

HELSINKI

U.S.S.R.

GERMANY   POLAND

Europe also present a number of interesting geographic variations. Denmark in the south consists of a peninsula on the European continent and three hundred nearby islands: low-lying, fertile agricultural land that today supports an effective industrial base as well. Denmark turns its long, open coast toward England and western Europe, and it is completely consistent that the special Danish variety of Scandinavian design shows the obvious influence of English arts and crafts. And what could be more natural than a country of farmers developing a rich ceramic tradition into a specialty? Copenhagen's early importance as a port and trade center also helped to bring Denmark into the cultural mainstream of Europe earlier than its sister countries.

Norway, too, with its long, magnificently lovely coast of deep fjords carved into mountains, turns west toward the ocean. It is a country for bold seamen. The primary local materials, wood and wool, were used masterfully in the medieval stave churches and in magnificent seventeenth- and eighteenth-century tapestries. In contrast to Denmark, where short distances between points and ever-present waterways have led to centralization, Norway is split topographically into innumerable small communities along the fjords and in the fell valleys. This has favored the emergence of a large number of quite varied local and regional traditions with highly developed popular crafts, which still form the country's greatest asset in design. A corollary of this emphasis on local tradition is the Norwegian's well-developed individualism and disinclination to listen to decrees from Oslo.

Iceland's special situation is clearly illustrated by its isolated position out in the Atlantic. The special cultural characteristics of the country have traditionally been manifested in magnificent epic poetry and literature rather than in design. For the past couple of decades, however, designers have worked with some success to gain on the sister countries' lead in this area, in particular by studying in Denmark and Norway, Iceland's closest neighbors.

Finland's geographic situation is radically different from that of all the others. Someone once said, "It is a country that lies between east and west, but somewhat more to the north." During more isolated periods, Finland was also called "the country behind God's back," which, as I will show later, was far from the truth. But under any conditions, Finland stands and has always stood in a political and cultural crossfire between East and West, and this position has often resulted in design assertively independent from that of its sister countries.

The largest country in this northern constellation is Sweden. Geographically, and thus historically, it is turned to the east and south—to Russia, the Baltic states, and Germany. The development of Swedish design has also been affected by this orientation. It should be noted, furthermore, that Sweden's size, major natural resources, and protected position framed by the other Scandinavian countries have afforded it some advantages over its Nordic neighbors.

Admittedly, the five countries have not always maintained the same good relationships they enjoy today. The past centuries have seen many conflicts and considerable drama. Today's peaceful competition over generally excellent design products was preceded by sharp confrontations. Far into this century, Scandinavian countries based their internal affiliations on the ancient principle that the sea, lakes, and rivers unite, while forests and mountains divide. This has had noteworthy consequences in our case. Even though Sweden and Norway lie "back to back" and share a long land border, Sweden has had a more important interchange with Finland on the other side of the Gulf of Bothnia, while Norway has had more contact with Denmark on the other side of the North Sea. In fact, Sweden and Finland formed one kingdom for six hundred years, right up to 1809, when Finland came under Russian domination as a favored and, in fact, fairly autonomous grand duchy. After the Russian Revolution in 1917, the country won its freedom. Norway depended in various ways on Denmark until 1814, when Sweden's kings assumed a rulership that lasted until 1905. If I also note that parts of southern Sweden belonged to Denmark until three hundred years ago, the reader will have an indication of the political ties among the countries.

In addition to geography and topography, climate has also been influential in the emergence of Scandinavian design. Despite a certain difference between the climate of Denmark in the south and that of the northernmost regions, all the countries share a relatively long, and in places hard, winter and a correspondingly short summer. This type of climate has engendered what I have already called winter design. It is apparent in architectural adjustments such as steep roofs and small windows; in sturdy equipment for outdoor use such as skis and snow shovels, insulated sportswear and work clothes; and in advanced machine design, covering everything from motor-powered ice drills to enormous icebreakers.

Above all, the Scandinavian climate nurtured an interest in the home and its furnishings unparalleled elsewhere in Europe. During certain periods, this interest has almost developed into a cult. The safe, warm, snug house huddled in the frost and snow under the starry winter sky abides as a nostalgic symbol even today, when international technology and communications make living in industrialized countries more and more uniform. In contrast to the social life of southern Europe, in which the streets and the squares figure as important meeting places, Scandinavian family and social life remains centered in the home.

Changes of season—chiefly the radical transition from winter to spring—explain the fixation on nature that has led, in Scandinavian design, to the use of organic forms and natural materials wherever possible. This emphasis contrasts markedly with the more cerebral character of most Continental design, even to the point of making Scandinavian design appear lacking in a certain intellectualism.

When signals emanating from the English theorists of design John Ruskin and William Morris were picked up in Scandinavia in the latter half of the nineteenth century, the response was strong everywhere, and—in a striking expression of how external conditions affect design—the reaction was especially dramatic in Finland. Not only literature and painting, but also architecture and design were mobilized in the increasingly intense struggle to establish Finland's national identity. The Finns exerted themselves vigorously to give expression to what many among them considered their national heritage, with magnificent results. The brilliant symbol of this fight for cultural freedom was the country's pavilion at the Paris Exposition of 1900; this pavilion was visited by far more people and written about more widely than any other. Even after Finland gained its independence in 1917, the country continued to foster such exceptional manifestations of design.

The depth of the external influences affecting Finland sometimes set it off from the other countries, where changes occurred more internally. In Denmark, developments took the form of a well-considered and in many ways temperate modification and renewal of the country's refined bourgeois culture, "perhaps the finest in Europe," to quote a Swedish expert. Denmark's design development thus evidenced a kind of stability that was largely absent from Finland's. In Norway, too, activity was considerable but concentrated in Oslo, where current trends were documented in Scandinavia's first museum of applied arts, founded as early as 1876.

Domestic interior, Stockholm Exhibition of 1930

Typically enough, Sweden had learned of developments in England primarily via Austria and Germany. In light of Sweden's greater resources and the nature of its government, which was more inclined toward administrative and organizational centralization, design evolved there in line with clearly formulated social goals. "More beautiful things for everyday use"—*vackrare vardagsvara*—became a well-known and representative slogan. It was also in complete accord with this social and aesthetic aim that the functionalist Stockholm Exhibition was organized in 1930. The exhibition evoked a variety of responses in the Nordic countries. In Sweden itself, where, according to perspicacious colleagues, people have a tendency to applaud a single view at a time, functionalism made its breakthrough after an admittedly violent debate. By 1940, partly as a result of the new social democratic regime's adoption of the principle (after some hesitation), Sweden had become functionalistic and has so remained. We can confidently say it was domestic policy that guided Swedish architecture and design in a direction that later resulted in a kind of "national international" style.

Functionalism quickly gained a foothold in Finland, too, but mostly for reasons of foreign policy. The young, dynamic republic had one overriding goal: to put the country on the world map as a respected member of the community of nations. Following more or less the same nationalistic motivation that had earlier inspired the architects and designers of the pavilion at the Paris Exposition, designers now fostered the new international style to show that Finland was keeping up with the times. Leading architects soon created functionalistic masterworks, which were promptly featured in international journals. The social aspect of functionalism, while perhaps not neglected altogether, did not gain the same dominant position in Finland as it did in Sweden.

In Denmark, too, an intensive and often brilliant debate on architecture and design—partly fueled by the Stockholm Exhibition—stimulated the world of design. There, however, the reaction was completely different from those in Sweden and Finland, among other reasons because of the geographic factors mentioned earlier. Sweden was directly influenced by the Bauhaus in Germany, while Denmark, with its English connections, was averse to large-scale uniformity in building and to small-scale uniformity in home furnishings. The reaction in Norway is difficult to interpret, in some measure because its regional divisions both slow down the arrival of new influences and, for good and bad, interpret and rework them to suit local conditions.

Another important external factor in the development of design is the economy. Here, too, Finland serves as a prime example. When the young republic started up its vigorous industrial expansion in the 1920s and 1930s, it made bold, major investments. Even the industrial arts—usually a quantitatively modest field—were given enormous support in Finland because large companies were involved. The Arabia porcelain company, established in the 1880s as a subsidiary of the Swedish Rörstrand, became an important enterprise soon after it broke away from the Swedish firm in 1916. For a period after World War II Arabia was Europe's largest manufacturer of ceramics, with a team of up to thirty artists—far more than any similar company in Scandinavia could support. Similarly, other large companies during this prosperous period attracted leading young talents and, as a result, there were almost no small workshops and studios in Finland.

Until the very end of the 1960s, Sweden, like Finland, had its leading work in design bound up with fairly dominant companies in the ceramics, glass, textile, woodworking, and metal industries. The external conditions influencing the development of design were quite different in Denmark. Its companies were small, and the economy had room for the widest variety of design enterprises, from nationalized furniture production to small workshops and one-man studios. With certain modifications, this was also true of Norway, though on a smaller scale.

World War II naturally caused an upheaval in the world of design, but while the course of development in Scandinavia was disrupted, there were certain consolidations as well. The exchange of ideas slowed but did not cease altogether. In addition to the contacts among Scandinavian refugees in Sweden, some exhibitions circulated among the countries. As a result, the industrial arts were at least partly prepared when, at the close of the war, they were hit by the enormous demand for the beautiful things of the "good life" that people had only dreamed of until then. Finland, which had to pay an enormous war debt to the Soviet Union, exploited design as an instrument of goodwill in its export efforts, providing generous state support and achieving excellent results. The other countries followed Finland's example with varying amounts of support—and with varying degrees of success. Although the exemplary quality of Scandinavian design gave it a competitive edge, without this extremely favorable postwar situation it is doubtful whether it would have been able to achieve such international prominence. This view is supported by the fact that Scandinavian design dominance declined during the 1960s, when other countries had regained their ability to compete. In fact, the pressure from abroad squeezed the Scandinavian producers so hard that the leading companies fell into serious difficulties around 1970. Partly because of this situation, studio production has increased in recent years on quite a large scale.

Basically, then, it is important external factors that account for the somewhat different roles assumed by designers in the separate Scandinavian societies. With some simplification these roles can be described as follows. In Denmark, they are architect/designers, who with great care consciously or unconsciously further a well-established tradition of quality. In Finland, during the glorious postwar period, they were star artists (often granted greater status than those in the fine arts), who with undeniable talent and magical names brought even the most trivial objects into the realm of art. In Iceland, designers are beginning to gain a respected status for their cultural contributions. In Norway, designers are well on their way to securing an established position and can look forward to increasing economic support from the state. In Sweden, designers have always been a large group, and their work has succeeded because of the practicality of their designs and their ability to satisfy the needs of the entire society. Only in Sweden does one know with statistical certainty that, for example, a three-person household in Stockholm in Social Group 3 lives in two rooms and a kitchen and owns over two thousand objects—the statistics do not reveal whether these objects are of Scandinavian design.

NORDIC DESIGN:
A MULTITUDE OF VOICES

HELENA DÄHLBECK LUTTEMAN
Curator, Department of Applied Art, Nationalmuseum, Stockholm

Simo Heikkilä and Yrjö Wiherheimo. *Armchair*, 1980
(no. 339)

The design histories of five different countries are included in this retrospective survey. While the American audience may see the Scandinavian countries as an entity, we see ourselves in a different way. We are indeed close relatives, but still distinct individuals: as similar and as different as five siblings. It is perhaps the differences—the individuality and distinctiveness of each country—that we choose to emphasize. It is certainly worthwhile, however, to look beyond the differences occasionally and to focus on our common features.

Montesquieu wrote about the significance of climate for a people, and Scandinavia's geographic position has naturally influenced design in our countries, which share elements of a common history and similarities of culture. Yet the political conditions in each have been fundamentally different.

I believe that the past few decades have been important to the way the Scandinavian countries perceive themselves and the way they are perceived by the world. Although Scandinavia took part in the international expositions at the turn of the century, it was only with the emergence of the concept "Scandinavian Design" after World War II that the Scandinavian countries became leaders in design. From the 1930s through the 1950s, Swedish design concepts won a great deal of international attention, which was later shifted to Finland and Denmark, in particular, with their bold touches and good products. After the 1950s, the Swedes, unfortunately a bit tamer in temperament, did not participate as fully as the others in deliberate external image-building. The Finnish and Danish desire to make the world aware of their new designs was simply not considered as important for Sweden. Perhaps this was because Sweden was neutral in World War II, thereby enjoying an uninterrupted development in design. The other countries, where many design activities were restricted if not curtailed, met the challenges of the postwar period with a new energy.

A feeling for materials seems to be something specially Scandinavian. It was certainly an important aspect of the crafts tradition, which was, in turn, fundamental to the development of Scandinavian design. We can also find a characteristic paradox here. In the 1930s, during the emergence of functionalism—that severe and dogmatic style with machine-inspired forms, steel tubes, and plain, unadorned surfaces—there was still a sensitivity to organic materials. The properties of glass—its mass, its ability to refract light, its weight—were considered important elements in glass design; textile and furniture designers took into account the structure of cloth and wood as materials. Perhaps one can claim that this emphasis on natural materials became a part of the functionalism of the Scandinavian countries: for example, the tubular steel furniture of the Bauhaus school held only a minor, indirect place in our designs. This was in sharp contrast with the attitude of the previous epoch of designers, whose products were characterized by decorative patterning, elegance, and an internationalism that sometimes suffocated independent expression. (It is incidentally interesting to note that we in Scandinavia never had any true Art Deco. Although classicism was clearly in evidence during the 1920s, it was never closely aligned with Continental Art Deco.)

Direct contact with a material results in a special kind of design. A good designer can create good things with different materials. Although he or she can also simply sit down at the drawing board and create good products, something different emerges by making direct contact with a material, getting a feel for it. A ceramist who creates one-of-a-kind pieces in a studio has unique qualifications for making serial products. The industrial arts in Scandinavia have in many cases been built upon this direct contact.

Recent changes in social and economic conditions in Scandinavia have radically altered the traditional relationship between the crafts and industry. Previously, crafts formed the basis for much of Scandinavian industrial art. This was, however, in a period when the economy was still developing. Now that the Scandinavian countries have achieved a high standard of living, combining crafts and industry is a problem. Today the wage scale in industry is so high that it is difficult for industry to turn out products at acceptable prices. There are always people willing to pay for exceptional outstanding objects, but some Scandinavian ceramics and glass, for example, can be matched by less expensive alternatives, often from other Scandinavian countries. The result is an untenable situation. Here is some food for thought: in Scandinavia, a completely handmade cup or a glass blown in a one-man workshop may be cheaper than an industrially produced cup or glass. Should we say that we have come full circle and be delighted with the renaissance of crafts? It is undoubtedly gratifying and paradoxical at the same time.

This economic situation also seems to be in keeping with an important trend of contemporary life: back to nature and to things that are genuine, to simple, primitive, and good forms of production. See! We don't need the big, dirty, ugly factories! Yet, we cannot deny that crafts production today can hardly serve as a viable alternative to industrial production. Because of our national economies, we need more rational and large-scale production units. We cannot go back to a few workshops and augment their products with imports from the developing countries; unemployment would be an even more ominous specter than it already is. And today, at least in Sweden, there is also a longing to return to natural materials, those on which Scandinavian industrial art was built. Linen, to mention just one example, is beginning to be used widely again.

It is interesting to present Scandinavian crafts, industrial arts, and industrial design in parallel, decade by decade, but this method of presentation has shortcomings in that only a small segment of the tradition must serve as representative of a much larger spectrum of activities. What I will try to do here is to briefly characterize each country, illuminating its special contribution to the history of Scandinavian design.

There is a Swedish word—*lagom*—which is difficult to translate precisely. It means moderate, sufficient, and, above all, not excessive. It always means that something is above reproach and good, but there are many shades of meaning to the term. Something that is *lagom* can seem dull and unin-

Domestic interior, Liljevalchs Art Gallery Exhibition, Stockholm, 1917

spired, but even then, it displays a balance not to be disdained. Much of the best that has been done in the past hundred years in Swedish design is *lagom*, and, I must hasten to add, good.

This *lagom* quality often resulted from a conscious effort to balance social needs and aesthetic demands. In 1917, the Swedish Society of Crafts and Design organized an exhibition in Stockholm that displayed small apartments furnished with good, simple things intended for blue-collar and lower-level white-collar workers. The unpretentious furniture was well suited to its purpose—to fit comfortably in the given space while serving several functions simultaneously. Far from being a hodgepodge of different styles, it drew from Swedish tradition to come up with a simple yet effective style. The same can be said of the ceramics, glass, and textiles at the exhibition. The ceramics and glass were jointly produced by industry and by artists who were commissioned to design objects with visual integrity and practical value. This was the first real and profound cooperation between industry and designers in Sweden. Although the exhibition proved to be a landmark in design, the workers for whom the objects were intended felt cheated. They wanted the "fine" things they identified with the upper classes: flowered porcelain dinner services and intricately patterned crystal. Ironically, it was primarily the initiated—architects and designers—who went out and bought the new objects.

The socially oriented design ethic remained important in the 1920s in spite of several exhibitions that featured luxury-oriented industrial arts and aimed to avoid "that social rubbish." In fact, it is precisely this social aspect that has become a distinct—and distinguished—theme in the history of Swedish design. Functionalism made its breakthrough at the famous Stockholm Exhibition of 1930, although, viewed critically, the architecture and ideology of the exhibition were far more radical than the industrial arts on display. The leading industries presented a resumé of 1920s classicism rather than new, fresh designs. Social commitment did surface, nevertheless, in designs for hospital rooms and other public buildings.

By 1955, when a major design exhibition was held in Hälsingborg, many of the goals formulated about 1917 had been achieved, but at the same time, a perfection had been attained that could be considered as bordering on the uninteresting. It was not just "more beautiful things for everyday use" that

Scandinavian Design Cavalcade: 1955. This page, above, a cooperative department store display from Sweden; below, the Danish section. Opposite, above, the Finnish section; below, the Norwegian section

had been created, but also faultless artistic pieces: ceramic vases that could not be improved upon and glass objects that had reached the optimum of elegance. The reaction was not long in coming: designers experimented with thick and blistered glass, textile clipped into pieces, ceramic sculptures whose expressive qualities overpowered aesthetic values, and even inelegant silver pieces.

This response, in turn, ushered in a new era characterized by a search in fresh directions and a need to use the classic craft materials to transmit a message. Central to this message, which gained currency in the 1960s, was an awareness of suffering around the world, of the shortage of resources, of environmental pollution. This awareness, when combined with a strong political commitment, proved paralyzing for some craftsmen. Unable to incorporate this social consciousness into their creative efforts and refusing to express themselves "conventionally," they stopped working.

Today the situation is different. Pure crafts have regained freedom of expression and a decidedly sensual quality; the aesthetic message is again current. For many, the interim was a time of inactivity and great anxiety. Seen in a larger context, however, the reaction and the new awareness were highly significant. In industrial design, they stimulated interest in such important areas as the needs of the handicapped and technology for developing countries. People reconsidered their goals and means, and found that issues of ergonomics, consumer interests, and the conscientious use of materials had been neglected in comparison with the flourishing consumer goods industry. As often happens during periods of fundamental change, the pendulum may have swung too far. Are we then on our way into a more balanced era, one in which we will take both matters of conscience and aesthetics into consideration? Are we on our way to a new *lagom*? This is perhaps where the movement toward a new sensuality will have its greatest impact.

The violent swings of the pendulum have not been felt as strongly in Denmark. On the other hand, no one would ever think of using the work *lagom* to describe Denmark's contribution to the history of design. Esprit and talent, even a certain radicalism and critical attitude, are primary traits of Danish design; yet, no abrupt breaks with the past can be seen in its course over the last hundred years. Denmark, perhaps the most cultivated of the five countries, has a design history firmly rooted in a secure bourgeois tradition. In the twentieth century, its design has used elements of the refined Empire style of the nineteenth century and even the classical idiom of the eighteenth century. From Kaare Klint's *Red Chair* to Poul Kjærholm's superb furniture of bent steel and cane, these influences may be seen. Danish architecture has developed smoothly, its styles and techniques transmitted from one generation of architects and designers to the next. The new generation has no need for a *tabula rasa*.

Nevertheless, the older generation has also made sure that research and criticism remain important elements of design. Research on design-and-use standards and concern about people's true needs go back to the early 1900s in Denmark. Poul Henningsen, a radical cultural critic, strongly affected the Danish intellectual climate in the 1920s and 1930s. And when the Swedes enjoyed a major success at the 1925 Paris Exposition with their elegant engraved glass, Henningsen was singled out for his prototype of the now-classic "PH" lamp, a superb innovation in lighting. On a small scale, this seminal design may even be compared with Le Corbusier's *pavillon de l'esprit nouveau*.

A special geniality often appears in Danish design, which favors curvilinear shapes, gently rounded forms, and a lively color sensibility. Perhaps these characteristics, epitomized by Copenhagen's Tivoli Gardens, put Danish design in a class all its own. To these characteristics must be added a precision of detail and a sure taste that neither overstates nor understates. Just look at a Danish street sign or a printed currency note. The typography is most often perfect, simple, and matter-of-fact. No other Scandinavian country has such superbly painted signs, often built on little more than the expressive shapes of the letters themselves. Caring about the smallest details: perhaps some of the secret lies there.

Throughout Denmark, a concern for the quality of life is discernible in the immediate environment. Perhaps the Danes realize that beauty is a necessity of life. This is something Ellen Key in Sweden discussed at the turn of the century. Her philosophy was that beauty should be accessible to all and that people work better and are happier if they live in an aesthetically satisfying milieu, surrounded by lovely things. Such a concept may seem naive today, when much more is

Kaare Klint (Denmark). The Red Chair, *1927*

required: acceptable social conditions and economic parity, to begin with. But since Scandinavians have come so far in many respects—a car, a boat, and a summer vacation, for instance, can now be had by the great majority—perhaps beauty is once again something to consider.

When we speak about Sweden, it seems essential to focus on developments at a few major Swedish exhibitions and the ambitions that were associated with them. When we speak about Denmark, it is just as natural to emphasize the strength of design in certain areas during certain specific times. Who can forget the Royal Copenhagen Porcelain Manufactory's Art Nouveau pieces with their shimmering underglaze decorations, or the stoneware produced at the Saxbo studio, or Gertrud Vasegaard's classic table services? And yet furniture and silver are generally considered the most important areas of Danish design.

After World War II, the Snedkerlauget in Copenhagen became one of the world's most noteworthy producers of furniture. It achieved this status by fostering a spirit of close and harmonious cooperation between architects and master cabinetmakers—thereby establishing an important aspect of what was to become known as Scandinavian Design. The typical furniture of this period was exclusive, well made, and stylish. It was not insignificant that one of Hans Wegner's chairs was christened "The Chair." After World War II, Danish furniture was exported all over the world, and it has stood the test of time as a product that combines fine crafts and industry. Any part of the furniture that could be done just as well by machines was produced industrially, while details were handled by the craftsmen themselves.

Among the design products of Scandinavia, those of Sweden and Denmark perhaps have become the most familiar to foreign audiences. Yet the contribution of the other three Nordic countries to Scandinavian design cannot be underestimated. Iceland has recently been making a concerted effort in the field of design, and it is now producing many interesting objects, particularly in the area of crafts.

Norway enjoys closer ties with traditional popular art than any other Scandinavian country, with the possible exception of Iceland. But there, too, an ambition for "more beautiful things for everyday use" has made itself felt. The Norwegian Society of Arts and Crafts and Industrial Design, founded in

1918, has as its goals to "encourage the development of Norwegian crafts and Norwegian industry in an artistic direction" and to create "effective ties among crafts, industry, and art." The goals are familiar, but Norway's peripheral location and small and dispersed population make them difficult to carry out. Nonetheless, the goals are there, clearly stated, and the country has produced some major designs in the last century.

Although not as well known for its design as other Scandinavian countries, Norway is sovereign, and practically alone, in one area: enamel. Their translucent enamels set up an interplay of light with the metal to create a marvelous effect of radiance and life. To quote one Norwegian, "The powerful and pure enamel colors bear a marked similarity to the colors in the Norwegian landscape. They are the same hues that can be seen in Norwegian textiles and Norwegian painting." Characteristically, the Norwegian designer has worked with nearly every material and has been able to apply his or her talents in various craft areas without losing a feeling for different materials.

Finland brings a youthful freshness and power to the Scandinavian design community. Back at the turn of the century, the Finns created impressive examples of architecture, the industrial arts, and crafts. Unlike Denmark with its cultivated history, Finland drew its style from the popular tradition and the national character, fed by an unspoiled, natural source that is stronger than history alone. A powerful purity and magnificent frankness characterize a Finnish attitude to design. Past poverty and the drab, gray workaday world have not given birth to meager simplicity but rather to a powerful extravagance of color and form. This is particularly evident in all Finnish textiles, from the glowing *ryijys* to the stylish printed fabrics of Marimekko and Vuokko. Finnish design often approaches an "art for art's sake" attitude.

Designers in Finland have specialized in the fields of architecture and industrial design, finding in them a liberation that transcends the ordinary. Especially after World War II, Finland made a name for itself in the industrial arts, most notably in textiles and glass, although the innovative and now classic designs of Alvar Aalto cannot be overlooked. The Finns continued to reap medals at the Milan Triennale time after time with magnificent, striking, and superaesthetic installations. The marked differences between the Finnish style and those of the other Scandinavian countries prompted much discussion in Finland, particularly after the 1955 exhibition in Hälsingborg. While the displays of the other countries reflected the prevailing attitude of social commitment, Finland's entries concentrated on aesthetics. Many felt that everyday objects had been kept, wrongly, in the background; yet, on the other hand, Finland's successes abroad had nourished the development of the best designers. A revision in design focus took place during the 1960s with a new emphasis on everyday products, which gradually became a standard aspect of the Finnish design image.

Perhaps it is our most important task in Scandinavia—the task of the five siblings—to maintain the position we have achieved with the entity known as Scandinavian Design. To this end, we must develop good, basic ideas still further, broaden our field of social commitment, already evident in consumer goods, and extend our ideas to producers and their products within a larger world view of human needs and resources.

Aesthetic quality gave us a place on the world map, but it is not an end in itself. Our products also stood for a style of living. That Scandinavian Design has become something of a term denoting style, rather like the term Art Deco, is undoubtedly exciting. But, in its truest sense, Scandinavian Design must stand for more than how things look: it must stand equally for the ideas behind them.

VIKING REVIVAL AND ART NOUVEAU: TRADITIONS OF EXCELLENCE

ELISABET STAVENOW-HIDEMARK
Curator, Nordiska Museet, Stockholm

1. Jens Ferdinand Willumsen (1863–1958). *Vase.* 1898–99. Denmark. Produced at Bing & Grøndahl, Copenhagen. Porcelain, 15 × 10¾″ (38 × 27.5 cm). Bing & Grøndahl, Copenhagen

Willumsen was Bing & Grøndahl's artistic director from 1897 to 1900. Only four of these unusual vases were made at the factory, and one of them was deposited in the town hall of Copenhagen. The vase is inscribed "JFW forsøg med dobbelt billede 1898" (Trial with a double motif). It was quite difficult to fire this ambitiously pierced design, and most versions suffered firing cracks.

Note: The order of the dimensions is always height by width by depth. Unless otherwise specified, dates given for objects refer to the year of their design.

Those who view the Scandinavian countries from outside often see them as a cultural entity, their individual differences blurring at a distance. We who look at cultural manifestations at closer range, from Scandinavia itself, discern the differences more easily. At the end of the nineteenth century and the beginning of the twentieth, these differences, largely due to the political situation in each country, were unusually distinct and were underlined by the urge for national self-assertion. Norway, which since 1814 had been a subordinate partner in a union with Sweden, ruled by the Swedish kings, was striving for independence. The union was dissolved in 1905, occasioning an identity crisis for the Swedes as well as for the Norwegians. Finland had formed part of Sweden up to 1809, when it came under Russian domination as a grand duchy. At first the czars favored Finland's economy and granted the grand duchy considerable autonomy. But changing conditions in the 1890s came to a head in 1899, when Finland's autonomy was sharply curtailed. Denmark still bore traces of the bloody war with Germany during the period 1863–64, which ended with Denmark's loss of Schleswig and Holstein. Yet, despite these struggles for independence, Scandinavian artists paid little attention to border lines. Even in other European countries, they banded together in colonies. The kindred languages of Scandinavia also facilitated contacts.

The dominant styles in Scandinavian design in the late nineteenth century, architecturally and artistically, were revivals of the Rococo and the Renaissance, not unlike those that could be found in many other European countries. The strong influence of Germany on Scandinavia can be seen in the particular popularity of the Renaissance mode, which had become a symbol of political unification in Germany. Another important style current in the late nineteenth century was the Viking revival, also called the dragon style or the Old Nordic style. A peculiarly Scandinavian version of a revival style, it fired the imaginations of many artists and designers because of its unmistakable national overtones.

The Old Nordic style had its roots in the early nineteenth century, particularly in the realm of literature. Artists, poets, and scholars, deeply interested in Nordic mythology, wrote heroic epics, taking their themes from the world of the Vikings. It took longer for those in the art world to embrace the style. Although elegant ornamentation with serpentine dragon bodies appeared as decorative borders in interior design as early as 1841 in a royal apartment outside Christiania (as Oslo was then called), only after the middle of the century did Old Nordic motifs become common in the pictorial arts. Archaeological excavations, especially of the Norwegian ships in Tune in 1867 and in Gokstad in 1880, generated a widespread enthusiasm for the style.

The Viking revival meant different things to each Scandinavian country. In Sweden, it was fostered by a small but influential circle of artistically oriented persons, who took it up around 1870, but it never became truly popular. This group in Stockholm, however, gave new power to the style by applying Old Nordic motifs to architecture and crafts.

Two well-known Swedish doctors, professors Carl Curman and Axel Key, built summer houses with Nordic motifs derived from Norwegian farm buildings. Dragon heads at the end of the gables adorned the exteriors of these houses, and friezes with saga motifs based on the heroic Norwegian *Hávamál* poems of the ninth and tenth centuries decorated the interiors. Painter August Malmström designed oak furniture with carved braided ornamentation; together with Daniel J. Carlsson and architect Magnus Isaeus, he also devised ceramic tablewares with borders featuring dragon ornamentation.

This Swedish group also included the Norwegian Lorentz Dietrichson, a well-known lecturer in aesthetics and the doyen of art critics, especially those surrounding the royal court. It was after his return to Christiania in 1875 as professor of art history that the dragon style made its breakthrough on a broader

48

2. August Malmström (1829–1901) and Daniel J. Carlsson (1853–1922). *Tureen and stand.* 1877. Sweden. Produced by Gustavsberg. Ironstone ceramic, enamel decoration, *tureen:* 11 × 16″ (28 × 40.6 cm); *stand:* diameter 12¾″ (32.5 cm). Nordiska Museet, Stockholm

Colorful designs in the Nordic style were produced at Gustavsberg from the 1870s until about 1900. Malmström designed the forms of this tureen and stand, and Carlsson provided the decoration. The bold dragon handles and finials of such pieces were emphasized with brilliant enamel decorations based on Viking interlaced knots.

3. Torolf Prytz (1856–1938). *Jardiniere.* 1900. Norway. Produced by J. Tostrup, Oslo. Silver, cast and chased, 13¾ × 20⅞″ (35 × 53 cm). Oslo Kunstindustrimuseet

Although Viking revival or dragon style designs could be found in several Scandinavian countries during the late nineteenth century, such designs were particularly favored by metalworkers in Norway. This jardiniere, inspired by archaeological finds, echoes the shape of a Viking ship. It was intended to be shown at the Paris Exposition of 1900, but was not completed in time.

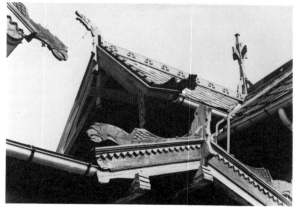

Hunting lodge roof in the "dragon" style, Bergen, designed by P. A. O. Digre, 1898

Bedroom, Professor Carl Curman's house, Lysekil, Sweden, c. 1883

2

3

front in Norway. There the dragon style, as a means of expression in the struggle for national identity, became a national phenomenon and came to be considered Norwegian property.

In its first phase, the dragon style was heroic, but this emphasis soon gave way to purely aesthetic or decorative concerns. The most important sources of inspiration were archaeological finds and medieval Norwegian wooden architecture. Although such medieval buildings (along with what was then the modern Swiss style) constituted the point of departure, architecture still had its basis in neo-gothic principles current at the time. On the other hand, tourist hotels in the fells presented such vivid examples of the dragon style that foreigners took it to be the expression of a distinct Norwegian character.

Ornamental designs from archaeological finds were adapted to work in silver and cast iron and appeared in prints as well. Dragon motifs were figured into embroidered decorative cloths and white damask cloths. The new Viking ornamentation enriched both Neo-Renaissance forms and objects that had no prototypes in ancient culture. Modern objects such as the coffeepot, creamer, and sugar bowl sat on dragon feet and had spouts in the shape of dragon heads; borders with dragons or braids in bas-relief encircled the bodies of hollow ware pieces. Norway's leading goldsmithing firms, J. Tostrup and David Andersen in Christiania, were primary exponents of the style and were followed by many others, especially those in the souvenir industry.

At the same time, the revival of old techniques was espoused and encouraged. In his book *Den Norske Træskjærerkunst* (The Norwegian Art of Carving) published in 1878, Dietrichson praised the rich carving style of Norwegian peasant art and spoke of the possibilities of reviving the art by reviving the old ornaments. His call was heeded and instruction in this traditional art began.

Although the Viking revival did not have the nationalistic impact in Denmark that it had in other countries, certain designs, such as those for jewelry, clearly revealed its influence. Goldsmiths found inspiration in the jewelry and other objects of metalwork excavated at numerous archaeological sites, and they used these rich finds to develop a new vocabulary of decoration and design. Such goldsmiths as E. F. Dahl and

Holmenkollen Tourist Hotel, near Oslo, 1892

4. Gerhard Munthe (1849–1929). *Tapestry:* The Three Suitors. 1897. Norway. Executed by Augusta Christensen at Nordenfjeldske Kunstindustrimuseum Tapestry Studio, Trondheim. Linen (warp) and wool (weft), 72 × 87⅛" (183 × 221.5 cm). Vestlandske Kundstindustrimuseum, Bergen

Trained as a painter, Munthe studied in Düsseldorf and Munich before returning to his native land. In the latter years of the nineteenth century, he turned to flat, abstract designs based on Norwegian folk motifs and legends. Munthe's tapestries reveal his strong coloristic sense and flattened linear style. The tapestry was originally woven for the Exposition Universelle in Paris in 1900.

4

Anton Michelsen in Copenhagen freely imitated these archaeological objects in their armbands and clasps covered with a filigree of gold and silver threads. In Denmark, as in Norway and Finland, the style roused an interest in old techniques, and complex patterns that combine filigree with minute granulation mark the finest Danish jewelry in the revival style.

In Finland, as in Norway, the Old Nordic style was seized on as an expression of nationalism. The Finns even had their own term—Karelianism—to describe the style. Karelia, an area in eastern Finland, was the source of the ancient dramatic national epic, the *Kalevala*, which had existed only in the oral tradition until it was systematically collected and set down in the nineteenth century.

In the late 1800s, Finland was a country seething with unrest. Increasing Russian oppression roused the Finns to regenerate their national language and restore it to a paramount position. While Finnish had been the language of the common people for hundreds of years, the educated classes and people in the western and southern coastal districts spoke Swedish. Many artists had Swedish names and spoke Swedish at home. A large number of them now turned to Finnish and sought power and inspiration in the old myths and unspoiled wilds of Finland. The untamed forests of Karelia, which were considered genuinely Finnish, attracted many architects and painters in search of traditional motifs.

Among the first to make an artistic pilgrimage to Karelia, in 1890, were painter Axel Gallén (who later took the Finnish form of his name, Akseli Gallen-Kallela) and the Swedish artist Louis Sparre. In the national romantic spirit, many artists who followed them built log houses in the wilderness. These houses, often inspired by the Karelian building tradition, had balconies and high ceilings, but their interiors reflected modern English ideas of room division and furnishing. Gallen-Kallela's studio home, Kalela, and the large wooden "castle," Hvitträsk (built by the architects Gesellius, Lindgren, and Saarinen in 1901–3), are perhaps the best-known examples of such buildings.

Work in textiles also profited from the new movement. The Friends of Finnish Handicraft (Suomen Käsityön Ystävät), founded in 1879 along the same lines as the somewhat older Friends of Textile Art Association in Sweden, collected old Finnish—especially Karelian—embroidery and weaving motifs,

Hall at Suur Merijoki, 1901–3, designed by Gesellius, Lindgren, and Saarinen; watercolor by Eliel Saarinen

5. Gustav Gaudernack (1865–1914). *Candelabra.* 1898. Norway. Produced by David Andersen, Oslo. Silver, height 19¾" (50.5 cm). Collection Lennart Nisser, Sweden

Although Bohemian by birth, Gaudernack moved to Norway in 1891 and became one of that country's most respected designers of metalwork. He produced an extensive number of silver objects, many incorporating enamel in the designs. Gaudernack's work is distinguished by its technical complexity of ornament and attention to detail.

6. Emil Ferdinand Dahl (1819–1879). *Bracelet.* Denmark. c. 1875. Gold, 1¼ × 2⅞" (3.5 × 7.5 cm). Det Danske Kunstindustrimuseum, Copenhagen

7. F. W. Knoblich (1808–1879). *Pair of brooches.* 1870. Denmark. Produced by A. Michelsen, Copenhagen. Gold, 2⅝ × 2¾" (6.6 × 7 cm). Det Danske Kunstindustrimuseum, Copenhagen

These opulent pieces of jewelry clearly evoke the romantic appeal of Viking ornamentation. The renewed interest in metalworking techniques employed in Viking designs is seen in the use of both filigree work, consisting of tiny twisted wires, and granulation of minute gold beads.

5

6

7

9

8. Gerhard Munthe (1849–1929). *Armchair*. 1895–1907. Norway. Designed for the "Fairy Tale Room" of Holmenkollen Turisthotell, Oslo, and produced by "Cabinetmaker Borgersen," Oslo. Wood, painted, and fabric, 43¼ × 23¾ × 23⅝" (110 × 60.5 × 60 cm). Vestlandske Kunstindustrimuseum, Bergen

The vigorous sculptural treatment of this chair and the brilliant colors used in its decoration indicate the extremes that the Viking revival could attain. The interior of the Turisthotell was decorated with bold carvings of Nordic sagas and legends in a style that is noteworthy for its exuberance and liberated ornament, out of which functional forms were created.

9. Gabriel Engberg (1872–1953). *Rug*. 1905. Finland. Executed by Suomen Käsityön Ystävät (Friends of Finnish Handicraft). Wool, *ryijy* technique, 122⅞ × 70⅛" (312 × 178 cm). Taideteollisuusmuseo, Helsinki

Ryijy rugs have a long and distinguished history in the Scandinavian countries, particularly in Finland. Besides making colorful additions to interiors, these large rugs, long enough to drape from the wall over a bench or seat below, were also designed to provide maximum warmth. Engberg, along with Akseli Gallen-Kallela and Jarl Eklund, contributed to the revival of interest in this folk art.

intending to develop modern Finnish textile art in a national vein. A traditional Swedish and Finnish knotting technique used by peasants in making bedcovers, called *rya* in Swedish and *ryijy* in Finnish, was revived and used to make a combined rug, bench cover, and wall hanging. The first modern *ryijy* was Gallen-Kallela's *Flame*, shown at the Paris Exhibition of 1900; other designers such as Gabriel Engberg produced boldly geometric patterns exemplifying the vitality of the tradition.

Karelianism profoundly affected young Finnish artists. A bond that transcended the boundaries of their different fields —painting, sculpture, architecture, crafts, and music—was formed between them. In their effort to express the Finnish identity, they raised Finnish art to a new level.

A new international style called Art Nouveau flourished on the Continent, particularly in France and Belgium, during the second half of the century and made its way to Scandinavia during the 1890s, where it became known as Jugend in Sweden. Although a large number of German and French art periodicals circulated its message, its most influential advocate was the English periodical *The Studio*, first published in 1893. Artists also encountered new trends on their travels abroad.

In most Scandinavian countries, the new foreign influence was joined to the awareness of traditional crafts that grew out of the recent Viking revival. While Finland and Sweden enthusiastically adopted the new style, it never became as popular in Norway, which held on to the dragon style. However, Norwegian arabesques did take on an increasingly clear Art Nouveau character. The influence of the new style was strongest in two long-established craft areas that had already won for Norway an international reputation—enamel work and tapestry weaving.

In Sweden, the impulses from abroad were fused with particular national goals. An ethnological museum, the Nordiska Museet, had been founded in 1873 primarily in order to preserve peasant culture. The Handarbetets Vännar (Friends of Textile Art Association), founded in 1874, worked for a revival of textile art by bringing back old Swedish techniques and patterns. This association was the first to accept the new style. The Föreningen Svensk Hemslöjd (Swedish Handicraft

10

11

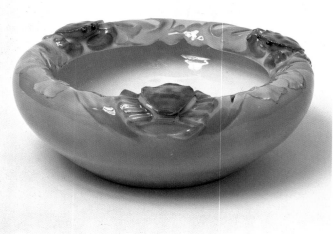

12

10. Gunnar Wennerberg (1863–1914). *Bowl.* 1900. Sweden. Produced at Kosta Glasbruk. Overlay glass, wheel cut, 4¾ × 7⅛″ (12 × 18 cm). Nationalmuseum, Stockholm

The prolific Wennerberg, well known for his ceramics, was also a designer of overlay glass. Inspired by Continental artists such as Gallé and those of the school of Nancy, Wennerberg's work also shows an affinity with the softly modeled cutting of the English overlay designers of Stourbridge.

11. Alf Wallander (1862–1914). *Tea and coffee service.* c. 1900. Sweden. Produced by Rörstrand, Lidköping. Porcelain, underglaze decoration, *coffeepot:* height 10″ (25.4 cm); *tray:* length 18″ (45.7 cm). Collection Robert and Sherry Schreiber, United States

Each piece of this service is ornamented with one or more delicately tinted dragonflies, each of which forms a functional part of the design as a handle or finial. This popular design remained in production at the Rörstrand factory until the 1920s.

12. Alf Wallander (1862–1914). *Bowl.* c. 1900. Sweden. Produced by Rörstrand, Lidköping. Porcelain, underglaze decoration, height 4¾″ (12 cm). Collection Robert and Sherry Schreiber, United States

Wallander's interest in nature as a source of design also extended to the world of undersea life. The extremely naturalistic crabs modeled on the edge of this bowl are painted subtly to contrast with the watery blue of the bowl itself.

13. Algot Eriksson.(1868–1930). *Vase.* c. 1900. Sweden. Produced by Rörstrand, Lidköping. Porcelain, underglaze decoration, height 11¾″ (30 cm). Collection Robert and Sherry Schreiber, United States

The artists and modelers at the Rörstrand factory were responsible for some of the most luxurious wares in the naturalistic style of the late nineteenth and early twentieth centuries. This vase is formed as a partially opened blossom, the sensuous shape emphasized by the subtle gradation of colors.

14. Pietro Krohn (1840–1905). *Tureen, plate, and knife from the* Heron *service.* 1888. Denmark. Produced at Bing & Grøndahl, Copenhagen. Porcelain, underglaze and gilded decoration, *tureen:* 7⅛ × 11¾ × 9⅞″ (18 × 30 × 25 cm); *plate:* diameter 9⅛″ (23.5 cm); *knife:* length 10¼″ (26 cm). Bing & Grøndahl, Copenhagen

The *Heron* service, each piece of which depicts a variation on the heron motif, is a virtuoso masterwork of stylized naturalism. Krohn served as artistic director of the Bing & Grøndahl factory from 1885 to 1897 and became the first director of the Danish Museum of Decorative Art (Det Danske Kunstindustrimuseum) in Copenhagen.

13

14

Society), founded in 1899, studied old crafts all over the countryside to provide a basis for new work. Skansen, the world's first open-air museum, opened in Stockholm in 1891 with a collection of household objects, folk art, and folk costumes housed in old peasant buildings. In the early 1900s, eighteenth-century designs found in Swedish manor houses became the inspiration for applied designs.

Under the influence of Art Nouveau, crafts attained an equal footing with other forms of art; artists and architects experimented with various mediums (painters, for example, turned to pottery or ceramics design) in an effort to create a unified design statement that ranged from architecture to domestic utensils. Nowhere in Scandinavia was the idea of the habitat as a total work of art cultivated so much as in Finland. Its leading architects, Herman Gesellius, Armas Lindgren, and Eliel Saarinen, working in close collaboration, designed large country houses and their furniture, electric fittings, wrought-iron fixtures, and textiles. Saarinen's watercolor interiors in the spirit of the English Arts and Crafts architect Baillie Scott appeared repeatedly in such German art periodicals as *Moderne Bauformen* and *Die Kunst*.

The initial response of Finnish artists to the new style was to adapt it to works of a national character. But in 1904, a heated debate ensued when architect Sigurd Frosterus, who had been trained by the Belgian leader of Art Nouveau Henri Van de Velde, claimed that it was time for constructively rational architecture, social responsibility, and a break with national romanticism. From then on, the influence of the Otto Wagner school in Vienna became stronger: construction was more clearly emphasized and the ponderous symbolism in applied decoration was toned down.

The Arts and Crafts movement in England was particularly influential, since it had stressed vernacular features in architecture and furniture. Many Arts and Crafts designs emphasized simple, clearly constructed forms, restrained two-dimensional decoration, and carefully chosen colors, an approach that struck a sympathetic chord in Sweden. Through their contacts with the Arts and Crafts movement in England, Swedish architects and artists took a fresh look at their own heritage. Inspired by William Morris, the writer and ethical philosopher Ellen Key wrote a little book in 1899 entitled *Skönhet för alla* (Beauty for All) in which she spoke out on the significance

15. Alf Wallander (1862–1914). *Vase*. 1897. Sweden. Produced by Rörstrand, Lidköping. Porcelain, height 27⅝" (70 cm). Collection Robert and Sherry Schreiber, United States

A multitalented designer, Wallander excelled in the sculptural handling of ceramics. Two swans form the body of this large and impressive vase, a virtuoso effort shown in the Stockholm Exhibition of 1897 and again in Paris in 1900.

16. Helmer Osslund (1866–1938). *Vase*. c. 1900. Sweden. Produced at Höganäsbolaget, Höganäs. Glazed earthenware, height 14¼" (36.5 cm). Höganäs Museum

Osslund, like many artists who turned their attention to ceramic design during the late nineteenth century, was trained as a painter. The forceful treatment of color and texture in this vase is typical of Osslund's work, as is the use of a stylized flame motif that also suggests organic growth.

17. Thorolf Holmboe (1866–1935). *Covered jar*. 1900–1905. Norway. Produced at Porsgrunds Porselænsfabrik, Porsgrunn. Porcelain, underglaze decoration, height 6⅞" (17.3 cm). Oslo Kunstindustrimuseet

Holmboe's designs for the Porsgrund factory drew heavily on the flora and fauna of the surrounding countryside. Although technically and stylistically related to the work of the Royal Copenhagen factory, the technique of underglaze painting as practiced at Porsgrunds was distinctive in its restraint.

18. Arnold Krog (1856–1931). *Vase*. 1889. Denmark. Produced at the Royal Copenhagen Porcelain Manufactory Ltd., Copenhagen. Porcelain, underglaze decoration, height 13¼" (33.7 cm). The Royal Copenhagen Porcelain Museum

Krog's interest in Japanese designs is indicated in the carefully delineated isolated figure of the bird. This vase—one of the landmark works in Krog's oeuvre of underglaze-painted porcelains—was shown with several other of his pieces at the Exposition Universelle of 1889 in Paris, moving the critic Roger Marx to compare Krog with Emile Gallé in his handling of decorative form.

15

16

17

18

19. Andreas Ollestad (1857–1936). *Vase.* 1899. Norway. Produced at Egersunds Fayancefabrik, Egersund. Glazed earthenware, height 10¾" (27.5 cm). Oslo Kunstindustrimuseet

Ollestad worked at the Egersund factory for fifty years, from 1886 until his death in 1936. This vase exemplifies the superb integration of painted and modeled relief typical of Ollestad's work; the waves and emerging fish are modeled in relief, creating textures that are emphasized by the rich, transparent glazes.

20, 21. Gustav Gaudernack (1865–1914). *Two drawings for a compote.* 1904. Norway. Pencil and watercolor on paper, 20: 17⅜ × 12¼" (44 × 31 cm); 21: 11½ × 10" (29.5 × 25.5 cm). Oslo Kunstindustrimuseet

Many of the detailed drawings that Gaudernack made for his enameled works have, fortunately, survived. The intricate nature of the *plique à jour* technique is clearly indicated in these drawings, which display the same jewel-like quality that distinguishes his completed objects.

22. Effie Hegermann-Lindencrone (1869–1945). *Covered vase.* 1923. Denmark. Produced at Bing & Grøndahl, Copenhagen. Porcelain, pierced and underglaze decoration, height 21¾" (55.5 cm). Bing & Grøndahl, Copenhagen

A leading figure in the development of pierced, molded decoration, Hegermann-Lindencrone continued to work in a late-nineteenth-century naturalistic style well into the twentieth century. This vase was cast in a mold, with supplementary piercing and detailing added by hand. The depth of color and delicacy of the natural forms are typical of Hegermann-Lindencrone's finest works.

23. Attributed to Gustav Gaudernack (1865–1914). *Bowl.* c. 1900–1905. Norway. Produced at David Andersen, Oslo. Silver and *plique à jour* enamel, 6½ × 6" (16.6 × 15.5 cm). Collection Ruth and Leo Kaplan, United States

Interest in enameling revived in Norway during the latter part of the nineteenth century. The medium found its primary exponent in the Bohemian-born Gaudernack, whose work in the *plique à jour* technique was outstanding.

19

20

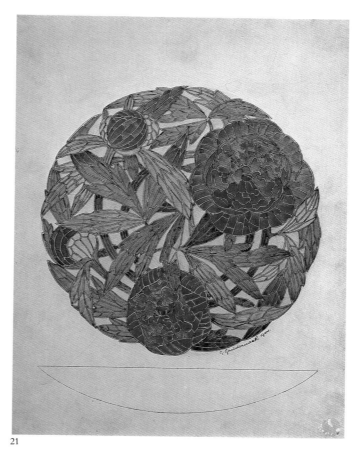

21

22

23

of the habitat. That same year, painter Carl Larsson published watercolors of his home in the Dalarna in a book that also became very popular in Germany. Larsson championed a down-to-earth, unpretentious style in the home and the use of abundant color. Houses built in growing suburban areas borrowed elements of vernacular architecture, especially the red-washed wooden siding and white trimming of simple country dwellings. This is the side of Swedish Art Nouveau embraced by many young artists and other enthusiastic supporters of the style who were drawn to its combination of a passion for nature with a concern for aesthetic quality and national integrity.

The other side of Swedish design in this period reflected a sophisticated internationalism. It adopted the new art idiom and the idea of transforming the habitat, but in a style that paralleled Continental developments without clear reference to the new nationalism. The leading representative of this trend was architect Ferdinand Boberg, who created refined and elegant interiors such as that designed for King Oscar II shown in the Paris 1900 exhibition. He also designed furniture, silver, glass, ceramics, and textiles.

The stylistic features of Art Nouveau were adapted as well to the Scandinavian sensibility. In France and Belgium, compositions based on flowers and plants undulated on the surfaces of ceramics, glass, and metalwork, but the abstract, sweeping lines of their patterns appeared less frequently in Scandinavian designs. More geometrically stylized motifs, which flourished in Scotland and Vienna, left their clearest marks in Finnish—and, to a certain degree, in Swedish—architecture and crafts well into the twentieth century. The unspoiled Nordic landscape—its forests, snow, wildlife, and wildflowers—became symbols of the artistic and spiritual heritage in the same way that vernacular log buildings and woven textiles did.

As on the Continent, flora and fauna provided a rich vocabulary of motifs for Scandinavian designers, and Nordic designs, in particular, depicted the forms and patterns of native plants and animals with great sensitivity and faithfulness. The implied organic growth in these designs was restrained and often understated, and the taut drawing lines defined the forms rather than becoming a calligraphic exercise for its own sake.

Carl Larsson, "The Nursery," from Ett hem *(A Home), 1899*

24. Gunnar Wennerberg (1863–1914). *Vase.* 1908–9. Sweden. Produced at Kosta Glasbruk. Overlay glass, wheel cut, height 9⅞" (25.1 cm). Collection Eva Polland, Sweden

The design of fern fronds, arranged asymmetrically on the surface of the vase, stands out in a green glass that contrasts with the frosted clear glass beneath. The surface of the glass has been carefully wheel cut to achieve a "hammered" texture that lends distinction to Wennerberg's designs.

25. Georg Jensen (1866–1935). *Brooch: Dragonfly.* 1904. Denmark. Produced by Georg Jensen Sølvsmedie, Copenhagen. Silver and opals, 3⅛ × 1¾" (8 × 4.5 cm). Det Danske Kunstindustrimuseum, Copenhagen

26. Erik Magnussen (1884–1935). *Brooch: Grasshopper.* 1907. Denmark. Silver and coral, 2 × 3½" (5 × 9 cm). Det Danske Kunstindustrimuseum, Copenhagen

Jewelry produced in Scandinavia around the turn of the century reveals the fascination of designers with plants and animals of unusual shape. In jewelry like these brooches, the soft patina of silver was emphasized in the surface textures and played against the vibrant color of semiprecious stones. Magnussen designed in Denmark until 1925, when he came to the United States, where he worked for the Gorham Company, among others. He used natural forms for his jewelry design, into which he often incorporated amber and stones.

27. Anna Boberg (1864–1935). *Vase.* 1902. Sweden. Produced at Reijmyre Glasbruk, Rejmyra. Blown glass, applied detail, wheel cut, height 6" (15.2 cm). Collection Prins Eugens Waldemarsudde, Sweden.

The wife of the architect and designer Ferdinand Boberg, Anna Boberg composed unusual glass designs using a variety of techniques. The juxtaposition of abstract and natural motifs—here, small fish—remains a feature of Swedish glass design.

The country least affected by the Art Nouveau influence was

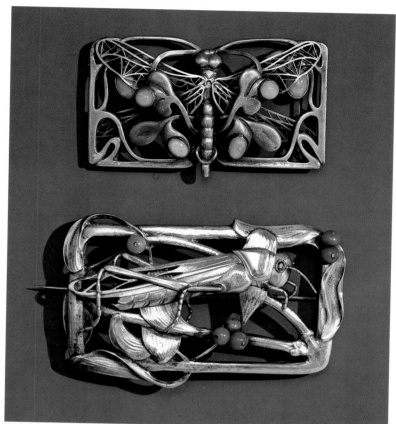

24

25 26

27

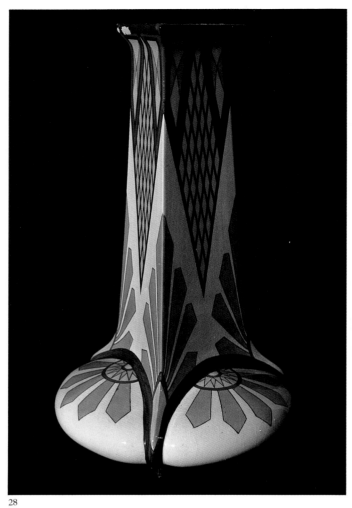

28

29

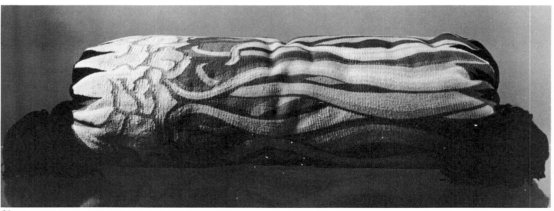

30

28. *Vase from the* Fennia *series.* c. 1902. Finland. Produced at Arabia, Helsinki. Earthenware, enamel decoration, height 12⅝" (32 cm). Arabia Museum, Helsinki

Karelian designs produced during the late nineteenth century in Finland were often striking in their geometric patterning and free use of strong color. The *Fennia* series of vases is decorated with motifs related to Karelian folk art. The actual designer of these vases, unfortunately, is unknown.

29. Eliel Saarinen (1873–1950). *Armchair.* 1918. Finland. Produced by Boman, Turku. Oak and leather, 33½ × 20⅞ × 20⅛" (85 × 53 × 51 cm). Gerda and Salomo Wuorio Foundation, Hvitträsk

When the three leading Finnish architects of the turn of the century—Herman Gesellius, Armas Lindgren, and Eliel Saarinen—designed their famous residence/studio at Hvitträsk, they also considered virtually every detail of the interior furnishings. Saarinen's suite of furniture for the dining room, of which this chair is one example, relied on sinuous organic forms of provocative design. Each chair is inscribed "Hvitträsk 1918" on the back splat.

30. Akseli Gallen-Kallela (1865–1931). *Cushion cover.* 1913. Finland. Executed by Suomen Käsityön Ystävät (Friends of Finnish Handicraft). Wool, width 33½" (85 cm). Taideteollisuusmuseo, Helsinki

Like his *ryijy* rugs, Gallen-Kallela's designs for textiles often featured flamelike patterns arranged asymmetrically over the surface of the work. The design of this cushion cover combines the linear flame motif with abstract floral patterns.

The Iris Room, Finnish Pavilion, Paris Exhibition of 1900

Denmark, which had an unbroken tradition of excellence in the crafts. During this period—called "Skønvirke" ("aesthetic activity"), also the name of a major design periodical—Danish crafts retained a distinct profile. A few versatile artists were responsible for crafts production in many fields. Although their style was often restrained and elegant, recalling the early nineteenth-century "golden age" of refinement and sophistication, it often revealed a new, sensuous appreciation of materials. The work of leading craftsmen showed no trace of the undulating lines of Van de Velde's style or of geometrically composed motifs. Instead, Danish artists were particularly influenced by the Japanese art they had seen in Paris in the 1880s. Although Danish crafts of this time do not resemble those in other countries, they share the same spirit.

The large world's fairs, or expositions, played an important role in the world of design in at least two ways: they opened up new contacts for participating Scandinavian artists, and they directly affected production. In an effort to win the highly coveted gold and silver medals awarded during the expositions, companies hired artists and began producing new collections several years in advance of the events. Their efforts were rewarded: many Scandinavian companies and artists garnered prizes at the expositions in Paris in 1900, in Turin in 1902, in St. Louis in 1904, and in St. Petersburg in 1908.

Finland had its own stunning success at the Paris Exposition of 1900. Its pavilion, built by Gesellius, Lindgren, and Saarinen, suddenly made Finland a current topic in European cultural circles. The pavilion's overall plan, which took into account the ideas of Wagner in Vienna, achieved a brilliant modernity; yet the great granite doorway, the ornamentation with bears, squirrels, and pine cones, and a tower whose form is said to have been taken from that of Finnish rural church towers conferred on it a distinct national character. The harmonious form and artistic treatment of details aroused admiration. The interior, to which the leading Finnish design talents contributed, was no less carefully composed. One room contained furnishings designed by Gallen-Kallela, including his *ryijy Flame*, and the Friends of Finnish Handicraft provided other *ryijys* as well as draperies and upholstery fabrics. The elegant silhouettes of the furniture were emphasized by the natural qualities of its light birch wood, for the most part left undecorated.

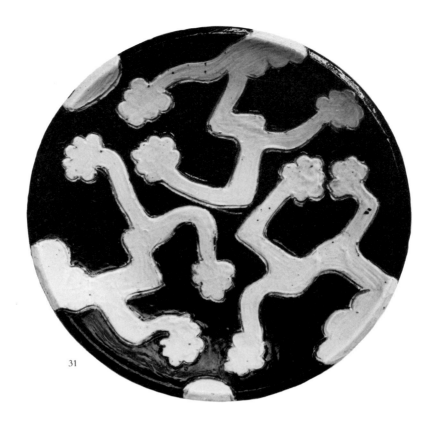

31

32

33

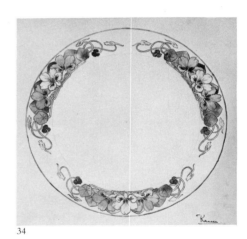

34

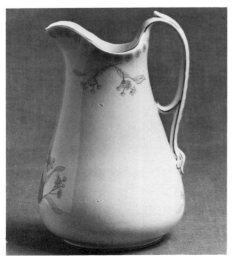

35

36

31. Thorvald Bindesbøll (1846–1908). *Plate*. 1901. Denmark. Produced at Københavns Lervarefabrik, Copenhagen. Glazed earthenware, diameter 17¾" (45 cm). Det Danske Kunstindustrimuseum, Copenhagen

Trained as a classical architect, Bindesbøll became one of the most innovative designers of ceramics, metalwork, furniture, and textiles. He formulated his designs with the eye of a painter and sculptor, producing boldly expressionistic patterns highlighted with earthy colors. In this plate, for example, the black-and-white glazes accentuate the strongly calligraphic design.

32. C. F. Liisberg (1860–1909). *Plate*. 1890. Denmark. Produced at the Royal Copenhagen Porcelain Manufactory Ltd., Copenhagen. Porcelain, underglaze decoration, diameter 11⅜" (29 cm). The Royal Copenhagen Porcelain Museum

Liisberg, employed by the Royal Copenhagen Porcelain Manufactory as early as 1885, was an innovator in the use of slip (a creamy mixture of clay and water) as a painting medium. This technique can give a three-dimensional texture to the surface, as seen in the figure of a swimming male on this plate.

33, 34. Gunnar Wennerberg (1863–1914). *Two designs for plate borders*. c. 1895–1900. Sweden. Watercolor on paper, 33: 12½ × 12¼" (31.8 × 31 cm); 34: 12¼ × 12⅝" (31.2 × 32 cm). Gustavsberg Museum

Wennerberg's designs for floral borders for standard production tableware manifest a fresh and sensitive appreciation of native flora. Although the blossoms and leaves are stylized to permit them to be repeated around the borders of the plates, they still retain their natural forms and colors.

35. Gunnar Wennerberg (1863–1914). *Pitcher*, Lindlof *pattern*. 1899. Sweden. Produced by Gustavsberg. Flintware, enamel decoration, height 8⅜" (21.5 cm). Gustavsberg Museum

Wennerberg was artistic director of the Gustavsberg factory from 1895 until 1908, during which time he introduced many new naturalistic patterns. Among the most popular was the *Lindlof* pattern of native Swedish buttercups, which was applied to extremely simple standard forms.

36. Gunnar Wennerberg (1863–1914). *Tureen*, Snödroppe *pattern*. 1897. Sweden. Produced by Gustavsberg. Bone porcelain, enamel decoration, 5⅛ × 12⅝" (13 × 32 cm). Gustavsberg Museum

A great champion of Swedish naturalism, Wennerberg created a wide variety of designs for the decoration of production tableware. Although Wennerberg did not radically revise the general shape of domestic utensils, he did pioneer the decorative use of patterns based on the world of Swedish flora to be mass-produced for a large consumer audience.

Besides participating in international expositions, Sweden held its own art and industrial exhibitions. Three of these, each of which occasioned large economic and artistic investments, are mileposts in the history of the Art Nouveau style in Sweden. The Stockholm Exhibition of 1897, which revealed a breakthrough in ceramics, gave the new style its first public recognition. The 1909 Stockholm Exhibition not only marked a high point in Swedish design, above all in textile art, but it also officially confirmed that the new style was fully established. The final milestone, the Baltic Exhibition in Malmö in 1914, met with devastating criticism because its displays were thought to lack innovation and social commitment. Only textile art was considered to have come up to expectations.

The leading figure of the age—perhaps the epitome of the artist in a period of interdisciplinary activity—was the Danish artist Thorvald Bindesbøll, whose multiplicity of talents carried him into the fields of architecture, graphic arts, and the design of ceramics, silver, furniture, books, and embroidery patterns. Everything he made, whether it was a chair or an embroidery pattern, has an architectonically clear form that is given breadth, warmth, and life by its sensual decorations. Bindesbøll used generous, swelling forms, rounded surfaces, and abstract decoration which bring to mind clouds gathering or leaves against the light. Color, form, and decoration were completely thought out in everything, and there is a clear consistency in all his work. He designed ceramic pieces for several companies. His bowls and platters, done mainly between 1891 and 1904, are large, rough, and powerful, and many are decorated in bold patterns of black and white.

Denmark, a pioneer in experimental ceramics, continued as a leading force in the field. As far back as 1889, Arnold Krog had presented underglaze-painted ceramics at the Paris Exposition, winning a worldwide reputation for the Royal Copenhagen Porcelain Manufactory. Krog, working with C. F. Liisberg, made underglaze decorations with a blue-gray color scale, taking his motifs from the Danish flora and fauna. Flowering branches, willow leaves, or birds in pale, soft colors, inspired by Japanese painting, were set asymmetrically on classically simple pieces. Under the direction of Pietro Krohn, Bing & Grøndahl, the Royal Copenhagen Porcelain Manufactory's traditional competitor, also designed pieces to be decorated with underglaze painting. Without doubt, Krohn's 67 most famous work is the extensive *Heron* service, each piece of which is modeled or painted with a bird motif.

J. F. Willumsen, architect, painter, and sculptor, joined Bing & Grøndahl in 1897 and periodically served as its artistic director. His work in ceramics, often highly sculptural, was symbolically and poetically expressive. Willumsen also developed new glazes at the firm. One of his co-workers, Effie Hegermann-Lindencrone, specialized in vessels with intricate openwork surfaces. Leaves and flowers, carefully delineated and finely painted, luxuriate on the surfaces of these works.

At Herman A. Kähler's workshop in Næstved, painter K. Hansen Reistrup infused his decorative friezes with images of birds and the sea. Kähler himself often used exotic reptile forms as fully modeled decoration on his work. His son, H. C. Kähler, made decorative platters, each individually fashioned on the wheel, bearing motifs with fluid contours that suggest fruit and leaves. His pieces, glazed in deep and luminous colors, unite form and ornamentation in a perfect harmony.

During this period, Norway's ceramic production drew largely on the style set by Denmark. The Porsgrund porcelain factory produced underglaze art wares using the customary blue-gray color scale in many nuances. Decorative motifs, especially those of Theodor Kittelsen and Thorolf Holmboe, depicted Norway's flora and fauna, typically, snow-covered spruce, fells, and animals in the snow.

Andreas Schneider was the first Norwegian ceramist with his own experimental workshop, in Slemdal outside Christiania. Originally a painter, he became interested in ceramics during a stay in Copenhagen, where he undoubtedly studied the works of Danish potters. The coloristic richness of Schneider's glazes and the fluid sculptural quality of his forms reflect his knowledge of Danish pottery and of Japanese ceramics, which he also greatly admired.

Sweden's two major porcelain companies, Gustavsberg and Rörstrand, hired the painters Gunnar Wennerberg and Alf Wallander before the Stockholm Exhibition of 1897. (Both artists were to become leading designers in several fields.) Wennerberg, working for Gustavsberg, took his inspiration from Japanese floral arrangements in his use of Swedish wildflowers as the source for designs on table services. He also did pioneering work in sgraffito ceramics, in which

37. Arnold Krog (1856–1931) and Erik Nielsen (1857–1947). *Dish.* 1890. Denmark. Produced at the Royal Copenhagen Porcelain Manufactory Ltd., Copenhagen. Porcelain, underglaze decoration, width 8″ (20.2 cm). The Royal Copenhagen Porcelain Museum

Naturalism and Japanese designs inspired this unusual leaf-shaped dish; both leaves and frog probably were cast from nature. When the dish is turned upside down (*right*), it is possible to see the remainder of the frog's body as well as a snail, which forms the supporting foot of the dish.

38. Thorvald Bindesbøll (1846–1908). *Design for a large vase.* 1893. Denmark. Watercolor on paper, 24 × 23¾″ (61 × 60.5 cm). Det Danske Kunstindustrimuseum, Copenhagen

This early watercolor study foreshadows Bindesbøll's arresting designs of the turn of the century; the floral ornament of the vase is highly stylized and depicted with an exuberant sense of movement. Also, the strong sculptural form of the vase, revealed in the sensuously rippling outline, was to become a pronounced feature of Bindesbøll's subsequent designs.

39. Herman A. Kähler (1846–1917). *Vase.* c. 1895. Denmark. Produced at H. A. Kähler, Næstved. Glazed earthenware, 8¾ × 11¾″ (22.5 × 30 cm). Röhsska Konstslöjdmuseet, Göteborg, Sweden

Kähler's experiments with naturalistic forms and new glazing techniques resulted in a body of highly unusual works. The lizard encircling the body of this vase is fully three-dimensional; the vase is covered with an iridescent glaze of deep plum modulating to pale green.

37

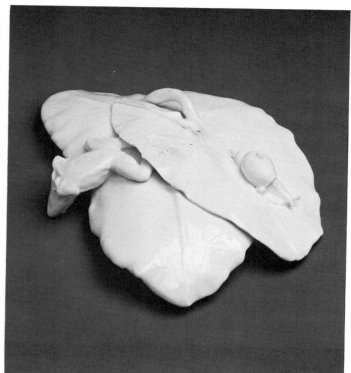

38

39

40. Alfred William Finch (1854–1930). *Vase.* c. 1900. Finland. Produced at the Iris factory, Porvoo. Glazed earthenware, height 8⅜″ (21.5 cm). Taideteollisuusmuseo, Helsinki

41. *Jug.* c. 1900. Finland. Produced at the Iris factory, Porvoo. Glazed earthenware, height 8″ (20.5 cm). Taideteollisuusmuseo, Helsinki

Finch's work was brought to the attention of Louis Sparre in Brussels about 1897, and Sparre invited the English ceramist to work at the Iris factory in Porvoo, Finland. The Iris factory was launched by Sparre and Akseli Gallen-Kallela to produce quality domestic objects, including furniture, textiles, metalwork, and ceramics. Finch's designs for Iris are boldly abstract, with little reference to actual organic forms.

42. *Covered dish and plate.* 1909. Finland. Produced by Arabia, Helsinki. Earthenware, *dish:* width 13¾″ (35 cm); *plate:* diameter 8¼″ (21 cm). Arabia Museum, Helsinki

The Arabia factory often employed simple, flat patterns of stylized organic forms to decorate mass-produced ceramics. Arabia, which began as a subsidiary of the Rörstrand factory of Sweden, maintained an important export trade, and somewhat conservative and restrained designs such as these figured as important stock items.

41

42

43

44

45

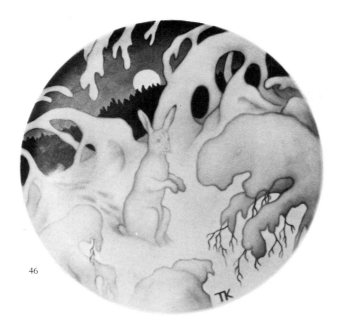

46

43. Jenny Meyer (1866–1927). *Vase*. 1908. Denmark. Produced at the Royal Copenhagen Porcelain Manufactory Ltd., Copenhagen. Porcelain, underglaze decoration, height 13¾″ (35 cm). The Royal Copenhagen Porcelain Museum

Meyer worked at the Royal Copenhagen factory from 1892 until her death in 1927; nearly all her work exhibits the subtle delicacy displayed in this vase, which depicts moths circling a flame. The stylization of the motifs, particularly the swirling candle flame, relates more closely to Continental examples of Art Nouveau than to designs by other artists at the firm.

44. Andreas Schneider (1867–1931). *Vase*. 1899. Norway. Produced at the Schneider workshop, Christiania (Oslo). Glazed earthenware, height 12¼″ (31 cm). Nordenfjeldske Kunstindustrimuseum, Trondheim

Schneider was a leading figure in the development of studio pottery in Norway, and his influence can be felt even today. Characteristically, his work combines powerfully modeled abstract forms with vivid and liquid glazes.

45. Arnold Krog (1856–1931) and Valdemar Engelhardt (1869–1915). *Vase*. 1894. Denmark. Produced at the Royal Copenhagen Porcelain Manufactory Ltd., Copenhagen. Porcelain, crystalline glaze, height 16½″ (42 cm). The Royal Copenhagen Porcelain Museum

Krog designed the shape of this vase; the glaze was the creation of Engelhardt, who had succeeded Adolphe Clément as the technical manager of the Royal Copenhagen factory. Engelhardt, influenced by French ceramics from the Sèvres factory, was a leading figure in the development of such crystalline glazes. The emphasis on pure shape and richly colored glaze—a marked departure from the naturalistic painted decorations so familiar during the late nineteenth century—represented a new tradition at the Royal Copenhagen factory.

46. Theodor Kittelsen (1857–1914). *Plate*. c. 1900–1905. Norway. Produced at Porsgrunds Porselænsfabrik, Porsgrunn. Porcelain, underglaze decoration, diameter 15½″ (39.3 cm). Nordenfjeldske Kunstindustrimuseum, Trondheim

Kittelsen was one of the most popular illustrators of folk tales and children's stories in Norway during the late nineteenth and early twentieth centuries. The simplified, almost naive drawing of this plate recalls the domestic charm of Kittelsen's illustrations, prints, and paintings.

designs were scratched or incised through the upper surface of the vessel. His work, always balanced, has a refined, poetic touch.

Rörstrand's more temperamental Wallander exploited the Danish technique of underglaze painting to express his powerful ideas. In the 1890s, fascinated by motifs from the sea, he reproduced fish and mythical beings in swirling waters, the whole form conceived as an organic entity. In addition to brilliant aquatic and floral designs, Wallander incorporated insects, such as the dragonfly, into his tableware designs.

Finland's ceramic production reached for a more independent character. Its large porcelain company, Arabia, was founded in 1874 as a subsidiary of the Swedish Rörstrand. After having largely copied production in Sweden, it strove in the 1890s to find a national style of its own. Consciously attempting to apply old Karelian motifs to table services in a strict, modern idiom, Arabia came up with patterns in the spirit of Saarinen, Lindgren, and Gallen-Kallela. These handpainted pieces, called *Fennia* ware, were produced at the factory for about a decade beginning in 1902. The stark, geometric decoration is, of course, a parallel development with that seen in Germany, but the nationalistic intention of the *Fennia* ware gives it a particular distinction.

The Iris factory, founded by Louis Sparre in 1897 in Porvoo, was the first industrial arts enterprise in Finland to set for itself the goal of refining the public taste. Although the factory specialized in furniture (it made the pieces for the Finnish pavilion at the 1900 Paris Exposition), it also engaged the painter and ceramist Alfred William Finch. Born in England and raised in Belgium, where he became friends with Van de Velde, Finch created ties between Finland and both the English Arts and Crafts movement and Belgian Art Nouveau.

While his ceramics maintained many traditional forms, such as jugs, pitchers, and bowls, Finch set up an interesting tension between these familiar, even homely, shapes and his treatment of them. His ornamentation often consisted of an abstract, wavy line, and he used glaze in powerful colors, without nuances. The products were always made in series. In spite of the Iris factory's reputation and some exports, notably to St. Petersburg, it had to be closed for economic reasons in 1902.

73

In metalwork, Denmark reigned supreme. Georg Jensen was not only the most famous Danish silversmith, he was also the most internationally famous of all Danish craftsmen. Originally trained as a sculptor, he profited from the work done by Bindesbøll and Willumsen, who paved the way for a freer style in crafts, and probably developed his style under the influence of the Wiener Werkstätte as well. In 1904, he opened his own studio in Copenhagen. With an extraordinary sensitivity to the possibilities of his material, Jensen used silver's softness to advantage in restrained, swelling forms and exploited its ability to reflect light by covering its surface with nearly imperceptible hammer marks. This sensitivity to the material was matched by a sensitivity to form. For example, the undecorated surface of a coffeepot, water pitcher, or bowl would be enriched by a sculpturally formed finial in the shape of a stylized flower or a lush cluster of grapes. His jewelry designs drew on such motifs as fruit, leaves, and insects and frequently employed semiprecious stones, such as fire opals, or honey-colored amber, cut in the cabochon style. Jensen created so many design classics that certain of the objects originated early in his firm's history are still in production.

In 1906, Johan Rohde began to work with Jensen. Rohde was a painter who had become involved with design when he took an interest in creating everyday objects for his own use at home. In this way, he began to work with many materials. His furniture is pure and strict in form—incorporating elements of the early nineteenth century—and exquisite in execution. For Jensen, Rohde designed tableware, bowls, and other objects to be made in silver, all with simple and undecorated forms. Jensen's opulent style clearly influenced the jewelry designs of silversmith Erik Magnussen, who also worked in the United States for an extended period.

Norwegian silver in this period is particularly distinguished because of its colorful and proficient use of enamel. As early as about 1880, J. Tostrup started to work with this material, and somewhat later it was taken up by David Andersen. In the 1890s, they specialized in a technique called *plique à jour*, which reached its zenith of popularity about 1900. In this technique, a network of silver threads supported transparent "windows" of brilliantly colored enamel. Bowls with thin walls shaped like transparent flowers were borne up by the most delicate stems and leaves; insects with outspread wings

47. Thorvald Bindesbøll (1846–1908). *Bowl.* 1900. Denmark. Produced by A. Michelsen, Copenhagen. Silver, 3½ × 2¾″ (9 × 7 cm). Det Danske Kunstindustrimuseum, Copenhagen

The swelling organic forms devised by Bindesbøll were equally successful as flat patterns and three-dimensional designs. The consistent approach to form and ornament so distinctive in Bindesbøll's work set a precedent that became an important principle of modern Danish design.

48. Aron Jerndahl (1858–1936). *Covered bowl:* The Dance. 1903. Sweden. Produced by Fabriks Herkules, Stockholm. Pewter, 6¾ × 11″ (17 × 28 cm). Nationalmuseum, Stockholm

The rhythmic movement of Jugend designs serves a strong folk-culture purpose in this bowl: the handles are formed of couples dancing to the fiddler who composes the finial of the cover. Thus, a strong nationalistic reference is paired with an overall style of international character.

49. Alf Wallander (1862–1914). *Wine pitcher.* 1899. Sweden. Produced by Schreuder & Olsson, Stockholm. Pewter, height 14⅝″ (37 cm). Nationalmuseum, Stockholm

The Jugend style in Sweden affected most aspects of design, including nonprecious metalwork. This wine pitcher is virtually alive with organic ornament: a fish arising from the swirling base. It is valid to draw comparisons between Wallander's ceramics and metalwork objects, for the same principles of design were in operation in both mediums.

47

48

49

50

51

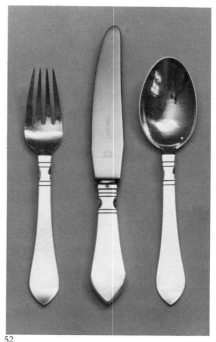

52

53

50. Arthur David-Andersen (1875–1970). *Ewer*. 1901–4. Norway. Produced at David Andersen, Oslo. Silver, height 11½″ (29.5 cm). Oslo Kunstindustrimuseet

The influence of Continental Art Nouveau is evident in this work by the young Arthur David-Andersen, second in the line of silversmiths who have maintained one of the most important workshops in Norway.

51. Georg Jensen (1866–1935). *Necklace*. 1908. Denmark. Produced by Georg Jensen Sølvsmedie, Copenhagen. Silver and amber, length 17¾″ (45 cm). Det Danske Kunstindustrimuseum, Copenhagen

Jensen's jewelry makes maximum use of the softness of silver, often contrasting highly reflective surfaces with velvety patination. Additional color and texture are provided here by the smooth cabochon amber.

52. Georg Jensen (1866–1935). *Cutlery*, Continental *pattern*. 1906. Denmark. Produced by Georg Jensen Sølvsmedie, Copenhagen. Silver, *spoon:* length 7⅝″ (19.4 cm). Georg Jensen Sølvsmedie A/S, Copenhagen

This simple and elegant design achieves its effect through the subtle hammered texture of the silver and the purity of the shapes—a striking and important departure from the many revival styles of flatware then current, and from the more elaborate patterns produced by Jensen. *Continental* is still in production today, attesting to its timeless appeal.

53. Walle Rosenberg (1891–1919). *Covered sugar bowl and ladle*. 1911. Finland. Produced by Alm, Porvoo. Silver, 9⅞ × 6⅞″ (25 × 17.5 cm). Taideteollisuusmuseo, Helsinki

Finnish silver of the early twentieth century is less frequently seen than that of other Scandinavian countries. Pieces such as this sugar bowl display features of the Arts and Crafts movement, particularly the overall clarity of form and construction and the careful limitation of ornament to flat rectangular panels.

54. Carl Wilhelm Vallgren (1855–1940). *Hand mirror*. c. 1895. Finland. Bronze and glass, 10¾ × 5¾″ (27.3 × 14.6 cm). The Cleveland Museum of Art. James Albert and Mary Gardiner Memorial Fund

"Ville" Vallgren, one of the most prominent sculptors in Finland during the national romantic period, designed small free-standing sculptures that reflected strains of Continental Art Nouveau. Vallgren's interest in the formal and textural qualities of bronze enlivens his designs for objects that also served a practical function. He often imbued his work with a symbolic and expressionistic content.

54

sat on the edges of these little decorative vases. One artist above all others made this ethereal art his own. Gustav Gaudernack, who was trained in Vienna, came to Christiania in 1891, and one year later was hired by David Andersen. A skilled draftsman—many of his drawings have been preserved—Gaudernack was also greatly interested in the technical side of his work and often exceeded even René Lalique in technical audacity.

Among the metalwork designers in Finland were Walle Rosenberg and Carl Wilhelm Vallgren. Vallgren's work in bronze included designs for a number of domestic items, such as architectural hardware and hand mirrors, into whose sculptural forms he often incorporated human figures. Richly patinated, these small-scale sculptures evoke an unmistakable sense of mystery.

An exhibition of modern furniture in Stockholm in 1899 confirmed the breakthrough of the new style in this field, although earlier styles were still sometimes softly echoed. Ferdinand Boberg, who included the royal family among his clients, often based his furniture on historical styles, but these he filtered through a modern sensibility. What he arrived at was organically shaped furniture, usually decorated with clearly delineated reliefs emphasizing composition. Another leading furniture designer was Carl Westman, whose interiors showed definite English influences.

A more radically modern approach was taken by other designers. As early as 1899, open-air painter J. A. G. Acke began designing chairs in a highly modern style. Tall and slender, they combine a strict line with an organic sense of shape. Carl Bergsten, Acke's junior by several years, had been trained in Vienna, where he became familiar with the ideas of architect Josef Hoffmann. For a large exhibition in Norrköping in 1906, Bergsten designed a café interior in what was at the time a shockingly modern style. Flame-colored walls and a green floor vied for attention with café chairs that had geometrically formed black bentwood frames.

Furniture for an elite clientele in Norway showed clear features of French-influenced Art Nouveau at the end of the 1890s, particularly in the work of architect Harald Olsen. The soft lines of his elegant furniture played down the construction in order to accentuate the curvilinear silhouette. His work provides a striking contrast to that of Gabriel Kielland,

55

55. Jacob Prytz (1886–1962). *Vase.* c. 1914. Norway. Produced at J. Tostrup, Oslo. Silver and turquoise, 8¼ × 4⅜" (21 × 12.1 cm). Vestlandske Kunstindustrimuseum, Bergen

One of the preeminent Norwegian silversmiths of the early twentieth century, Jacob Prytz created designs that exploited the various textural possibilities of silver by the skillful use of organic ornament. The vase is fitted with two stones, one on each side. Prytz's daughter Grete Prytz Kittelsen is one of the most important enamelists in Norway today.

56. Henrik Krogh (1886–1927). *Tapestry:* Woodland Scene. 1911. Sweden. Executed by Märta Måås-Fjetterström, Båstad. Linen (warp) and wool (weft), 112¼ × 97¼" (285 × 247 cm). Röhsska Konstslöjdmuseet, Göteborg

Krogh studied as a painter and applied an abstract and stylized sense of design to his compositions for woven tapestries. This image of nature represents the majesty of the forest as bold contoured patterns in shades of green, yellow, brown, and blue. The continual process of growth is recorded by the delicate details of the small branches budding new shoots.

57. Thorvald Bindesbøll (1846–1908). *Cushion cover:* Split Peas. c. 1890. Denmark. Executed by Elise Konstantin-Hansen at Bindesbøll-Konstantin Broderiforretning. Embroidery, cross-stitch technique, silk, and wool, 15⅜ × 22⅞" (39 × 58 cm). Det Danske Kunstindustrimuseum, Copenhagen

With his fertile imagination, Bindesbøll could transform even a mundane subject into a dynamic pattern. The strength of the design relied on simple forms arranged asymmetrically to evoke a sense of rhythm. Even Bindesbøll's small embroideries, such as this, possess an air of monumentality.

56

57

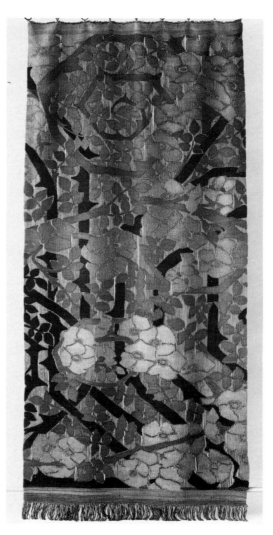

58

59

60

61

58. Frida Hansen (1855–1931). *Portieres*. 1900. Norway. Executed by Det Norske Billedvæveri, Oslo. Wool, 100¾ × 43¼″ (256 × 110 cm). Nationalmuseum, Stockholm, Sweden

Probably Norway's most important weaver of the late nineteenth and early twentieth centuries, Hansen achieved an international reputation for her innovative work and particularly for the special techniques, such as "transparent" weaving, that she developed. She left areas of the warp exposed to create a transparent structure, and these were often contrasted with broad expanses of rich color.

59. J. A. G. Acke (1859–1924). *Chair*. c. 1900. Sweden. Produced by Carl Johanssons Möbleringsaffär, Stockholm. Oak and linen, 44⅞ × 20⅛ × 20⅛″ (114 × 51 × 51 cm). Nationalmuseum, Stockholm

Acke was primarily known as a painter of realistic landscapes, but he also devoted his attention to the design of furniture. The elongated and attenuated profile of this chair shares many characteristics with Continental furniture developments, but it also suggests the clean and sensuous line that was to become a hallmark of Swedish furniture in the twentieth century.

60. Carl Westman (1866–1936). *Armchair*. 1898. Sweden. Wood and cotton, 36¼ × 23¾ × 24⅜″ (92 × 60.5 × 62 cm). Nordiska Museet, Stockholm

Carl Westman's furniture, and his designs for interiors as well, drew heavily on elements of English design, particularly those of the Arts and Crafts movement. Yet the silhouette of this chair exhibits a distinctly Swedish elegance, and, in keeping with the Scandinavian sensitivity to materials, the natural grain of the wood is brought out.

61. Louis Sparre (1863–1964). *Chair*. 1906–7. Finland. Produced by the Iris factory, Porvoo. Pine, stained, 33⅝ × 15½ × 18½″ (85.5 × 39.5 × 47 cm). Kustannusosakeyhtiö Otava, Helsinki

Some of the most forceful of Finnish designs emerged from the studio of Louis Sparre, who, along with Akseli Gallen-Kallela, sought to revitalize Finnish textiles, ceramics, and furniture. A founder of the influential Iris factory in Porvoo, Sparre contributed bold and striking furniture in a highly geometric style that parallels but does not imitate the constructional furniture of the Continent and England.

62. Alf Wallander (1862–1914). *Tapestry*. 1906. Sweden. Executed by Frida Lönngren at Svensk Konstslöjdsutställning Selma Giöbel. Wool, 86⅝ × 66⅞″ (220 × 170 cm). Nationalmuseum, Stockholm

Wallander sought his motifs from the world of nature, which served him for designs in a variety of materials, including ceramics and textiles. The rich coloration and complex motifs in this tapestry join with the stylized natural forms to produce a striking abstract pattern of color and texture. *(See frontispiece for an illustration of this work.)*

who furnished his buildings along the lines of the English version of Art Nouveau. His furniture is simple and powerful. Using wood in unmodulated sections, Kielland played with the relationship between structural support and weight-bearing potential to create an unusually honest and direct effect.

Finland's Iris factory produced furniture of strong, solid Scandinavian wood. It has a powerfully simplified form without ornamentation, although its handmade metal fittings are prominent.

Swedish textile art enjoyed a golden age during this period. The naturalistic Jugend style appeared about 1892 and flourished by the middle of the decade. Designs derived from nature, primarily flowers, were especially prevalent in embroidery. Clearly delineated forms of foliage and blossom ranged rhythmically over the surface of the textile. Around the turn of the century, the studio of the Friends of Textile Art Association produced traditionally woven tapestries, often from designs provided by leading artists. Textiles for the home modeled more closely on foreign examples came from the studio Svensk Konstslöjdsutställning Selma Giöbel, managed from 1898 by Wallander. His models for tapestries often involved large-figured, dense, and almost three-dimensional greenery and blossoms.

Since the eighteenth century in Norway, professional weavers among the peasantry had woven tapestries with stylized motifs taken from the Bible. Their power and artistic expression had made them national treasures, and the new Norwegian tapestry art was firmly grounded in this tradition. Frida Hansen wove tapestries with motifs from the Norwegian sagas until 1895, when she traveled to Paris and encountered the new style. In 1897, she founded a company in Oslo which from 1899 was called Det Norske Billedvæveri (The Norwegian Tapestry Weaving Studio); she combined its initials, DNB, with her own to form her signature. Hansen invented a method of "transparent" weaving in which certain sections of the warp were left exposed and others were filled with large, stylized flowers and leaves. Her luminous colors, forceful draftsmanship, and expansive rhythm combined to create works of a great liveliness.

Hansen was greatly appreciated in countries outside Norway, gaining an international reputation for her narrative and pictorial designs. In Norway, however, the most popular design-

63

64

65

63. Christian Knag (1855–1942). *Wall shelf.* 1909. Norway. Walnut and stained inlaid woods, 21¼ × 40⅛″ (54 × 102 cm). Oslo Kunstindustrimuseet

The landscape as a pictorial motif in the decorative arts found a persuasive advocate in Knag. The overall form of this wall shelf and the use of tinted inlays recall the work of Emile Gallé.

64. Gabriel Kielland (1871–1960). *Armchair.* 1900. Norway. Produced by the Nordenfjeldske Kunstindustrimuseum Carpenter Workshop, Trondheim. Oak and leather, 36 × 25¼ × 24″ (91.5 × 64 × 61 cm). Nordenfjeldske Kunstindustrimuseum, Trondheim

The strength and vitality of Kielland's furniture—in part, springing from its simple and straightforward construction—offered a striking alternative to Art Nouveau–inspired pieces by designers such as Harald Olsen. Kielland's emphasis on structure and undecorated wood pointed ahead to a set of principles that were to be reasserted throughout twentieth-century furniture design.

65. Thorvald Bindesbøll (1846–1908). *Chair.* 1899. Denmark. Wood, painted and gilded, and embroidery, 33½ × 17½ × 17¾″ (85 × 44.5 × 45 cm). Det Danske Kunstindustrimuseum, Copenhagen

This chair illustrates the internal consistency of Bindesbøll's designs: the stylized "cloud" motifs on the apron and back bring to mind the experimental sgraffito ceramics that he produced about the same time. The decoration of this chair was carried out by R. P. Rasmussen, and the fabric, also a Bindesbøll design, was made by Elise Konstantin-Hansen and Johanne Bindesbøll.

66. Carl Bergsten (1879–1935). *Chair.* c. 1906. Sweden. Designed for Strömsholmens Restaurant at the Norrköping Exhibition, 1906. Bent birch, painted, and leather, 41¾ × 18⅛ × 22⅛″ (106 × 46 × 56.5 cm). Collection Martin Lundgren, Sweden

Viennese avant-garde furniture, which depended on great clarity of geometric form, found an important echo in Sweden in the work of Bergsten. An unusually early example of the Austrian influence, this chair is also noteworthy since its employment of bentwood anticipates later Scandinavian furniture designs.

66

er was probably Gerhard Munthe, whose highly stylized saga motifs appeared in paintings from which his tapestries were woven. The appeal of these tapestries was such that multiple copies were often woven of each design.

Besides being an important ceramics designer, Gunnar Wennerberg also made a contribution as a glass designer, working for the Kosta glassworks in Sweden. He designed overlay glass, which was certainly inspired by the works of Emile Gallé. Overlay glass, consisting of a core covered with one or more layers of glass in different colors, was wheel cut or etched through these layers to produce a raised pattern of a color that contrasted with the ground. Wennerberg's glass often exploited the textural possibilities inherent in this technique; certain of his pieces appear to have a "hammered" surface.

Alf Wallander also designed art glass and lamps, for both Kosta and the Reijmyre glassworks. Influential artists in glass during this period include Betzy Ählström and Anna Boberg. Boberg's glass mingled various colors in the body, with decoration applied, impressed, or cut to create organic patterns.

Artists at the turn of the century believed it their task to improve man by surrounding him with things of beauty. While the new respect for crafts as an artistic endeavor did release powerful creative forces in this field, ultimately social awareness and the aesthetic impulse ended up at odds. Unique handmade objects were produced, but only the well-educated, the wealthy, the aesthetically inclined—a severely limited segment of the population—could afford to, or wanted to, make them a part of their daily lives.

Although the new style, with its attendant message of a new aesthetic consciousness, did not give rise to any wholesale changes in the large industrial design companies, mass-produced goods were not left unaffected. Companies with a keen sense for shifts in style quickly adopted the new fashions in wallpaper, printed matter, electric fittings, and household ceramics. However, while the "elite production" had sought its models in England, Belgium, France, and Vienna, mass-culture design largely came from Germany. The German design style is difficult to pinpoint, since production was scattered in many manufacturing centers, but Germany clearly functioned as a melting pot for foreign influences. For a long time, Scandinavian industrial leaders had bought patterns for their prod-

67

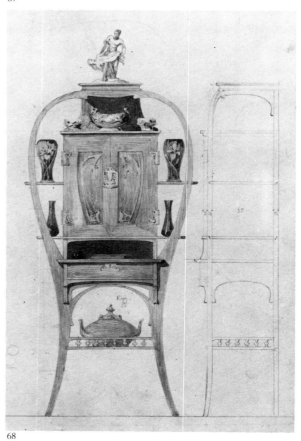

68

67. Harald Olsen (1851–1910). *Furniture design: sofa.* 1901. Norway. Designed for Christiania Haandværks og Industriforening. Watercolor on paper, 9⅝ × 12⅝" (24.5 × 32 cm). Oslo Kunstindustrimuseet

68. *Furniture design: cupboard.* 1903. Norway. Designed for De Samvirkende Fagforeninger. Watercolor on paper, 14⅝ × 9½" (37 × 24 cm). Oslo Kunstindustrimuseet

Olsen's furniture designs reflect a strong French and Belgian influence, particularly in the exaggerated curvature of the silhouettes. The elaborate carving and construction formed part of the furniture's cosmopolitan appeal.

Produced by A. Michelsen, Copenhagen. Silver and ivory, 10⅝ × 6¼″ (27 × 16 cm). Det Danske Kunstindustrimuseum, Copenhagen

Also known for his work in ceramics, Slott-Møller captured in his silver designs the evanescent and delicate beauty of turn-of-the-century designs inspired by nature.

continued in this way to dominate Scandinavian mass production at the beginning of the twentieth century as well. Aesthetically attuned Scandinavians turned down their noses at German mass-produced goods and German taste. As time progressed, however, interest in this sort of simple, mass-produced everyday object and its relationship to "elite production" continued to grow.

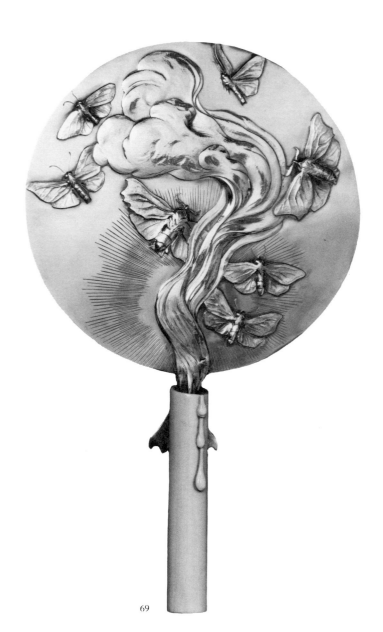

69

THE EARLY 20TH CENTURY: DESIGN IN TRANSITION

ERIK LASSEN
Director, Det Danske Kunstindustrimuseum, Copenhagen

70. Johan Rohde (1856–1935). *Pitcher.* c. 1925. Denmark. Produced by Georg Jensen Sølvsmedie, Copenhagen. Silver, height 8¾″ (22.4 cm). Det Danske Kunstindustrimuseum, Copenhagen

If purity of form and line can be taken as the yardstick of fine Danish silver in the twentieth century, few artists surpassed Rohde in this field. Although fabricated separately from the body, the handle appears to emerge from the lip of the pitcher as an organic extension of the metal, while the carefully hammer-textured surface coruscates with light.

In the early decades of this century, the Scandinavian countries were undergoing a period of readjustment following a number of fundamental political changes. The union between Norway and Sweden had been dissolved in 1905, when Norway became a sovereign state and chose a Danish prince as its king. Finland, discontent in its century-long status as a grand duchy with its own constitution under Russian domination, did not achieve independence until after the Russian Revolution in 1917. Although Denmark granted independence to Iceland in 1918, Iceland elected to remain under the protection of the Kingdom of Denmark until 1944. The struggles for political freedom waged in those countries led to an intellectual movement aimed at cultivating popular cultural traditions, and crafts became one of its means of expression, especially in Norway, Finland, and Sweden. National romanticism, the slightly derogatory term applied to this style by later generations, also emerged in Sweden, where peasant culture survived for some time in an increasingly industrial setting and where industry was closely bound up with the country's natural resources of wood, ores, and hydropower. The style was least widespread in Denmark, with its predominantly bourgeois urban culture centered in Copenhagen.

In discussing trends in Scandinavian crafts in the period from 1910 to 1930, it is important to keep in mind that such trends were only ripples on the surface of the whole cultural scene. Despite the many associations, exhibitions, periodicals, and active critical voices, only a small percentage of the population was involved in the sphere of crafts.

No single tendency or program in crafts predominated during the period, either in the individual Scandinavian countries or in Scandinavia as a whole. The previous period had embraced Art Nouveau and national romanticism; the following period was to be devoted to functionalism and industrial design. The span of twenty years that separated these two distinct trends was a time of transition. Each country, caught up in its own problems, had little to contribute to a broad-ranging movement.

Like fashions, highly exaggerated art styles have a tendency to burst into the public eye in a shower of sparks, fire and flame brightly, and quickly burn out. This held true for the Rococo revival in the eighteenth century and, equally, for Art Nouveau in the nineteenth. The Art Nouveau style emerged in several places at the beginning of the 1890s, reached its zenith at the Paris Exposition of 1900, and disappeared completely a few years before World War I. It played a relatively brief but fruitful role in the Scandinavian countries.

National romanticism, on the other hand, continued to exert an important influence because of prevailing political and social conditions. As their country confronted political independence, Norwegians increasingly pursued their passion for their own history, looking to the Middle Ages, when Norway was a powerful, independent land, and to peasant culture, which kept medieval traditions alive into modern times. In Finland, certain artists strove to move out from under the shadow of Swedish culture, which permeated Finnish society—and, to a lesser degree, of Russian-influenced traditions—by seeking inspiration in the Finno-Ugric peasant culture and in its ancient *Kalevala* epic. The Arts and Crafts movement in Sweden preserved the traditions of peasant culture; the paintings of Carl Larsson idealize country values in his home in the Dalarna with a decorative talent and personal treatment of color.

Another enduring aspect of Scandinavian design was that the work of several outstanding artists and craftsmen carried a weight that transcended current styles. This was most prominent in Denmark in the highly personal styles of such artists as Thorvald Bindesbøll in ceramics, Georg Jensen in silver, and Johan Rohde in furniture.

During this period, Iceland's creative energies were focused on the areas of literature, painting, and sculpture. In design, this country still depended largely on foreign influences.

71. Patrick Nordström (1870–1929). *Vase.* 1913–14. Denmark. Produced at the Royal Copenhagen Porcelain Manufactory Ltd., Copenhagen. Stoneware, uranium glaze, height 7⅛" (18 cm). The Royal Copenhagen Porcelain Museum

In 1911, the Swedish-born Nordström began to work at Royal Copenhagen, where he carried out important experiments with glazes, particularly those of the *flambé* variety. Nordström drew his inspiration primarily from two important sources: the new stoneware tradition of French potters, in which the glaze was the sole decoration, and the Chinese tradition of *flambé* glazes—the ultimate inspiration for both French and Danish potters.

72. Gerhard Henning (1880–1967). *Figural group:* Eventyr (Adventure). 1914. Denmark. Produced by the Royal Copenhagen Porcelain Manufactory Ltd., Copenhagen. Porcelain, enamel and gilded decoration, height 8¼" (21 cm). Nationalmuseum, Stockholm, Sweden

The sculptural works of Henning fuse the traditions of the eighteenth century with those of the twentieth, an approach particularly notable in his figural groups. The refinement and delicacy of his figures are emphasized by the bold and often exotic costuming, which evokes an Oriental mood.

73. Wilhelm Kåge (1889–1960). *Vase.* 1920. Sweden. Produced by Gustavsberg. Earthenware, underglaze decoration, 8 × 9⅞" (20.5 × 25 cm). Nationalmuseum, Stockholm

Kåge's fertile imagination in the field of ceramic design encompassed not only practical vessels but also ornamental wares. Inexpensive materials and exuberant painted patterns distinguish his earthenware of the 1920s. Many of the motifs painted on such objects hark back to folk motifs that held a special appeal for Swedish audiences.

74. Wilhelm Kåge (1889–1960). *Tableware,* Liljeblå *pattern.* 1917–18. Sweden. Produced by Gustavsberg. Earthenware, underglaze decoration, *plate:* maximum diameter 11¾" (30 cm). Nationalmuseum, Stockholm

The concern expressed by many designers for the quality—or lack of it—in mass-produced consumer goods was among the more important stimuli for the production of this service. Kåge hoped to remedy the situation with his "workers' service," as it was also known, inexpensive and attractive tableware in a blue-and-white pattern intended for the common man—who, however, appreciated the philosophy a great deal less than the theorists and designers. The service was introduced to the public at the "Hemutställningen" (Home Exhibition) held at the Liljevalchs Art Gallery in Stockholm in 1917.

71

72

73

74

75

75. Nora Gulbrandsen (1894–1978). *Tureen*. 1927. Norway. Produced by Porsgrunds Porselænsfabrik, Porsgrunn. Porcelain, enamel and gilded decoration, height 7⅜" (18.8 cm). Oslo Kunstindustrimuseet

Gulbrandsen was one of the revolutionary potters who rejected the soft and organic Art Nouveau mode for a more clearly modern aesthetic. With several other young designers, she took part in the 1927 Bergen exhibition sponsored by the Norwegian Society of Arts and Crafts, and was subsequently employed by Porsgrund as its artistic director. The clean and disciplined forms she introduced there, such as seen in this tureen, are purely modern in style, with no lingering vestiges of the old traditions.

While the crafts were in a period of transition, they still managed to consolidate many of the gains made under the Art Nouveau and national romantic movements. For one thing, they became better organized than before. In Norway, the Foreningen Brukskunst (Society of Applied Arts)—now called the Landsforbundet Norsk Brukskunst (Norwegian Society of Arts and Crafts and Industrial Design)—was founded in 1918 in order to promote cooperation among artists, manufacturers, and consumers. In 1910, the Finnish Association of Designers, ORNAMO, was organized. In Sweden, the Svenska Slöjdföreningen (Swedish Society of Industrial Design), now called the Föreningen Svensk Form (Swedish Society of Crafts and Design), had been founded back in 1845. Under its secretary, Erik Folcker, the society carried out the ideas of the German critic and theorist Hermann Muthesius on "the modern reevaluation of our concepts of beauty." In Denmark, the Landsforeningen Dansk Brugskunst Og Design (Society of Applied Art and Industrial Design) was founded in 1907. The Danish periodical, *Skønvirke*, published between 1914 and 1927, offered a forum for the discussion of design issues.

The early part of the twentieth century was filled with new possibilities and old associations. National romanticism in Norway culminated in Gerhard Munthe's decoration of the medieval Håkon Hall in Bergen (unfortunately, the building's interior was destroyed during World War II). The young and vital republic of Finland created a monument to its newly won independence in the stately, neoclassical House of Parliament and its interiors. Exhibitions proliferated. The Stockholm Exhibition of 1909 proved Sweden's strength in textile art. Denmark's Århus Exhibition in the same year was especially important because of its architecture: designers Anton Rosen and Valdemar Andersen produced structures that relied on a pale palette of colors, primarily light wood and white. Even in the field of industrial design, great changes were occurring. Architect Knud V. Engelhardt anticipated functionalism in his 1910 design for the first Copenhagen trolley car.

The Baltic Exhibition held in Malmö in 1914 was dominated by Sweden, which filled the fairgrounds with numerous halls, pavilions, and restaurants. Although the exhibition was intended to be international, Finland and Norway did not participate. Because of their absence, the displays of Sweden and Denmark were thrown into prominence, prompting critics to compare the applied arts in the two countries.

76

77

76. Christian Joachim (1870–1943) and Arno Malinowski (1899–1976). *Tureen and stand.* 1925. Denmark. Produced by the Royal Copenhagen Porcelain Manufactory Ltd., Copenhagen. Porcelain, enamel and gilded decoration, 10⅝ × 11¾" (27 × 30 cm). The Royal Copenhagen Porcelain Museum

Joachim designed the sleek neoclassical form of this tureen. The simple purity of the shape is emphasized by the restrained linear decoration contributed by Malinowski. The sophisticated refinement of such designs attests to the internationalism that pervaded Danish and Swedish design so forcefully in the 1920s.

77. Edward Hald (1883–1980). *Tureen and stand,* Still Life *pattern.* 1922. Sweden. Produced by Rörstrand, Lidköping. Porcelain, enamel and gilded decoration, 13 × 9⅝" (33 × 24.5 cm). Nationalmuseum, Stockholm

Although today Hald is known primarily for his brilliant glass designs for Orrefors, his work in ceramics during the 1920s cannot be overlooked. The design for this tureen features a modern finesse of shape, a pictorial central motif, and folk-art elements used in the decorative borders.

78, 79. Simon Gate (1883–1945). *Two drawings for a bowl.* 1921. Sweden. Pencil on paper, 78: 9⅞ × 17¾" (25 × 45 cm); 79: 8 × 10⅝" (20.5 × 27 cm). Orrefors Glasbruk Museum

80. *Bowl and plate.* 1924. Sweden. Produced at Orrefors Glasbruk. Glass, engraved, *bowl:* 4½ × 15⅛" (11.5 × 38.5 cm); *plate:* maximum diameter 12¼" (31 cm). Smålands Museum, Växjö

Gate and Edward Hald both executed virtuoso works in engraved glass for Orrefors at the same time, but, with their distinctive ornamental styles, it was impossible to confuse them. Whereas Hald's works, for the most part, reveal a highly painterly and graphic approach, Gate's engraved decorations are more sculptural in effect. Elegant and expensive works such as this bowl were among the most popular features at the Paris 1925 exhibition.

78

79

80

A leading Swedish critic, Erik Wettergren, argued that Denmark was stronger, pointing to the fact that several important Danish artists worked in industries relating to the applied arts. Exhibited at Malmö, for instance, were porcelain figurines by Swedish-born Gerhard Henning, who worked at the Royal Copenhagen Porcelain Manufactory, and the designs of the prominent Danish sculptor Kai Nielsen, employed at Bing & Grøndahl. (The most important Swedish artists working in industry before this time, Gunnar Wennerberg and Alf Wallander, both died the year of the exhibition; in any case, their work was considered to belong firmly to an earlier period.) In his article on the industrial arts at the Baltic Exhibition, Wettergren repeatedly praised Danish achievements, and he did all he could to generate corresponding achievements in Sweden. When Wettergren became secretary of the Swedish Society of Industrial Design, he lobbied, at first unsuccessfully, to have Swedish artists engaged by porcelain companies and glassworks. He encountered strong resistance from the companies. Gustavsberg, a reputable ceramics manufacturer, told him he shouldn't trouble himself, "since we buy the models we need at the Leipzig Fair."

In the next several years, however, Swedish companies came around to Wettergren's way of thinking. Wilhelm Kåge was hired by Gustavsberg, and Edward Hald joined Rörstrand. The recently established glassworks, Orrefors, engaged first Simon Gate and then Hald. Edvin Ollers came to the Kosta glassworks and Arthur Percy to the Gefle ceramics company. The "Home Exhibition" at Liljevalchs Art Gallery in Stockholm in 1917 was decisive in establishing Sweden's resolution to prove itself in the field of design. On display were more than a score of interiors, fitted out with unpretentious furniture by, among others, architects Gunnar Asplund and Carl Malmsten, and ceramics designed by Kåge for Gustavsberg. Of particular importance was Kåge's *Liljeblå* pattern, known as the "workers' service," intended as practical, attractive, and inexpensive tablewares for the average person.

Another Swedish critic, art historian Gregor Paulsson, assumed an attitude of greater social consciousness than Wettergren. He was interested less in individual, sophisticated craft creations than in industry's ability to produce household objects with good design "as cheaply as industry now produces ugly things." The title of his book *Vackrare vardagsvara* (More Beautiful Things for Everyday Use), published in 1919, in a way

81, 83. Sverre Pettersen (1884–1958). *Decanter and glasses*. 1929. Norway. Produced by Hadelands Glassverk, Jevnaker. Blown glass, engraved, *decanter*: height 7⅞" (20 cm). Oslo Kunstindustrimuseet

After joining the Hadelands glassworks in the late 1920s, Pettersen revised the styles of both unique and production glassware. Many of his innovations for mass-produced wares involved simplifying decorative additions. In the process, he engendered designs that are classically restrained and elegant; the decorations enhance rather than compete with the forms.

82. Simon Gate (1883–1945). *Decanter, glasses, and bowl*. c. 1920. Sweden. Produced by Sandvik Glasbruk, Hofmanstorp. Blown brown glass, *decanter*: height 12¾" (32.3 cm). Nationalmuseum, Stockholm

Gregor Paulsson's book *Vackrare vardagsvara* (More Beautiful Things for Everyday Use), published in 1919, became the rallying point around which many designers gathered during the third decade of this century. Gate's tablewares are elegant of line yet permit ease of manufacture, thereby satisfying aesthetic ideals and suiting the reality of the consumer market.

81

82

83

84

85

84. Edvin Ollers (1888–1959). *Covered bowl*. 1917. Sweden. Produced by Kosta Glasbruk. Blown soda glass, 8¼ × 5⅝" (21 × 14.5 cm). Nationalmuseum, Stockholm

The new social concerns of the early twentieth century affected designers of glass as well as ceramics; they undertook the fabrication of practical, inexpensive, and attractive table glassware. Ollers made designs to be mass-produced in simple soda glass whose bubbles and blisters, typical of unrefined glass, are used to create their own patterns.

85. Edward Hald (1883–1980). *Plate:* The Broken Bridge. 1921. Sweden. Produced at Orrefors Glasbruk. Glass, engraved, diameter 10¾" (27.3 cm). The Newark Museum, Newark, New Jersey

Hald's innate sense of composition, refined under the tutelage of Henri Matisse, is unmistakable in this engraved plate. Orrefors' finest wares of the 1920s bear the mark of Hald's elegant draftsmanship, which was certainly partly responsible for the appellation "Swedish Grace" that the English critic Morton Shand, in his review of the Paris 1925 exhibition, bestowed on Swedish designs.

86. Edward Hald (1883–1980). *Vase*. c. 1923. Sweden. Produced at Orrefors Glasbruk. Glass, *graal* technique, height 12¼" (31 cm). Smålands Museum, Växjö

Edward Hald and Simon Gate at Orrefors set the tone for several generations of glass designers, with both their strong compositions and their experimentation with new techniques. In the early part of this century, Hald developed a special technique of blowing glass with colored decoration trapped within the body of the glass itself. This technique, known as *graal*, has continued to be significant in Orrefors's production, particularly in the work of Eva Englund (see no. 311).

became a trumpet call of Swedish industrial arts propaganda, but his philosophy gained only a partial victory. Among the works reflecting Paulsson's ideas were Malmsten's simple wooden furniture, Kåge's *Liljeblå* pattern, and the cloudy, inexpensive soda glass that Hald and Gate developed for Orrefors at the Sandvik glassworks in Hofmanstorp. But during the years between the two world wars it was not such functional everyday objects that gained fame for Swedish industrial arts but, rather, their expensive, one-of-a-kind luxury items like the engraved art glass from Orrefors.

A significant portion of Orrefors's renown stemmed from its production of this type of art glass. Hald, who had studied painting under Matisse and had had a brief career in ceramics, was the designer who set its style. Characterized by elegance and fine ornamentation, these objects shared the overall designation "Swedish Grace." Included in Orrefors's line of art ware were several pictorial pieces engraved in crystal following artists' designs. These pieces were highly successful in international exhibitions, but so were other, less ambitious ones which to some extent watered down the genre.

87

88

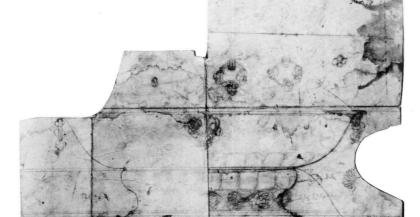

87. Jacob Ängman (1876–1942). *Coffee service.* 1917–18/1927. Sweden. Produced by Guldsmedsaktiebolaget, Stockholm. Silver, *pot:* height 7½″ (19 cm). Röhsska Konstslöjdmuseet, Göteborg

Ängman's conscientious designs for table silver successfully married a rich sense of tradition with modern taste, often resulting in objects of a timeless quality. In employing octagonal forms in these pieces, Ängman avoided rigid geometry by softening the ribs that define the sections and by treating the upper edge as a continuous, wavelike curve.

88. Georg Jensen (1866–1935). *Bowl.* 1919. Denmark. Produced by Georg Jensen Sølvsmedie, Copenhagen. Silver, 5¼ × 14⅝ × 10⅜″ (13.5 × 37 × 26.5 cm). Georg Jensen Sølvsmedie A/S, Copenhagen

The judicious use of cast ornament notable in Jensen's work resulted from continuous refinement of the design. The accompanying drawing, actually used in the studio by the craftsmen in the fabrication of the design, shows several variations on the grape-cluster theme and its final resolution as a tripartite motif.

89. Kay Fisker (1893–1965). *Covered box.* 1926. Denmark. Produced by A. Michelsen, Copenhagen. Silver and ebony, 3¼ × 4¾″ (8.5 × 12.1 cm). Det Danske Kunstindustrimuseum, Copenhagen

Trained as an architect, Fisker was in demand for silver and furniture designs as well. Although this box, like other of Fisker's designs, follows in the traditional mode, it evinces a peculiarly modern quality in that form and ornament are inseparable.

Henning and Nielsen were not the only artists to work in the Danish industrial arts. In 1912, Bing & Grøndahl hired Carl Petersen, who, during his short stay at the firm, was instrumental in starting up the company's stoneware production. Petersen insisted that every piece be thrown by hand and be modeled in the clay body itself. Believing that glazing effects were to some extent contingent on the caprices of the kiln, he concentrated instead on ornamental decoration. A young ceramist, H. O. Busch-Jensen, aided Petersen in his work and remained at Bing & Grøndahl after his departure. Busch-Jensen's knowledge and experience were of great value to the artists working after World War II to rejuvenate Bing & Grøndahl's stoneware production. Indirectly, Petersen also influenced Danish furniture design. He hired Kaare Klint, who was to become recognized as the leading theorist and practitioner of good furniture design, and assigned him the job of designing furniture for the Fåborg Museum's archives room. Klint's work there has become a classic example of his combination of traditional and modern design principles.

Georg Jensen remained the supreme interpreter of silver. Like most craftsmen in Denmark, he flourished during World War I, in which the country was not involved. Jensen was more than an excellent craftsman: he brought his knowledge of sculpture to bear on his work. During these years, he created a whole series of lavish works notable for their swelling, plastic exuberance. His closest co-worker was Johan Rohde, whose designs for silver were realized at the Jensen factory.

The spectacular success of Sweden's Orrefors overshadowed Denmark's glass production. Nonetheless, the Holmegaard glassworks hired such artists as Jacob E. Bang to create a line of art glass. Taking his example from Orrefors's Sandvik soda glass rather than from the Swedish company's more bravura numbers, Bang designed a range of simple glassware decorated through linear wheel cutting alone.

After the national romantic wave had peaked in Norway with Munthe's work for Håkon Hall and with textiles by Oluf Wold-Torne, crafts entered a period of quiescence and new trends did not begin to be felt until much later. Although the skilled Sverre Pettersen reworked Hadeland's everyday glass ranges and art glass beginning in 1927, and the ceramics factories in Egersund and Porsgrunn continued their standard lines, Norway's strengths during this time lay more in decoration than in the applied arts. Gustav Vigeland's wrought-

89

91

90. Märta Måås-Fjetterström (1873–1941). *Wall hanging: Perugia (detail)*. 1927. Sweden. Executed by Atelier Märta Måås-Fjetterström, Båstad. Wool, 96½ × 59″ (245 × 150 cm). Nationalmuseum, Stockholm

One of the most influential textile designers in Sweden during the early twentieth century, Måås-Fjetterström combined a passionate interest in traditional textiles and a fascination with Middle Eastern patterns to create flat-woven rugs and wall hangings of a distinctive character. The workshop that she founded continued to be the most significant producer of woven textiles well into the twentieth century.

91. Ivar David-Andersen (b. 1903). *Coffeepot*. 1928. Norway. Produced by David Andersen, Oslo. Silver, height 6⅜″ (16.3 cm). Oslo Kunstindustrimuseet

The son of Arthur David-Andersen and the representative of the third generation of the major firm of David Andersen, Ivar David-Andersen fashioned silver that recalls the grace of French designs of the early nineteenth century yet conforms to the aesthetics of the 1920s, seen here in the bold, unmodulated surface of the coffeepot.

iron work, stained glass by Emmanuel Vigeland and Frøidis Haavardsholm, and colored wood reliefs by Dagfin Werenskiold typify Norway's most distinguished achievements.

As in Norway, the national romantic style had more or less played its role before World War I in the Grand Duchy of Finland. It was as if all of Finland's strength was being gathered for the final struggle to win freedom and sovereignty from Imperial Russia. Finland was, in addition, a poor country. Not until more favorable economic conditions were restored in the 1920s did crafts in the young republic win back something of the position they had held during the time of Akseli Gallen-Kallela, Louis Sparre, and Eliel Saarinen.

The single most significant force in Finland's industrial arts—furniture, glass, and textiles—was Arttu Brummer. A great teacher, he had claim more than anyone else to the honor of having raised the generation of Finnish craftsmen and designers who were to make Finnish industrial arts internationally famous after World War II. Brummer helped to furnish the House of Parliament in Helsinki, but his best-known work was done in the following decades.

From the beginning of the 1920s, artists and companies in the industrial arts gathered forces for the Paris Exposition of 1925. Denmark and Sweden each had its own pavilion, in addition to stands in the Grand Palais, while Finland exhibited only in the joint facilities. Denmark received no crafts from Iceland, and Norway did not participate in the exposition.

Not unexpectedly, Sweden triumphed in the field of engraved art glass. Orrefors won many medals, and its success opened the way to the American market. Handwoven ornamental picture weaves by Märta Måås-Fjetterström also earned considerable praise, drawing attention to Sweden's strong position in crafts as well as in the industrial arts. Both glass and textile art were firmly rooted in tradition in Sweden: the substantial glassworks industry grew from a crafts tradition dating back to the eigthteenth century; women weavers and textile artists derived a wealth of motifs from old peasant textiles.

Finland had had neither the time nor the money to make a major effort in its presentation at the Paris Exposition, but it did offer a few pieces of furniture designed by Arttu Brummer and a selection of textiles. It was then, in the 1920s, that Brummer reiterated the importance of old Finnish textile tech-

92

niques, primarily the ancient *ryijy* and also the double weave and the tapestry.

The Danish committee had taken great pains with its pavilion. The ceramics on display showed a wide range of talent: Axel Salto's work in biscuit porcelain with enameled decorations for Bing & Grøndahl; Jais Nielsen's vases and figurines in chamotte stoneware, made for the Royal Copenhagen Porcelain Manufactory; and ceramics by Jean Gauguin and animal sculptures by Kai Nielsen and Knud Kyhn, which aroused the most comment. Georg Jensen's work dominated the silver section, but new trends surfaced in pieces by Evald Nielsen, Kay Bojesen, and Anton Michelsen. Young Danish architects designed heavy, neoclassical luxury furniture for the furnished interiors at the Esplanade des Invalides. Danish industrial art found its most forceful expression, however, in Poul Henningsen's lamps for Louis Poulsen & Co. The six model lamps shown were the predecessors of the highly successful "PH" lamps, probably the most significant functional design produced in Denmark in the first half of the century.

In the late 1920s, functionalism as espoused by the Bauhaus asserted itself in the Scandinavian countries. This influence

92. Georg Jensen (1866–1935). *Teakettle on stand.* 1915. Denmark. Produced by Georg Jensen Sølvsmedie, Copenhagen. Silver and ebony, height 12¼" (31 cm). Georg Jensen Sølvsmedie A/S, Copenhagen

Jensen—the acknowledged dean of Danish silversmiths in the early twentieth century—retained in his mature work the soft and sensuous outlines of his earlier pieces. The ambiguous organic forms that are combined to make up this teakettle and stand are vegetal in inspiration. In addition, small, seedlike details enhance the expansive surfaces and are repeated in the carved ebony handle. The present whereabouts of the original version is, unfortunately, unknown; this example dates from the 1950s.

93. Archives Room, Fåborg Museum, Denmark. Designed by Kaare Klint and Carl Petersen, 1914

94. Kaare Klint (1888–1954) and Carl Petersen (1874–1923). *Chair.* 1914. Denmark. Produced by N. M. Rasmussen, Copenhagen. Oak and woven cane, 28⅜ × 22 × 22½" (72 × 56 × 57 cm). Det Danske Kunstindustrimuseum, Copenhagen

Klint probably has influenced more Danish furniture designers than any other single individual in the twentieth century. Starting with a thorough examination of the qualities that made certain types of traditional furniture successful (such as the English eighteenth-century chair), Klint developed his designs along the lines of anatomical functionalism. This chair was designed with the architect Carl Petersen to be used as public seating in the Fåborg Museum.

95. Carl Malmsten (1888–1972). *Armchair.* 1915. Sweden. Walnut and woven cane, 33¼ × 22⅛ × 19" (84.5 × 56.5 × 48.5 cm). Nationalmuseum, Stockholm

Malmsten's importance in the development of modern design in Sweden is twofold. His designs, based on the distillation of traditional qualities of form and comfort, advance a directness in the use of materials and a simplification of structure. Secondly, his insistence that quality in design could only succeed if quality in production was maintained—an attitude passed on to his students—reinforced the tradition of fine craftsmanship.

96. Gunnar Asplund (1885–1940). *Armchair.* 1925. Sweden. Produced by David Blomberg, Stockholm. Mahogany, leather, and ivory, 44⅛ × 35⅜ × 59" (112 × 90 × 150 cm). Nordiska Museet, Stockholm

Scandinavia boasted a profusion of architects who turned their attention to furniture design. Among the most important was Asplund, who championed the new aesthetic creed of simplification with his expressive forms. This chair belonged to a suite of furniture shown at the Paris 1925 exhibition.

93

94

95

96

97

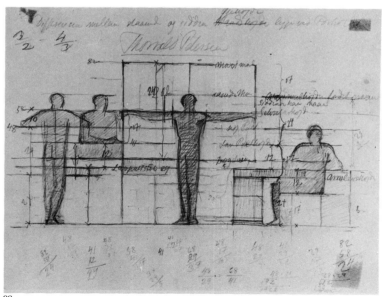

98

99

100

97. Alvar Aalto (1898–1976). *Armchair*. c. 1929. Finland. Bentwood, laminated and painted, 25¼ × 23⅝ × 33½" (64 × 60 × 85 cm). Collection Touko Saari, Finland

Few chairs are as universally popular as this masterly one by Aalto. Designed along highly functional lines, the chair captures the practicality and lightness of metal tubular furniture without sacrificing comfort, and adds its own pleasing grace with its natural wood and sinuous curves.

98. Kaare Klint (1888–1954). *Proportion study*. c. 1916–17. Denmark. Pencil on paper, 7 × 8¾" (17.8 × 22.5 cm). Library of the Royal Academy of Fine Arts, Copenhagen

Klint's landmark proportion studies for furniture were based on careful examination of the functional requirements of the human figure. Many of these studies significantly predate those of other European furniture designers. The drawing is inscribed: "The difference between the eye-levels of a standing person and a sitting person is located around the relations 3/2–4/3."

99. Herman Munthe-Kaas (1890–1977). *Armchair*. 1929. Norway. Produced by Christiania Jernsengfabrikk (Oslo). Steel and fabric, 29½ × 19⅝ × 21¼" (75 × 50 × 54 cm). Oslo Kunstindustrimuseet

Functionalist designs produced in early-twentieth-century Norway are less familiar than those of the sister countries. Among the designers who took a functional approach to design was the little-known Munthe-Kaas. Although the basic form of this chair owes a great deal to the innovative work of Marcel Breuer (and the tubular steel base used by Aalto in the first of his Paimio Sanatorium chairs), this design is unusual for its metal-strap back construction and the use of simple ring hooks to support the upholstered seat.

100. Poul Henningsen (1894–1967). *Hanging lamp*. 1926. Denmark. Produced by Louis Poulsen & Co., Copenhagen. Opal glass and brass, diameter 19⅝" (50 cm). Louis Poulsen & Co. A/S, Copenhagen

Two Scandinavian designers are responsible for major innovations in lighting design in the early decades of the twentieth century: Jac. Jacobsen in Norway designed the *Luxo* lamp (adapted from an English prototype) in 1937, and Henningsen of Denmark conceived in the mid-1920s the first of what would become the now-famous "PH" lamps. Several variations on this design, all complying with the principle that lighting fixtures should provide general illumination without glare from the naked bulb, were shown in Paris in 1925. In 1957 a new version was introduced as the "PH 5" lamp (see no. 204).

was least apparent in Denmark and strongest in Sweden, which was more open to influences from Germany. Some of the most fruitful and artistic ideas from the Bauhaus school emerged in the famous Stockholm Exhibition of 1930, which signaled functionalism's breakthrough in Scandinavia.

At the same time, designers in Denmark moved into new areas of experimentation which provide a parallel texture to the functionalist impulse in Sweden. Kaare Klint began to make furniture based on research into practical qualities, materials, and economy. His first independent commission was to design several kinds of exhibition cases and the seats for the Danish Museum of Decorative Art. Gerda Henning and her pupil Lis Ahlmann did innovative work in the weaving of carpets and upholstery fabrics, and the Danish Handcraft Guild, founded in 1928, revived cross-stitch embroidery. Bang, working at Holmegaard, proved to be less interested in art glass than in "beer glasses for Denmark's Hansen," the common man. Kay Bojesen, one of Jensen's apprentices, conceived Den Permanente, an exhibition and sales facility which presented a wide range of well-designed products. In 1931, Bojesen abandoned the rich, decorative style in silver in favor of smooth, functionally designed pieces, especially flatware. Together with the artist Gunnar Nylund, Nathalie Krebs, a chemist and ceramist trained at Bing & Grøndahl, founded a stoneware workshop called Saxbo in 1929. It thrived for nearly half a century with its restricted line of pieces in simple forms using only a few rich glazes.

Similar trends, although less prominent, surfaced in Norway. Nora Gulbrandsen, hired by the Porsgrund porcelain company in 1927, significantly transformed table service designs by simplifying forms and decoration. At the studios of both J. Tostrup and David Andersen, silver underwent a process of purification and simplification that led to a new, French-inspired, Art Deco style. Nevertheless, the Norwegians' strength still lay in their expansion of decorative, artistic ornamentation along national lines.

All of these trends culminated in functionalism's show of strength at the Stockholm Exhibition of 1930—but Scandinavian designers met the new movement on their own terms, fully prepared. The growing strength of industry, the confidence of talented young artists, and an active craft tradition all combined in Scandinavia to pave the way for an intense and highly productive future in design.

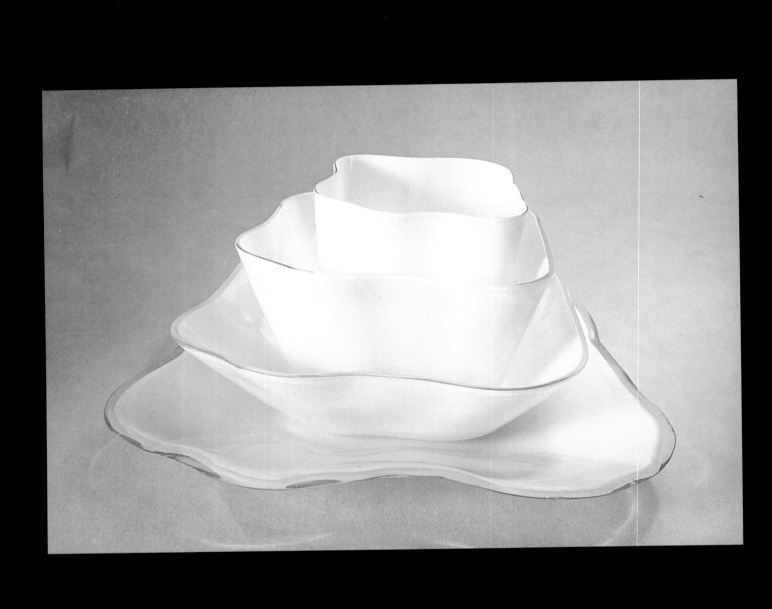

THE 1930S: A NEW FUNCTION FOR DESIGN

JARNO PELTONEN
Director, Taideteollisuusmuseo, Helsinki

101. Alvar Aalto (1898–1976). *Nesting bowls.* 1939. Finland. Produced by Iittalan Lasitehdas, Iittala. Cased glass, maximum height 6¼″ (16 cm); maximum diameter 15¾″ (40 cm). Taideteollisuusmuseo, Helsinki

Aalto's guiding principle of organic design also applied to his work in glass; in addition to the celebrated *Savoy* vases, he produced a series of gracefully curvilinear vessels. Although these bowls can be used individually, together they constitute a glass sculpture that captures the blossoming of a flower in a "stop-motion" effect.

The decade began dramatically. The economy had collapsed, and did not make even a slow recovery until the middle of the 1930s. Progress during this decade was marked both by a cautious optimism and by an unmistakable pessimism that was a natural result of the Depression. In the field of design, new products could be clearly distinguished from those of the "old" tradition, thus reflecting the enormous changes occurring in other cultural and intellectual spheres.

Certain of the changes in society and politics that had begun after World War I continued to be felt, and a new awareness of social responsibility was perceptible in the art and culture of Scandinavia. Social differences between groups and classes in Scandinavian society became less marked, and Social Democratic governments appeared in Denmark (1929), Sweden (1932), Norway (1935), and Finland (1937). Distinctions between the political Left and Right became clearer in domestic affairs as Nazism and Fascism emerged as undercurrents in Europe. The technological progress that followed World War I escalated; it was a time of industrial and scientific innovation. The contrasts between new and old, modern and old-fashioned, industrialization and the crafts became sharper than ever before.

An increasingly urbanized society required more adequate public facilities—more movie houses, libraries, theaters, restaurants, and stadiums—which provided opportunities and challenges to designers of the 1930s. Department stores proliferated, and as travel became more common and ultimately necessary, new service facilities were needed for rail, bus, boat, and air traffic. Everything from vehicles to hotels had to be designed as well. The press, radio, and films helped to give culture a more international and technological character. A new awareness of hygiene and health spurred the development of modern hospitals; Alvar Aalto's Paimio Sanatorium, designed in 1928, served as an important model in Finland.

The technical achievements of the decade were celebrated in a great number of national and international exhibitions. The Paris Exposition of 1937 and the New York World's Fair in 1939 showed the major powers in competition with each other for technological supremacy, and, viewed in retrospect, suggested that a second world war was not far away. The decade ended even more dramatically than it had begun.

The 1920s bequeathed to its succeeding decade a fully formulated ideology in the planning and exploitation of the man-made environment; one of the tenets of this ideology was the idea of "functionalism," in which design technology and social customs were guided by the principles of fitness for purpose, both in materials and style. By the 1930s, because of technological and industrial advances as well as a greater ability to utilize available natural and human resources, society was better prepared to accept and adapt this ideology.

An exploration of the relationship between design and use and a full exploitation of new materials and technology were key to the development of functionalism. Behind the idea were the aims of the Bauhaus—linking architecture, the pictorial arts, and the industrial arts and encouraging their vital interaction. The forms and even the colors used in both architecture and interiors accorded with new trends in the visual arts, particularly Cubism and Abstract Constructivism.

Bauhaus ideals of design and construction made a dramatic appearance in Scandinavia at the 1930 Stockholm Exhibition. This exhibition revealed a revolutionary attitude toward domestic design, with special emphasis on residential architecture and furnishings. In keeping with modern concerns for practicality, flexibility, and hygiene, dwellings at the exhibition had large windows, light walls, and a minimum of furnishings. Furniture shown was simple and lightweight, with clear colors, restrained decoration, and basic geometric forms.

The aim of functional design for domestic living was to produce dwellings that were livable and inexpensive and furnishings that could be mass-produced and thus available to a wider

102. Wilhelm Kåge (1889–1960). *Bowl*, Argenta *ware*. 1930. Sweden. Produced at Gustavsberg. Stoneware, silver inlay, 10⅝ × 16⅛″ (27 × 41 cm). Gustavsberg Museum

103. *Drawing for a bowl*. 1927. Sweden. Pencil and watercolor on paper, 10½ × 15¼″ (26.8 × 38.7 cm). Gustavsberg Museum

During the 1920s, Kåge developed a new form of stoneware that was similar in quality and texture to patinated bronze. Examples of this ware were shown in Stockholm and in New York in 1926 and 1927. In the 1930 Stockholm Exhibition, however, Kåge displayed the refined version of these ceramics —called *Argenta* after the silver inlay that described figures and patterns on the surface.

104. Wilhelm Kåge (1889–1960). *Tableware*, Praktika *pattern*. 1933. Sweden. Produced by Gustavsberg. Earthenware, *canisters:* 6⅜ × 4⅜″ (16.5 × 11 cm); *largest bowl:* maximum diameter 12⅝″ (32 cm). Gustavsberg Museum

After Kåge introduced his "workers' service" in 1917, many other functionalist designs for tableware followed. Kåge himself was responsible for an important series of designs from the early 1930s, whose basic shapes were known as *Praktika*. Those with green enamel borders were marketed as *Weekend*. Consumers did not readily accept this service when it first appeared, but its functional virtues of easy cleaning and stackability have made it a classic.

105. Kurt Ekholm (1907–1975). *Tableware*, Sinivalko *pattern*. 1936–40. Finland. Produced by Arabia, Helsinki. Glazed earthenware, *pitcher:* height 6⅞″ (17.5 cm); *bowls:* diameter 7¼″; 6½″ (18.3 cm; 16.6 cm). Taideteollisuusmuseo, Helsinki

Ekholm was artistic director of the Arabia factory between 1932 and 1948, and during that time he contributed many new designs to the production. An early example of highly functional everyday wares, this service was easily mass-produced by molding, and the simple blue decoration at the lip was rapidly and efficiently applied. The horizontal ridges of the bowls reiterate the geometric forms in the same manner as those found on the early pressed glass by Aino Aalto.

106. Gudhmundur Einarsson (1895–1963). *Pierced vase*. 1939. Iceland. Produced at Listvinahusid Ltd., Reykjavik. Stoneware, height 15″ (38 cm). Collection Lydia Palsdottir Einarsson, Iceland

Einarsson was the first Icelandic ceramist to establish a workshop in that country, an event that occurred in 1927. After studying in Munich from 1921 to 1926, Einarsson returned to Iceland and produced a number of works with stylized "Viking" decoration, incorporating pierced strapwork and animal figures in his double-walled vessels. This vase was shown at the 1939 World's Fair in New York.

102

103

104

105

106

107

108

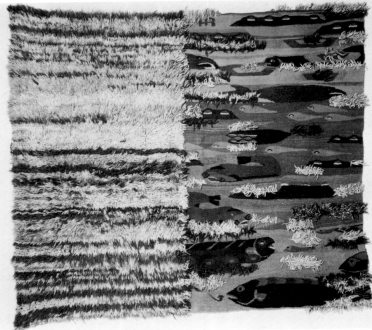

109

110

107. Impi Sotavalta (1885–1943). *Rug.* c. 1930. Finland. Executed by Suomen Käsityön Ystävät (Friends of Finnish Handicraft). Wool, *ryijy* technique, 83½ × 61″ (212 × 155 cm). Taideteollisuusmuseo, Helsinki

The *ryijy* tradition, which was revived in the late nineteenth century, continued to be an important aspect of Finnish textile arts in the twentieth century. Sotavalta's rug, with a lower pile than usually found in *ryijys,* employs a strong abstract geometric pattern that is clearly modern in design.

108. Arthur Percy (1886–1976). *Covered bowl.* 1930. Sweden. Produced at Gefle Porslinsfabrik, Gävle. Glazed earthenware, 14⅛ × 17¾″ (36 × 45 cm), including handles. National-museum, Stockholm

Although somewhat overshadowed by the illustrious Wilhelm Kåge at Gustavsberg, Percy produced a line of ornamental wares in the 1930s that are exceptional for their lively and expressive use of both modeled and painted decoration.

109. Hannah Ryggen (1894–1970). *Tapestry:* Fog-Fishes. 1938. Norway. Wool, 55⅛ × 59″ (140 × 150 cm). Oslo Kunstindustrimuseet

Born in Sweden, Ryggen settled in 1924 in Norway, where she established her own studio. She spun and dyed her own yarns and wove all her pieces herself. The "seaweed" section of this weaving is actually an old *rya* rug, interwoven with flat tapestry and supplemental *rya* knots.

110. Oskar Sørensen (b. 1898). *Liqueur decanter.* 1937. Norway. Produced by J. Tostrup, Oslo. Silver, height 10⅝″ (27 cm). Oslo Kunstindustrimuseet

Even ornamental designs produced in Norway during the 1930s reflect the discipline of functionalism; this sleek and streamlined decanter in the form of a bird creates sculptural form through the interplay of geometric planes. Sørensen was also a leading designer of spun- and pressed-aluminum products around the middle of the century.

consumer audience. Environments, buildings, rooms, and objects were designed to be aesthetically pleasing as well as inexpensively produced. All of these principles implied a new form of social equality among those who were to incorporate these designs into their daily lives. Since dwellings were necessarily smaller because of the increased cost of production and decreased availability of urban space, studies were made of dimensions, proportions, and usage. Designers abandoned furniture "suites" and evolved innovative concepts—sofa beds, stacking chairs, and multipurpose stackable dining utensils—to reflect the new use of dwelling space.

The Stockholm Exhibition engendered reactions throughout Scandinavia. Since the Scandinavian countries shared similar economic, political, climatic, and social conditions, as well as languages so similar as to put up few barriers, the new principles of functionalism were applied in the same way in each country. Joint Scandinavian exhibitions, various forms of cooperation on social and cultural levels, and the growth of ideological and vocational organizations within the field of industrial arts also played major roles in the dissemination of new ideas. Exhibitions and competitions were organized periodically, and each country published journals that set design issues not only before professionals but also before a large segment of the general population.

Functionalism in its most extreme forms did not, in fact, reach great numbers of the population. Tubular metal furniture and oftentimes cold basic forms found their most suitable place in public buildings rather than in the home. Furniture, glass, ceramics, and textiles intended for domestic use often had a softer, more human touch than did the functionalist designs. Although a small and dedicated group of sophisticated design consumers did embrace functionalism with enthusiasm, those who still preferred the traditional status symbols of the upper classes chose revival-style furnishings that offered a readily apparent sense of luxury. Between these two groups were a substantial number who chose "softened" versions of functionalist designs which did not always correspond to the disciplined character of the original ideal.

New furniture forms developed by the architects of the Bauhaus had an international impact on design quite early in the 1930s. The introduction of bent tubular steel, for example, was enormously influential throughout Europe. Scandinavian 111

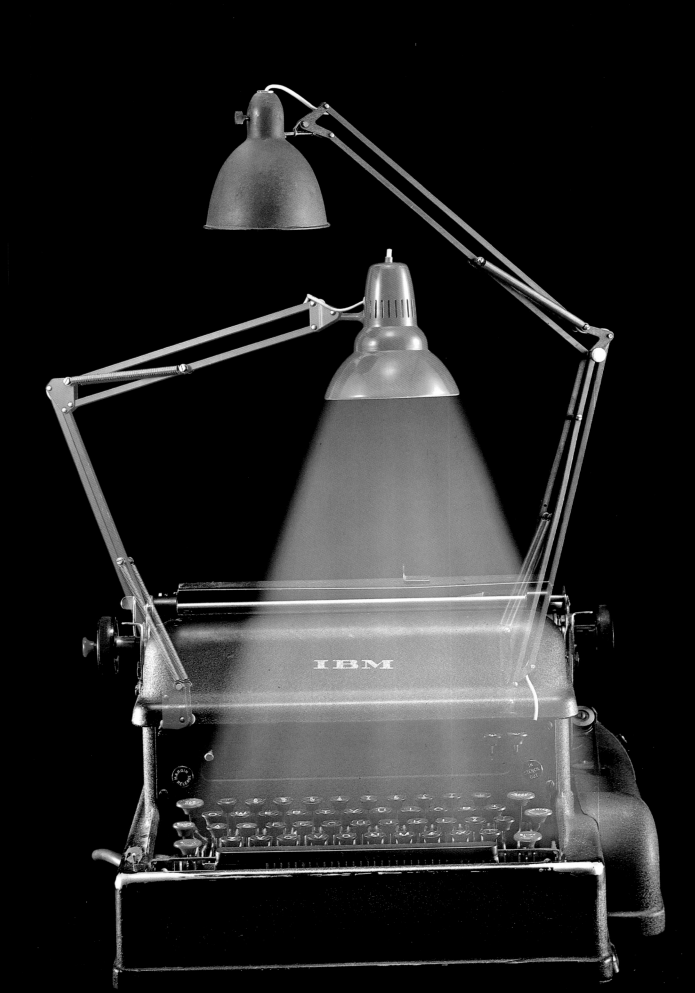

112

111. Jac. Jacobsen (b. 1901). Luxo *lamp.* 1937. Norway. Produced by Jac. Jacobsen, Oslo. Enameled metal, length when extended 45¼" (115 cm). Collection Jac. Jacobsen

In the late 1930s, Jacobsen saw an English lamp called the *Anglepoise,* which featured a counterbalanced armature that could be adjusted to direct the light. After securing the patent rights for Norway, Jacobsen made alterations to the design, and by the beginning of the 1940s he had established a virtual monopoly on what has become one of the most familiar of lighting devices in the twentieth century.

112. Kay Bojesen (1886–1958). *Cutlery,* Grand Prix *pattern.* 1932. Denmark. Produced by Kay Bojesen, Copenhagen. Silver, *knife:* length 7⅞" (19.9 cm). Det Danske Kunstindustrimuseum, Copenhagen

Without doubt the most influential design for cutlery produced in Scandinavia during the first half of the century was this one, designed by Kay Bojesen. Each of the implements has been reduced to its essentials, with no decoration to interrupt the smooth and expressive linear flow.

designers who kept abreast of such developments often opted for a course of design that retained the bold, innovative spirit of functionalism but also employed traditional materials such as wood in a manner that made serial production possible. Furniture designs of the period—especially the chair, which was the most prominent piece of furniture at the Stockholm Exhibition—clearly affirmed the supremacy of the new style in their simple construction techniques, predominance of straight lines, visual and physical lightness of shape, and use of natural materials like leather and cloth for construction and upholstery. Prior to the Stockholm Exhibition, tubular furniture had been included in some architectural interiors, such as the café in the newly completed House of Parliament in Helsinki. Alvar Aalto had at first experimentally combined a tubular base with a curved plywood seat in a chair designed for the Paimio Sanatorium, but shortly afterward had returned to a structure made entirely of wood. Tubular furniture was made only by special factories and workshops, while furniture manufacturers continued to use wood and gradually reworked their production line designs to conform more closely with functionalist principles.

Two designers were particularly influential in Scandinavia in the middle of the decade, and their influence continues to this day. One is Kaare Klint of Denmark and the other is Alvar Aalto, genius of Finland. Klint's *Red Chair,* designed in 1927 for the Danish Museum of Decorative Art, did not actually become famous until the early 1930s. Aalto's now-classic Paimio Sanatorium armchairs—made entirely of plywood and laminated bentwood—won international acclaim at an exhibition in London in 1933. Although both designed in the late 1920s, these pieces of furniture already exhibited the clear structures and forms of the new design ideology.

It was Klint's influence, as well as his country's traditional emphasis on the quality of materials and craftsmanship, that won special recognition for Danish furniture design. Klint respected tradition: his point of departure in designing a chair was often an analysis of a chair from another particular culture or period (such as the English eighteenth century). A thorough study of the essence of the chair, its form, purpose, and ability to serve the practical and aesthetic needs of the user, was a standard part of Klint's approach to design. For him, a good piece of furniture was an object that could be 113

113

114

115

113. Vicke Lindstrand (b. 1904). *Sculpture:* The Pearl Fishers. 1931. Sweden. Produced at Orrefors Glasbruk. Blown glass, applied detail, wheel cut, height 15¾" (40 cm). National-museum, Stockholm

Following the lead of Gate and Hald, the glass designers employed at Orrefors launched into a series of experiments that combined several decorative techniques. Exploiting the qualities of thick optical-quality glass, Lindstrand created purely sculptural works with no reference to the functionalist tradition.

114. Elis Bergh (1881–1954). *Vase.* 1934. Sweden. Produced by Kosta Glasbruk. Blown glass, 6¾ × 6¼" (17 × 16 cm). Nationalmuseum, Stockholm

Designing both practical and ornamental glass, Bergh provided Kosta with a series of innovative designs that virtually revised their production during the period of his artistic leadership from 1929 to 1950.

115. Aino Marsio-Aalto (1894–1949). *Tableware.* 1932. Finland. Produced by the Karhula glassworks. Pressed glass, *pitcher:* height 5⅝" (14.5 cm); *tall glass:* height 3⅝" (9.5 cm). Taideteollisuusmuseo, Helsinki

Aino Aalto's innovative glass designs inspired many others working in the field. Displaying concerns not unlike those of her husband, Alvar Aalto, Aino Aalto presented a design that combines the quest for quality with the reality of mass production. She won a design competition sponsored by the Karhula glassworks in 1932 with this service; when subsequently put on the market, it proved very popular.

116. Jacob E. Bang (1899–1965). *Vase.* 1931. Denmark. Executed by Holmegaards Glasverk, Holmegaard. Blown glass, wheel cut, 9⅞ × 5⅛" (25.2 × 13.2 cm). Det Danske Kunstindustrimuseum, Copenhagen

Bang's calligraphic style of glass decoration exemplifies the finest works produced at Holmegaard during the 1930s. Working well within the framework of modernism, Bang applied rapid wheel-cutting techniques to achieve a faultless balance of form and ornament.

116

compared to a good tool. Among the important new types of chairs he designed was the *Safari Chair* (1933), developed from the British officers' chair used in Africa. Klint's version can be folded, stored, carried—its structure fits its use perfectly. Other Klint chairs from the 1930s include a deck chair and a collapsible stool. Klint was also one of the first designers to work with storage units; his excellent sideboard (1929) admirably fulfilled the needs of a typical family.

In Denmark, furniture design interested both professionals and, gradually, the public at large, even though industrial serial production got under way slowly. Through the efforts of the active Cabinetmakers Guild, exhibitions and competitions for new designs began in the late 1920s, and designers became aware of the long tradition of furniture craftsmanship in Denmark and the skills available in the field. More and more designers worked in industry to create models for large-scale production.

Danish furniture is beautifully finished; even pieces made by machine have a soft, handmade look. Klint in particular was influential in making such warm-colored materials as teak, mahogany, and leather a popular feature of Danish furniture.

In Finland, Alvar Aalto became famous for using the industrial processes of furniture-making to create inexpensive, well-designed pieces. Particularly innovative was his employment of thin, tough, malleable plywood, a material easily made industrially from the woods so readily available in Finnish forests. From this material Aalto created light, comfortable, compact, and modern furniture like his stool from the early 1930s, a close cousin to the pieces he had designed for the Paimio Sanatorium. This stool was admirably suited to the new concept of "free" furnishing: it was easily movable and highly versatile. Its seat could be upholstered or painted. The stools could be easily stacked when necessary, forming the favorite pattern of functionalists—the spiral. In 1935, Aalto, Maire Gullichsen, and Nils-Gustaf Hahl founded Artek to sell furniture designed by Aalto and his first wife, Aino, along with a select range of standard products.

At the time, professionals were engaged in a redefinition of the industrial arts and interior design. Aalto stressed that standard products should not be considered "final," but that their users should interact with them to "complete" their forms. Hahl believed that the industrial arts should seek to satisfy

Interior in Alvar Aalto's Villa Maire, 1938–39

117. Wiwen Nilsson (1897–1974). *Vase*. c. 1930. Sweden. Produced at A. Nilsson, Lund. Silver, height 11⅞″ (30.3 cm). Röhsska Konstslöjdmuseet, Göteborg

118. *Water jug*. 1941. Sweden. Produced at A. Nilsson, Lund. Silver and ebony, height 8⅜″ (21.5 cm). Nationalmuseum, Stockholm

The ultimate extension of functionalist and abstract design is pure geometry, a position most closely approached in Swedish design of the 1930s by Wiwen Nilsson. However, he often softened the sharp faceting of his forms by adding a reeded molding at the edge or by introducing a gentle curve to the design.

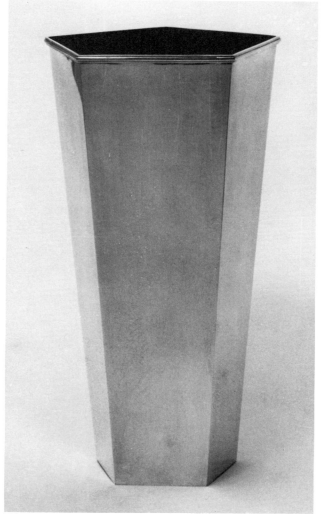

117

118

119

120

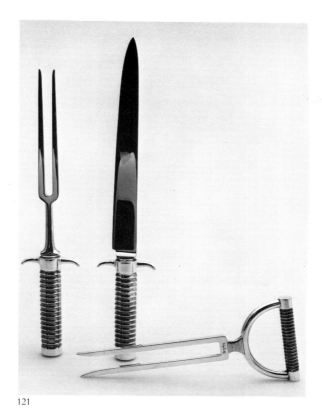

121

119. Marie Gudme-Leth (b. 1910). *Printed fabric:* Landsbyen (Village). c. 1935–40. Denmark. Produced by Dansk Kattuntrykkeri, Copenhagen. Linen, width 52″ (132 cm). Det Danske Kunstindustrimuseum, Copenhagen

In 1935, Gudme-Leth founded the Dansk Kattuntrykkeri, where she printed fabrics of striking graphic effect. The motifs for *Village* recall folk patterns of buildings and animals; the changing industrial landscape in Denmark during the 1930s is acknowledged by the factory with large smokestacks.

120. Thorbjørn Lie-Jørgensen (1900–1961). *Jug.* 1934. Norway. Produced by David-Andersen, Oslo. Silver and ebony, 4⅞ × 8¼″ (12.5 × 21 cm). Oslo Kunstindustrimuseet

The absence of applied decoration emphasizes the robust proportions and gentle curves of this jug, making it a felicitous exemplar of the functionalist ideal. The jug performs as a stable and capacious container for liquids, with a handle that affords secure balance when in use.

121. Sigvard Bernadotte (b. 1907). *Carving implements.* 1939. Denmark. Produced by Georg Jensen Sølvsmedie, Copenhagen. Silver and stainless steel, *knife:* length 13⅜″ (34 cm). Georg Jensen Sølvsmedie A/S, Copenhagen

Bernadotte, son of King Gustavus VI Adolphus of Sweden, began his career as a designer with Georg Jensen in 1930. His functionalist designs are of notable grace. The ribbed handles of each utensil here not only provide a visual contrast to the smooth, uninterrupted metal cutting and piercing ends but also assure a firm grasp.

long-term needs, especially those created by deep social changes, rather than catering to demands of the moment. It was his contention that each nation's contribution to the industrial arts would depend on the extent to which it provided universal forms.

In Sweden, functionalism at first took a simple form in the wood furniture of such designers as Axel Larsson and Sven Markelius. Bruno Mathsson introduced a more original approach: his *Eva* armchair (1934), fashioned to suit the shape of the sitter, presented a soft, organic line. This soft line was immediately taken up by Larsson and Josef Frank. Perhaps as a result of Danish influence, warm-toned woods gained in popularity in Sweden as well.

Alf Sture's armchair (1941) reflects a similar soft trend in Norwegian furniture design, but its innovations—a separate seat and backrest, the latter anatomically molded—made it something of a model in the field. Functionalism was slow to move into the realm of industrial production in Norway, and only came into its own at the end of the decade. Until then, the new ideology was nurtured by a handful of architects working in furniture design.

The trend toward softness in international furniture design in the latter half of the decade was bolstered by a touch of romanticism. This impulse was partly a function of a general reaction against strict functionalism (particularly strong in the case of the Nazis) and partly a result of the active sponsorship of the Dutch Delft school. The new softness had some features in common with Alvar Aalto's early ideas and with the direction functionalism had taken in Scandinavia. Indeed, the achievements of Scandinavian functionalism can perhaps be seen most clearly in Aalto's work. The organic materials he favored not only lent his work a warm, human touch, but also helped to minimize costs. Aalto's humanist approach to public architecture also permeates his interiors for Villa Maire (1938–39) even though this private dwelling was custom-designed for its owners.

The field of ceramics resisted functionalism more than furniture design did. In an effort to keep costs down, companies retained traditional shapes and decorations and hired only a few new artists. As a result, the Stockholm Exhibition of 1930 had no innovative ceramics on display. Gradually, the industry began to revise its products and rethink its design

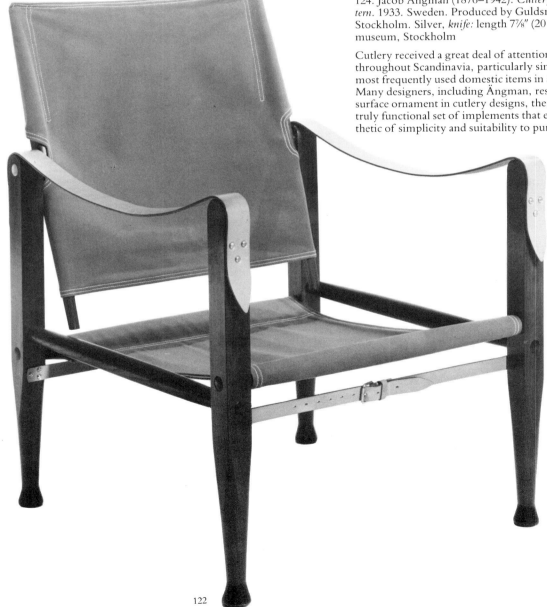

122. Kaare Klint (1888–1954). *Chair:* Safaristol. 1933. Denmark. Produced by Rud. Rasmussens Snedkerier, Copenhagen. Ashwood, fabric, leather, and metal, 31½ × 22½ × 22½″ (80 × 57 × 57 cm). Collection Rudolf Rasmussen, Copenhagen

Klint's perceptive studies of the furniture of other eras and cultures furnished him with many ideas for designs based on models that had already passed the test of time. Among traditional furniture forms analyzed and adapted by Klint was the collapsible safari chair used by nineteenth-century explorers. This form proved highly accommodating to modern demands: it was light, easily stored, comfortable, and inexpensive—and it became the first chair produced in Europe to be sold "knockdown" to facilitate shipping.

123. Maija Kansanen-Størseth (1889–1957). *Tapestry:* The Red Madonna. 1935. Norway. Wool, linen, cotton, and silk, 57½ × 40½″ (146 × 103 cm). Nordenfjeldske Kunstindustrimuseum, Trondheim

With the technique of flat-weaving and the mixture of various fibers, Kansanen-Størseth achieved a painterly effect in her works. The Finnish weaver, also active in Norway, won numerous design awards.

124. Jacob Ängman (1876–1942). *Cutlery,* Rosenholm *pattern.* 1933. Sweden. Produced by Guldsmedsaktiebolaget, Stockholm. Silver, *knife:* length 7⅞″ (20 cm). Nationalmuseum, Stockholm

Cutlery received a great deal of attention from designers throughout Scandinavia, particularly since it was among the most frequently used domestic items in any household. Many designers, including Ängman, restricted the use of surface ornament in cutlery designs, thereby realizing a more truly functional set of implements that expressed a new aesthetic of simplicity and suitability to purpose.

123

124

principles, resulting in several table services designed along functionalist lines: Ebbe Sadolin's porcelain service for Denmark's Bing & Grøndahl (1932); Nora Gulbrandsen's modern service for Norway's Porsgrund porcelain factory (1932); Wilhelm Kåge's *Praktika*, a faience service for everyday use for Sweden's Gustavsberg (1933); and Kurt Ekholm's *Sinivalko*, also for everyday use, for Finland's Arabia (1936).

Sadolin's service was meticulously designed, adhering to the principles of the Bauhaus in its simplicity and lack of decoration. The services by Kåge and Ekholm (Arabia's artistic director) possessed the virtues of clean-lined basic forms, light colors, and simple ornamentation—*Sinivalko* had a simple blue-and-white pattern—and were versatile and easy to store as well. *Praktika* had bowls that could double as covers for the jar-shaped storage pieces. Its only decorative elements were the inherent "softness" of ceramics and a stripe that harmonized well with contemporary linen towels and tablecloths. This original service was soon pulled off the market, and only scored some success in the latter half of the decade.

Kåge and Ekholm continued to work on simple, basic services. Kåge designed an earthenware service called *Kadmium* in 1935, and shortly afterwards, Ekholm came up with *Aino*, a simple, "soft," straw-colored service. At the end of the decade, Kåge developed a new basic service with "soft forms," which marked the breakthrough of a more relaxed but more highly stylized design in industrially made products.

The artists in the art ceramics departments found in most of the famous porcelain companies were not hampered by the restrictions of industrial production; they were given a free hand to develop and create one-of-a-kind pieces. In this area, functionalism was defined more loosely, but here, too, powerful, basic forms predominated. Compact shapes and clear outlines constituted the most salient features of the modern style. Glazes, surface structures, plastic decoration, and the material's special characteristics received special attention.

The most important designers of art ceramics were Axel Salto in Denmark and Wilhelm Kåge in Sweden. Kåge's highly classical work enjoyed a popularity that extended to the general public. In the late 1920s, his decorations and glazes won him a special reputation. His *Argenta*, introduced at the Stockholm Exhibition of 1930, presented decorations painted in silver on a glazed body that was made to resemble oxidized bronze. 121

Salto achieved a powerful expressiveness by exploiting form and surface. Taking his motifs from the plant world, he created pieces with surface structures that rippled with dynamic energy and a dramatic liveliness. (Kåge later displayed the same sculptural dynamism in his work.) Another leading art ceramist, Arthur Percy, made expressive pieces with opulent molded decoration and brilliant polychromy for Gefle in Sweden. Art ceramists in Iceland included Gudhmundur Einarsson, whose decorative motifs were drawn from national romanticism and realized in a plastic and ribbonlike style.

New ceramic influences surfaced in the late 1930s. A fresh, decorative, pictorial touch—also found in the textile art of the period—appeared in smooth decorative platters, wall plaques, and vases, reflecting aspects of Expressionism, on the one hand, and retrospective styles, including the Pre-Raphaelites and the early Renaissance, on the other. In addition to functional wares, several designers gave a new vigor to the sculptural tradition in ceramics, producing ornamental works depicting stylized animal and human figures.

Like the ceramics industry, Scandinavia's glass industry was at first reluctant to accommodate the new style by changing its production. Norway's Hadeland glassworks was one of the first to issue, in serial production, glassware in the new style. Designed by Sverre Pettersen in 1927, the series used thin, bright glass to accentuate the simple, elegant forms, well within the precepts of the Bauhaus. The glasses conformed perfectly with the undecorated white services that were also being produced as a result of the German influence. Compared with the Hadeland series, the new glass in Denmark and Finland of the same time seemed old-fashioned, still entrenched in the classic style of the 1920s.

The early 1930s saw certain artists gravitate toward design for mass production. In glass, they were spurred by competitions such as the one organized in 1932 by Finland's Karhula glassworks for both art glass and everyday glassware; this competition marked the breakthrough of functionalism in glass in Finland. The top prize was awarded to Aino Aalto for her entry, a pitcher and tumblers made of pressed glass, a material that was inexpensive and admirably suited to the design. The wide rims and narrow bases of the glasses made them easy to stack, and with their simple design and sturdy construction, they were practical as well as aesthetically sound. Karhula

125

125. Jacob Prytz (1886–1962). *Cutlery,* Parisersølv *pattern.* 1938. Norway. Produced by J. Tostrup, Oslo. Silver, *knife:* length 9″ (23 cm). Vestlandske Kunstindustrimuseum, Bergen

Made for the Paris World's Fair of 1938, this cutlery service reveals the elegance of functionalist design. The handles of each implement are gracefully tapered to fit the hand and to provide balance when in use. With its shortened tines and extended bowl, the fork presages designs that exaggerated these features in the 1950s.

126. Mogens Koch (b. 1898). *Folding chair.* 1933. Denmark. Produced by Interna, Frederikssund. Beech and canvas, 34¼ × 22 × 20½″ (87 × 56 × 52 cm). Det Danske Kunstindustrimuseum, Copenhagen

The simplicity of its construction makes this innovative design one of the most efficient of folding chairs. It has retained its appeal for nearly half a century—the model illustrated was produced in 1960.

126

soon put the set into production, and it became popular with a wide segment of the population.

Other designers followed this trend. They applied new ideas not only to drinking glasses and sets of glasses with pitchers—tableware remained the most important form of household glass produced in the 1930s—but to plates and bowls as well. The same spirit informed the smooth, transparent glass services produced by Karhula and by Orrefors in Sweden. Smooth glass was the specialty of Göran Hongell in Finland and Vicke Lindstrand in Sweden. Colored glass was also popular; Aalto's glasses were available in blue, smoke topaz, and green. Following the tenets of functionalism, glass developed into an important material in furniture as well, especially for tops of serving carts and coffee tables.

More exclusive art glass remained conservative in its design until after the Stockholm Exhibition of 1930. Simon Gate, for one, embraced the new trend and created crystal vases with simple, bulbous forms that drew attention to the material itself. The glass was of such a purity that its reflective and optical qualities gathered light and created a jewel-like atmosphere. Other designers, who previously had concentrated on the decorative engraving, now worked with the characteristics of glass—particularly its mass and its ability to refract light—to create expressive, free, powerful forms. Vicke Lindstrand and Edvin Öhrström at Orrefors and Elis Bergh at Kosta promoted such an approach in Sweden. In Denmark, Jacob E. Bang collaborated closely with glass blowers to fabricate his modern pieces. Sverre Pettersen, one of Norway's major glass designers, incorporated severe wheel-cut decorations into his work.

Finland's art glass designers arrived at a similarly free and expressive style in a more roundabout fashion. Initially, they took from functionalism their basic, highly geometrical forms and smooth surfaces, using bright, thick glass as their material. Some designers added bubbles or decorative etchings of figures similar to those found in traditional woodcarving. Soon, however, Gunnel Nyman, Arttu Brummer, and Göran Hongell exploited the expressive quality of glass, imbuing their forms with movement and fluidity. Alvar Aalto upheld this spirit in his set of art glass pieces, which could be placed one inside the other or used separately as bowls and vases.

Bauhaus designers had found textiles a fruitful medium for experimentation. They studied the characteristics of various

127. Bruno Mathsson (b. 1907). *Chair:* Eva. 1934. Sweden. Produced by Firma Karl Mathsson, Värnamo. Bent beech and fabric, 32¾ × 19¼ × 29⅛" (83.5 × 49 × 74 cm). Nationalmuseum, Stockholm

Mathsson's experiments with bent and laminated wood, combined with his studies of function and maximum comfort, have resulted in several twentieth-century design classics that have been in continuous production since their conception. The *Eva* chair, sculpturally molded to fit the human body, gives the impression of lightness with its minimal structural parts and fabric support.

128. Alvar Aalto (1898–1976). *Stacking stools.* 1930–33. Finland. Produced by Korhonen, Turku. Bent birch, laminated, 17¾ × 13¾" (45 × 35 cm). Taideteollisuusmuseo, Helsinki

The simplicity of the idea expressed in these stools, coupled with the use of readily available materials, has assured their success in both the home and export markets. The stools are practical, are adaptable to a variety of settings and purposes, and can be easily stacked.

materials and played with different combinations in works produced both by hand and industrially. As a result of their influence, art textiles became prominent in interior design, finding their way into the home as wall hangings, rugs, upholstery, and curtain fabrics. In Scandinavia, with its long tradition in textiles, designers who took up the modern style achieved particularly good results. Among the artists specializing in textile design were Greta Skogster-Lehtinen, Laila Karttunen, and Maija Kansanen-Størseth in Finland; Barbro Nilsson and Astrid Sampe in Sweden; and Lis Ahlmann in Denmark. As directors of small weaving shops and studios, they either worked under the auspices of department stores that had their own decorating departments or formed their own small companies. Most of their work, whether in art textiles or in upholstery and curtain fabrics, was commissioned for specific projects. However, they also designed a number of extremely popular *ryijy* patterns that were available to the general public to be made at home. Gradually, artists began to work more closely with industry, designing such soft furnishings as tablecloths in addition to upholstery and clothing fabrics.

Since art textiles were considered an art form closely akin to painting, the interchange between the two was particularly active. In the late 1920s and early 1930s, Scandinavian textile artists incorporated the abstract trends of painting in their work. Freely applied to *ryijys* in Finland, this style turned the traditional textile into a modern art form. In making their *ryijys* and other large art textiles, artists once again called upon such organizations as the Friends of Finnish Handicraft, and artist and weaver often worked together. Typical projects like monumental tapestries for city halls, banks, and company headquarters displayed stylized compositions with human figures or townscapes.

One of the legacies of the Bauhaus influence was an emphasis on the physical structure of upholstery and curtain fabrics. The predominance of natural colors focused attention on the weave of the fabric and deemphasized supplementary patterns. Printed textiles, which could be mass-produced readily and more inexpensively than woven patterns, assumed a new importance in the 1930s; hand-printed textiles for the home did not become generally accepted until the 1940s. The Austrian-born architect Josef Frank, who worked in Sweden beginning in 1932, introduced in his printed textiles a vigorous use of bright colors, several of which he combined in surprising ways. The abstract style made inroads into production textiles in the early 1930s, but decorative plant motifs and human figures in smaller scale later reappeared.

Denmark, long the leader in silver design, retained its preeminence in this field. While continuing their outstanding line of handmade, one-of-a-kind pieces, Danish companies now began the serial production of cutlery, which took on soft forms, functional proportions, and smooth surfaces. The pronounced emphasis on materials so integral to functionalism here, too, had its effect. A concern with silver's special characteristics—reflectiveness, softness, and luster—particularly marked the work of Kay Bojesen, who in the 1930s produced Denmark's most individualistic cutlery, characterized by clean lines and simple forms. A carving set designed in 1939 by Sigvard Bernadotte for Denmark's Georg Jensen was more functionalist in spirit; despite its strict and streamlined contour, however, it had a festive look, implying the ritualistic and ceremonial nature of the act of carving.

Similar work was being done in Norway by Jacob Prytz, in Sweden by Jacob Ängman, and in Finland by Gunilla Jung. In the 1930s, Sweden's Wiwen Nilsson created cubistic, streamlined silver with severe, simple forms well suited to serial production. Objects not necessarily intended for mass production also revealed the importance of flat, undecorated surfaces and the geometric composition of forms. Artists such as Thorbjørn Lie-Jørgensen and Oskar Sørensen in Norway produced memorable designs in this style.

Functionalism—the internationally proclaimed ideology for design in the 1930s—undoubtedly pervaded the work of Scandinavian designers. Overall, however, it turned out to be more important in providing a set of principles to be followed than in establishing a particular style. As a design ethic, functionalism proved to be rigid in its application of formal rules, leaving little room for further development. Yet, its principles had a lasting influence. Even when designers adopted a softer and more organic approach, they continued to make careful studies of form, construction, materials, and functions.

For the Scandinavian countries, the decade of the 1930s was a time to search, to experiment, to adapt. It was a time when design and function became two sides of the same concept, resulting in an unimpeachable harmony. Many of the achievements of the 1930s became classics, and many have served as inspiration for designers to this very day.

129. Lisa Johansson-Pape (b. 1907) and Greta Skogster-Lehtinen (b. 1900). *Chair.* c. 1935. Finland. Produced by Stockmann/Keravan Puusepantehdas, Kerava. Wood, lacquered, and fabric, 26⅜ × 23¾ × 24¾" (67 × 60.5 × 63 cm). Taideteollisuusmuseo, Helsinki

A multitalented designer of furniture, ceramics, glass, and lighting, Johansson-Pape produced this striking chair design quite early in her career. The simple counterbalance structure ensures both stability and strength. The fabric, designed by Skogster-Lehtinen, is specially woven to adapt perfectly to the contours of the chair.

129

MID-CENTURY:
YEARS OF INTERNATIONAL TRIUMPH

PETER ANKER
Director, Vestlandske Kunstindustrimuseum, Bergen

130. Josef Frank (1885–1967). *Printed fabric:* Vegetable Tree. 1944. Sweden. Produced by Svensk Tenn, Stockholm, 1981. Linen, width 51⅛" (130 cm). AB Svensk Tenn, Stockholm

Viennese-trained Josef Frank came to Sweden in 1932 and became established as a major influence in textile, furniture, and interior design. Frank's assured sense of composition, expressed in rich patterns, and his use of bright and surprising color combinations inspired interior design throughout Scandinavia.

World War II reached the Scandinavian countries in the winter of 1939–40, but in such diverse ways that it was to have different effects on the applied arts from country to country during the early postwar period. Sweden remained neutral while Denmark and Norway were invaded by Germany. Finland fought two wars against the Soviet Union to retain its independence and also ended up fighting the Germans. Especially toward the end of the war, conditions were quite hard in Finland and Norway.

What crafts production there was relied on various substitute materials: fish skin and wood for shoes, for instance, and paper and birch bark for textiles. In Finland, this brought about some original works—Dora Jung's furniture fabrics woven from paper thread, Greta Skogster-Lehtinen's wall hangings and wallpapers made from birch bark—that are aesthetically interesting as well as imaginative in their use of materials.

There is a certain contrast between these creations and the elegance and variety of Finland's design products only a few years after the war. What happened in that country, and in the other Scandinavian countries? How much time was spent on reestablishing the crafts and bringing the production of domestic furnishings to a normal, that is, prewar, level? To answer these questions we must first examine the countries separately.

In Norway, a new periodical, *Bonytt* (Interior News), was started in January, 1941, by a group of young architects, artists, and designers. Its first issue after the war, in May, 1945,

131

131

133

132

134

131. Friedl Holzer-Kjellberg (b. 1905). *Bowl and vase.* 1948. Finland. Produced at Arabia, Helsinki. Porcelain, *bowl:* diameter 8¼" (21 cm); *vase:* height 7½" (19 cm). Arabia Museum, Helsinki

A multifaceted artist, Holzer-Kjellberg is best known for her adaptation of the Chinese "rice porcelain" technique, in which patterns are cut away from the eggshell-thin porcelain bodies of bowls and vases, the interstices covered by a translucent film of glaze.

132. Wilhelm Kåge (1889–1960). *Vase from the* Surrea *series.* 1940–50. Sweden. Produced at Gustavsberg. Flintware, height 13⅜" (34 cm). Gustavsberg Museum

Kåge's lively imagination brought forth an astonishing variety of forms. The angularity of several geometric vessels in the *Surrea* series, which recall Cubist painting and sculpture, stands in striking contrast to the "soft forms" of organically shaped tableware produced at the same period of time.

133. Axel Salto (1889–1961). *Vase.* 1943. Denmark. Produced at the Royal Copenhagen Porcelain Manufactory Ltd., Copenhagen. Stoneware, height 8" (20.2 cm). The Royal Copenhagen Porcelain Museum

Active over several decades, Salto never abandoned his experiments with unusually rich glazes and evocative organic forms. The bitter yellow-green streaks of the "solfatara" glaze used on this vase are typical of Salto's classic style.

134. Wilhelm Kåge (1889–1960). *Tableware,* Gray Lines *pattern.* 1945. Sweden. Produced by Gustavsberg. Flintware, *plate:* diameter 9⅝" (24.5 cm); *bowl:* diameter 7½" (19 cm). Nationalmuseum, Stockholm

The sculptural softness of *Gray Lines* anticipates the sensuous and organic shapes that became a pronounced feature of Scandinavian design during the 1950s. The bands of soft gray encircling the outer edges of each piece gently point up the subtlety of the shapes.

contained a major article by Håkon Stenstadvold entitled "Our National Character." In it, Stenstadvold maintained that while future Norwegian design should remain open to new impulses, its primary aim should be to search out and express a national identity based on its own traditions. The sentiment of this article may well represent a general attitude, indicating why Norwegian design, like its architecture, continued to be relatively isolated for some time after the war, lagging behind developments in other Scandinavian countries.

In contrast, the Finns, who had been harder hit by the war, turned devastation and impoverishment into a creative challenge. Even during the precarious situation in 1940 and 1941, the Finnish design organizations managed to hold two important exhibitions in Copenhagen and Stockholm. Then, in the first years after the war, a new generation of young talents emerged, many of whom are still prominent in design. Their first achievement was the Finnish contribution, designed by Tapio Wirkkala, at the Milan Triennale of 1951, where Finland received more medals and awards than any other nation.

In Denmark, the arts were hardly affected by the war. They continued to develop, during the forties, from the very solid foundation of the preceding period. Established personalities such as Axel Salto, Kay Bojesen, Kaare Klint, and Poul Henningsen remained in the forefront of design, but, of course, younger talents presented themselves, especially in the fields of furniture design, silver, and ceramics. New designers like Arne Jacobsen, Hans Wegner, Ole Wanscher, Henning Koppel, Magnus Stephensen, Gertrud Vasegaard, and Eva Stæhr-Nielsen carried Danish design into the fifties with a great self-confidence.

No dramatic changes occurred in Sweden, the country least touched by the war. There was no press censorship, as in other countries, to hamper free critical discussion. While entire cities were being destroyed on the Continent, Sweden continued to build houses. Designers from the occupied neighboring countries found a refuge there. With its unbroken activities of a normal art life and its continued achievements in design, Sweden served as a frame of reference as well as a source of inspiration for the other Scandinavian countries in the first years after 1945.

From the Swedish point of view, however, the 1940s were years of national isolation, of broken contacts. To some extent, 133 the decade was what art historian Dag Widman has called "a period of idyllic retrospection and decorative formalism," especially in light of functionalism and the other advanced trends of the 1920s and 1930s.

This split among various trends is apparent in the works of Wilhelm Kåge. With his flintware vases titled *Surrea*, Kåge made an artistic joke pointing back to Cubist sculpture, whereas in his stoneware table service called *Soft Forms* he pointed forward to the fifties. The attitude of "idyllic retrospection" in the 1940s was clearly evident in textiles: in printed fabrics like Josef Frank's lush *Vegetable Tree* and in richly textured tapestries like Barbro Nilsson's *Snails*. Yet, in the same period, the Swedish furniture industry embraced a moderate, commonsensical modernism expressed in such designs as Carl-Axel Acking's bentwood and veneer chair of 1944.

Iceland's isolation during the war profoundly affected developments in the fields of crafts and design there. Its designers traditionally had sought their education abroad, and because the war made that impossible, the Icelandic School of Applied Art (founded in 1939) became the focal point of Icelandic design. For the first time, native designers began to formulate a concerted approach to design theory and practice, and its influence was evident in the marked progress made in Icelandic applied arts and design after World War II.

Widman's characterization of the 1940s may be valid for all the Scandinavian countries. In the fifties, however, the whole Scandinavian world of applied arts was suddenly on the move again. Following Finland's early triumph at Milan in 1951, the first full show of renewed vigor in Scandinavian design came at the Triennale of 1954. Four Scandinavian countries participated, and all shared in the success. Also in those years, the various national design organizations in Scandinavia established a policy of cooperation. Their first major achievement was the exhibition "Design in Scandinavia," which traveled to leading museums in the United States and Canada from 1954 to 1957 under the auspices of the American Federation of the Arts. The design organizations of Denmark, Finland, Norway, and Sweden worked together in the planning and implementation of the show. In the course of its tour, the exhibition was shown in twenty-two cities. Then, if not before,

135. Stig Lindberg (1916–1982). *Plate*. 1942–49. Sweden. Produced at Gustavsberg. Glazed earthenware, diameter 16⅞″ (43 cm). Gustavsberg Museum

In his ceramic designs, Lindberg chose unexpected motifs and patterns, to which he applied brilliant colors. The unsophisticated charm of even a subject as humble as laundry lines offered the artist inspiration for the exercise of bold colors in contrasting shapes.

135

136

136. Arttu Brummer (1891–1951). *Vase:* Finlandia. 1945. Finland. Produced by Riihimäen Lasi glassworks, Riihimäki. Molded blown glass, wheel cut, height 12¼″ (31 cm). Riihimäen Lasi glassworks, Riihimäki

Through his work and his teaching at the School of Applied Art in Helsinki, Brummer had a tremendous impact on the careers of many designers in Finland. The *Finlandia* vase, in its angular strength and irregularity of surface, embodies the lyrical quality of Jean Sibelius's music and the breaking up of the winter ice in Finland.

137. Helena Tynell (b. 1918). *Vase.* 1949. Finland. Produced by Riihimäen Lasi glassworks, Riihimäki. Blown glass, height 5⅝″ (14.5 cm). Finnish Glass Museum, Riihimäki

Tynell often chose simple shapes for her glass designs, relying on the optical distortion of the material to produce an effect both sculptural and liquid in quality. Some of the gentle forms are gracefully asymmetrical, evoking a sense of movement.

138. Göran Hongell (1902–1973). *Glassware,* Aarne *pattern.* 1948. Finland. Produced by Iittalan Lasitehdas, Iittala. Molded glass, maximum height 3½″ (9 cm). Iittalan Lasitehdas, Iittala

These designs by Hongell express an important trend in Finnish glass design of the mid-twentieth century: the exploitation of the crystalline material exclusive of additional ornament or texture. The purity of the glass itself is matched by the rigorous clarity of the forms.

139. Gunnel Nyman (1909–1948). *Glassware.* 1946. Finland. Produced by Nuutajärvi-Notsjö Glass, Nuutajärvi. Blown glass, maximum height 4⅜″ (11 cm); maximum diameter at lip 2¾″ (7 cm). Taideteollisuusmuseo, Helsinki

140. *Vase:* Baroque. c. 1947. Finland. Produced by Riihimäen Lasi glassworks, Riihimäki. Glass, engraved, height 9⅛″ (23.2 cm). The Newark Museum, Newark, New Jersey

Nyman created both art glass and tableware during her short but prolific career, working at three of the major glassworks of Finland—Riihimäki, Notsjö, and Iittala. Strong and animated forms composed with a sculptural boldness characterize her art ware, while her restrained and functional glassware aimed for a more subtle effect, achieved by the gradual progression from thick supporting elements to a thin edge.

141 *(overleaf).* Sven Palmqvist (b. 1906). *Bowl from the* Ravenna *series.* 1949. Sweden. Produced by Orrefors Glasbruk. Blown glass, 5⅛ × 12⅝″ (13 × 32 cm). AB Orrefors Glasbruk

Palmqvist began his work at the Orrefors factory in 1936; not only did he expand the range of designs for art glass but he also introduced new techniques of fabrication. The *Ravenna* series of vessels incorporated brilliant mottled red panels into a deep blue body, producing an effect not unlike that of stained-glass windows.

137

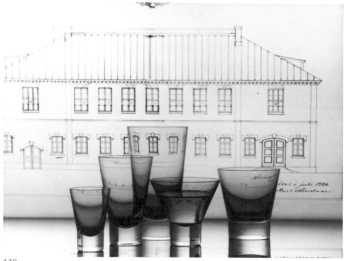

138

139

140

142

143

144

142. Thorbjørn Lie-Jørgensen (1900–1961). *Coffee service.* 1945. Norway. Produced by David-Andersen, Oslo, 1960. Silver, *coffeepot:* height 7⅞″ (20 cm). Oslo Kunstindustrimuseet

The gentle shapes of Norwegian silver reflect both an appreciation of organic form and an awareness of functionalism. Lie-Jørgensen, who embodied this tradition in his designs while working at David-Andersen, passed it on to subsequent generations of Norwegian silversmiths in his role as a teacher.

143. Tapio Wirkkala (b. 1915). *Vases:* Chanterelles. 1946–47. Finland. Produced by Iittalan Lasitehdas, Iittala. Blown glass, heights 8¼″; 5⅛″ (21 cm; 13 cm). Iittala Museum

Wirkkala has established the Iittala factory in Finland as a leading producer of art glass. His designs often reflect natural forms, translated into pure and elegant contours. These vases, based on the modest shape of a mushroom, were among the most popular of designs introduced by Wirkkala and were in production from 1947 until 1960.

144. Arne Korsmo (1900–1968). *Cutlery.* 1949. Norway. Produced by J. Tostrup, Oslo, from 1953. Silver, *dinner knife:* length 8″ (20.5 cm). Vestlandske Kunstindustrimuseum, Bergen

Although Korsmo's designs for table cutlery are highly functional, they also display the unmistakable "softness" of mid-century design, seen here in the gentle opposition of the curves that form the handles of the pieces. This design won a gold medal at the Milan Triennale of 1954.

the image of "Scandinavian Design" achieved international currency.

Another aspect of Scandinavian collaboration was the Lunning Prize, instituted in 1951 by Frederik Lunning, founder of the New York City branch of Georg Jensen. Awarded to two Scandinavian designers annually until its termination in 1972, this prize not only served to stimulate excellent design work but also established, in the public's mind, the idea of design as a joint Scandinavian concern.

In their campaign for modern functional design, the Scandinavian design organizations arranged numerous exhibitions of home furnishings both on a national and on a local level. In retrospect, this activity can be seen as a main characteristic of the fifties. The most significant was probably "H 55," a large exhibition magnificently installed on Hälsingborg pier, facing Øresund, in Sweden. It included a housing section with an international sampling of furnished apartments as well as areas devoted to design from other Scandinavian countries and the design of public spaces. Later, annual exhibitions called "Scandinavian Design Cavalcades" were organized to rotate among the Scandinavian countries, and their success ensured their continued showings. Along with the press and the design journals, these exhibitions contributed to the exchange of ideas and influences within the Scandinavian design world—perhaps to such an extent that they isolated it somewhat from external developments.

The design organizations did more than arrange exhibitions: they became prominent advocates for their field. They encouraged industry to invest in enlightened product development; they lobbied the governments to support good design in their export policies; and they educated the general public to be aware of better design and "more beautiful things for everyday use." Their exertions were not without effect and continued to be important in the development of design in the fifties and early sixties.

Beyond the efforts of the organizations, however, forces operating in the social and economic life of the fifties had a more profound influence on the future of design. With industrialization, urbanization, and the growth of the cities, the entire population structure changed and a rising standard of living affected most people and their life-styles. A general feeling of optimism, a belief in growth and progress, obtained. 141

Certain ideals came to be commonly shared, including the conviction that ordinary people had a right to a comfortable home that was not only salutary but also functional and aesthetically satisfying. During the 1950s, the welfare state was finally established in Scandinavia; modern design came to be considered the visual expression of the socially just society.

One factor significant in design development was the great advance in housing, both privately built and government-supported. The sheer volume of construction demanded rational solutions, in which rational furnishings naturally played an important role. Architects, designers, and critics concentrated their thinking in this direction. Of course, their concepts and ideals had their roots in the 1920s and 1930s—and even further back into the past—but it was during the 1950s and early 1960s that modern design theories were translated into practical solutions on a broad scale. Only then did society fully accept the modern style and its underlying assumptions and attempt to integrate them into its fabric. Such fundamental and material changes fed one into the other to bring industrial design, also, to a turning point.

During the thirty years under discussion, Scandinavia presented a consistent style to the world at large; within this period, a number of stylistic developments can, however, be discerned. It is easier to perceive the common denominators of Scandinavian Design from abroad than from within. And the decisive events in its early stages become clearer when viewed in retrospect than in the period when they actually occurred. Internationally, by the 1920s and 1930s, Swedish design had already made a certain impression: terms like "Swedish Grace" and slogans like "Swedish Modern—a movement toward sanity in design" were in use before 1940. The label "Scandinavian Design" was first applied to the achievements of the entire Scandinavian design area in the mid-1950s in connection with the Milan Triennale and the traveling exhibition in America. Since then it has become more or less accepted that "Scandinavian Design" is also the name of a *style*. Although such a statement is debatable, one can attempt to defend it and give the style a common description, while taking into consideration national differences and other factors.

Generally speaking, the style known as Scandinavian Design is based on functionalism. Its forms are simple and geometric, its materials and technical solutions clearly visible. Ornament is more or less restricted, especially that derived from nature

145. Lisbet Jobs-Söderlund (1909–1961). *Bowl.* 1939. Sweden. Produced at Jobs Keramik, Västanvik. Glazed earthenware, 2¾ × 12¼" (7.1 × 31 cm). Nationalmuseum, Stockholm

In her lively and freely painted nature studies, Jobs-Söderlund treated the ceramic surface as if it were a canvas. The bowls and plates she designed in floral patterns afford a striking parallel to the textiles designed by her sister, Gocken Jobs.

146. Gocken Jobs (b. 1914). *Printed fabric:* Trollslända (Dragonfly). 1945. Sweden. Produced by Ljungbergs Textiltryck, Dala-Floda. Linen, width 53⅛" (135 cm). Nationalmuseum, Stockholm

During the war years, Sweden's textile industry set out to provide designs that would lend a breath of color to interiors; few patterns introduced during the period are as rich in color and detail as those produced by Jobs in the family studio. Fresh and unprepossessing, the Jobs designs are meticulously printed.

147. Sven Arne Gillgren (b. 1913). *Covered box.* 1942. Sweden. Produced by Guldsmedsaktiebolaget, Stockholm. Silver and gold, height 3⅞" (10.1 cm). Nationalmuseum, Stockholm

During the difficult years of World War II, Sweden's neutrality permitted certain luxury crafts, among them silversmithing, to flourish. Gillgren's designs during this period echo trends current in ceramics and textiles, including an interest in folk-art patterns.

145

146

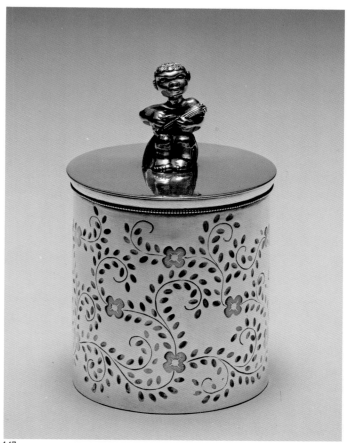

147

148. Alvar Aalto (1898–1976). *Printed fabric:* Siena *(detail)*. 1954. Finland. Produced by Artek, Helsinki. Cotton, width 51⅛″ (130 cm). Artek Oy AB, Helsinki

Aalto designed his fabrics, intended as upholstery or window hangings, with their architectural role in mind. This simple geometric pattern, employing the motif of brickwork to obtain a compositional unity, is entirely consistent with the humanized functionalism of Aalto's buildings and furniture.

149. Greta Skogster-Lehtinen (b. 1900). *Weaving (detail)*. 1945. Finland. Birchbark and paper, 108¼ × 38⅛″ (275 × 97 cm). Collection Timo Arjas, Helsinki

Shortages of supplies during the war years in Finland encouraged designers to seek alternate materials. Many weavers of the period experimented with paper; Skogster-Lehtinen's exploitation of the color and texture of native Finnish birchbark yielded a particularly striking pattern.

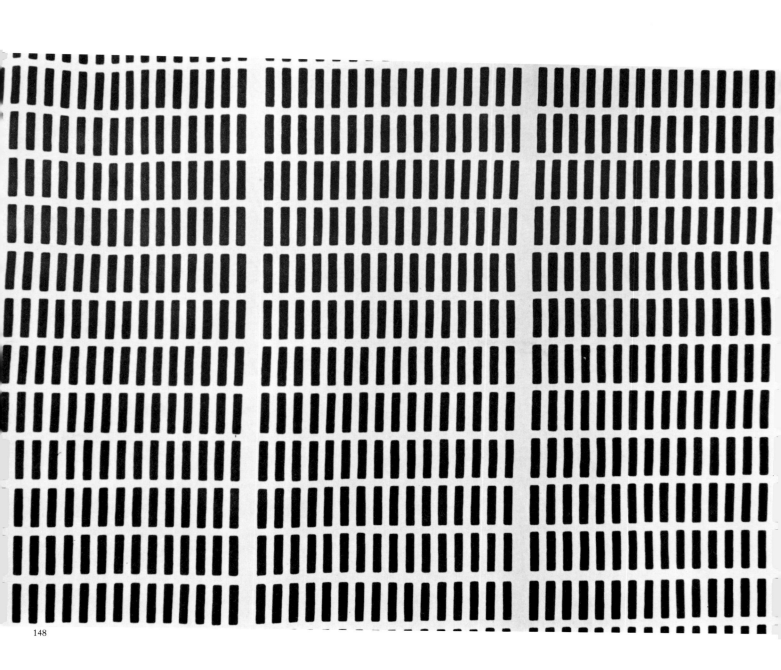

150

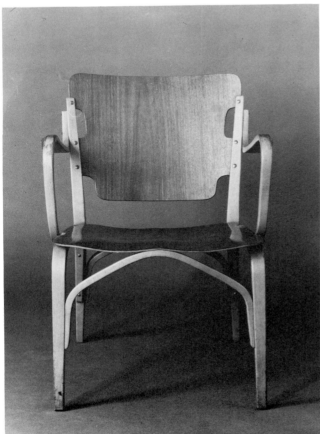

151

150. Barbro Nilsson (b. 1899). *Rug*: Shells. 1943. Sweden. Executed by AB Märta Måås-Fjetterström, Båstad. Wool, 74¾ × 66⅞″ (190 × 170 cm). Nationalmuseum, Stockholm

Nilsson combined traditional textile techniques with a new painterly approach in her tapestries and rugs. The abstract quality of her designs, along with an intensity of color, transcended pictorial or narrative qualities and gave a new impetus to the art of woven textiles.

151. Carl-Axel Acking (b. 1910). *Armchair*. 1944. Sweden. Produced by Svenska Möbelfabrikerna, Bodafors. Bent mahogany and beech, laminated, 31⅛ × 24¾ × 25⅝″ (79 × 63.2 × 65 cm). Nationalmuseum, Stockholm

That Acking acknowledged functionalist principles is evident in this chair, but it also expresses a movement toward less formalistic design. The laminated wood used for the back and seat has been gently curved, as have the arms and stretchers, to produce an effect at once energetic and suggestive of comfort. The rivets that secure the sections of the chair were left exposed, underlining the clarity of construction.

152. Finn Juhl (b. 1912). *Armchair*. 1945. Denmark. Produced by Nils Vodder, Allerød. Teak and fabric (by Vibeke Klint for C. Olesen), 32 × 16½ × 18⅞″ (81.5 × 42 × 48 cm). Det Danske Kunstindustrimuseum, Copenhagen

The graciousness of mid-century Danish furniture, evinced in its inviting curves, is exemplified by this chair, the work of Finn Juhl—the acknowledged master of the sculptural style of furnishings. The sensitive modeling of the wood to denote both firm support and repose profoundly affected the field of furniture design the world over.

motifs. In textiles, a slightly different situation may be seen. The decoration of interiors has always required the services of a textile designer, and these designs are clearly related to current tastes and interests. Motifs derived from nature continued to be used in textiles, and the postwar wave of abstract and Constructivist painting also strongly influenced their design. In Sweden, where abstract art made its first breakthrough in Scandinavia, the impulse was particularly fruitful, resulting in such objects as the wall hangings designed by the abstract painter Olle Bærtling for NK (Nordiska Kompaniet, Sweden's leading interior design firm). The abstract style also inspired Karl Axel Pehrson and Astrid Sampe in Sweden, and, to a lesser degree, Vibeke Klint in Denmark, Bjørn Engø in Norway, and Dora Jung in Finland.

The Scandinavian functionalism of the 1940s and 1950s was much less severe and dogmatic than that of the 1930s. Geometric forms softened, corners and flat planes smoothed into S-like curves and waves. Often described as "organic," this trend might be considered one in which the forms became more human, more sensitive. The movement of the 1940s toward national retrospection and a certain romanticism, often expressed in rustic and deliberately unsophisticated forms, spurred on this "softening" process. Instead of the simple, primary color schemes of early functionalism, gradations of color were introduced in the 1940s. Coarser textures were employed in fabrics, natural wood was favored in furniture, and simpler forms were cultivated in ceramics. The Danish tradition of fine craftsmanship, another retrospective trend, gained strength in Sweden and Norway in the first years after 1945.

This "mellowing" of the early functionalist style contained an implicit element of reaction against the previous period. As a natural consequence, designers looked further back into the past; thus, by the middle of the 1950s, after a generation of disfavor and scorn, Art Nouveau had been rediscovered. Whether consciously inspired by Art Nouveau or not, Finn Juhl's furniture, with its organic shapes and curved contours (especially evident in his armchairs), contains echoes of the style. Other resonances of Art Nouveau can be found in Wirkkala's glass "mushroom" vases, Henning Koppel's large silver dish and cover, Stig Lindberg's earthenware bowls, and Tias Eckhoff's coffee service. Even the silverplate cutlery of Arne Korsmo displays this linear-organic trend.

153. Alf Sture (b. 1915). *Armchair.* 1943. Norway. Produced by Hiorth & Østlyngen, Oslo. Elm and woven paper string, 28½ × 20⅛ × 24″ (72.5 × 51 × 61 cm). Oslo Kunstindustrimuseet

Radically simple in its construction, this chair, designed during the lean years of World War II, uses twisted and woven paper in lieu of upholstery. The back is angled to promote a relaxed posture, and the gentle curve to the seat furnishes additional comfort.

154. Kaare Klint (1888–1954). *Lanterns:* Frugtlygte. 1944. Denmark. Produced by Le Klint, Copenhagen, 1981. Folded paper, 14⅛ × 10⅝″ (36 × 27 cm); 20⅞ × 16½″ (53 × 42 cm); 17⅜ × 13⅜″ (44 × 34 cm). Le Klint, Copenhagen

Klint experimented with folded paper to provide an inexpensive and aesthetically satisfying lighting fixture. These innovative lanterns, designed to be suitable for mass production in simple materials to keep their prices low, realized his purpose. The lamps soon appeared in many public and domestic interiors and remain in use today.

155. Hans Wegner (b. 1914). *Folding chair.* 1949. Denmark. Produced by Johannes Hansen, Copenhagen. Oak and cane, 31⅛ × 24 × 17¾″ (79 × 61 × 45 cm). Det Danske Kunstindustrimuseum, Copenhagen

Over the course of his long working career, Wegner has continued to develop chairs that have become classics, of which the familiar folding chair is one of the best examples. Designed with a strict regard for comfort while in use, the chair folds extremely flat for easy storage, with handles ingeniously built into the structure of the support frame.

156. Hans Wegner (b. 1914). *Armchair.* 1949. Denmark. Produced by Johannes Hansen, Copenhagen. Walnut and cane, 29⅞ × 24¾ × 20½″ (76 × 63 × 52 cm). Det Danske Kunstindustrimuseum, Copenhagen

The finest traditional qualities of Danish design—meticulous craftsmanship, subtle exploitation of materials, concern for comfort—are conspicuous in Wegner's furniture. This design, with its embracing back support, gently curved seat, and soft contours, so successfully fulfills the most stringent requirements of function and aesthetics that it has become popularly known as "The Chair."

153

154

155

156

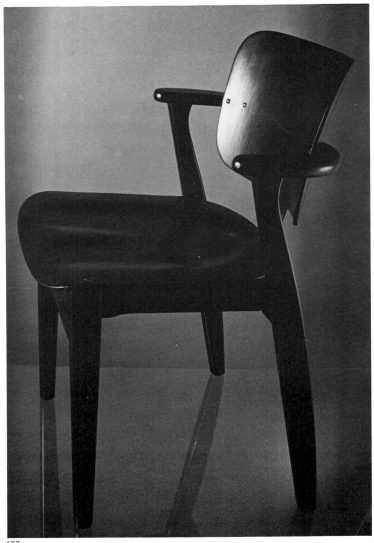

157

158

157. Ilmari Tapiovaara (b. 1914). *Armchair:* Domus. 1946. Finland. Produced by Wilhelm Schauman, Jyväskylä. Wood and pressed wood, painted. 29½ × 22½ × 22½" (75 × 57 × 57 cm). Taideteollisuusmuseo, Helsinki

This highly functional design by Tapiovaara is constructed of simple parts that were easily mass-produced. The innovative use of curved laminated plywood brings to mind Charles Eames's landmark chair of the same year.

158. Finn Juhl (b. 1912). *Bowl.* 1949. Denmark. Turned by Magne Monsen for Kay Bojesen, Copenhagen. Teak, 6⅞ × 14⅝" (17.5 × 37 cm). Det Danske Kunstindustrimuseum, Copenhagen

This simple wooden bowl profits from the sculptural quality with which Juhl also endowed his furniture: the full and gentle curve of the body is played off against the strong grain of the wood. While the form suggests the traditional rustic wooden bowl, it does so with a sophistication of design that speaks of its own decade.

Another, strikingly different, trend emerged from the rising importance of industrial design and the influence of Constructivist art. "Hard-edged" and matter-of-fact, this style marks Kaj Franck's *Kilta* table service and Arne Jacobsen's domestic designs in stainless steel. As a simple, logical design, the style also suited the new plastic materials being developed at the time.

While the Scandinavian countries shared many ideas about design in this period, each country displayed its own variations. Finnish crafts, for example, are generally intended for a more elite audience than those in the other countries. Thus, in the middle of the 1950s, a lively discussion arose in the press and design organizations about the ways and means of Finnish design. Industry's lack of interest in everyday products and the marked difference between mass-produced objects and the more prestigious artistic creations bore most of the criticism. The promotion of "star designers" was also the subject of debate.

Timo Sarpaneva's elegant glass vases and dishes from the early 1950s embody the sophisticated Finnish style, as does Wirkkala's leaf-shaped, laminated wood dish. The latter was proclaimed, after the Milan Triennale in 1951, "the world's most beautiful object" for that year—for whatever that was worth. (Three years later, Sarpaneva's glass sculpture was similarly honored.) In spirit such pieces are closer to modern sculpture than to the idea of a functional, applied art in its stricter sense.

Yet a range of other products counterbalanced the impression of exclusiveness. Kaj Franck's *Kilta* table service, produced by Arabia beginning in 1953, combined elegant forms with simple materials; Lisa Johannson-Pape's electric fittings and Carl Johan Bomann's stacking chairs also derived from the more functional trend. By the end of the 1950s, a whole generation of young talents had the opportunity to realize their artistic ambitions as designers for various industrial firms. Antti Nurmesniemi, Saara Hopea, Nanny Still-McKinney, and later Oiva Toikka and Björn Weckström created new table glass series for the leading glassworks Iittala and Nuutajärvi-Notsjö. Nurmesniemi's high-polished steel and leather chairs and Yrjö Kukkapuro's bold swivel armchair made of metal and welded plastic turned Finnish furniture design toward a decisively international style.

In the early 1960s, Maija Isola, Marjatta Metsovaara, Liisa

159

160

159. Toini Muona (b. 1904). *Vases.* 1952–55. Finland. Produced at Arabia, Helsinki. Glazed earthenware, heights 17⅜"; 15¾"; 15" (44 cm; 40 cm; 38 cm). Arabia Museum, Helsinki

The poetry of nature was a distinctive aspect of Muona's works in the 1950s; these three slender vases recall the gentle movement of the wind through water reeds. They were designed to be shown in groups or arrangements rather than individually.

160. Bjørn Wiinblad (b. 1918). *Plate.* 1954. Denmark. Earthenware, diameter 7⅞" (20 cm). Det Danske Kunstindustrimuseum, Copenhagen

Wiinblad, still one of the most prolific of Danish designers, has stamped his personal and often whimsical style on designs for ceramics, silver, textiles, posters, and the theater. The stylization of the human figure for which Wiinblad is best known attains an elegance at once medieval and urbane.

161. Wilhelm Kåge (1889–1960). *Vase.* 1952. Sweden. Produced at Gustavsberg. Stoneware, 8⅝" × 8" (22 × 20.5 cm). Röhsska Konstslöjdmuseet, Göteborg

Kåge's *Farsta* ware (stoneware fired at about 1,200° C) pieces of the 1950s are the culmination of his lifelong experiments with organically derived forms and rich glazes.

162. Nathalie Krebs (1895–1978) and Eva Stæhr-Nielsen (1911–1976). *Vase.* 1954. Denmark. Produced at Saxbo, Copenhagen. Stoneware, height 13⅞" (35.5 cm). Det Danske Kunstindustrimuseum, Copenhagen

Working at Saxbo, their studio, Krebs and Stæhr-Nielsen created stoneware vessels of superb grandeur and presence. Stæhr-Nielsen designed the forms and Krebs developed the glazes; their joint efforts produced a body of work with a distinctive and characteristic texture that arises from the unity of shape and glaze.

163. Carl-Harry Stålhane (b. 1920). *Bowl.* 1955. Sweden. Produced at Rörstrand, Lidköping. Stoneware, 2⅞" × 16⅞" (7.5 × 43 cm). Collection Carl-Harry Stålhane

Engaged by the Rörstrand factory at the age of nineteen, Stålhane supplied art and production wares of singularly powerful design. The abstract geometry inside the bowl is accomplished through a pattern of overlapping curves, which echo the streamlined silhouette of the outer edge of the vessel.

161

162

163

Suvanto, and Vuokko Eskolin startled the world of design with their excitingly vivid and colorful printed textiles. Firms like Armi Ratia's Marimekko (Mary's frock) and later Vuokko Eskolin's company marketed such prints with tremendous success, and their popularity gave birth to a new, informal manner of wearing clothes, "more like a life-style than a fashion," to quote Ulf Hård af Segerstad.

While refinement and cultivation of form may be said to characterize Danish design as well, Denmark created a broader range of design products than did Finland. Unique products of fine craftsmanship were supplemented by industrial products made in larger series and aimed at an extended market.

Danish furniture design provides a good illustration. It has strong links with traditional cabinetmaking; indeed, exhibitions of the Cabinetmakers Guild in Copenhagen were annual events in which leading furniture designers presented their new models. Ole Wanscher and Børge Mogensen, both one-time assistants of Kaare Klint (who died in 1954), derived their styles from the principles of craftsmanship espoused by Klint in the 1930s. Wanscher cultivated the careful shaping of wood into forms of great refinement, whereas Mogensen concentrated on extremely simplified basic structures. Hans Wegner, like Wanscher, expressed his functional ideas in sculptural form, and, in the process, created a classic, now known as "The Chair." Finn Juhl, also a furniture sculptor—"although a sybaritic one" according to Hård af Segerstad—emphasized linear rhythm in his own particular way. Of course, the results of this sophisticated design depended entirely on the quality of the craftsman's execution.

The work of Arne Jacobsen and Poul Kjærholm may be juxtaposed to the fine craft pieces of Wanscher, Wegner, and Juhl. Jacobsen, an architect who controlled every detail of his buildings, including the furniture and equipment, drew his designs from industrial technology. Kjærholm favored steel, with its flexibility and elegant surface finish, for his furniture. His use of industrial materials points back to such primary exponents of functionalism in furniture design as Le Corbusier and Mies van der Rohe. Although mass-produced, the furniture designed by Jacobsen and Kjærholm is still intended for the rather sophisticated buyer.

Danish metal design displays the same breadth, ranging from simple but exquisite forms in silver to equally elegant, mass-

154

164

164. Anders Liljefors (1923–1970). *Sculpture.* 1956. Sweden. Produced at Gustavsberg. Stoneware, height 8⅜" (21.5 cm). Nationalmuseum, Stockholm

As early as the 1950s, an impulse to free potters from their traditional role so that they could develop the creative potential within traditional craft areas began to take hold. A new school of independent artists arose that included Liljefors among its earliest proponents. His potent and often shocking forms and glazes, which had no association with a functional or decorative tradition, foreshadow the separation of art and design that would become so prominent in Scandinavia during the 1970s.

165. Stig Lindberg (1916–1982). *Cooking pan:* Terma *and dishes:* Spisa Ribb. 1955. Sweden. Produced by Gustavsberg. Stoneware, *pan:* length 11½" (29.5 cm); *dishes:* diameters 11⅜" × 4⅜" (29.8 × 11 cm); 7⅜" × 5¾" (18.7 × 14.8 cm). Nationalmuseum, Stockholm

Lindberg's production designs for cooking and serving ware during the 1950s have become standards of functional design. The cooking pan, made of high-fired stoneware, is equally suitable for frying or baking and can go directly from stove to table. Nearly all of Lindberg's designs are carefully planned to encourage the mixing of patterns and shapes at table, a development of the twentieth century that made expensive services of a single pattern unnecessary.

166. Kaj Franck (b. 1911). *Tableware,* Kilta *pattern.* 1952. Finland. Produced by Arabia, Helsinki. Glazed earthenware, *square dish:* 1⅝" × 5⅜" (3.9 × 13.6 cm); *rectangular dish:* 1⅝" × 12¼" × 8¼" (3.9 × 30.9 × 20.9 cm). Taideteollisuusmuseo, Helsinki

Restricted to a modular system of shapes and a limited range of colors, *Kilta* proved to be one of the most successful of Arabia's standard production lines, from the points of view of consumer and critic alike.

165

166

167

168

167. Eystein Sandnes (b. 1924). *Tableware,* Jubileum *pattern.*
1959. Norway. Produced by Porsgrunds Porselænsfabrik,
Porsgrunn. Porcelain, *coffeepot:* height 6¾″ (17 cm); *large
plate:* diameter 7⅝″ (19.5 cm); *cup:* 2¾ × 3⅞″ (7.1 × 9.9 cm).
Vestlandske Kunstindustrimuseum, Bergen

This simple and functional tableware pattern was awarded
the silver medal at the Milan Triennale in 1960. Sandnes
frequently chose to understate his designs, and their simple
yet expressive forms could serve in a variety of settings.

168. Ulla Procopé (1921–1968). *Covered cooking dishes,* Liekki
pattern. 1957. Finland. Produced by Arabia, Helsinki. Stoneware, maximum diameter 9″ (23 cm). Taideteollisuusmuseo,
Helsinki

Engaged by Arabia from 1948 to 1967, Procopé designed
numerous tablewares, of which this service fully deserves the
appellation "classic." Entirely functional, these dishes can be
used for cooking or serving, and their shapes are strong,
balanced, and perfectly proportioned. The lustrous uninterrupted surfaces of the bowls emphasize the self-assured
elegance of the design.

169. Nils Landberg (b. 1907). *Glasses from the* Tulip *series.*
1957. Sweden. Produced by Orrefors Glasbruk. Blown
glass, heights 14⅛″; 16½″; 16½″ (36 cm; 42 cm; 42 cm). AB
Orrefors Glasbruk

From 1925 until 1972, Landberg served on the design staff of
Orrefors, where he developed art glass in addition to functional glassware. The *Tulip* series, among his best-known
designs, won admiration for the attenuated grace of the tall
and elegant goblets, attained through technical virtuosity: the
foot and stem are made of a single gather of glass, pulled into
an elongated bubble.

170. Ingeborg Lundin (b. 1921). *Vase:* Apple. 1957. Sweden.
Produced by Orrefors Glasbruk. Blown glass, 13⅜ × 14⅛″
(34 × 36 cm). AB Orrefors Glasbruk

Lundin contributed innumerable designs for art glass and
tableware during her career at Orrefors from 1947 to 1971.
Although ornamented designs constituted an important part
of her repertoire, she chose in the *Apple* vase a purity of form
that exploits the clarity of the lead crystal to an extraordinary
degree.

169

170

171

172

173

174

175

171. Kaj Franck (b. 1911). *Pitchers*. 1958. Finland. Produced by Nuutajärvi-Notsjö Glass, Nuutajärvi. Blown glass, 9 × 3⅛" (23 × 8 cm). Finnish Glass Museum, Riihimäki

Franck has provided designs for many Finnish companies, including Arabia, Iittala, and Notsjö. The straightforward simplicity of much of Franck's work lends a charm to the highly functional designs. These pitchers, produced in a range of colors that include ruby red and smoke gray, elegantly state their purpose.

172. Per Lütken (b. 1916). *Bowl*. 1955. Denmark. Produced by Holmegaards Glasverk, Holmegaard. Blown glass, 4⅜ × 7¼" (11 × 18.5 cm). Det Danske Kunstindustrimuseum, Copenhagen

The soft and gentle forms of much Danish glass of the 1950s parallel a similar development in silver. Lütken's forms are exceptionally organic in shape, the clear glass appearing to expand in the manner of a large soap bubble. His production wares and table glass often exhibit the same relaxed quality.

173. Saara Hopea (b. 1925). *Glasses*. 1952. Finland. Produced by Nuutajärvi-Notsjö Glass, Nuutajärvi. Molded blown glass, 3¼ × 2¾" (8.5 × 7 cm). Taideteollisuusmuseo, Helsinki

Hopea's career as an artist and designer has embraced design activities in the fields of furniture, glass, enamel, and jewelry. The stacking glasses of 1952, produced in a broad range of colors, are easily gripped while in use.

174. Arne Jon Jutrem (b. 1929). *Vase*. 1958. Norway. Produced by Hadelands Glassverk, Jevnaker. Blown glass, height 7¾" (19.7 cm), diameter at lip 6⅛" (15.8 cm). Nordenfjeldske Kunstindustrimuseum, Trondheim

During the 1950s, Jutrem, a prolific designer who won a gold medal at the 1954 Milan Triennale, achieved international acclaim for his art glass. Strong sculptural forms are effectively combined with intense or subtle coloration, which gives even his simple shapes an inner vitality.

175. Willy Johansson (b. 1921). *Bowl*, Peach *pattern*. 1956. Norway. Produced by Hadelands Glassverk, Jevnaker. Pressed glass, diameter 11" (28 cm). Nordenfjeldske Kunstindustrimuseum, Trondheim

In 1947, Johansson joined the Hadelands glassworks in Jevnaker as head of the team of designers working on both unique and production items. His innovative designs for production in the traditional pressing technique brought a new aesthetic interest and quality to the medium.

176, 177. Erik Höglund (b. 1932). *Vases*. 1953–59. Sweden. Produced by Boda Glasbruk. Blown glass, 176: 8⅛ × 4⅜" (20.6 × 11.1 cm); 177: 5¼ × 5" (13.3 × 12.7 cm). Cooper-Hewitt Museum, New York. Gift of Harry Dennis, Jr.

Höglund has pursued a career as a sculptor and glassblower. His designs for simple blown-glass vessels of the 1950s made use of metallic occlusions in the glass, which produce fine or crude bubbles. The rusticity of Höglund's mid-century designs contrast strikingly with the elegant, sophisticated glass typical of the period.

176

177

178. Tapio Wirkkala (b. 1915). *Decanter and glasses,* Romantica *pattern.* 1959. Finland. Produced by Iittalan Lasitehdas, Iittala. Molded glass, *decanter:* height 9⅛″ (23.4 cm). *Glasses:* Iittala Museum; *decanter:* Taideteollisuusmuseo, Helsinki

Even in his simple designs, Wirkkala contrasts a massive base with the transparent fragility of the body. In this service, the solid, flaring base of each vessel lends stability to the rhythmically curved glass.

produced steel cutlery. Henning Koppel and Magnus Stephensen were leading designers in the field of silver and were joined in metalwork design by Arne Jacobsen. Jacobsen, Koppel, and Herbert Krenchel also designed table settings using the new hard plastic.

As Danish design reached its peak, in the 1950s and early 1960s, the fields of furniture and metalwork were particularly noteworthy. This should not, however, overshadow the continued high achievements in ceramics, glass, and textiles. Gertrud Vasegaard, Ingrid Dessau, Nanna Ditzel, Grethe Meyer, Per Lütken, Lis Ahlmann, Finn Lynggaard, and numerous other respected designers contributed to the high level of Danish applied arts during this period.

The Danish ceramics industry simultaneously carried a line of one-of-a-kind pieces and objects in large series. The design studios of the Royal Copenhagen Porcelain Manufactory and Bing & Grøndahl could be described as pottery workshops in the broadest sense. This phenomenon was not peculiar to Denmark. The ceramic and glass industries of all the Scandinavian countries in the 1950s and 1960s succumbed to an enlightened policy of running studio production parallel to mass production. Thus the designers of the industrial series were also freely creating their own single works of art, either completely by their own hand or in close collaboration with the craftsmen of the factory.

Sweden is the country in which the idea of "more beautiful things for everyday use" materialized first and went furthest. Early on, industry accepted quality as a goal of inexpensive mass production, and the turn-of-the-century slogan "artists into industry" achieved significant results. Even more than in Denmark, designers were employed by industry in a wide spectrum of activities. At first they concentrated on the traditional areas of home furnishings, but later they expanded their concerns to encompass all the surroundings of the human being—"society, home and furnishing, work and leisure environment," as it was stated in the program of the "H 55" exhibition. Their goals were to shape the environment so that it would express the democratic ideals of society and to develop the potentialities of technology in order to make better commodities available for everyone. At the same time, the more exclusive crafts continued to attract wide public attention.

Among Sweden's exemplary achievements in design for mass

179

179. Tapio Wirkkala (b. 1915). *Vases.* 1955. Finland. Produced by Iittalan Lasitehdas, Iittala. Molded and cased glass, maximum height 7⅞″ (20 cm). Iittala Museum

The bold, sculptural forms of these vases, made of heavy and solid glass, engender an optical jewel-like effect through the refraction of light. Although Wirkkala has contributed many designs for practical tablewares, he is known for the art-glass style—direct, virile, and uncompromising—that made vases such as these classics of Finnish modern design.

180. Berndt Friberg (1899–1981). *Vase.* 1954. Sweden. Produced at Gustavsberg. Stoneware, height 6⅜″ (16.5 cm). Nationalmuseum, Stockholm

The Swedish glass and ceramics industries hired artists not only to design production wares but also to work independently in creating unique art objects. At Gustavsberg, Friberg concentrated on making unique stoneware vessels of exceptionally refined form, using ineffably beautiful glazes in the Oriental manner.

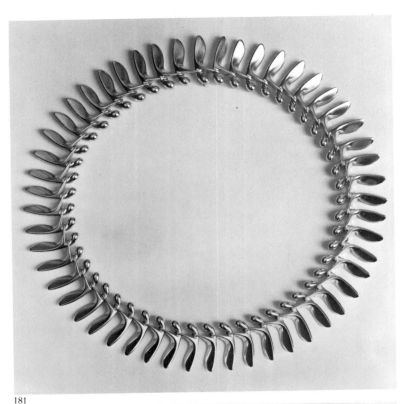

181

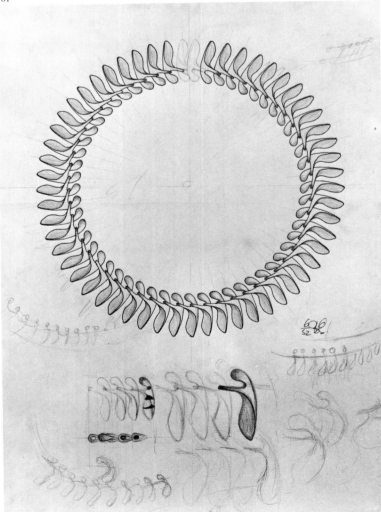

182

181. Bent Gabrielsen (b. 1928). *Necklace*. 1959. Denmark. Produced by Georg Jensen Sølvsmedie, Copenhagen. Silver, diameter 6¼″ (16 cm). Georg Jensen Sølvsmedie A/S, Copenhagen

182. *Drawing for a necklace*. 1952. Denmark. Pencil on paper, 11¾ × 8¼″ (30 × 21 cm). Collection Bent Gabrielsen

Designed in 1952, this necklace was put into production at Georg Jensen in 1959; it subsequently won a gold medal at the Milan Triennale in 1960. Each of the cast links, echoing the natural forms of winged seeds, is interlocked to provide maximum flexibility so that the necklace will conform to the neck of the wearer.

183. Aune Siimes (1909–1964). *Bowl*. 1952. Finland. Produced at Arabia, Helsinki. Porcelain, 2⅜ × 9″ (6 × 23 cm). Taideteollisuusmuseo, Helsinki

The inherent qualities of porcelain—translucence, delicacy, and resonance—were exploited fully by Siimes, who worked at the Arabia factory beginning in 1932. Siimes tended toward fragile shapes, relying on carefully modulated raised or incised patterns and eggshell thinness of body for the effect of her pieces.

184. Kyllikki Salmenhaara (1915–1981). *Bowl*. 1959–61. Finland. Produced at Arabia, Helsinki. Stoneware, 4¾ × 15″ (12 × 38 cm). Taideteollisuusmuseo, Helsinki

A leading figure in the development of art ceramics in Finland, Salmenhaara was first engaged by Arabia in 1947. She used rough stoneware, to which she gave mottled surface textures and intense colors, imbuing her vases and bowls with a natural vitality and evocative strength.

185. Henning Koppel (1918–1981). *Fish platter and cover*. 1954. Denmark. Produced by Georg Jensen Sølvsmedie, Copenhagen. Silver, 6¾ × 26¾ × 12⅝″ (17 × 68 × 32 cm). Det Danske Kunstindustrimuseum, Copenhagen

Koppel's designs for silver are among the most timely and timeless, embodying with sculptural vigor the organically inspired forms of mid-century. The swelling contours of this fish platter suggest either a fish or a shell without resorting to literal translation of the shape. Koppel has received many design awards, including medals at the Milan Triennale.

183

184

185

165

production are the printed fabrics of Astrid Sampe and Sven Markelius designed for NK; Stig Lindberg's tableware for Gustavsberg; and the polished steel cutlery of Sigurd Persson, a leading goldsmith since the 1950s.

The Danish cabinetmaking tradition visibly influenced Swedish furniture design, but in Sweden it was translated into mass production of high quality. Designers like Bruno Mathsson continued their work in new furniture materials and forms to be applied to standard mass production. By the early 1960s, large furniture exhibitions and sales fairs, arranged by industry with considerable publicity, began to replace the earlier, less commercial exhibitions of the design organizations. The concentrated commercial marketing of modern furniture design turned it into a thriving business in Sweden, and the Danish and Norwegian furniture industries quickly followed suit.

A corresponding artistic specialization appears in other fields of design as well. In ceramics, Lindberg, Hertha Bengtson, and Karin Björquist were most successful with their tableware series for Gustavsberg and Rörstrand starting in the 1940s. At the same factories, there was also a stable of artists, including Berndt Friberg, Carl-Harry Stålhane, and Anders Liljefors, who devoted themselves to creating individual and unique works. Although Liljefors was making nonfunctional ceramic sculpture as early as the mid-1950s—and despite the achievements of such other independent creative designers as Hertha Hillfon and Britt-Ingrid Persson—free sculptural forms did not, or could not, develop until the 1960s. Only then did some ceramists, like Signe Persson-Melin, begin to set up their own workshops, a trend which grew in strength in the succeeding decade.

Similarly, glass production in the 1950s spanned a range from everyday tableware to the unique vases of Sven Palmqvist, Ingeborg Lundin, and Erik Höglund for Orrefors and Boda. In the mid-1960s, glass became a challenging art medium employed in purely decorative sculpture.

Developments in Swedish silver design foreshadowed later events in the other Scandinavian countries. The leading creative silversmiths in Sweden had always set up workshops of their own; industrial firms that hired artists to design for large-scale mechanized production never played an important role. This may explain the remarkable display of individually formed and richly varied hollow ware silver produced at a time when

186

186. Nanna Ditzel (b. 1923). *Bracelet*. 1956. Denmark. Produced by Georg Jensen Sølvsmedie, Copenhagen. Silver, diameter 3⅞" (10 cm). Georg Jensen Sølvsmedie A/S, Copenhagen

Working with her husband Jørgen, Nanna Ditzel supplied extremely disciplined and expressive designs for Georg Jensen. This bracelet depends entirely on a shape that creates tension between the circle and the oval. The simplicity of design, merging traditional and contemporary aesthetics, makes this bracelet timeless.

187. Sven Palmqvist (b. 1906). *Bowls from the* Fuga *series.* 1954. Sweden. Produced by Orrefors Glasbruk. Glass, centrifugally spun, 4⅞ × 8⅜" (12.5 × 21.5 cm); 4⅜ × 7½" (11 × 19 cm); 2½ × 4½" (6.5 × 11.5 cm). AB Orrefors Glasbruk

In addition to developing specialized techniques of glass decoration, Palmqvist introduced the *Fuga* technique of production, in which the molten glass is spun centrifugally to form the spherical shapes of the bowls. Besides facilitating the production of large spheres, the technique gave an unusual surface texture to the glass.

188. Sigurd Persson (b. 1914). *Cutlery,* Servus *pattern.* 1953. Sweden. Produced by Kooperativa Förbundet (The Cooperative Society of Sweden), Stockholm. Stainless steel, *knife:* length 7⅛" (18 cm). Kooperativa Förbundet, Stockholm

As an independent designer and craftsman in silver and gold, Persson has created many exuberant designs for jewelry and hollow ware. This simple and highly functional cutlery pattern reflects a concurrent development in Persson's work: the cultivation of sculptural and tactile forms that realize their effect through understatement. This service has gained the distinction of being one of the most generally accepted patterns in cutlery since its introduction.

187

188

189

190

191

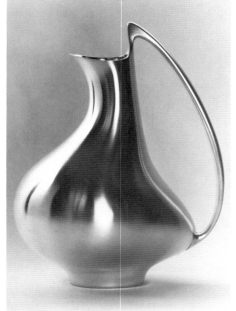

192

189. Gertrud Vasegaard (b. 1913). *Tea service*. 1957. Denmark. Produced by Bing & Grøndahl, Copenhagen. Porcelain and bamboo, *teapot:* height 5½″ (14 cm). Bing & Grøndahl, Copenhagen

Although active as an independent potter, Vasegaard worked at Bing & Grøndahl from 1947 to 1959. Her designs for both unique and production pieces combine the Danish tradition of unpretentious pottery with the subcurrent of Oriental influence that had such an impact on the Danish tradition.

190. Magnus Stephensen (b. 1903). *Covered pot*. 1951. Denmark. Produced by Georg Jensen Sølvsmedie, Copenhagen. Silver and cane, 5⅛ × 6¾″ (13 × 17 cm). Det Danske Kunstindustrimuseum, Copenhagen

From 1938 to 1952, Stephensen designed for Kay Bojesen; then he joined the staff of Georg Jensen. His metalwork and furniture designs are distinguished by their simplicity and directness, particularly in the exposed constructional elements.

191. Arne Jacobsen (1902–1971). *Cutlery: AJ pattern*. 1957. Denmark. Produced by A. Michelsen, Copenhagen. Stainless steel, *spoon:* length 7⅞″ (20 cm). A. Michelsen A/S, Copenhagen

Trained as an architect, Jacobsen designed functional cutlery entirely devoid of ornament, electing to accentuate clarity of form and refinement of detail. These sleek utensils suggest their purpose through minimal reference to traditional forms, such as the tines on the fork; what references remain Jacobsen translated into a unified sculptural statement. This service is still in production today.

192. Henning Koppel (1918–1981). *Ewer*. 1952. Denmark. Produced by Georg Jensen Sølvsmedie, Copenhagen. Silver, height 11¼″ (28.7 cm). Georg Jensen Sølvsmedie A/S, Copenhagen

Although a functional vessel, this ewer by Koppel succeeds as a purely sculptural statement. Koppel's silver always reflects the handcraft tradition, each form carefully raised, planished, and polished to achieve a luster that fully complements the softly curvilinear forms.

193. Antti Nurmesniemi (b. 1927). *Coffeepots*. 1957. Finland. Produced by Wärtsilä, Helsinki. Enameled metal and plastic, height 5⅞″ (15 cm). Taideteollisuusmuseo, Helsinki

A designer equally competent in the fields of furniture and domestic utensils, Nurmesniemi contributed a distinctive variation on one of the most traditional of forms—the standard coffeepot—which has become a classic in the Finnish design tradition. The simple form of the body clearly expresses its function, while its gently rounded edges give the pot a domesticated grace. The handle permits a firm grasp while keeping the hand well away from the heat.

194. Sven Markelius (1889–1972). *Printed fabric: Pythagoras*. 1952. Sweden. Printed by Erik Ljungberg, Floda, for Nordiska Kompaniet, Stockholm, 1965. Cotton, width 51⅛″ (130 cm). Nationalmuseum, Stockholm

Markelius was involved in the design of the 1930 Stockholm Exhibition and served as the architect for the Swedish pavilion at the 1939 World's Fair in New York. His architectural training can be detected in his bold printed fabrics, seen to their best advantage in extended lengths. The complex geometry of *Pythagoras,* based on the triangle, occasions a highly varied interlocking pattern of line and color.

193

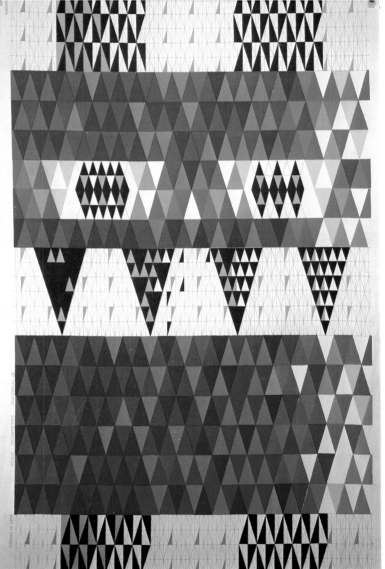

194

169

195

196

197

195. Sigvard Bernadotte (b. 1907). *Ice-water jug*. 1952. Denmark. Produced by Georg Jensen Sølvsmedie, Copenhagen. Silver and ebony, height 6⅞″ (17.2 cm). Georg Jensen Sølvsmedie A/S, Copenhagen

Schooled in the functionalist tradition, Bernadotte often endowed his functional designs with an unmistakable elegance of outline and detail. The unusual triangular form of this pitcher is gently tapered from the base upward to provide stability, while the hinged spout cover, pierced with a lozenge pattern, accents the simple shape.

196. Kaj Franck (b. 1911). *Bowls*. 1956. Finland. Produced by Wärtsilä, Helsinki. Enameled metal, maximum height 4″ (10.5 cm); maximum diameter 9″ (23 cm). Taideteollisuusmuseo, Helsinki

Exemplifying Franck's understated and functional designs, these award-winning bowls (Grand Prix, Milan Triennale of 1957) unite a sophisticated form with durability, lightness of weight, and stackability. Franck's domestic utensils rarely depart from the demands of disciplined functionalism, but with their exuberance of color they transcend the label of "everyday" wares. These bowls were originally produced in a range of six colors—pale blue, dark blue, red, yellow, green, and white—meant to be mixed and matched.

197. Bertel Gardberg (b. 1916). *Cooking pan,* Canton *pattern*. 1957. Finland. Produced by Hackman & Sorsakoski, Sorsakoski. Stainless steel and teak, 2¾ × 7⅞″ (7 × 20 cm). Taideteollisuusmuseo, Helsinki

Gardberg, the recipient of numerous design awards, including prizes from the Milan Triennale in 1954, 1957, and 1960, has joined wood to metal in a variety of domestic utensils from cookware to cutlery. In the *Canton* pattern, the richly grained wood of the handle contrasts visually with the sleek polished steel while serving as an effective insulation against conducted heat. Characteristically, the forms are elegantly simple, and the cover carries a recessed finger grip, a refinement of detail typical of the designer's style. The *Canton* pattern remained in production until 1965.

198. Olli Borg (1921–1979). *Armchair*. 1952. Finland. Produced by Keravan Puusepänteollisuus, Kerava. Acrylic, metal, and fabric, 31½ × 26⅜ × 23⅝″ (80 × 67 × 60 cm). Taideteollisuusmuseo, Helsinki

The Finnish have promptly adopted new materials and processes for their industrial furniture designs. Two molded acrylic sections form Borg's armchair; these simple curvilinear shapes are held in place by exposed rivets, which become integral elements of the design.

199. Tapio Wirkkala (b. 1915). *Light bulbs*. 1959. Finland. Produced by Airam, Ltd., Helsinki. Glass and metal, 7⅞ × 3⅛″ (20 × 8 cm); 5½ × 3⅞″ (14 × 10 cm). Taideteollisuusmuseo, Helsinki

Wirkkala's interest in the aesthetic potential of lighting led to important experiments with the shape of the light bulbs themselves. While standard-shaped bulbs had always been used inside a fixture, Wirkkala's design made the bulb into its own fixture. The outer surface of the bulb is translucent to prevent glare, but the bottom end is left clear to direct the light downward. Wirkkala received a Grand Prix at the 1960 Milan Triennale, where these bulbs were shown.

198

199

new hollow ware models had disappeared in Denmark, Finland, and Norway.

Designers Sven Arne Gillgren and Sigurd Persson, who in the 1950s succeeded the generation of Erik Fleming and Wiwen Nilsson, led the renaissance of hollow ware. From about 1960, they were joined by Torun Bülow-Hübe and Bengt Liljedahl, and a little later, by Olle Ohlsson, to mention only a few of the astonishing number of gifted artist-craftsmen in the field. The association of Nutida Svensk Silver (Contemporary Swedish Silver) was especially active in promoting the works of these new free-lance silversmiths.

Marika Hausen characterized Swedish design of the period in the following way: "One might say that Sweden, for a short while during the fifties, attained a sort of balance, when it seemed that the ideas and efforts of the thirties had been realized.... There was still a belief in consumer information, in good taste and quality." One might add, also, that the negative consequences of technology, industrialization, and urbanization had not yet become apparent.

In a way, Norwegian design is more difficult to assess in this period. As mentioned before, the national and retrospective attitude taken up by the established designers of the 1940s may have had more lasting consequences in this country than elsewhere. Even designers of a more enterprising spirit, like Alf Sture in furniture and Thorbjørn Lie-Jørgensen in silver, had problems finding their "national" identity, since the Danish influence was so strong in their fields. The earlier Norwegian functionalism was not extinct, however—its flame was fed by a group of designers and architects headed by Arne Korsmo. The progressive trend in Norway in the beginning of the 1950s is largely due to Korsmo. In 1949 he designed a set of silverplate cutlery that was elegant and unconventional, even by Scandinavian standards. At about the same time, his wife, Grete Prytz, developed special techniques for enameling large silver vessels. In 1954, Korsmo was architect for the Norwegian section at the Milan Triennale, where Prytz received the Grand Prix for her rich and lustrous enamels.

The Porsgrund porcelain factory reorganized its art department around 1950. Promising young designers like Tias Eckhoff, Eystein Sandnes, and Arne Lindaas were recruited from design school even before they had graduated and in the following years left their mark on ceramic, glass, and metal design.

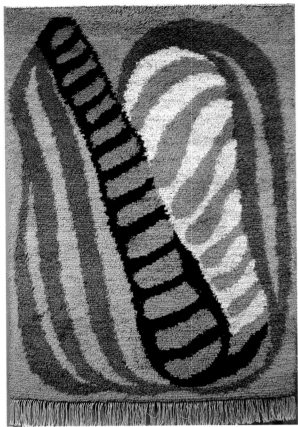

200

200. Juliana Sveinsdottir (1889–1966). *Tapestry:* The Snake. 1957. Iceland. Wool, *ryijy* technique, 75¼ × 53½″ (191 × 136 cm). Collection Leifur Sveinsson, Iceland

Although weaving and knitting are firmly established in the Icelandic craft tradition, the Danish-trained Sveinsdottir, who won a gold medal at the 1951 Milan Triennale, was among the first Icelandic textile artists to achieve international prominence. Sveinsdottir's compositions of the 1950s rely on sinuous abstract shapes and a distinctive range of colors that come from natural dyes or the richly colored—deep browns, black, and gray—undyed sheep's wool of Iceland.

201. Uhra-Beata Simberg-Ehrström (1914–1979). *Rug:* Four Colors. 1958. Finland. Executed by Suomen Käsityön Ystävät (Friends of Finnish Handicraft). Wool, *ryijy* technique, 70⅞ × 51⅛″ (180 × 130 cm). Ministry of Education, Helsinki

Although active in weaving and fabric design since the 1930s, Simberg-Ehrström gained international acclaim during the 1950s for her unique colors and compositions using the traditional *ryijy* technique. Her palette of carefully controlled colors tended toward the darkly lustrous hues; the subtlety of color was balanced by a simplicity of composition.

202

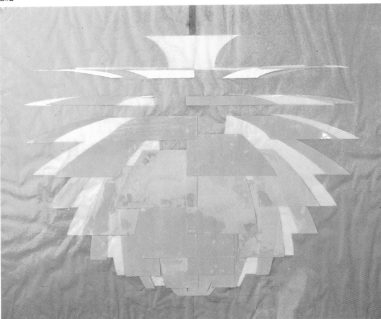

203

202. Poul Henningsen (1894–1967). *Lamp:* PH Artichoke. 1958. Denmark. Produced by Louis Poulsen & Co., Copenhagen. Copper, 27⅛ × 33⅛″ (69 × 84 cm). Louis Poulsen & Co. A/S, Copenhagen

203. *Collage: Lamp design.* 1957. Paper. Louis Poulsen & Co. A/S, Copenhagen

The collage studies for the *Artichoke* lamp reveal Henningsen's skillful fusion of the functional and the aesthetic. Originally designed for use in public spaces, this lamp has been produced in smaller versions for domestic use. The overlapping "leaves" spread bright general illumination to a large area, while, with their copper color, they cast a warm and inviting light. Henningsen carefully arranged the leaves with two goals in mind: to maximize the amount of reflected light and to protect the viewer from glare.

204. Poul Henningsen (1894–1967). *Lamp:* PH 5. 1957. Denmark. Produced by Louis Poulsen & Co., Copenhagen. Enameled metal, 9⅞ × 19⅝″ (25 × 50 cm). Louis Poulsen & Co. A/S, Copenhagen

Henningsen's innovative lighting fixtures of the 1920s (see no. 100) served as models for the now-classic "PH" series of hanging and table lamps. This conscientiously planned lamp reflects Henningsen's commitment to the principles of functionalism: the shade can be easily mass-produced from sheet metal; the curvature of the circular flanges distributes the light evenly and efficiently; the bulb is entirely covered to prevent glare; and the upper section of the fixture casts a general illumination that further eliminates downward glare.

205. Grete Prytz Kittelsen (b. 1917). *Bowl.* 1953–54. Norway. Produced at J. Tostrup, Oslo. Enameled silver, 2⅞ × 9″ (7.5 × 22.9 cm). Vestlandske Kunstindustrimuseum, Bergen

Heir to the Norwegian tradition of excellence in enameling, Kittelsen, who received her training in the United States as well as in Norway, has brought new vigor to the field. She exploits the transparency of the richly colored enamel by applying it over a metal field of delicately engraved lines, creating a myriad of reflected-light surfaces. The quality of her work—including an equally important number of jewelry designs in addition to large-scale works—won her the Lunning Prize for outstanding contribution to the field of design in 1952 and the Grand Prix at the 1954 Milan Triennale.

204

205

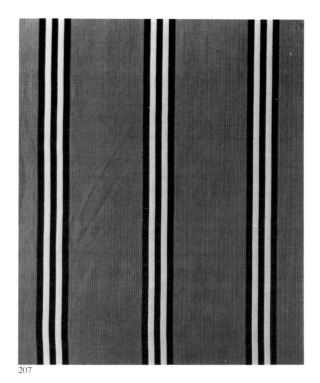

207

206. Poul Kjærholm (1929–1980). *Chair*. 1957. Denmark. Produced by E. Kold Christensen, Copenhagen. Steel and cane, 28⅛ × 13¾ × 16⅞" (71.5 × 35 × 43 cm). Det Danske Kunstindustrimuseum, Copenhagen

Most twentieth-century Danish furniture stresses the beauty of wood; Kjærholm's innovative designs in steel and cane represent an important departure from this tradition. The artist's individual approach to functional design gained him a Grand Prix at the 1957 Milan Triennale, followed a year later by the award of the Lunning Prize. The employment of strong tempered steel makes possible the pared-down structure of this chair, and the caning gives firm, resilient support while accentuating the linear quality of the silhouette.

207. Vibeke Klint (b. 1927). *Woven fabric (detail)*. 1952. Denmark. Cotton, width 44⅞" (114 cm). Det Danske Kunstindustrimuseum, Copenhagen

The simplest of patterns—the stripe—can be the most demanding for a designer, and few artists have handled this pattern as effectively as Vibeke Klint. Klint's work reveals a full and sensitive gift for subtle color combinations, for which she often uses natural dyes. Although Klint has designed for production, many of her finely woven fabrics are entirely produced by hand, her skill evident in the smooth flat weave, which requires an especially controlled technique.

In this connection one should mention such versatile designers as Hermann Bongard and Bjørn Engø, who made important contributions in graphic, glass, and textile design, and in other areas from about 1950 on.

The Hadeland glassworks held a position in its field similar to that of Porsgrund in porcelain. In the 1950s the firm's advanced policies brought forth a new generation of designers. Some, like Willy Johansson and Severin Brørby, had practical backgrounds as glassblowers; others, like Arne Jon Jutrem, Benny Motzfeldt, and, in later years, Gro Bergslien and Gerd Slang, arrived fresh from design school. Jutrem made glass sculpture in the early 1950s, while Motzfeldt and Bergslien, with their freer forms, left a distinct mark on Norwegian glass in the 1960s.

The leading silver and enamel designers of the 1950s were Thorbjørn Lie-Jørgensen, Oskar Sørensen, Sigurd Alf Eriksen, and Grete Prytz. Although hollow ware production more or less vanished about 1960, jewelry came into prominence from about 1965 onward with the rich designs of Tone Vigeland and Christian Gaudernack. Eckhoff, who made designs for both Norwegian and Danish manufacturers, introduced the use of steel in quality cutlery.

If Norwegian furniture was a somewhat late starter in the postwar years, it had attained a respectable position by the end of the 1950s. Most designers concentrated their attention on quality rather than on startling, individual pieces. Sture, who began his career in the late 1930s, was still—with Sven Ivar Dysthe, Bjørn Engø, Rolf Rastad, and Ingmar Relling— among the leaders of the 1950s and 1960s. The younger designers Arne Halvorsen and Fredrik A. Kayser joined their ranks in the 1960s. More experimental in their attitude were Tormod Alnæs, with his innovative *Pony Chair*, and Jan Lunde Knudsen, who developed a standardized system for office furniture, which, unfortunately, did not become widely known.

The original talents in Norwegian design have always expressed themselves best in free, creative invention rather than in disciplined collaboration with industry. A field like textiles, and especially tapestry weaving, which thrives on such independent endeavor, is thus particularly strong there. Hannah Ryggen, prominent in the field in the 1950s, was followed by Synnøve Aurdal and Britt Fuglevaag, among others, in the 1960s.

208

209

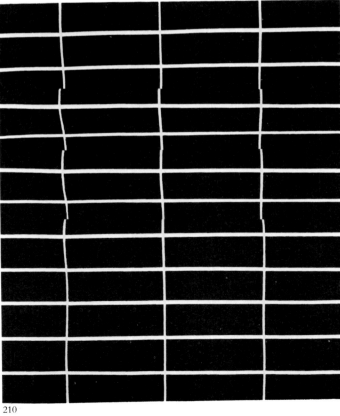

210

211

208. Birger Dahl (b. 1916). *Lamp*. 1955. Norway. Produced by Sønnico Fabrikker, Oslo. Enameled aluminum and brass, 9½ × 6½″ (24 × 16.8 cm). Oslo Kunstindustrimuseet

Like other designers specializing in lighting fixtures and interior decoration, Dahl sought to produce fixtures that effectively fulfilled their functional role yet contributed to the overall visual integrity of an architectural space. In pursuit of this objective, he created a number of sophisticated hanging fixtures whose shapes and colors blended with their surroundings.

209. Arne Jacobsen (1902–1971). *Chair: Ant*. 1952. Denmark. Produced by Fritz Hansens Eftf., Allerød. Wood, laminated and pressed, steel, and rubber, 30¼ × 18⅞ × 18⅞″ (77 × 48 × 48 cm). Det Danske Kunstindustrimuseum, Copenhagen

Masterly and economic treatment of means and materials resulted in this important chair. The simple press-molded one-piece seat and back compose a resilient and comfortable support; with its overall lightness, the chair is easy to move and to stack. These features, along with modest cost and simple maintenance, have made this chair especially popular for public seating areas, such as airports and restaurants. The unusual three-legged design is surprisingly stable, since the weight-bearing elements find a center of gravity toward the back of the seat.

210. Armi Ratia (1912–1979). *Printed fabric:* Prickstone. 1952. Finland. Produced by Marimekko, Helsinki. Cotton, width 51⅛″ (130 cm). Marimekko Oy, Helsinki

Ratia's firm, originally called Printex, introduced an entirely new range of Finnish fabric designs that have become synonymous with modern design in that country. The firm originally sold its products, many of which were made into clothing, through its subsidiary Marimekko, a name familiar to American consumers since the 1950s and 1960s. Ratia's designs—and those of her staff designers Vuokko Eskolin (who subsequently founded her own company) and Maija Isola—are distinguished by their unexpectedly powerful large-scale patterns, printed with consummate skill in intense colors or in striking black and white.

211. Alvar Aalto (1898–1976). *Floor lamp:* A 805. 1954. Finland. Produced by Artek, Helsinki. Enameled metal and leather, 68⅞ × 20½″ (175 × 52 cm). Artek Oy AB, Helsinki

Aalto's lighting fixtures often parallel in small scale his architectural ideas, particularly that of organic continuity of form. Exemplifying this philosophy of design, the strongly sculptural form of this lamp provides an efficient source of light distribution.

212. Astrid Sampe (b. 1909). *Printed fabric:* Windy Way. 1954. Sweden. Printed by Erik Ljungberg, Floda, for Nordiska Kompaniet, Stockholm. Cotton, width 46½″ (118 cm). Nationalmuseum, Stockholm

Head of the Nordiska Kompaniet Textilkammare from its founding in 1936, Sampe has enormously influenced the history of modern Swedish textile design, particularly in the field of fabrics created especially for architectural settings. Her designs draw their strength from a vigorous and assured handling of abstract pattern and an equal skill in the use of color. A subtle range of tones from black to white gives *Windy Way* the effect of fluted shadows in movement. The recipient of many major design awards and citations, including a Grand Prix at the 1954 Milan Triennale, Sampe has achieved an international reputation through her work with firms such as Knoll International.

212

213

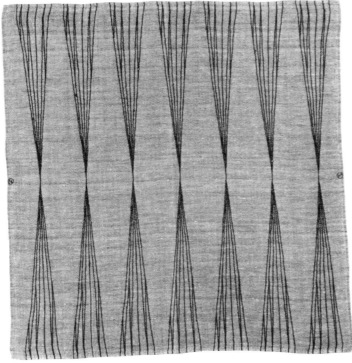

214

213. Dora Jung (1906–1980). *Weaving:* Shells IV. 1957. Finland. Linen, 23⅜ × 22½″ (59.5 × 57 cm). Cooper-Hewitt Museum, New York. Au Panier Fleuri Fund

214. *Napkin,* Line Play *pattern.* 1956. Finland. Produced by Tampella, Tampere. Linen, 19⅜ × 18⅛″ (49.5 × 46 cm). Cooper-Hewitt Museum, New York. Gift of Elizabeth Gordon

For almost half a century, Dora Jung was one of the master weavers of Finland. Both in unique pieces and in production designs, Jung assiduously maintained the highest standards of technical quality in craftsmanship, often restricting the range of colors to form patterns through the weave itself—as in *Shells IV,* from a series of abstract woven compositions. The linen napkin, in which a strong graphic pattern emerges with an economy of color, typifies her production designs; it was awarded a Grand Prix at the Milan Triennale of 1957.

215. Arne Jacobsen (1902–1971). *Chair:* Egg. 1957. Denmark. Produced by Fritz Hansens Eftf., Allerød, 1967. Steel, leather, and foam, 38¼ × 35⅛ × 31⅛″ (97.5 × 89.5 × 79 cm). Det Danske Kunstindustrimuseum, Copenhagen

Jacobsen's range of designs included furniture, lighting fixtures, textiles, and domestic utensils, many produced in tandem with his major architectural commissions. The now-famous *Egg* and *Swan* chairs first appeared in Jacobsen's Royal Hotel in Copenhagen. The seductive and inviting grace of these chairs clearly expresses comfort in repose as well as stability; at the same time, their form, line, and detailing make a strong sculptural statement.

216. Yki Nummi (b. 1925). *Lamp:* Modern Art. 1955. Finland. Produced by Stockmann/Orno, Kerava. Acrylic, 15¾ × 9⅞″ (40 × 25 cm). Taideteollisuusmuseo, Helsinki

Like several other designers of the 1950s, Nummi specialized in lighting fixtures. He explored fully the new plastics of the twentieth century; in this lamp, acrylic tubing serves as a "transparent" structure for the translucent shade. Many later designs took this idea as a point of departure.

217. Peter Hvidt (b. 1916) and Orla Mølgaard-Nielsen (b. 1907). *Chair:* Ax. 1950. Denmark. Produced by Fritz Hansens Eftf., Allerød. Wood, laminated wood, and leather, 29⅞ × 23⅝ × 26⅜″ (76 × 60 × 67 cm). Collection Peter Hvidt and Orla Mølgaard-Nielsen

Hvidt and Mølgaard-Nielsen, both trained as cabinetmakers in Denmark, joined in partnership in 1944. Among their numerous designs for seating furniture, the *Ax* chair stands out for its application of new production methods: one sheet of laminated wood forms the seat frame and arms, the latter from sections that are bent upward. Although fabricated separately, the legs are integrated into the support structure to yield an uninterrupted visual line.

218. Børge Mogensen (1914–1972). *Armchair.* 1958. Denmark. Produced by Fredericia Stolefabrik. Oak and leather, 26¾ × 32¼ × 23⅝″ (68 × 82 × 60 cm). Det Danske Kunstindustrimuseum, Copenhagen

In his furniture designs, Mogensen clearly defined and underlined materials and composition so that the object became a direct statement of structural principles. This armchair exemplifies such a conception to an unusual degree: the capacious frame with broad, flat arms provides comfort and flexibility; the leather seat and back are self-supporting and replaceable; the detailing of the thick leather, including buckles and stitching, is treated as an important element in the overall design and lends the chair a casual, rustic appearance.

215

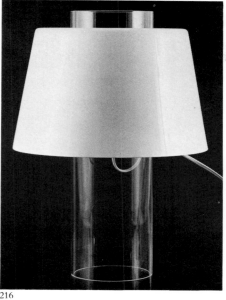

216

217

218

219

220

219. Ole Wanscher (b. 1903). *Folding stool.* 1957. Denmark. Produced by A. J. Iversen, Copenhagen. Palisander wood and leather, 16⅜ × 21⅝ × 12⅝″ (41.7 × 55 × 32 cm). Det Danske Kunstindustrimuseum, Copenhagen

Wanscher's abiding interest in historical furniture, his adherence to the highest standards of woodworking and cabinetry, and his appreciation of sculptural and experimental forms mark his furniture designs of the 1950s with a special elegance. His fondness for rare woods, sculpted and polished to emphasize the richness of the grain, enhances the elegance of his designs and confers on them an air of luxury. Based on an Egyptian folding stool, this object maintains the tradition of Danish furniture design that integrates maximum refinement of form with the requirements of use and storage.

220. Sveinn Kjarval (1919–1981). *Chair.* 1953. Iceland. Produced by Nyvirki Ltd., Reykjavik. Bent oak, laminated, and wool, 27⅝ × 23⅝ × 25⅝″ (70 × 60 × 65 cm). Collection Gisli Asmundsson, Iceland

Kjarval was the most important furniture designer in Iceland during the middle years of this century, although his work is not frequently seen. His training in Copenhagen unmistakably influenced his work. This armchair combines a rustic form with an unusual structure, in which the back support and armrests are treated as a continuous curve set at a steeply inclined angle.

221

222

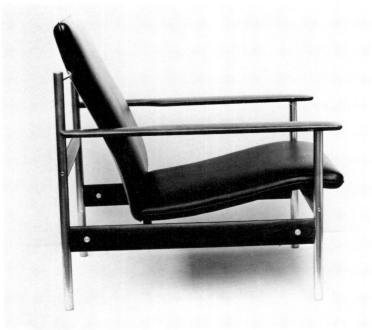

223

221. Alvar Aalto (1898–1976). *Stool:* Y 61. 1954. Finland. Produced by Korhonen, Turku. Birch and leather, 17¾ × 17¾″ (45 × 45 cm). Artek Oy AB, Helsinki

This stool by Aalto grew out of his much earlier designs for a three-legged stool and represents a more highly refined idea of the structural unity of the form. Earlier stools had been constructed with three separately attached legs, but the "y"-shaped legs of this stool are integrated completely into the seat, achieving a notable visual continuity. However, more material was required to fabricate the curved laminated sections than was needed for the earlier stool.

222. Tapio Wirkkala (b. 1915). *Platter.* 1951. Finland. Executed by Martti Linqvist at Soinne et Kni, Helsinki. Laminated wood, maximum diameter 17¾″ (45 cm). Taideteollisuusmuseo, Helsinki

Experimenting with laminated wood as a sculptural medium, Wirkkala developed a variety of strikingly elegant designs for functional utensils. In this leaf-shaped platter, the striations are treated as veins, and they set off the gentle curvature of the concave shape. Wirkkala, awarded a Grand Prix at the 1951 Milan Triennale, won international recognition for his designs in this material.

223. Sven Ivar Dysthe (b. 1931). *Armchair.* 1959. Norway. Produced by Dokka Møbler. Steel, palisander wood, and leather, 30¼ × 28 × 29⅛″ (77 × 71 × 74 cm). Nordenfjeldske Kunstindustrimuseum, Trondheim

Their designs may be less familiar than those from Denmark, but Norwegian furniture designers of the 1950s were equally concerned with sculptural and architectural forms. In this armchair, Dysthe establishes a visual relationship between the disciplined geometry of the support structure and the invitingly tilted seat. The clearly delineated sections underline the different materials—wood, leather, and steel—that went into the chair's construction.

224. Antti Nurmesniemi (b. 1927). *Sauna stool.* 1952. Finland. Produced by G. Söderström, Helsinki. Birch, laminated, and teak, 19⅝ × 13¾ × 13¾″ (50 × 35 × 35 cm). Palace Hotel, Helsinki

Commissioned by the Palace Hotel to furnish seating for use following the sauna, Nurmesniemi designed a traditional and rustic form with a comfortable seat ideally suited to its purpose. The laminated wood of the seat is both sturdy and attractive, the striations created by lamination becoming an essential part of the design. The exposed joints of the teak legs contribute to the stool's air of rusticity.

Since many of Iceland's designers continued to be educated abroad, its design development during this time had much in common with that in the other Scandinavian countries. At the same time, designers began to seek their own voices as Icelanders, and they achieved significant results.

Iceland's relatively conservative production lines in furniture were largely based on the Danish tradition of craftsmanship. In the 1950s, Sveinn Kjarval worked within this mode, but he brought to it an interest in the older traditions of Icelandic architecture. This approach, combined with his use of native, natural materials, makes his designs quite distinctive. In the 1960s, younger designers attempted, with mixed results, to apply modern ideas of design to industrial production, an impulse that continues to be strong.

Textile and metalwork designers, drawing on a long and distinguished crafts tradition in these fields, were more successful in asserting their creative independence. Icelandic metalworkers applied traditional techniques and understanding of materials to modern pieces using sculptural or abstract forms. In this period, the less developed fields of ceramics and glassmaking began to equal those of the other Scandinavian countries in achievement.

In the second half of the 1960s, a new climate in design and crafts was felt in Scandinavia. The triumph of industrial design had created a new situation: the designer in industry had become a specialist within the wider field of design. Significantly, his specialty was one in which a talent for collaboration was as important as artistic talent. Thus, the craftsman-designer of the previous period had had to choose sides, and by the late 1960s the ties between the crafts and industry had loosened. This development was not without its positive aspects. New areas opened for the designer—office equipment, household implements, all sorts of electronic commodities; modern aesthetics spread to areas like ship design, sporting goods, and machine tools; and new materials, notably synthetics, were introduced in traditional design areas. Freeing themselves from industry, the crafts renewed the system of independent workshop production throughout Scandinavia.

This polarization between crafts and industrial design can be explained in a larger context. For one thing, many firms in

225

225. Grethe Meyer (b. 1918). *Tableware,* Blue Line *pattern.* 1962. Denmark. Produced by the Royal Copenhagen Porcelain Manufactory Ltd., Copenhagen. Earthenware, *plate:* diameter 10″ (25.5 cm). The Royal Copenhagen Porcelain Manufactory Ltd., Copenhagen

Meyer has designed glassware for Kastrup Glassworks of Denmark and tableware for the Royal Copenhagen Porcelain Manufactory. Her *Blue Line* service is of stunning simplicity, with generous yet restrained forms that express their purpose without pretension. The creamy white body of the wares is highlighted by a thin cobalt blue line at the lip of each vessel and dish.

226. Jens von der Lippe (b. 1911). *Tureen.* 1960. Norway. Earthenware, height 10⅜″ (26.5 cm). Oslo Kunstindustrimuseet

Von der Lippe's ceramics refer poetically to the time-honored folk tradition of Norwegian pottery but also display a fully independent appreciation of form. This tureen is wheel-thrown, with the impressions of the hands clearly visible under the richly colored glaze. The rotund shape, expressive handles, and amusing cover form an object that is at once universal and highly personal.

227. Stig Lindberg (1916–1982). *Tableware.* 1968. Sweden. Produced by Gustavsberg. Molded plastic, *largest container:* 4 × 7½″ (10.5 × 19 cm). Gustavsberg Museum

The author of a wide variety of ceramic designs, Lindberg also developed the pattern for one of the most successful plastic services. Following in the functionalist tradition, these utensils are stackable and unbreakable and have covers that can also serve as dishes.

228. Signe Persson-Melin (b. 1925). *Teapot.* 1963. Sweden. Stoneware, height 7⅛″ (18 cm). Nationalmuseum, Stockholm

An independent studio potter since she established a workshop in Malmö in 1950, Persson-Melin has specialized in domestic utensils and wall decorations. She studied with Nathalie Krebs in Denmark and rapidly developed a distinctive style emphasizing massive forms, often with unglazed surfaces that reveal the rich natural colors of the ceramic body. Faceted forms, such as this teapot, are decorated with simple herringbone patterns that give them an archaic and timeless quality.

226

227

228

229

230

231

229. Timo Sarpaneva (b. 1926). *Glassware*, Ripple *pattern*. 1964. Finland. Produced by Iittalan Lasitehdas, Iittala. Molded blown glass, maximum height 4½" (11.4 cm); maximum diameter 3" (7.6 cm). Iittalan Lasitehdas, Iittala

Sarpaneva endowed this glassware pattern with a characteristic sophistication of form and subtlety of decoration. The cylindrical purity of the vessel shape is interrupted by a gentle double ripple forming a central band, which also serves as a comfortable rest for the hand when the glass is in use. The squat and sturdy stems imply a weight-bearing potential, and the glasses stack easily for efficient storage.

230. Tias Eckhoff (b. 1926). *Coffee service,* Regent *pattern*. 1961. Norway. Produced by Porsgrunds Porselænsfabrik, Porsgrunn. Porcelain, *coffeepot:* height 5⅝" (14.4 cm); *large plate:* diameter 6¾" (16.9 cm). Vestlandske Kunstindustrimuseum, Bergen

The designer of award-winning tablewares of impeccable form as well as of stainless steel cutlery, Eckhoff has received gold medals at the Milan Triennale exhibitions of 1954, 1957, and 1960 and the Lunning Prize in 1953. The *Regent* service, often cited as a Norwegian design classic, presents substantial and modest forms equally at home in casual and formal settings.

231. Richard Lindh (b. 1929). *Flowerpots*. 1963. Finland. Produced by Arabia, Helsinki. Stoneware, 5⅞ × 7½" (15 × 19 cm); 5⅛ × 6¼" (13 × 16 cm). Arabia Museum, Helsinki

Lindh joined the Arabia firm in 1955 and became the head of its industrial art production in 1960. These flowerpots afford a good example of Lindh's industrial designs—the supremely straightforward cylindrical forms are fitted with a self-contained water tray, a simple idea that has been adopted by many other ceramic manufacturers and remains popular even today.

232. Timo Sarpaneva (b. 1926). *Vase*. 1964. Finland. Produced by Iittalan Lasitehdas, Iittala. Molded glass, height 11" (28 cm). Iittala Museum

In this classic vase, Sarpaneva captured the world of nature in the malleable medium of glass. Molds for such "wood-patterned" vases were made from slabs of rough-hewn wood, charred into strong patterns by the red-hot glass. The resulting objects emphasize the strength and mass of the material.

233

234

233. Lars Hellsten (b. 1933). *Sculpture:* The Red Square. 1965. Sweden. Produced at Skrufs Glassworks, Skruf. Blown glass, hotworked, 19¼ × 11⅜ × 5½″ (49 × 29 × 14 cm). Nationalmuseum, Stockholm

During the 1960s, many glass artists in Sweden restored the sculptural integrity of studio glass, creating works with no reference to the functional tradition that had guided Swedish glass production since the 1920s. In his sculptures, Hellsten aims for a purely visual effect, exploiting the ability of the transparent material to attract and disperse light. His works are often composed of delicate globular forms, arranged in complex patterns and structures that have a baroque architectural quality.

234. Oiva Toikka (b. 1931). *Tableware,* Flora *pattern.* 1966. Finland. Produced by Nuutajärvi-Notsjö Glass, Nuutajärvi. Molded glass, *pitcher:* height 9½″ (24 cm); *bowl:* diameter 9⅝″ (24.5 cm). Nuutajärvi-Notsjö Glass, Nuutajärvi

Since 1963, Toikka has contributed to the Nuutajärvi glassworks designs for production ware as well as for unique vessels and sculpture in glass. Toikka depicts his motifs, often taken from nature, with an exuberant naiveté, and his designs express a whimsical delight that gives them a special charm.

the last half of the 1960s reduced their design staffs for economic reasons. At the same time, a new, critical attitude toward tradition, the cultural establishment, technocrats, and expertise also won broad support among artists, and the negative aspects of industry became one of their main targets. Experienced designers who had felt torn between their own artistic ideas and the demands of their firms now left to begin working on their own; the younger generation simply rejected the role of industrial designer altogether.

By the end of the decade, this process was well established. Typical was the case of glass designer Benny Motzfeldt, who left her position as chief designer at the Hadeland glassworks about 1968 to fulfill her artistic goals at a smaller factory. Eventually, she took over a small glass workshop with one or two glassblowers in order to devote all her time to her designs. This disengagement of the artist-craftsman from industry originally took place in Sweden and Norway, but in the 1970s spread to Denmark and Finland also.

As a phenomenon, this development cannot be seen only as a simple question of the organization of design and its role in the general social structure. It is closely linked with artistic development as well. The quest for artistic liberty may or may not have been its driving force; a number of forces were in action and interaction simultaneously. But the phenomenon does direct our attention to the question of style—or, rather, of styles.

In the 1950s and early 1960s, the two leading styles, the "organic" and the "hard-edge," achieved a balance for a time. Looking back from the 1980s, one realizes that the "organic" trend finally predominated. The emancipated designers of the second half of the 1960s adopted for themselves the ideal of creative freedom, one that is taken for granted in the pictorial arts. Moreover, new directions in painting and sculpture had a double effect. Such trends as Tachism and Informalism were directly reflected in crafts: in ceramics, for example, this was the period of heavy stoneware in darkish glazes. But, more broadly, every new experimental style strengthened the reaction against industry and the industrial look.

Thus, the period of the mid-1960s experienced a diversity of styles, some the results of Scandinavian developments, some imported from abroad. Even the "Pop" and "Op" fashions arrived there. A renewed interest in decor and a certain anti- 189

235

236

235. Ann Wärff (b. 1937) and Göran Wärff (b. 1933). *Bowl.*
1970. Sweden. Produced at Kosta Glasbruk. Flashed glass,
etched, 7⅞ × 12¼″ (20 × 31 cm). Nationalmuseum, Stockholm

While working at the Kosta glassworks, Ann and Göran
Wärff together produced many flashed-glass bowls with
complex decoration and vivid colors. The transparent layers
of color are "peeled" back through an etching process to
expose layers of color trapped beneath; the entire form
radiates with transmitted light. Both artists have gone on to
independent work in the field of studio glass.

236. Kaj Franck (b. 1911). *Plate.* c. 1965. Finland. Produced
at Nuutajärvi-Notsjö Glass, Nuutajärvi. Glass, diameter
16⅛″ (41 cm). Taideteollisuusmuseo, Helsinki

Although primarily recognized as a designer of mass-produced
domestic designs, Franck has developed a body of unique
studio objects that cannot be overlooked. This plate, rich in
color and texture, reveals another side of the inventive
designer even while the sensitivity to the potential of the
material and the exuberant sense of pattern remain consistent
with Franck's principles of design.

237. Tapio Wirkkala (b. 1915). *Vases,* Paadar's Ice *pattern.*
1960. Finland. Produced by Iittalan Lasitehdas, Iittala. Molded
glass, heights 6¼–11¾″ (16–30 cm). Iittala Museum

Wirkkala's versatility as a designer of art glass is exemplified
in these unusual vases based on the changing shapes of
melting ice slabs. Although Wirkkala regards the poetry of
nature as a potent force in guiding the hand of the designer,
he goes well beyond the simple imitation of natural forms.

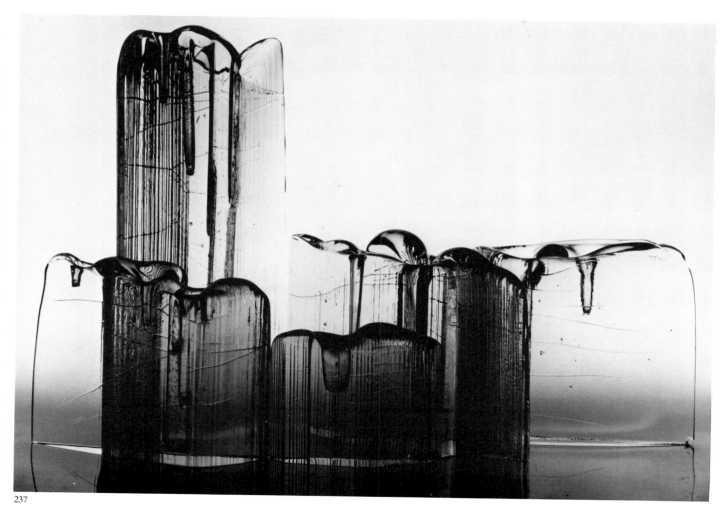

perfectionism also became apparent at this stage. Then, the new realism in painting and sculpture found expression in the crafts in serious, satirical, or political motifs, particularly noticeable in tapestry weaving. Practicing weavers became creative artists who rejected the role of simple craftsmen. In particular, Hannah Ryggen's independent and dedicated work inspired an entire generation of weavers. Some of them—Maria Adlercreutz and Helena Hernmarck in Sweden, for example—introduced motifs derived from newspaper photographs and contemporary painting into their work, thus bringing a traditional craft into the mainstream of modern concern.

As weavers, ceramists, and glassmakers participated in the ideological struggles of this period, industrial designers also moved into a new, more powerful position. Increasingly, they demanded that architects, engineers, financiers, and politicians collaborate with them in achieving the goal of good and acceptable design.

One now looks with nostalgia on the dream of the 1950s: the hope of a rational, yet human world, shaped with simplicity for the well-being of everyone. The design style of the 1950s—which, in fact, was still strong around 1970 (and even longer)—is an achievement of all the Scandinavian countries in common. More than just an expression of a certain politico-historical situation, the style grew out of the social, human, and artistic ideals that were shared by the Scandinavian peoples at that time. It would be rash to believe that these ideals are now extinct. Shaping the human environment by artistic means still offers a valid challenge, but one more difficult to achieve now than it was three or four decades ago.

238. Gerd Slang (b. 1925). *Bowl.* 1968. Norway. Produced by Hadelands Glassverk, Jevnaker. Blown glass, etched, 5½ × 9⅝" (14 × 24.3 cm). Nordenfjeldske Kunstindustrimuseum, Trondheim

A poetic gentleness, conveyed by relaxed and simple forms and soft etched decoration, suffuses the work of Slang. Etched motifs, often transparent flowers or stylized butterflies, appear to be freely drawn on the thin surface of the objects.

239. Gunnar Cyrén (b. 1931). *Glass: Pop.* 1967. Sweden. Produced by Orrefors Glasbruk. Glass, height 6¾" (17 cm). AB Orrefors Glasbruk

Trained as a silversmith, Cyrén began to work at Orrefors as a glass designer in 1959, designing both *graal* and cut glass. The *Pop* glasses reveal Cyrén's response to the bold antitraditional aesthetics of the 1960s; strident colors are combined in a vessel with a unique ritualistic quality that goes well beyond simple functional requirements.

240. Birger Kaipiainen (b. 1915). *Plate.* c. 1965. Finland. Produced at Arabia, Helsinki. Earthenware, diameter 20⅞" (53 cm). Arabia Museum, Helsinki

Unique among modern Finnish ceramists, Kaipiainen approaches the medium as a painter, bringing the surfaces of simple forms to life with radiant color and iridescent glazes. Drawing on Eastern design traditions, Kaipiainen decorates his work with naive and stylized representations of flora and fauna, expansively celebrating the forms, colors, and textures of nature.

241. Severin Brørby (b. 1932). *Vase.* 1962. Norway. Produced by Hadelands Glassverk, Jevnaker. Blown glass, 8¾ × 1¾" (22.5 × 4.5 cm). Nordenfjeldske Kunstindustrimuseum, Trondheim

From the beginning of his career at Hadeland in 1956, Brørby has explored the sculptural qualities of thick, colored glass. Utilizing the intensity of color and the optical distortion of the material, he unites mass and light in works of architectonic presence, even those as small-scale as this vase.

239

240

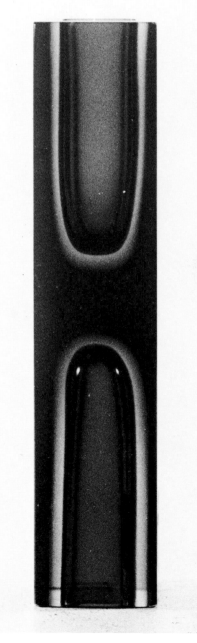

241

242

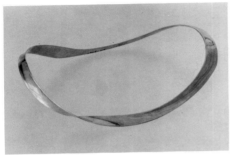

243

244

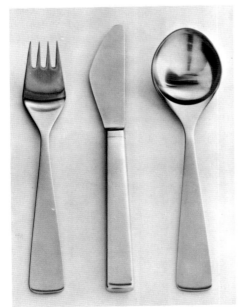

245

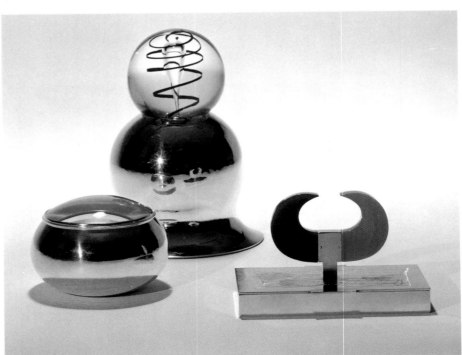

246

242. Bengt Liljedahl (b. 1932). *Bowl.* 1965. Sweden. Silver, 3⅛ × 7⅝″ (8 × 19.5 cm). Nationalmuseum, Stockholm

In the 1960s, a style of informality and directness in Swedish silver challenged the sleek and sophisticated forms of the previous decade. The new movement, which stressed uneven surfaces and rougher textures, was spearheaded by Liljedahl, who uses the hammering process by which a hollow vessel is produced from a flat sheet of silver for textural and sculptural effect.

243. Torun Bülow-Hübe (b. 1927). *Necklace.* 1964. Sweden. Silver, maximum diameter 10″ (25.5 cm). Nationalmuseum, Stockholm

Bülow-Hübe, winner of a gold medal at the Milan Triennale of 1960 and the Lunning Prize in the same year, has experimented with unorthodox shapes for jewelry. Yet her pieces, which may be free form and asymmetrical, are carefully designed to rest comfortably on the body, their gentle curves following the contours of the wearer.

244. Timo Sarpaneva (b. 1926). *Cooking pot.* 1961. Finland. Produced by W. Rosenlew & Co., Porin Konepaja. Cast iron and teak, 6⅜ × 8″ (16.5 × 20.5 cm). Taideteollisuus-museo, Helsinki

Sarpaneva is probably best known for his glass, but he has developed important designs for domestic utensils as well. The sculptured wooden handle of this cooking pot may be easily removed and used to lift the cover, not unlike the way the cooking plates of old wood-burning cookstoves were removed with a handle.

245. Tias Eckhoff (b. 1926). *Cutlery,* Maya *pattern.* 1961. Norway. Produced by Norsk Stålpress, Bergen. Stainless steel, *knife:* length 7⅞″ (20 cm). Nordenfjeldske Kunstindustri-museum, Trondheim

In the course of his distinguished career, Eckhoff has worked in Denmark for Georg Jensen. The *Maya* pattern cutlery was Eckhoff's first design for mass production in his native country, and has proven to be one of the most successful. The refined forms of simple outline, ideal for industrial production, conscientiously fulfill the demands of efficiency and ease of handling.

246. Birger Haglund (b. 1918). *Three boxes*. 1964–70. Sweden. Silver, glass, gold, and plastic, maximum height 6" (15.5 cm). Collection Birger Haglund

In his innovative designs of the 1960s, Haglund often took different materials, such as silver and plastic, and played them off against one another, contrasting the reflectiveness of silver with the transparency or translucence of glass and synthetics. The effect he achieved was heightened by his use of color to punctuate his simple shapes. His small sculptured boxes, with their ambiguous forms, project a mysterious and symbolic quality.

247. Bjørn Engø (1920–1981). *Plate*. 1965–66. Norway. Enameled copper, diameter 7" (17.6 cm). Vestlandske Kunstindustrimuseum, Bergen

Engø's work, in the classic enamel tradition, emphasizes the brilliant translucence of the material as illuminated by light reflected from the supporting metal. The patterns formed by the enamel, often nonrepresentational, play upon textural contrasts between surface and foundation.

248. Arne Jacobsen (1902–1971). *Ice bucket, ice tongs, and ashtray*, Cylinda *series*. 1964–66. Denmark. Produced by Stelton, Gentofte. Stainless steel, *ice bucket:* 5⅝ × 7⅛" (14.5 × 18 cm); *tongs:* length 6¾" (17 cm); *ashtray:* 2½ × 2⅞" (6.5 × 7.5 cm). Stelton A/S, Gentofte

In aiming for design quality in mass-produced consumer goods, Scandinavian designers turned the goal into reality. Among designs that thus gained international acclaim, Jacobsen's *Cylinda* series of domestic wares stands out. Their purely functional forms share a distinctive compatibility with the material and with the industrial processes required for fabrication.

247

248

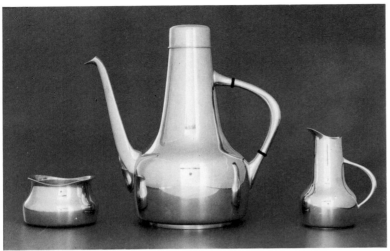

249

249. Bjørn Sigurd Østern (b. 1935). *Coffee service.* 1962. Norway. Produced by David-Andersen, Oslo. Silver, *pot:* height 8⅜" (21.5 cm); *creamer:* height 3⅞" (10 cm); *sugar bowl:* height 2¾" (6.9 cm). Nordenfjeldske Kunstindustrimuseum, Trondheim

Østern realized a fluid profile in this design by accentuating and elongating the forms. A broad and stable base balances the tapered necks of coffeepot and cream jug, while a gently everted lip relieves the necessarily squat shape of the sugar bowl. The elegance of the service results from the graceful manipulation of the material.

250. Kirsti Ilvessalo (b. 1920). *Rug:* Shadows in the Snow. 1968. Finland. Wool, *ryijy* technique, 76¾ × 59" (195 × 150 cm). Taideteollisuusmuseo, Helsinki

The *ryijy* technique of rug making, adapted to changes in the aesthetic climate with particular effectiveness in the work of Ilvessalo, provides continuity to the history of Finnish design. Although the textural quality of the knotting technique here softens the pronounced graphic quality of the geometric pattern, the visual effect is strikingly optical.

251. Helena Hernmarck (b. 1941). *Tapestry:* Sverige (Sweden). 1966. Sweden. Wool, 70⅛ × 35" (178 × 89 cm). National-museum, Stockholm

In her tapestries, Hernmarck marries tradition to modernity; while revitalizing many old and respected techniques of flat weaving, she employs them to give the woven surface a compositional structure entirely individual to her work. A variety of woven textures and a skillful handling of color enliven the nationalistic theme of this tapestry.

250

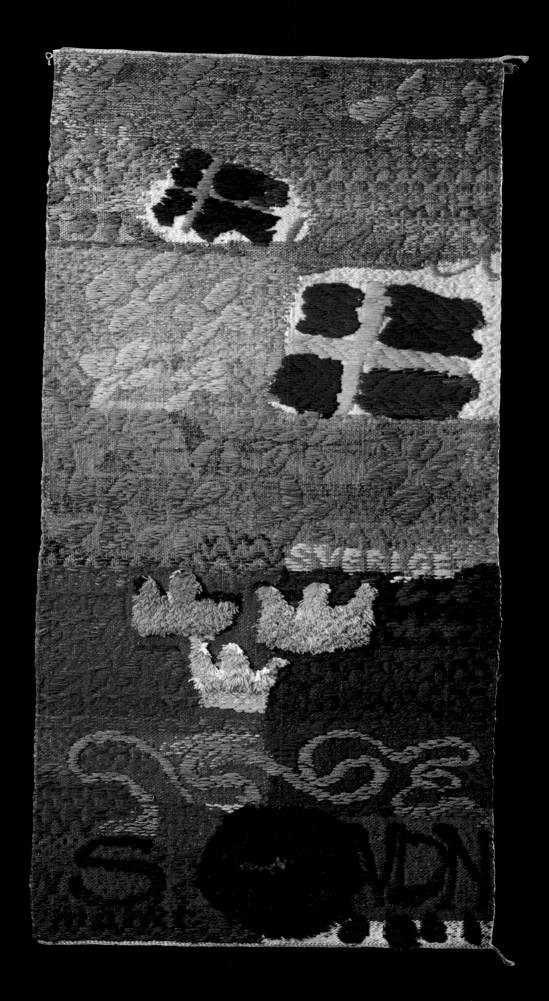

252

252. Vuokko Eskolin-Nurmesniemi (b. 1930). *Printed fabric:* Pyörre. 1964. Finland. Produced by Vuokko, Helsinki. Cotton, width 51⅛" (130 cm). Vuokko Oy, Helsinki

With its boldness of scale and dynamic informality, this pattern is a classic of modern Finnish textile design. The unusually large motif, which establishes a calligraphic rhythm, defines and accentuates the shape it surrounds when used for clothing and upholstery, while it becomes an uncompromisingly graphic image when used flat.

253. Gunila Axén (b. 1941). *Printed fabric.* 1968. Sweden. Produced by Borås Wäfveri for KF Interiör, Stockholm. Cotton, width 35⅜" (90 cm). Nationalmuseum, Stockholm

The engaging design, composed of "cutout" shapes, has a fresh and unsophisticated appeal that arises from the basic technique of negative image printing, in which only the background is printed in color.

254. Nanna Ditzel (b. 1923). *Necklace.* 1966. Denmark. Produced by Georg Jensen Sølvsmedie, Copenhagen. Gold, diameter 7½" (19 cm). Georg Jensen Sølvsmedie A/S, Copenhagen

With this necklace, Ditzel typically repeats a simple shape to create a harmonic pattern. The unlabored construction of the individual links, offering maximum flexibility when worn, exploits the reflectiveness of the material and gives this necklace an unpretentious elegance.

255. Olof Bäckström (b. 1922). *Scissors.* 1965. Finland. Produced by Fiskars, Helsinki, from 1967. Steel and plastic, maximum length 8⅜" (21.5 cm). Taideteollisuusmuseo, Helsinki

The Fiskars scissors claim the distinction of being among Finland's most internationally accepted designs from the 1960s to the present day. Besides offering a precision cutting edge, the scissors are carefully molded to fit the hand so that they provide maximum leverage while putting a minimum of pressure on the tissues of the fingers.

253

254

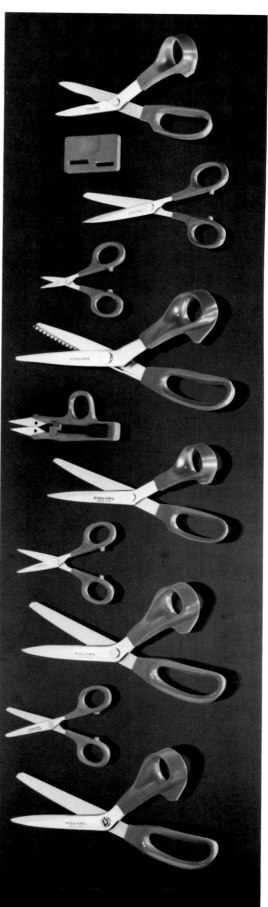

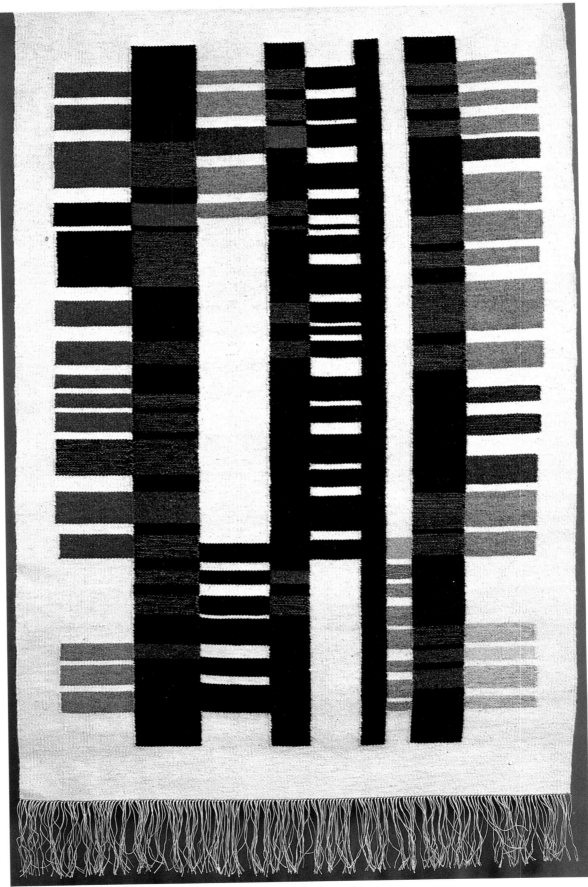

256

256. Asgerdur Ester Buadottir (b. 1920). *Tapestry:* Weaving 1. Iceland. Wool, 65¾ × 44⅞″ (167 × 114 cm). Collection Asgerdur Ester Buadottir

The subtle colors ranging from white to deep black-brown in this tapestry come entirely from natural, undyed Icelandic wool. Buadottir is internationally known for her strong abstract compositions and her technical competence.

257. Sven Fristedt (b. 1940). *Printed fabric:* Oppo. 1966. Sweden. Produced by Borås Wäfveri. Cotton, width 47¼″ (120 cm). Nationalmuseum, Stockholm

One of the younger generation of Swedish textile designers, Fristedt attuned his work of the mid-1960s to international developments in painting. To the strong Op art quality of his designs, however, he added an adroit handling of the repeat pattern.

258. Synnøve Anker Aurdal (b. 1908). *Tapestry:* Night. c. 1967. Norway. Wool and linen, 91 × 83½″ (231 × 212 cm). Vestlandske Kunstindustrimuseum, Bergen

Over the course of four decades, Aurdal has injected new life into the tradition of Norwegian weaving, in the process establishing for herself a special position in the movement of painterly weaving in that country. The artist effectively contrasts large expanses of color with complex small patterns, unifying the composition through an exceptionally sensitive use of color.

257

258

259

260

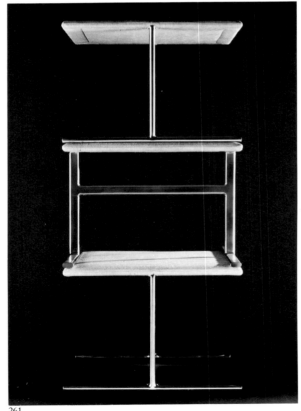

261

259. Maija Isola (b. 1927). *Printed fabric:* Silkkikuikka. 1961. Finland. Produced by Marimekko, Helsinki. Cotton, width 52″ (132 cm), repeat length 100″ (254 cm). Taideteollisuus-museo, Helsinki

Isola exploited the dramatic potential of both color and line in this printed fabric. The spirited colors acquire added individuality through the active linear patterns that suggest brushstrokes of ink on the surface. Although mass-produced in repeat lengths, this fabric has the air of a unique production, one of the distinguishing features of the Marimekko line.

260. Erik Magnussen (b. 1940). *Folding chair:* Z. 1968. Denmark. Produced by Torben Ørskov and Co., Copen-hagen. Steel and fabric, 28⅛ × 26⅜ × 18⅞″ (71.5 × 67 × 48 cm). Det Danske Kunstindustrimuseum, Copenhagen

Characteristically, Magnussen combines a noteworthy visual clarity with industrial technology in his designs. This chair—a major extension of the research into folding furniture carried on decades earlier by Danish furniture architects such as Kaare Klint, Mogens Koch, and Poul Kjærholm—is formed of two continuous lengths of tubing, bent and joined in an ingenious manner.

261. Antti Nurmesniemi (b. 1927). *Stool.* 1964. Finland. Produced by Vuokko, Helsinki. Steel and fabric, 13⅞ × 19⅝ × 19⅝″ (35.5 × 50 × 50 cm). Vuokko Oy, Helsinki

The simple "I" frame construction of this stool furnishes strength and stability to the seating unit while, with its minimal detailing, it imparts refinement to the design. The reflective steel of the structure effectively contrasts with the broad expanse of natural material on the thin seat. Compatible with both public and domestic settings, the stool has received international acceptance.

262. Börge Lindau (b. 1932) and Bo Lindekrantz (b. 1932). *Stool:* S 70-3. 1968. Sweden. Produced by Lammhults Mekaniska, Lammhult. Chrome-plated and enameled steel, 28 × 18⅞ × 17⅜″ (71 × 48 × 44 cm). Lammhults Mekaniska AB, Lammhult

Over the last twenty years, Lindau and Lindekrantz have developed a series of innovative seating furniture that utilizes the industrial process to create forms that are light, attractive, and functional in many settings. Chrome-plated steel, a favored material of these designers, is handled in a manner that recalls early functionalist designs while maintaining a contemporary look.

262

263

263. Petur B. Luthersson (b. 1936). *Lamp*. 1969. Iceland. Produced by Amundi Sigurdhsson, Ltd., Reykjavik. Aluminum, 13¾ × 20⅞" (35 × 53 cm). Collection Malmsteypa A. Sigurdhsson, Reykjavik

One of the most important Icelandic furniture designers, Luthersson has specialized in highly functional office furniture and lighting fixtures. This lamp offers bright general illumination without glare, and is particularly appropriate for mass production in spun aluminum.

264. Ingmar Relling (b. 1920). *Chair and footstool:* Siesta. 1965. Norway. Produced by Vestlandske Mobelfabrikk, Ørsta. Bent beech, laminated, canvas, and leather, *chair:* 39⅜ × 24⅜ × 33½" (100 × 62 × 85 cm); *stool:* 16½ × 23⅝ × 19⅝" (42 × 60 × 50 cm). Oslo Kunstindustrimuseet

Relling added new interest to the extremely popular material of laminated bentwood in his *Siesta* series, exploiting its resiliency and strength in a counterpoised weight-bearing structure. A seat and back laced to the frame *(below)* support the softly upholstered leather cushions.

265. Poul Kjærholm (1929–1980). *Folding stool*. 1961. Denmark. Produced by E. Kold Christensen, Copenhagen. Steel and fabric, 14⅝ × 23⅝ × 17¾" (37 × 60 × 45 cm). E. Kold Christensen A/S, Copenhagen

Kjærholm's designs of mid-century were innovative in their use of industrial materials and processes; the designer particularly favored the mixture of industrial steel and natural materials such as leather and canvas. In his classic folding stool of 1961, still in production, he reinforced the weight-bearing strength of steel by twisting the support members; the same twist allows the chair to fold perfectly flat.

264

265

266. Verner Panton (b. 1926). *Lamps,* Flower Pot *series.* 1968. Denmark. Produced by Louis Poulsen & Co., Copenhagen. Enameled metal, 5⅞ × 8⅜" (15 × 21.5 cm). Louis Poulsen & Co. A/S, Copenhagen

A multifaceted designer, Panton has introduced many new ideas in the fields of furniture design and lighting. The *Flower Pot* series of lamps, simply designed in a variety of bright enamel colors, yields efficient direct lighting without glare. Used singly or in groups, the lamps strike a balance between geometric restraint and informal domesticity.

267. Fredrik A. Kayser (1924–1968). *Armchair.* 1965. Norway. Produced by Vatne Lenestolfabrikk. Bent oak, laminated, and wool, 29⅛ × 22½ × 20½" (74 × 57 × 52 cm). Vestlandske Kunstindustrimuseum, Bergen

Kayser's design unites industrial expertise and the cabinet-maker's craft. In this chair, the sinuous and inviting curve of the arm terminates in perpendicular legs, and the gentle curve is echoed in the parallel back slats.

268. Åke Axelsson (b. 1932). *Armchair.* 1968. Sweden. Produced by Herbert Andersson, Gärsnäs. Red beech and leather, 29½ × 21¼ × 18⅞" (75 × 54 × 48.5 cm). Collection Åke Axelsson

Axelsson's free interpretation of traditional furniture forms has resulted in chairs that evoke the past while conveying a contemporary refinement and simplicity. The structural clarity of the design is heightened by the exposed interlocking supporting members, and the energetic curves add a quality of resilient lightness to the design.

269. Gunnar Magnusson (b. 1933). *Armchair:* Inca. 1963. Iceland. Produced by Nyvirki, Ltd., Reykjavik. Pine and fabric, 27⅝ × 25⅝ × 29½" (70 × 65 × 75 cm). Nyvirki Ltd., Reykjavik

Two qualities common to all of Magnusson's furniture are directness of form and exposed construction. The squared and joined leg and arm structure render this chair particularly stable, and the interlocking back support provides visual continuity to the geometric design.

267

268

269

CONTEMPORARY DESIGN: CHALLENGE AND RENEWAL

JAN-LAURITZ OPSTAD
Director, Nordenfjeldske Kunstindustrimuseum, Trondheim

270. Ulla Forsell (b. 1944). *Pierced vessel.* 1982. Sweden. Blown glass, 6¼ × 7⅞″ (16 × 20 cm). Collection Ulla Forsell

A splendid color sensibility and an exuberant joy in the liquidity and malleability of molten glass combine to make Forsell's works vividly personal statements. The artist mostly eschews conventional ornamentation in favor of freely "painted" abstract forms that float within the body of the glass.

The decade of the 1970s was a troubled time, and events far distant from Scandinavia had a strong impact there. Uncertainty and divisiveness marked domestic and international relations. Wars arose in various parts of the world. A new economic order entailing a radical redistribution of money and resources was promoted by the third world countries. Global problems—human rights, atomic energy, nuclear arms, pollution, diminishing resources—captured attention, but conflicting views on how to deal with them created a new source of tension.

On a personal level, changing life-styles called into question old standards and values. Different segments of the population, each pursuing, often relentlessly, separate interests, inevitably met in head-on collisions. Individuals paused in the mad rush for progress and asked themselves if this was what they really wanted.

The 1970s was a troubled decade for the applied arts as well. This essay will deal with the important changes that took place in this realm by describing the characteristics of design and crafts in Scandinavia today in general rather than specific terms.

Any discussion of Scandinavian applied arts in the 1970s must begin with the concept of "Scandinavian Design."

Does this concept still have validity?

That depends on what it is taken to mean. The designation, created outside the Nordic countries, was understood abroad to denote a stylistic category. Within Scandinavia, on the other hand, it was regarded in the 1950s and early 1960s as a method

—a particularly Scandinavian attitude toward objects themselves that was shared among the Nordic countries. However, in the course of the 1970s it came to be seen in Scandinavia, too, as a description of a style and specifically as a designation of a chronological period.

Many Scandinavians even now try to keep the idea alive, employing it not only in production but also for promotional purposes, since the style has gained a high degree of international recognition. But the ideas behind the products of today are so different from the ideology of the 1950s that the term "Scandinavian Design" can hardly be used nowadays without entailing grave misunderstandings. These new ideas in Scandinavian applied arts came out of changing social and economic conditions since World War II. Simply put, the concept "Scandinavian Design" belongs to a society quite different from today's.

In the Scandinavian Design period, artists were mainly concerned with the needs of private individuals. They concentrated on domestic design—furnishings and objects for everyday use. At the end of the 1960s, a new social consciousness prompted designers to question whether these forms of design were really the most important. At the same time, an ever-expanding bureaucracy and the encroachment of government upon previously private realms resulted in product design's reaching a new level of public interest and accountability.

Scandinavian applied arts of the 1950s and 1960s were quite sophisticated and enjoyed a position of world leadership. Toward the end of the 1960s this was no longer true. International attention turned away from Scandinavia and toward Italy with respect to design and toward the United States with respect to craft. The reason for this was not that the quality of Nordic products declined but that new ideas arose in other countries which found their expression in the fields of design and crafts.

Perhaps the most striking phenomenon in applied arts of the 1970s, distinguishing it clearly from the preceding decade, was the erection of distinct boundaries between the various trade groups within the field of applied art—in particular, between the designers and the artisans. In Scandinavia, this led to the breakdown of the design organizations, up to then the supporting factor in Nordic cooperation. In Denmark, the Danish design organization, the Landsforeningen Dansk

271

271. Gertrud Vasegaard (b. 1913). *Bowl.* 1978. Denmark. Stoneware, 6¾ × 13¾″ (17 × 35 cm). Det Danske Kunstindustrimuseum, Copenhagen

Vasegaard's distinguished career in ceramics began in the mid-1930s, when she established an independent workshop in Bornholm. Since that time she has evolved a highly personal and disciplined style that is dependent upon a consummate handling of pattern and glazes. In addition to studio work, she has designed production tableware.

272. Karin Björquist (b. 1927). *Table service, BV pattern.* 1978. Sweden. Produced by Gustavsberg. Bone porcelain, *plate:* maximum diameter 9½″ (24 cm); *cup:* maximum diameter 3⅛″ (8 cm). AB Gustavsberg

Although Karin Björquist has contributed a wide variety of designs for production at Gustavsberg, she shows a special interest in everyday tablewares. The functional *BV* service offers stackability and strength; a subtle refinement in the design of the cups is the small thumb rest that assures a firm grip.

273. Åsa Hellman (b. 1947). *Plate.* 1980. Stoneware, 2¾ × 18⅛″ (17 × 46 cm). Collection Taideteollisuusmuseo, Helsinki

The simple and robust shape of this plate, calling to mind the Finnish rustic pottery tradition, stands in contrast to the bold stripes of the glaze. The disciplined abstract ornamentation of Hellman's work brings tradition in line with contemporary aesthetics.

272

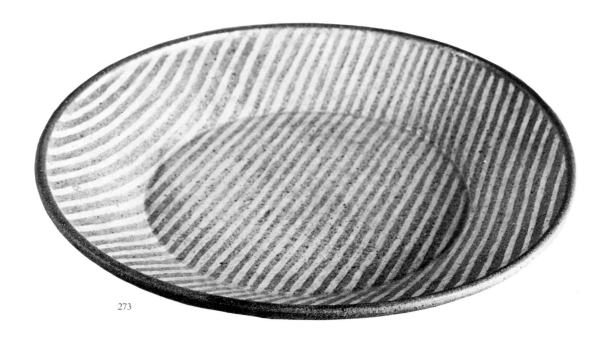

273

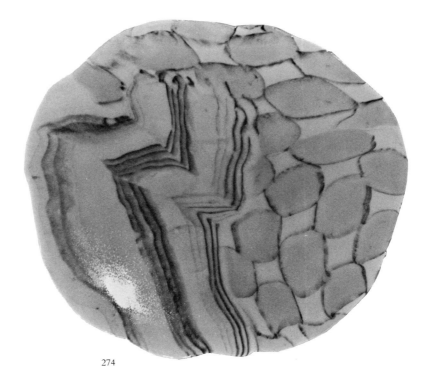

274

275

276

277

278

274. Arne Åse (b. 1940). *Plate*. 1980–81. Norway. Porcelain, diameter 16⅝″ (42.5 cm). Vestlandske Kunstindustrimuseum, Bergen

In the 1960s, the rougher, more powerful expression of stoneware and earthenware found favor over the refinement of porcelain. Recently, several Norwegian potters have worked to revitalize porcelain as a medium for ceramic art. Åse draws out porcelain's natural qualities—its translucence, its sheen, its ability to absorb color—in plates and vessels of exceptional fineness. His painterly patterns reveal the interaction between the material and the hand that fashions it.

275. Anna Maria Osipow (b. 1935). *Vase*. 1981. Finland. Earthenware, painted decoration, 23⅝ × 7⅞ × 15¾″ (60 × 20 × 40 cm). Collection Anna Maria Osipow

Osipow's striking geometric forms are constructed of angled slabs of clay, creating an internal structural pattern that parallels or contrasts with the strident painted decoration.

276. Ivan Weiss (b. 1946). *Covered jars*. 1981. Denmark. Produced at the Royal Copenhagen Porcelain Manufactory Ltd., Copenhagen. Stoneware, 8¼ × 9⅛″ (21 × 23 cm); 6⅜ × 7⅛″ (16.5 × 18 cm). The Royal Copenhagen Porcelain Manufactory Ltd., Copenhagen

Weiss went to Japan for training in the art of pottery, and this background has profoundly affected his work. The stoneware jars recall the elegant forms of Japanese ceramics and lacquer, and the rich and lustrous surfaces or delicately painted naturalistic decoration also point to the Japanese tradition.

277. Erik Pløen (b. 1925). *Vase*. 1972. Norway. Stoneware, 8¼ × 10¼″ (21 × 26 cm). Nordenfjeldske Kunstindustrimuseum, Trondheim

From the late 1950s to the present, Pløen has figured among the primary forces in Norwegian studio pottery. Intense glazes with a weathered, textured look enrich the organic forms of his pieces.

278. Reidun Sissel Gjerdrum (b. 1954). *Bowls*. 1979. Norway. Earthenware and silver, 4¾ × 4″ (12 × 10.5 cm); 6¾ × 6″ (17 × 15.5 cm). Nordenfjeldske Kunstindustrimuseum, Trondheim

Gjerdrum employs the Japanese *raku* (low-fired) technique for her earthenware vessels and produces a delicate crackle pattern in the glaze, giving an eggshell quality to the pieces. Each bowl, encircled by broad luster bands, is supported on a simple silver foot.

279. Steinunn Marteinsdottir (b. 1936). *Vase*. 1980. Iceland. Stoneware, 31½ × 15¾″ (80 × 40 cm). Collection Steinunn Marteinsdottir

One of the most distinguished native potters of Iceland, Marteinsdottir captures in her work the rugged and tenacious natural landscape of Iceland, interpreting in clay volcanic flows and the patterns left by centuries of wind and water erosion.

279

280

280. Jonina Gudhnadottir (b. 1943). *Wall relief:* Spring in the Air. 1979. Iceland. Stoneware and wood, 20⅞ × 18½″ (53 × 47 cm). Collection Jonina Gudhnadottir

Gudhnadottir often organizes her simple and rough-textured forms in wall reliefs that refer strongly to the world of nature. In these arrangements, she so effectively balances the heavy stoneware elements that the sculpture appears virtually weightless.

281. Leif Heiberg Myrdam (b. 1938). *Vase.* 1971. Norway. Stoneware, height 7½″ (19 cm). Oslo Kunstindustrimuseet

Swelling organic forms and sumptuously mottled glazes characterize the work of Myrdam. His vases consistently feature an off-center mouth, emerging from the clay like a volcanic rift in the surface. The sensitively applied glazes, which run and feather during the firing process, converge on this focal point.

282. Hertha Hillfon (b. 1921). *Sculpture:* The Expectation of Mary. 1974. Sweden. Earthenware, 11¾ × 20½″ (30 × 52 cm). Nationalmuseum, Stockholm

Among the craftsmen/artists who changed the course of ceramics during the 1960s, Hertha Hillfon holds a special place. Her translations of visual reality into the ceramic medium, frequently based on simple everyday objects such as clothing, achieve a poetic tranquillity and mystery.

281

282

283

283. Jane Reumert (b. 1942). *Teapot and creamer.* 1980. Denmark. Strandstraede Keramik, Copenhagen. Stoneware, *teapot:* height 6⅞" (17.5 cm); *creamer:* height 3⅝" (9.5 cm). Collection Jane Reumert

The exploration of limited serial production represents a special development within the field of contemporary ceramics in Scandinavia. The simple and strong forms—marked by a vital structural presence—of Reumert's stoneware are mold cast, then each piece is individually glazed in a range of subtle colors.

284. Gunhild Aaberg (b. 1939). *Bowl.* 1977. Denmark. Produced at Strandstraede Keramik, Copenhagen. Stoneware, 5⅛ × 16⅞" (13 × 43 cm). Det Danske Kunstindustrimuseum, Copenhagen

Both traditional and experimental ceramics emerge from Strandstraede Keramik—the cooperative studio of Gunhild Aaberg, Jane Reumert, and Beate Anderson—one of the most active ceramics centers in Denmark. Aaberg's work, nurtured by the tradition of Danish ceramics, displays a pronounced Oriental influence in its glazes and abstract patterns.

285. Minni Lukander (b. 1930). *Covered urn.* 1979. Finland. Stoneware, 15¾ × 7⅛ × 7⅛" (40 × 18 × 18 cm). Taideteollisuusmuseo, Helsinki

This covered urn by Lukander evokes a ritualistic meaning; the strong architectural form is ornamented with simple patterns that suggest an uncoded early language.

286. Seenat Group Pottery. *Bowls and covered bowls.* 1980. Finland. Stoneware, maximum height 5⅛" (13 cm); maximum width 6¼" (16 cm). Taideteollisuusmuseo, Helsinki

During the 1970s many designers and craftsmen established independent studios. Most of these produced one-of-a-kind works, but some turned toward limited production. The Seenat Group of Finland, consisting of several individual potters, signs each of its molded pieces with a cooperative mark rather than that of an individual artist.

287. Myre Vasegaard (b. 1936). *Bowl.* 1979. Denmark. Stoneware, 4⅞ × 22½" (12.5 × 57 cm). Statens Kunstfond, Copenhagen

Myre Vasegaard represents a second generation of Danish potters within the family. Sharing a studio with her mother, Gertrud Vasegaard, the ceramist has produced a series of large flat bowls often employing calligraphic ornamentation. On the surface of this bowl, a seemingly random pattern of quick strokes suggests the reflected patterns of birds in flight.

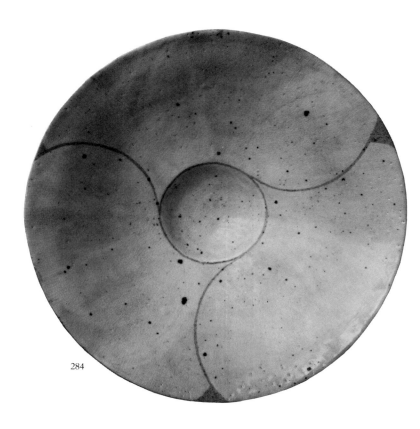

284

285

286

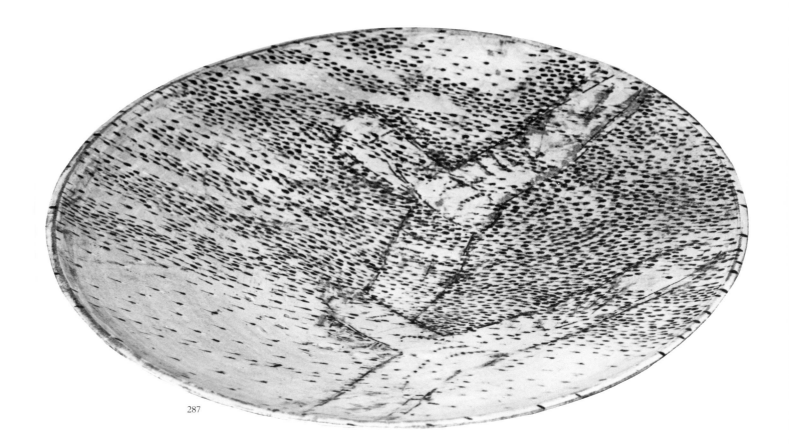

287

Brugskunst Og Design, was dissolved. Not until several years later were two new ones established: one for artisans and one for industrial designers. In Norway the artisans resigned from the Norwegian design organization—the Landsforbundet Norsk Brukskunst—and the industrial designers followed suit. In Sweden, the artisans withdrew from the Svenska Slöjdföreningen.

This strong polarization between the artisans and the designers in the applied arts is not a particularly Scandinavian phenomenon. In the Nordic countries, however, it had considerable impact since one of the basic ideas of the Scandinavian Design period had been the interplay between unique, handmade works and objects produced in series. Ideally, the artisan and the designer were to be one and the same person.

A major element in the pattern of our contemporary culture, industrial design, like many fields of culture in the Western countries, experienced a crisis about 1970. A new generation to whom World War II was history and the social and economic conditions of the 1930s hearsay had taken its place in the front ranks of design. It had grown up with prosperity, and the buy-and-throw-away mentality was part of its heritage. Yet, it was deeply concerned with the global problems that threatened people everywhere, rich and poor alike.

This new generation of designers was no longer solely interested in the right form and correct functional characteristics of the individual object, nor was it so set on the thought of making good consumer products intended for the home. Instead, it focused on the public environment, believing that objects and environments should be adapted to people and not the other way around. It also believed that industrial production should aim to satisfy the needs of all, not just those who can afford to buy the products.

Students at the craft schools, clearly champions of the new attitude, criticized the "self-centered" outlook toward design that permeated instruction in the field. They called for instruction that went beyond the aesthetic aspect of design to treat the total subject. Among other things, that meant learning the technical language so that they could work closely with technicians and engineers. In their view, design had become a matter of teamwork, demanding close cooperation at all stages of production.

288. Benny Motzfeldt (b. 1909). *Vase.* 1979. Norway. Produced at Benny Motzfeldt, Plus, Fredrikstad. Blown glass with inclusions, height 7½″ (19 cm). Oslo Kunstindustrimuseet

Motzfeldt early established a completely independent studio for serial production in Fredrikstad. This studio, plus her unique approach to the material, has earned her a prominent position in the history of modern Norwegian glass. She achieves richly varied abstract patterns by skillfully arranging inclusions—ranging from metallic screening to fiberglass, cut into random shapes—in the molten glass. The graphic textures thus produced contrast strikingly with the transparent body.

289. Edla Freij (b. 1944). *Vase.* 1979. Norway. Produced at Hadelands Glassverk, Jevnaker. Blown glass, etched, 10⅜ × 8½″ (26.5 × 21.8 cm). Nordenfjeldske Kunstindustrimuseum, Trondheim

Freij has contributed designs with both engraved and sandblasted decoration to the Hadelands glass factory. The etched border of this vase follows the pronounced curve of the rim, producing a subtle interplay of overlapping curves.

290. Gro (Sommerfeldt) Bergslien (b. 1940). *Dish and two vases.* c. 1973–74. Norway. Produced by Hadelands Glassverk, Jevnaker. Blown glass, *vases:* heights 11″; 10⅝″ (28 cm; 27 cm); *plate:* diameter 11¾″ (30 cm). Vestlandske Kunstindustrimuseum, Bergen

A prolific designer of textiles as well as glass, Bergslien favors softly organic forms for her glass designs, typified by these pieces. The apparent casualness of the forms results from careful control of the material during the blowing process. Here, Bergslien integrated striations of color into the velvety texture of the glass.

288

289

290

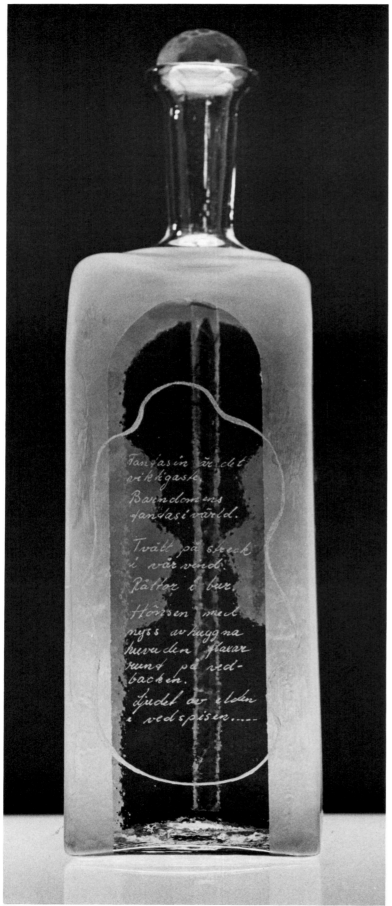

291

292

293

294

291. Åsa Brandt (b. 1940). *Bottle from the* Portrait of a Bottle *series*. 1981. Sweden. Blown glass, etched and engraved, 10⅝ × 2½″ (27 × 6.5 cm). Collection Åsa Brandt

The independent spirit of Swedish glass during the past decade is admirably expressed in the work of Brandt. Since 1968, she has overseen all aspects of production, including the blowing of the glass, in her own workshop—the first in the country to do so. Highly personal images and motifs in unexpected combinations with familiar forms give Brandt's work a special poetic quality. The poem inscribed on this bottle is entitled "The dreams of your childhood."

292. Finn Lynggaard (b. 1930). *Vase*. 1977. Denmark. Blown glass, 10¼ × 7⅛″ (26 × 18 cm). Röhsska Konstslöjdmuseet, Göteborg, Sweden

Independent studio glass is a relatively new phenomenon in Denmark, and much of the interest in the field has been generated by Finn Lynggaard, one of its earliest proponents. Lynggaard skillfully incorporates stylized floral ornamentation, using deep colors, into many of his objects, such as this vase.

293. Bertil Vallien (b. 1938). *Tableware,* Oktav *pattern*. 1977. Sweden. Produced by Kosta Boda, Kosta. Molded blown glass, *decanter:* height 9″ (23 cm); *bowl:* 5⅝ × 7½″ (14.5 × 19 cm); *glass:* height 6¾″ (17 cm). Nationalmuseum, Stockholm

The pictorial and poetic nature of Vallien's one-of-a-kind objects in overlay glass gives way to a classic simplicity in his production designs. The *Oktav* pattern is based on modified geometry, and the faceted sides of each piece make a smooth transition to a curve at shoulder or base.

294. Heikki Kallio (b. 1948). *Vase*. 1980. Finland. Blown glass, 4⅞ × 5¼″ (12.5 × 13.5 cm). Finnish Glass Museum, Riihimäki

In an unusual departure from Finnish glass tradition, which tends to emphasize the mass and solidity of the material, Kallio presents delicate cylindrical forms that capture and disperse light with an exceptional gentleness. The qualities of softness and sensuality are further heightened by jewel-like colors that give the impression of a rolling landscape in the glass.

295. Inez Svensson (b. 1923). *Printed fabric*. 1970. Sweden. Produced by 10-Gruppen, Stockholm. Cotton, width 59⅞″ (152 cm). 10-Gruppen, Stockholm

During the late 1960s and early 1970s, a pronounced trend toward geometry expressed itself in bold printed textiles—such as this one—throughout Scandinavia, but with particular vigor in Sweden and Finland. For over ten years, Svensson has been an active member of 10-Gruppen, an independent combine of ten artists who design and manufacture their own products. Many such independent groups in all the traditional fields of craft and design were set up in the 1970s to provide an alternative to the industrial mass-production system.

296. Ruth Malinowski (b. 1928). *Tapestry:* Sammenhæng I. 1977. Denmark. Wool, 63 × 61″ (160 × 155 cm). Det Danske Kunstindustrimuseum, Copenhagen

The international character of Scandinavian design is well documented in the person of Ruth Malinowski: born in Austria, she resides in Denmark and maintains a studio in Sweden. Malinowski's exceptionally forceful weavings depend entirely upon the uncompromising geometric composition. The artist restricts the color palette of her weavings to bring out the subtle differences of tonality and texture in the woven surface.

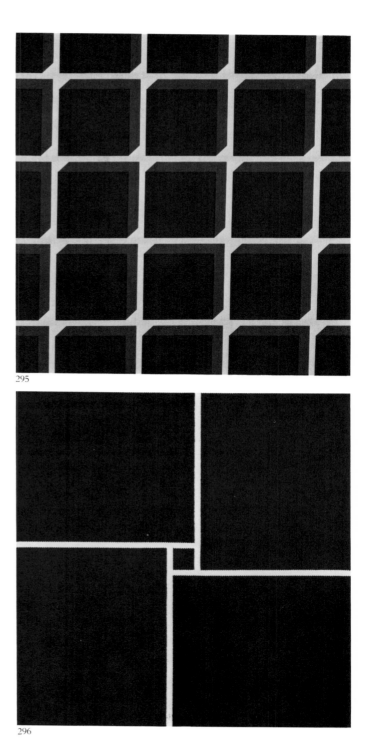

295

296

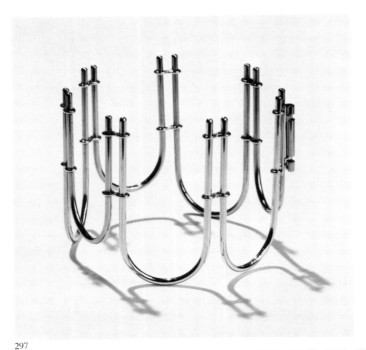

297

298

299

297. Ole Bent Petersen (b. 1938). *Bracelet*. 1980. Denmark. Gold and steel, height 2¾" (7 cm). Collection Ole Bent Petersen

298. *Bracelet*. 1980. Denmark. Gold and stones, length 7⅝" (19.5 cm). Collection Ole Bent Petersen

That a simple and direct statement may embody exceptional visual strength is borne out by the imaginative jewelry of Petersen. Working on an extremely small scale, the artist brings a vision of grandeur to his works—one bracelet captures the abstract architectural profile of a Danish street, while the diminutive crownlike bracelet has the impact of a large-scale sculpture.

299. Björn Weckström (b. 1935). *Pendant:* Kilimantšaro. 1974. Finland. Produced by Lipponia Jewelry, Helsinki. Silver and acrylic, diameter 2½" (6.5 cm). Lapponia Jewelry, Helsinki

Probably the most internationally known of Finnish jewelry designers, Weckström actually creates small wearable sculptures from precious metals, stones, and synthetics. A prolific designer, Weckström earned his international reputation with the variety and technical virtuosity of his designs.

300. Allan Scharff (b. 1945). *Covered bowl*. 1980. Denmark. Silver, 3¼ × 4¾" (8.5 × 12 cm). Det Danske Kunstindustrimuseum

Scharff's sleek and flowing abstract designs for silver hollow ware are often based on the shapes of birds. The cover of this vessel echoes the form beneath, establishing a parallel visual rhythm and lyrical quality. The sophistication of form and confident mastery of technique typify the Danish tradition of silversmithing.

301. Sigurd Persson (b. 1914). *Coffeepot*. 1970. Sweden. Silver and juniper wood, 7⅛ × 12¾" (18 × 32.5 cm), from spout to handle. Nationalmuseum, Stockholm

The bold sculptural forms of Persson's hollow ware reveal the hand of the master craftsman. The interplay of sharply defined planes and of generous curves endows the shape with an inner vitality. Persson's silver is always meticulously finished, the soft textures of the planished surfaces reflecting light from a myriad of small surface modulations.

300

301

This matter—a modern and specialized training for industrial designers—engendered considerable discussion during the 1970s among the professional design associations and institutions as well as among applied arts schools throughout Scandinavia. In 1971, the Nordic Cultural Commission sponsored a proposal for a joint Nordic institution at university level, but as yet it has not been acted on. In Denmark, the Academy of Art in Copenhagen provides theoretical instruction at the university level. At the applied arts schools in Helsinki, Stockholm, and Oslo, special instruction in industrial design is given at the university level.

The very concept of industrial design has yet to be clarified. No single comprehensive definition has won acceptance throughout Scandinavia. The description provided in 1976 by Alf Bøe, one of Norway's leading critics of art and design, can serve as a basis: "An industrial designer is not engaged in the production of a finished product, but in the production of the prototype for such a product—and, in addition, in the establishment of the work processes that make it possible to convert the prototype into finished products."

The modern industrial designer performs a wide variety of tasks, ranging from the production of consumer or capital goods to involvement in large-scale projects in such areas as public transport. The diversity of skills required for these different undertakings has led to the development of specialties within the field. Some industrial designers concentrate on graphics, others on materials or production techniques, still others on specific areas such as lighting, furniture, or human services (for example, hospitals). These activities demand a high degree of intersecting concerns and expertise.

The development of industrial design in Scandinavia in the 1970s is evinced in the joint Nordic expositions that have been shown abroad. The traveling exposition in Australia in 1968 was the last to offer a pure applied arts presentation, consisting of items selected by the organizers to represent model products from the Nordic countries. In the exhibition shown in Brazil and Mexico during 1970–72, products from the electronics and mechanical industries made up more than half of the displays, but the new design theme was neither developed in detail nor theoretically presented. This new approach finally prevailed in the organization of the exhibition traveling in Israel and Poland during 1974–75. Here, products and proj-

302

302. Gunnar Cyrén (b. 1931). *Bowl*. 1976. Sweden. Silver, 5⅜ × 7¾″ (13.7 × 19.7 cm). Röhsska Konstslöjdmuseet, Göteborg

Cyrén, also a noted designer of glass, emphasizes in his silver objects the reflectiveness of the highly polished metal. He accomplished the effect here by modeling the lattice-like pattern on the body to give a three-dimensional convexity to each lozenge-shaped panel. The swelling form of the body is carried through to the gently fluted and everted lip of the bowl.

303. Sigrun Einarsdottir (b. 1952). *Bowl*. 1979. Iceland. Blown glass, 4⅜ × 6¾″ (11 × 17 cm). Collection Sigrun Einarsdottir

304. *Bowl*. Iceland. 1979. Blown glass, 2⅞ × 10⅝″ (7.5 × 27 cm). Collection Sigrun Einarsdottir

An emerging craft in Iceland, studio glass recently has been furthered by Einarsdottir's establishment of the country's first hot-glass workshop. Trained in Denmark, Einarsdottir brings a thorough mastery of the techniques of glassblowing and a lively imagination to her work. In some of her pieces, she incorporates fluidly drawn human figures; in others, she allows the sound color composition to stand on its own.

305

306

307

308

305. Olle Ohlsson (b. 1927). *Teapot.* 1977. Sweden. Silver and pearwood, 7½ (with handle) × 7½" (19 × 19 cm). Private collection, Sweden

A vibrant surface and the seductively tactile quality of the malleable metal combine in this teapot to achieve an organic dynamism: the rippled and mottled surface of the upper portion of the pot presents an ever-changing display of reflected light. Much in the manner of a ceramic glaze, the patterns emerge from the body to gently embrace the shape.

306. Ulrica Hydman-Vallien (b. 1938). *Sculpture:* Animal and Man. 1974. Sweden. Earthenware, painted decoration, 12¼ × 13⅞ × 10¼" (31 × 34.5 × 26 cm). Nationalmuseum, Stockholm

Although German-born, Hydman-Vallien has become a major force in the development of ceramic sculpture in Sweden. Bright—often strident—colors add depth to the naive and visionary quality of her work, which can appear playful or menacing.

307. Britt-Ingrid Persson (BIP) (b. 1938). *Sculpture:* About Identities. 1970. Sweden. Stoneware, 13½ × 10¼ × 11¾" (34.5 × 26 × 30 cm). Nationalmuseum, Stockholm

During the 1970s, ceramics took off in new directions, including the growth of a free sculptural approach to the material. BIP often deals with the human condition in her work, exploring the relationships between individuals and society.

308. Gestur Thorgrimsson (b. 1920) and Sigrun Gudjonsdottir (Runa) (b. 1926). *Plate.* 1979. Iceland. Stoneware, painted decoration, 2⅛ × 12¼" (5.5 × 31 cm). Collection Gestur Thorgrimsson and Sigrun Gudjonsdottir (Runa)

Working in collaboration, Gestur supplies the thrown forms and Runa adds the decoration. Trained as a painter, Runa drew inspiration from many classical motifs, in which figural and animal subjects predominate. The elegant simplicity of the drawing parallels the purity of the form.

309 (*overleaf*). Hans Munck Andersen (b. 1943). *Bowl.* 1976. Denmark. Porcelain, 4¾ × 6¼" (12 × 16 cm). Det Danske Kunstindustrimuseum, Copenhagen

Andersen's extremely individual ceramics result from a special technique of fabrication that includes tinting the ceramic body prior to pressing strips of colored clay into a mold. This yields a primary pattern of strongly colored striations along with a subsidiary pattern of overlapping clay strips.

ects were thoroughly analyzed and linked together in a cogent presentation. However, in order to connect the new design ethic and Scandinavia's established style, a collection of older and well-known products was also displayed. At the Milan Triennale in 1973, the Scandinavian countries jointly participated in an installation dealing with the living conditions of children in a big-city environment—a problem-oriented rather than production-oriented theme.

In addition, an inter-Nordic exposition, titled "Nordic Industrial Design—What, Why, How," was set up to clarify the new situation in Scandinavian industrial design. Presented by the Olso Museum of Applied Art in connection with its centennial celebration in 1976, it exemplified the new cooperation among the Scandinavian museums of applied art, also an important factor in the organization of exhibitions traveling abroad. The exposition was equally divided between displays of contemporary, thoroughly analyzed products and classics from the Scandinavian Design period. As it traveled throughout the Nordic countries, the exposition offered Scandinavians a rare opportunity to familiarize themselves with the working tasks of the industrial designer.

This change in content and approach reflected the increasing involvement of industrial designers in projects within the metallic goods, mechanical, and electronics industries. Although it was initially due to the expansion of these industries into fields connected with home furnishing and private consumption, gradually the situation was reversed: industrial designers extended their functions to take in fields previously handled by purely technically trained engineers. Design ideals—form, color, and function—were now demanded in such objects as typewriters, office furniture, and machines—in fact, in the entire working environment.

One field that especially benefited from the contribution of Scandinavian designers in the 1970s is product development for special needs. In particular, designers worked on products for the handicapped that aimed at easing their everyday life and enabling them to participate in a wider range of activities.

The industrial designer's working situation in Scandinavia today is not much different from that in other Western industrialized countries. Certain large applied arts firms have their own design offices in which designers are engaged on a full-time basis, a common practice of the 1920s and 1930s. However, 227

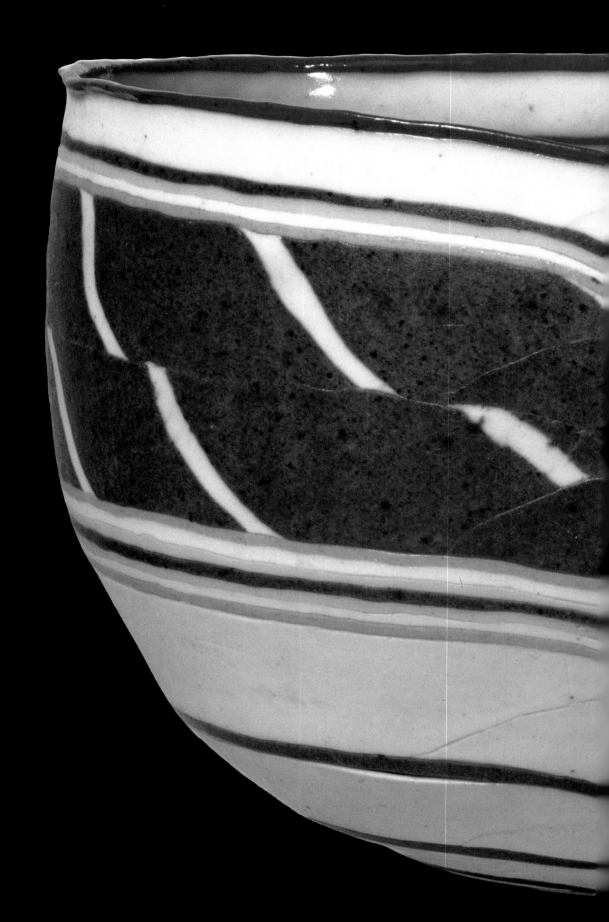

310

310. Lisa Bauer (b. 1920) and Sigurd Persson (b. 1914). *Bottle*. 1974. Sweden. Produced by Kosta Glasbruk. Blown glass, engraved, 10¼ × 5⅛ × 4⅜" (26 × 13 × 11 cm). Nationalmuseum, Stockholm

Exquisitely engraved glass, a strong Swedish tradition, has found a champion in Bauer. She endows her naturalistic designs with a tangible presence: these engraved leaves seem to be floating inside the body of the piece. Persson, noted for his metalwork, designed the form of this bottle.

311. Eva Englund (b. 1937). *Vase: Flower Bowl*. 1980. Sweden. Produced at Orrefors Glasbruk. Glass, *graal* technique, 9⅞ × 9⅛" (25 × 23.5 cm). AB Orrefors Glasbruk

The *graal* technique of glass decoration, which Edward Hald developed at Orrefors early in the twentieth century, has been revived with particular vigor by Englund. Whereas most decoration is applied to the surface, this technique traps the ornamentation within the glass, creating an intensity of color and a transparency rarely equaled by other methods.

312. Tapio Wirkkala (b. 1915). *Glassware,* Maaru *pattern*. 1980. Finland. Produced by Iittalan Lasitehdas, Iittala. Molded blown glass, maximum height 6" (15.5 cm); maximum diameter 4½" (11.5 cm). Cooper-Hewitt Museum, New York. Gift of Iittala Glassworks

In both his production and unique glass, Wirkkala exploits the natural and optical qualities of the material to an extraordinary degree. A near-perfect spherical shape forms the bowl of each glass in the *Maaru* pattern; the rippled surface expresses the liquidity both of the glass and of the contents each vessel is designed to hold.

311

312

313

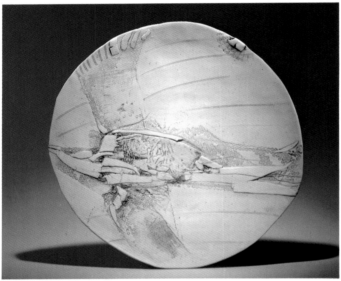

314

315

313. Signe Persson-Melin (b. 1925). *Table service,* Primeur *pattern.* 1978. Sweden. Produced by Rörstrand, Lidköping. Porcelain, *pitcher:* height 5⅞″ (15.1 cm); *plate:* diameter 9⅝″ (24.5 cm). Rörstrand AB, Lidköping

Having worked independently in her own studio since 1950, Persson-Melin in more recent years has created production designs for Kosta Boda glassworks and the Rörstrand porcelain factory. The *Primeur* service is decorated with a textural and calligraphic pattern of blue that lends a soft contrast to the simple forms.

314. Kari Christensen (b. 1938). *Plate:* Flying Bird. 1979. Norway. Porcelain, diameter 10¼″ (26 cm). Oslo Kunstindustrimuseet

Christensen, exploiting fully the fine texture and responsiveness of porcelain, forms vessels and plates by overlapping thin sections of the material, each impressed with textural patterns. She then stains and prints the pure white ceramic body with subtle gradations of soft color.

315. Bo Kristiansen (b. 1944). *Covered bowl.* 1981. Denmark. Stoneware, 6⅜ × 7⅞″ (16.5 × 20 cm). Det Danske Kunstindustrimuseum, Copenhagen

The letters of the alphabet, some picked out in colors and gilding, inscribed on the surface distinguish Kristiansen's ceramic bowls. Many of the sequences of letters, which often overlap, form words and phrases of ambiguous and multiple meanings.

316. Tone Vigeland (b. 1938). *Bracelet.* 1976. Norway. Silver and gold, length 7⅛″ (18 cm), width 2⅜″ (6 cm). Oslo Kunstindustrimuseet

317. *Necklace.* 1981. Norway. Steel, silver, gold, and mother-of-pearl, diameter 7½″ (19 cm). Nordenfjeldske Kunstindustrimuseum, Trondheim

Vigeland has become the foremost contemporary jewelry designer in Norway by virtue of her inventiveness and exceedingly high standards of technical competence. The necklace seems to be fashioned from soft and delicate feathers; each of these movable pieces, however, is an industrial blue-steel nail that has been hammered flat. The bracelet is composed of hundreds of individually fashioned and attached links and beads that form a soft and sensuous surface.

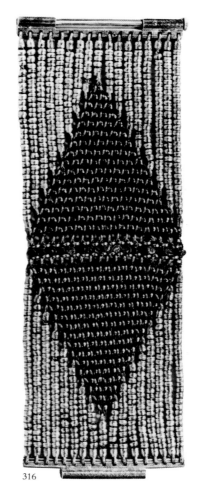

316

317

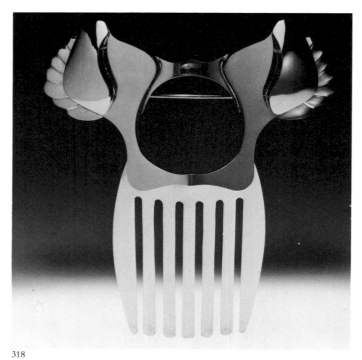

318

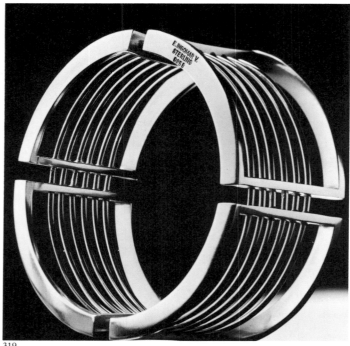

319

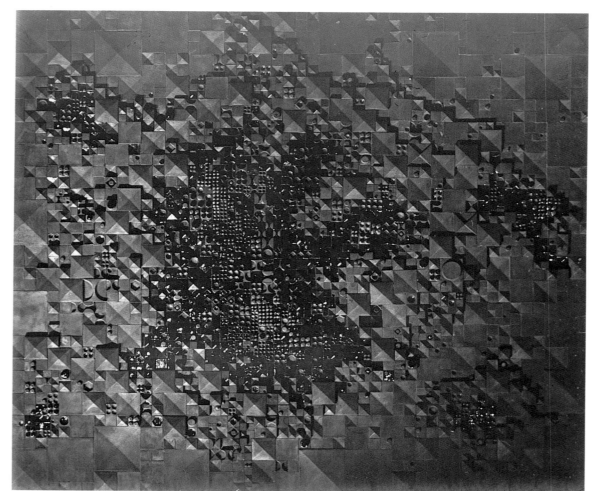

320

321

318. Jan Lohmann (b. 1944). *Brooch*. 1978. Denmark. Yellow and white gold, 3¼ × 3⅛″ (8.5 × 8 cm). Collection Jan Lohmann

Lohmann's work in jewelry attests to the continuation of high standards of craftsmanship in Danish metalwork. With its comblike teeth and stylized wings, this brooch evokes the quality of a magic amulet. The symmetry and balance of the design, the variations in surface levels and textures, and the effective utilization of positive and negative space give this small object a monumental power.

319. Erik Ingomar Vangsgaard (b. 1938). *Bracelet*. Denmark. 1979. Silver, 1¼ × 2½″ (3.5 × 6.8 cm). Collection Erik Ingomar Vangsgaard

The precision of construction and design that characterizes the work of Vangsgaard is evident in this bracelet, fabricated from a series of silver rods which support an architectural frame. Although handmade, the bracelet reveals the influence of technological development in the jeweler's art.

320. Rut Bryk (b. 1916). *Wall relief: Marsh Pond*. 1978–82. Finland. Produced by Arabia, Helsinki. Stoneware mosaic, 51⅛ × 59⅞″ (130 × 152 cm). Oy Arabia AB, Helsinki

Although Bryk's earlier ceramics include a number of wall reliefs, these were figural; more recently, she has concentrated on nonfigurative designs. Small mosaic tiles in a variety of patterns give this sculpture a dynamic textural surface. By virtue of their size and complexity, her wall reliefs assert an architectural presence.

321. Timo Sarpaneva (b. 1926). *Cookware*. 1970. Finland. Produced by Opa. Stainless steel, *cooking pot*: 5⅝ × 5⅝″ (14.5 × 14.5 cm); *platter*: diameter 12⅝″ (32 cm). Taideteollisuusmuseo, Helsinki

Known primarily for his work in glass, Sarpaneva readily applied to other materials his skill at creating functional forms of great visual strength. He eschewed all nonessential details for this well-proportioned cookware, choosing semicircular handles on the pots to allow an easy grasp and designing the cover to double as a serving container when reversed.

most designers work independently or as teams on a free-lance basis for both large and small companies. Some industrial designers have gained entry to public services on both the national and municipal levels.

There is still a great deal of room for the industrial designer's expertise in government, particularly in the preparation of complete design programs. Such areas as the state railroad systems and, in Norway, the emerging oil industry may require the skills of this new generation of designers.

While industrial designers in the 1970s were encouraged to extend their skills into more and more fields of industry, artisans found themselves increasingly isolated from industry. In all of Scandinavia, few positions for craft designers existed, although the situation was slightly better in Denmark, Finland, and Sweden than in Norway and Iceland. Yet, instruction in the crafts schools continued to function according to one of the aims of the Scandinavian Design period—that industry should employ designers with artistic training. This set up a dilemma for many of the students: where were they to work?

Another significant factor of crafts development in this period was public reaction against glossy, factory-made objects. In the course of the 1960s, handmade articles became an increasingly valued alternative. The general desire for the handmade look at any price led to objects widely varying in quality. Also related to this trend was the use of crafts to express political beliefs. The new social consciousness had considerable impact within crafts, and the results were often more interesting politically than artistically.

Around 1970, the crafts developed into a profession whose dominant characteristic was its opposition to industry. The newly trained artisans wished to create things in their own workshops, and the artistic content of these personal objects often became more important than their function. This reaction was directed not only against industry but also against traditional instruction in the crafts schools. The new assertiveness of craftsmen was not always easy to accept, particularly among those who staunchly defended the traditional role of the artist-designer.

In the 1970s, Scandinavian artisans also questioned the traditional marketing methods for crafts. Few of today's crafts are sold commercially—that is, over the counter, with a shop 235

323

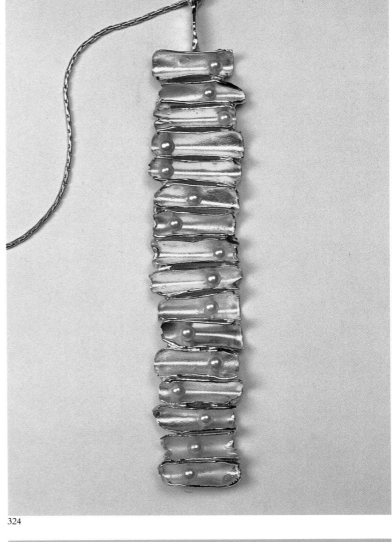

324

322. Jens Gudhjonsson (b. 1920). *Vessel*. 1969. Iceland. Silver, 9⅞ × 6¼″ (25 × 16 cm). Collection Jens Gudhjonsson

323. *Necklace*. 1972. Iceland. Silver, diameter 4¾″ (12 cm), length of pendant 9½″ (24 cm). Collection Jens Gudhjonsson

The craft of silversmithing in Iceland has flourished in recent decades, and much of this renewed interest can be attributed to the efforts of Jens Gudhjonsson, considered the dean of Icelandic metalworkers. The strongly textured surfaces of Gudhjonsson's work often recall the naturally sculptured forms of lava flows common to the Icelandic landscape.

324. Gudbrandur J. Jezorski (b. 1943). *Necklace*. 1981. Iceland. Gold and pearls, length 3⅛″ (8 cm). Collection Gudbrandur J. Jezorski

325. *Brooch*. 1981. Iceland. Gold and stone, diameter 2″ (5 cm). Collection Gudbrandur J. Jezorski

Like many members of the new generation of Icelandic craftsmen, Jezorski established an independent studio, located in Reykjavik. In his designs, he capitalizes on the textural possibilities of silver and gold, often adding inset stones or pearls for contrast. His distinctive vocabulary of motifs owes much to the extraordinary terrain of Iceland—an influence that similarly affects many Icelandic designers.

325

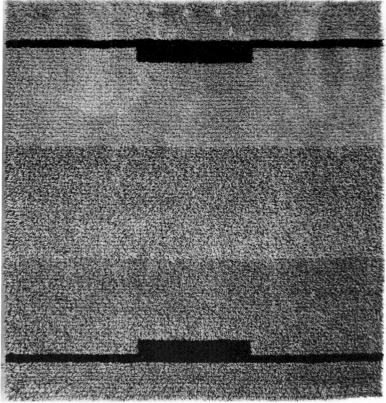

326

327

328

326. Maija Lavonen (b. 1931). *Rug:* Triad. 1977. Finland. Wool, *ryijy* technique, 47¼ × 47¼" (120 × 120 cm). Collection Ministry for Foreign Affairs of Finland, Helsinki

Lavonen's variations on the traditional *ryijy* rug format include strikingly graphic compositions with subtle gradations of color and tone. In *Triad,* the three unequal sections separated by unequivocal lines set up a dynamic tension across the surface of the rug, counterbalanced by the continuity of texture achieved in the *ryijy* technique.

327. Charlotte Block-Hellum (b. 1911). *Dish.* 1981. Norway. Enameled copper, diameter 13½" (34.5 cm). Collection Charlotte Block-Hellum

The rich colors that translucent enamels make possible have been exploited with particular skill by Block-Hellum, a specialist in this traditionally Norwegian field. She enamels her patterns, often abstract, in vibrant colors against a contrasting field. Beneath the translucent enamels, a variety of metallic textures add luster to the passages of pure color.

328. Maria Adlercreutz (b. 1936). *Tapestry:* In Her Eyes the Light of the People Is Reflected. 1971–72. Sweden. Wool, 33½ × 72⅞" (85 × 185 cm). Nationalmuseum, Stockholm

Much Scandinavian art of the late 1960s and 1970s reflects the pressing political and social issues of the time; among these, the war in Southeast Asia was singled out for particular attention. The powerful pictorial imagery of this weaving, taken from newspaper photographs of Vietnamese families who became helpless victims of the war, transforms life into art and promotes art as an important voice and conscience of society.

329. Saara Hopea (b. 1925). *Dish.* 1972. Finland. Enameled copper, 1⅝ × 7½" (4 × 19 cm). Taideteollisuusmuseo, Helsinki

A designer of furniture, glass, and ceramics, Hopea also extended her talents to enameling. The colors of the transparent enamels on this dish are particularly bright and clear, ranging from a deep red to a strong yellow. Beneath this brilliant surface an intense and warm internal luminosity, imparted by the copper, shines through. The asymmetrical oval bands of color provide a foil to the simple circular shape.

330. Bertil Vallien (b. 1938). *Bowl.* 1977. Sweden. Produced at Kosta Glasbruk. Blown and cased glass, sandblasted, 6¾ × 9⅞ × 7⅛" (17 × 25 × 18 cm). Röhsska Konstslöjdmuseet, Göteborg

Glass artist and ceramist, Vallien has experimented with layered or cased glass and sandblasting techniques, producing objects with a variety of surface textures and a deeply poetic visual imagery.

329

330

taking a certain profit. Instead, artisans have joined together to set up sales outlets for their workshop creations. This system has proved to be financially viable; in addition, since the artisans themselves take turns minding the shop, they come in close contact with the public. Crafts exhibitions have also become an increasingly important way for artisans to display and sell their wares directly to the public.

Since artisans in Scandinavia are generally in a low income bracket, many have had to take on other types of work in order to make ends meet. In this regard, artisans in one of the Nordic countries—Norway—have made a certain progress. A close look at what happened in Norway may illuminate the future of crafts and the goals of artisans in all of Scandinavia.

In 1974, Norwegian artists from a number of groups within the various art forms joined forces to establish a professional identity and to fight for their rights as professionals. Within the Artists' Movement, the artisans participated on equal terms with the other groups. The artists were successful in gaining the right to negotiate with the government on the same terms as a number of trade unions. Taking advantage of this concession, they achieved a system with a guaranteed minimum income for artists. The system has not been extended since, so a relatively small group receives a guaranteed income today. All the same, this income has meant that a number of artisans can concentrate solely on their art without having to take on other work.

The Artists' Movement also gained for artists financial compensation for articles displayed at all public exhibitions. The idea of artist-controlled art marketing began to take hold. In 1976, the artisans established their own marketing center, which sets up exhibitions and other outlets for selling crafts. The Art Marketing Center arranges, among others, the yearly national exposition and the yearly exhibition by applicants for scholarships. The center is also responsible for an archive of slides where consultants with decorating commissions can obtain professional assistance.

Perhaps the most important result of the Artists' Movement was that artisans received training in administration and cooperative action. (One of the various measures they took was to withdraw from the Norwegian design association in 1978.) Moreover, the movement has given the artisans pride in their

331. Erik Magnussen (b. 1940). *Thermal carafe*. 1976. Denmark. Produced by Stelton, Gentofte. Stainless steel, plastic, and glass, 11¾ × 4¾" (30 × 12 cm). Stelton A/S, Gentofte

This thermal carafe was designed with conscientious concern for practicality, performance, and visual clarity. The semicircular molded handle accentuates the simple cylindrical form; the counterbalanced stopper opens automatically when the carafe is tilted to pour and remains airtight when not in use; and the thermal liner may be easily removed by pressing the side buttons. The carafe was given the Industrial Design (ID) award in Denmark in 1977.

332. Karl Gustav Hansen (b. 1914). *Teapot*. 1978. Denmark. Produced by Hans Hansen Sølvsmedie, Kolding. Silver, height 4⅛" (10.7 cm). Hans Hansen Sølvsmedie A/S, Copenhagen

Karl Gustav Hansen, who headed the Hansen firm from 1940 to 1962, remains a major designer of silver hollow ware in Denmark. An exceptional clarity of form and flawlessness of surface inform his work. Each detail is meticulously planned and crafted, uniting in a practical form of distinctive finesse. The geometric and planar relationships of the various functional parts—handle, spout, body, and cover—create a unified and sophisticated effect.

331

332

333

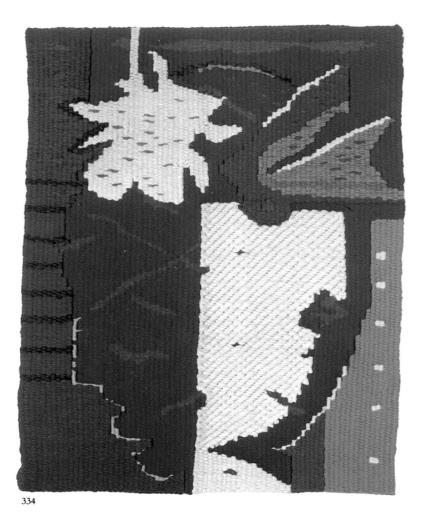

334

333. Ida Winckler (b. 1930). *Embroidered panel:* Nyhavn.
1973. Denmark. Made for the Danish Handcraft Guild.
Cotton on linen, cross-stitch technique, 7¼ × 70½″ (18.5 ×
179 cm). Det Danske Kunstindustrimuseum, Copenhagen

Needlework has remained a specialty of Danish textile designers, and the craft has been encouraged over the decades by
skilled artists such as Winckler. The panoramic view of
Nyhavn's waterfront architecture depicted in this embroidery is enlivened by a panoply of subtle colors and the
staccato rhythm of the simplified geometric forms.

334. Sigridur Johannsdottir (b. 1948) and Leifur Breidfjord
(b. 1945). *Tapestry.* 1980. Iceland. Wool, 23⅝ × 19⅝″ (60 ×
50 cm). Collection Sigridur Johannsdottir and Leifur
Breidfjord

Johannsdottir executes the designs for weavings supplied by
Breidfjord. The strong composition and pure colors of
Breidfjord's designs recall his work as an independent flat-
glass artist. Johannsdottir, with a similar color sensibility,
brings out the colors and forms of the surface pattern by
exploiting the textural possibilities of the woven structure.

335. Ulla Schumacher-Percy (b. 1918). *Tapestry:* Orfeus.
1975. Sweden. Silk, gold, artificial silk, and linen, 58¼ ×
56¼″ (148 × 143 cm). Nationalmuseum, Stockholm

Schumacher-Percy has contributed to the fields of rug design,
embroidery, and tapestry weaving in Sweden. A sure compositional sense informs all her work, whether abstract or, like
this tapestry, pictorial. Here, the artist successfully mixed
various types and weights of fiber to realize a rich surface
emphasized by the various woven textures that define major
passages in the composition.

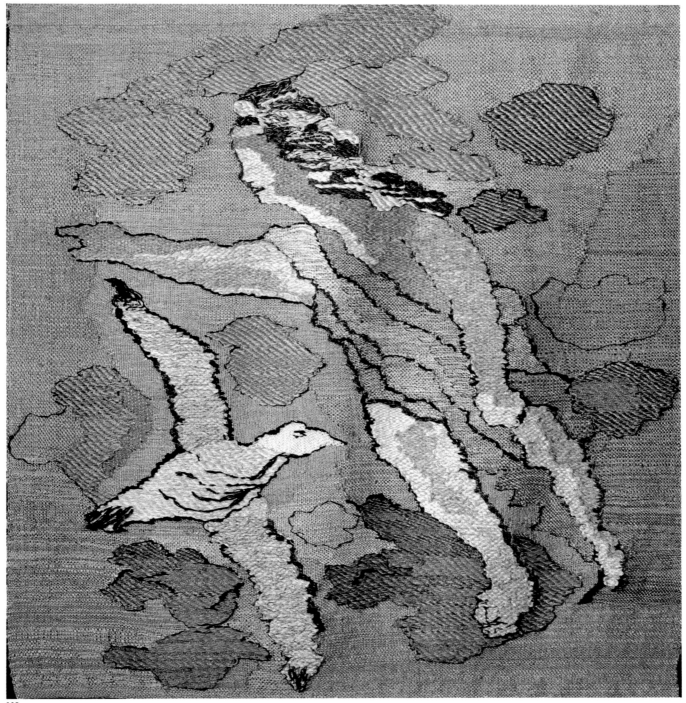

own profession. The romanticism too often associated with artisans, arts, and crafts has been replaced by a realistic attitude toward crafts as a profession on a par with all others. Artisans today sometimes serve as paid professional consultants for government projects.

In the last few years, the new strength of the artisans has been clearly expressed in production—by far the most satisfying effect of the movement. Artisans are making more and different kinds of objects, and without sacrificing quality. Those who receive the minimum income allowance have shown an especially impressive development, thereby contradicting the romantic notion that great art and poverty go hand in hand.

Although the same currents and trends that led to the Artists' Movement in Norway could be found in other Nordic countries at the same time, they have not been followed up in the same way. Nonetheless, the crafts throughout Scandinavia experienced a renaissance during the 1970s.

One striking feature of all modern crafts is their strong international character: it is difficult today to determine immediately where the different objects have been made. Distinctive national features have largely disappeared; new trends go beyond national boundaries, appearing in many places simultaneously and without any clear patterns. Additionally, the meetings of the World Craft Council have played an important role in the spread of new ideas in the 1970s. After each meeting, clear traces of the host country's culture showed up in crafts produced in the different Scandinavian countries.

In the 1970s, two distinct international impulses were particularly conspicuous in Scandinavian crafts. One influence came from the United States, where crafts have most forcefully freed themselves from traditional thinking. Iceland and Norway, which have always looked westward because of their geographical location, were most strongly affected by American ideas, while the other Nordic countries held on to the framework of Scandinavian tradition. Within this native tradition, studio crafts were particularly important, and an especially strong influence may be seen in the field of glass. Among new stylistic trends that have made their way into crafts is the "High Tech" look, and even an Art Nouveau influence can be detected in some work. Crafts of the 1970s have proven the futility of dividing applied arts and the fine arts into two separate fields.

336

336. Thorbjörg Thordardottir (b. 1949). *Printed fabric (detail)*. 1979. Iceland. Cotton, width 39⅜″ (100 cm). Collection Thorbjörg Thordardottir

The printing of textiles, a nascent craft in Iceland, is gaining recognition due to the work of Thordardottir. She effectively combines simple organic forms in stylized patterns with fresh and lively pastel colors.

337. Rud Thygesen (b. 1932) and Johnny Sørensen (b. 1944). *Armchair*. 1975. Denmark. Produced by Magnus Olesen, Durup. Bentwood, laminated, and fabric, 29½ × 23¾ × 18⅞″ (75 × 60.5 × 48 cm). Det Danske Kunstindustrimuseum

The design team of Thygesen and Sørensen has developed a major series of seating designs that apply industrial processes, such as lamination and pressure bending, to forms that are fresh and unexpected. This chair suggests earlier examples of bent and laminated wood—chairs by Alvar Aalto and Bruno Mathsson, for example—but introduces a new element in the cantilevered seat and support frame. Sturdy but flexible, it can function in many settings, in public as well as domestic spaces.

338. Claus Bonderup (b. 1943) and Torsten Thorup (b. 1944). *Floor lamp and table lamp*. 1979. Denmark. Produced by Focus Belysning, Holte. Enameled metal, heights 54⅜″; 19⅝″ (138 cm; 50 cm). Focus Belysning, Holte

The simple design of these lamps belies their efficiency as sources of directed light. Each lamp has a stabilizing base which supports the elongated curve of the body; the light source is a small high-intensity bulb set in an adjustable section at the head of the curve.

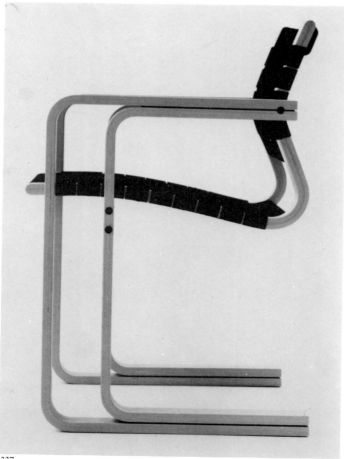

337

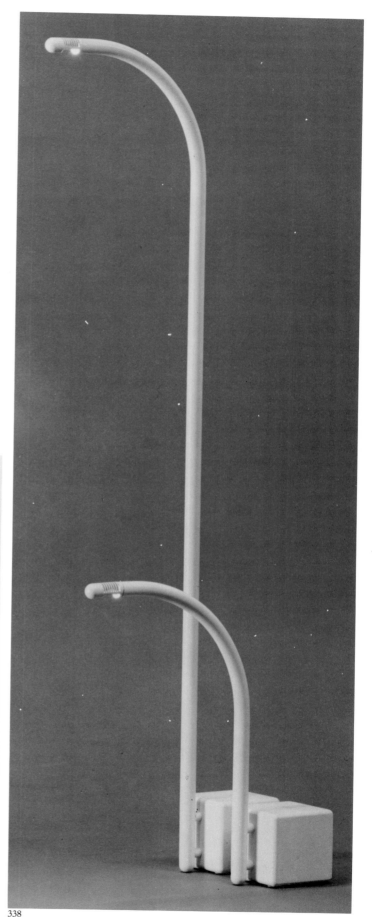

338

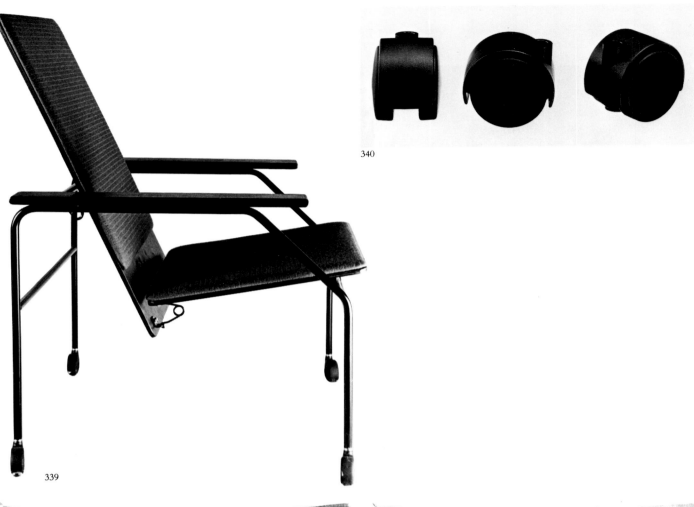

339

340

341

339. Simo Heikkilä (b. 1943) and Yrjö Wiherheimo (b. 1941). *Armchair.* 1980. Finland. Produced by Vivero, Helsinki. Metal, wood, and fabric, 35⅜ × 26 × 26″ (90 × 66 × 66 cm). Vivero Oy, Helsinki

With its unorthodox, frankly industrial appearance and its simplification of manufactured parts, this chair signals an important new trend in Finnish furniture design. Lightweight industrial metal tubing, welded with simple crossbars, forms the support structure; slabs of plywood with rounded corners, held in tension by a safety-pin spring of surprising strength, compose the seat and back, upholstered with thin foam pads. Beyond its functional virtues, the chair is comfortable in use.

340. Jørgen Rasmussen (b. 1931). *Wheel (caster).* 1965. Denmark. Produced by Kevi, Glostrup, 1969. Aluminum and nylon, 2½ × 1¾″ (6.2 × 4.5 cm). Kevi A/S, Glostrup

Rasmussen virtually reinvented the wheel; he substantially increased its flexibility of movement, safety, strength, and stability in this design, now in international use for office and domestic furnishings. Working for both Kevi and Knoll International, Rasmussen has contributed significantly to the development of functionally sound and comfortable furnishings for the modern office.

341. Kirsti Rantanen (b. 1930). *Two Tapestries:* My Soil *and* Bride in My Mind. 1978. Finland. Executed by Aino Käppi/ Helmi Vuorelma. Linen, each 45¼ × 43¼″ (115 × 110 cm). Collection Kirsti Rantanen

Within the past few years, Scandinavia has experienced an important revival in linen weaving, and Rantanen is a notable representative of this trend. Produced as flat double weaves, these tapestries show a reverse image on their backs. The complex patterns, derived from natural forms, suggest windswept fields in constant movement.

342. Svein Gusrud (b. 1944) and Hans Christian Mengshoel (b. 1946). *Chair:* Balans Activ. 1979. Norway. Produced by Håg, Oslo. Steel, plastic, fabric, and foam, 22 × 19¾ × 26¼″ (56 × 50.5 × 66.7 cm). Håg A/S, Oslo

343. Peter Opsvik (b. 1939) and Hans Christian Mengshoel (b. 1946). *Chair:* Balans Variable. 1979. Norway. Produced by Håg, Oslo. Wood, fabric, and foam, 19 × 20 × 28½″ (48 × 51 × 72.5 cm). Håg A/S, Oslo

Probably the most radical and successful of Scandinavian chairs to appear within the past few years, the *Balans* series is based on thorough posture studies. The design encourages the support of body weight on the knees—a position that relieves pressure on the spine—rather than the pelvic area as in ordinary chairs. Produced in several variations and sizes, the line includes rocking versions and others that may also be sat upon in a traditional manner. All of these chairs share simplicity of design, economy of materials, and a conscientious concern for function.

342

343

344

344. Anders Pehrson (b. 1912). *Lighting system:* Supertube. 1972. Sweden. Produced by Ateljé Lyktan, Åhus. Aluminum, length of section 38–144½″ (96.8–367 cm). Ateljé Lyktan AB, Åhus

Supertube affords maximum flexibility in lighting both commercial and domestic environments. The tube sections may be used individually—suspended as direct working lights for desks or tables—or may be assembled in elaborate configurations through the use of specially fabricated connecting joints. This allows the system to follow corners and reach other areas of difficult access.

The second international impulse was the growing interest in primitive cultures. Artifacts from the Orient, Africa, and South America inspired craft objects that contrasted strongly with the sleek, polished products of the United States—yet both share a boldness of design and a forceful character.

A delicate, more refined quality reappeared in crafts about 1980. Thin porcelain was favored over rougher ceramic bodies. Designers of printed materials dropped the bold motifs of the 1970s and returned to a more romantic mode, typically using small, delicate flowers and pastel colors. The crafts have plainly left the 1970s and moved into the 1980s.

The 1970s, marked by a tendency toward division, by a disposition to experiment, by widely divergent trends, are a phase that the Scandinavian applied arts have left behind. The polarization that split industrial designers and artisans into two self-assertive professional groups is a fact. A new spirit of assurance and determination has emerged in the fields of design and crafts, and this spirit has already made itself felt. But for the moment we are just on the threshold.

345. Maria Benktzon (b. 1946) and Sven-Eric Juhlin (b. 1940). *Kitchen knife and cutting board*. 1974. Sweden. Produced by Gustavsberg for Ergonomi Design Group, Stockholm. Plastic and steel, *knife:* length 13⅜″ (34 cm); *cutting board:* diameter 9⅞ × 5⅜″ (25 × 13.6 cm). AB Gustavsberg

Originally planned to fulfill the needs of the manually handicapped, this knife and cutting board have proven their integrity in general use. With its firm grasp, the knife can be easily wielded and controlled, and the cutting board holds a loaf of bread securely in place.

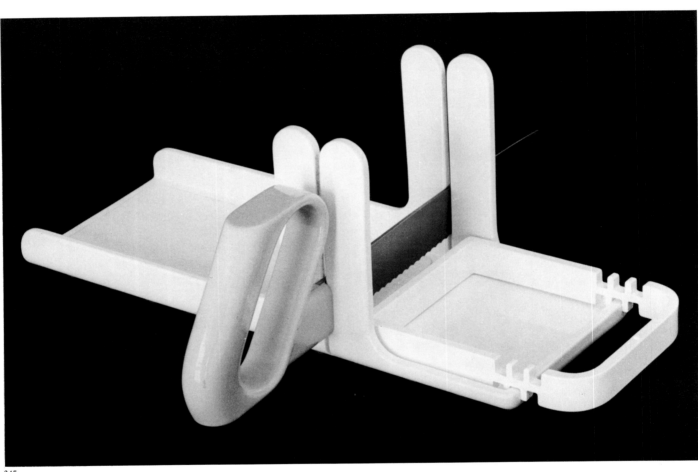

345

346. Ergonomi Design Group. *Tableware*: Eat and Drink. c. 1980. Sweden. Produced by RFSU Rehab, Stockholm. Plastic, metal, and glass, *plate:* diameter 7½″ (19 cm); *glass:* height 6¾″ (17 cm); *fork:* length 8⅝″ (22 cm). RFSU Rehab, Stockholm

Scandinavian designers have always considered the social and ethical responsibilities of design. In this context, contemporary designers turned their attention to the needs of the handicapped. The Ergonomi Design Group, a collaborative organization of several young designers, developed a series of innovative and highly functional utensils—cutlery, plates, and drinking vessels—especially designed for those with impairments that affect the use of the hands. Those who are not impaired can also use the objects efficiently, and this lends the design a dignity that specialized tools often lack.

346

DESIGN TODAY:
NATIONAL POINTS OF VIEW

DANISH DESIGN—TODAY/TOMORROW
Jens Bernsen
Director, M.Sc. EE, Danish Design Council

The lamp, the chair, and the wheel were not invented in Denmark. But Danish designers, by interpreting what these basic tools aspire to be, have created designs that so admirably fulfill their purposes that they are now considered "classics": *The* Lamp (Poul Henningsen, PH 5 Lamp, 1957), *The* Chair (Hans Wegner, 1949), and *The* Wheel (Jørgen Rasmussen, for Kevi, 1968). The fact that many Danish design classics, even those created twenty-five or thirty years ago, sell better than ever is sometimes taken as a sign of stagnation in the world of design. On the contrary, these products have set a standard of simplicity, quality, and truth to their purpose and materials that is difficult to surpass in new designs within the fields traditionally associated with Denmark—lighting, furniture, and everyday tools for the home.

As I see it, an unmistakable vitality underlies the principles of Danish design, and these principles reflect a continuous evolution rather than sudden change. These basic principles are as much alive today as they ever were, and they are being expressed in new areas of industrial creativity. In terms of new products, the design scene in Denmark today is generally dominated by industrial products, that is, by special-ized and often complex equipment for professional use, such as medico-technical machinery, building components, industrial hardware, computers, and production-control equipment.

Despite differences in application and technology, many of these new Danish products share an important quality with traditional Danish designs: they are perceived as rational and natural tools. To me, the demand that the user should identify with his tools is basic. This requirement should be a part of any design plan, which should also include an indication of how this need will be realized in different working situations and over a long product lifetime. Many of the new Danish products may be viewed as proof of the statement that meeting the demand for quality in function will mitigate the necessity to take a special interest in the aesthetics of the product. Beauty will come by itself—from within.

Naturally, working with more and more complex problems has changed the role of the designer, who has become a generalist member of a team of specialists. The designer's skill in identifying the design concept and visualizing the form of the new product is of vital importance, since it is the designer who synthesizes the ideas and expertise that all members of the team bring to the project.

Another tendency recognizable today is that entire 253

companies are becoming design-based. To such companies, good design is not only a goal to strive for but also a tool in itself that permits the goal to be reached. Design is viewed as a function of management, and the company itself as a design assignment in its own right. While this approach includes the products with which the company is concerned, it also extends to the graphics, architecture, production processes, offices, and internal organization of the company.

The industrial world is experiencing a recession at this time, among other reasons because of dwindling natural resources, ecological problems, technological development, social changes, and the alteration of consumer demands. For a design-based company, such problems are not obstacles to progress but stimulants for innovative and creative problem-solving. This may explain why a troubled economic period, in which simplicity, economy, and technical imagination are specially called upon, often gives rise to a rich development in the field of design. It may be happening again at this moment in a small country called Denmark, whose major natural resources continue to be skill, imagination, and a sense of quality.

FINNISH DESIGN TODAY
Dr. Tapio Periäinen
Director, Finnish Society of Crafts and Design

Certain universal facts about objects must be understood if we are to describe accurately the essence and significance of design and appreciate the characteristics of national form and material culture. Every object, work, or product made by man stems from an idea; it thus reflects the maker's personality, cultural background, and social and geographic environment. In any society, all objects designed and made reflect the economic, social, and cultural structure of the community, its values and aspirations. The same can be said for the groups of different objects that constitute material culture and the relationships that necessarily exist among them. At the same time—and alongside architecture and nature—these objects form our physical environment. Objects constitute the part of the environment that is closest to our immediate lives; in addition, every object is an "economic unit" with an investment or exchange value to the individual and to the society as a whole.

In this essay, the term "design" indicates the process by which objects are created and produced and is used, according to Finnish practice, to encompass art handicrafts, the industrial arts, and industrial design.

Finnish design is based on ancient folk traditions which, over the centuries, have developed from the interaction between the ecology of the country and the national character of its people. The significant point to note is that Finnish national culture is quite distinct from the "court cultures" of continental Europe, although influences from both Eastern and Western Europe have been incorporated into the Finnish national tradition after being stripped of the nonessential. Only the vital aspects of foreign cultures have thus been adopted, and this functionally and aesthetically "honed-down" tradition has survived, even despite World War II, because industrialization did not really arrive in Finland until quite recently. It has been claimed that the Finno-Ugric people, of whom the Finns are part, have a relationship with nature unlike that of any other Europeans. They are close to nature and attach great value to it. In the sphere of design this quality manifests itself in an inherent respect for materials and in a prevalence of organic forms. The folk tradition continues to be seen in the relationship between Finnish art handicrafts and industrial design, for the difference between the two is by no means sharply defined. In fact, many designers work simultaneously on art handicrafts and industrial product design.

One of the most prominent features of Finnish design today is the trend toward creating a comprehensive and well-planned environment, one that is not merely aesthetically unified but also suitable for everyone. (It must be admitted that there are large gaps between what we have achieved and what we would like to achieve; nevertheless, a definite trend is discernible.) When national creativity took postwar Finnish design to the very peak of international recognition, it did so specifically in the form of goods for the home, both industrial products and art handicrafts. Later, as industrialization spread, the field widened to cover industrial products for all purposes. Since high and reliable functional and aesthetic standards have been attained in these fields, the present trend is toward solving problems associated with specific areas, for instance, the particular equipment used by various groups in society, from children's toys and aids for old people to special equipment needed by the disabled. Also of importance today are designing the proper working environment, tools, and work clothes and meeting the requirements imposed by Finland's subarctic climate (Finland is at exactly the same latitude as Alaska). The latter need has focused design attention on ice-breakers and ice-reinforced ships; the machinery, equipment, and clothes needed by forest workers; winter clothing in general; and winter sports equipment.

Industrial arts today are represented by what are termed "design-intensive" industrial plants whose products are based on an extremely high standard of design: ceramics, glass, textiles, furniture, and clothing factories. Many firms in Finland are centered around a single design idea or the work of just one designer; thus, designers are given the freedom to put their ideas into practice while at the same time receiving immediate feedback both from others involved in the production process and from the users of their products. Many of these designers have also established a name for themselves outside Finland.

Some young designers have decided to devote themselves to art handicrafts as a way of life. They wish to create objects of beauty with their own hands and to be able to earn their own living in the country, away from the turmoil of urban life.

Like architecture, design has always been of immense significance for cultural and artistic life in Finland: it expresses our national identity in a material form. The national romanticism of the turn of the century was very much a part of Finland's struggle for independence. Once this independence was gained, in 1917, Finland adopted functionalism as its banner. In view of the fact that Finnish design attracted international attention during the difficult years following World War II, it is only natural that the new design should have also won recognition and acceptance here at home. At present, Finnish design embodies tendencies of the "new-old" folk tradition and the new creative design on a national basis as well as a more

anonymous general internationalism. Particularly noteworthy is the direction of design development: toward ways of saving energy and materials, toward forms and aesthetics that give greater flexibility and better serve the emotional needs of modern man, and toward a careful survey of those aspects of the environment and our material culture that have failed to keep abreast of progress. At its best, all the work being done in this field bears the characteristic marks of Finnish design: closeness to nature, an honest and open feel for materials, and a stark simplicity and refined frugality alongside the unrestrained and exuberant joy of creation.

ICELANDIC DESIGN: CONTINUITY AND CHALLENGE
Stefán Snaebjörnsson
Architect and design critic

It is often said that Iceland is a country of contrasts, a feature particularly noticeable in its geography and climate. Oppositions range from searing hot lava boiling up from the center of the earth to icy cold glacial expanses, and from completely calm seas to storms that rage with full power. This environment and the struggle for survival that it imposed over the centuries have played their role in forming the character and life-styles of the Icelanders for more than 1,100 years. They have also left their mark on the creative activities of our artists. Icelandic art, especially painting, may appear somewhat alien at first sight to those who live in milder climes; one must experience nature in Iceland to fully appreciate the vivid contrasts of forms and colors in the works of Icelandic artists.

Iceland was settled in the ninth century by Nordic Vikings and Celts who brought with them the ornamental arts of their homelands. The National Museum of Iceland in Reykjavik contains collections of silver and gold articles, carvings in horn, bone, and wood, and textiles and needlework, all of which illustrate the early Icelanders' efforts to preserve the artistic heritage carried with them from other parts of Scandinavia and the northern world. (These traditional designs were often repeated in materials native to the country.) The development of Icelandic folk arts can 255 be traced from its origins to the middle of the nineteenth century with little difficulty, but after this date the clear line of descent ends. Articles made in Iceland during the decades just before 1900 are extremely rare. This phenomenon is partly explained by the rapidly changing social and economic conditions in the country over the last century, the increased contact between Iceland and other countries, and the importation of mass-produced practical and decorative objects—all of these contributed to the decline of the folk tradition. It is ironic that while the rest of Scandinavia was experiencing a major reawakening within the applied arts, and while efforts were being made to put the heritage of the past to practical use in the present (exemplified by the establishment of crafts associations in Sweden in 1845 and in Finland in 1875), the applied arts of Iceland were entering a period of hibernation. The country was preparing itself for the transformation from a nation of self-sufficient farmers to a population of city-dwellers, and it would not be until much later that the influences that were so strong in the rest of Scandinavia around the turn of the century would be felt in Iceland.

In 1939 the Icelandic School of Applied Art was established by Ludvig Gudmundsson, a man of vision who understood the need for improvements in the arts and in human environments. The world situation at the time prevented many Icelanders from seeking education in the fields of craft and design at schools abroad. The founding of this school was an important landmark in Icelandic art history: the applied arts of Iceland, heretofore diffused and undefined, were brought into sharp focus, and an approach to design theory and practice that was to have a strong influence for years was formulated.

Since 1942 the school has served both fine and applied arts as a major educational force in these fields. Yet Icelanders still go abroad for education in several fields—furniture and industrial design, for instance. The people of this country have always been curious about what lies beyond the horizon; whether this is because of a need to travel inherited from their Viking forefathers or a need to combat the isolation of a small nation in a remote area cannot be determined. Most of the Icelandic designers who have sought education abroad have gone to the other Scandinavian countries, Germany, or Great Britain; some have pursued studies abroad after completing the course of training at the Icelandic school. In either instance, the influences from abroad cannot be underestimated.

Marked progress in Icelandic applied arts and design could be noted only after World War II. Notable artists, such as Gudhmundur Einarsson, a sculptor, had earlier pointed the way. Einarsson studied sculpture and painting in Copenhagen in 1913 and 1914 and in Munich from 1921 to 1926. On his return to Iceland in 1927, he established the first ceramic workshop in the country and experimented there with native Icelandic clays. Other later ceramic craftsmen have followed his lead—Gestur Thorgrimsson and Sigrun Gudjonsdottir, who work as a team, and the sculptor Ragnar Kjartansson, the founder of Glit, Ltd., the only ceramic factory in the country. Today, imported raw materials are used almost exclusively by Icelandic potters because of the expense and difficulty of preparing and mixing the ingredients.

The first native furniture designers in Iceland received their education in Stuttgart in the 1930s. Upon their return, most went directly into production rather than pure design, and their influence was felt more as leading master craftsmen within the industry. Following the war, a new generation of furniture designers and other potential craftsmen and designers studied abroad, especially in Denmark and Sweden, where the applied arts were flourishing. The influence of this group of designers begins to be felt in Iceland during the 1950s and is particularly noteworthy in the field of furniture design. Undoubtedly the most important figure in the field is Sveinn Kjarval, who began his career as a cabinetmaker, in keeping with the Danish tradition of emphasizing practical and technical knowledge as the foundation for design. Kjarval sought to bring older traditions of Icelandic architecture to bear on his designs and often managed to meld a classic Scandinavian look with the traditional feel of an Icelandic turf farmhouse. This effect is seen both in the construction of his pieces and in his use of materials—his favorite wood was pine and he often used calfskin or specially woven Icelandic wool for upholstery.

In 1960–61 and in 1968, the Association of Furniture

and Interior Designers held important exhibitions that were unique in the history of Icelandic design in that only prototypes and models of furniture were shown. This was an attempt to forge a pathway into the relatively conservative production lines of the furniture industry. Some of the designs shown were striking; the participating designers had been students of leading Scandinavian furniture designers, and their work showed this training. However bold the idea of these exhibitions, the results were disappointing in terms of the industry as a whole. Only a handful of designs were put into production, but some of these have proven successful and are today still manufactured. Current designers, led by such innovators as Petur Luthersson and Gunnar Magnusson, are still attempting to increase the influence of design within the industry.

The wool industry in Iceland has an age-old heritage. As early as the tenth century, woolen textiles were the most important export of the country, and this remained true until about 1300. Even today, the wool industry is still a major commodity in Iceland's international commerce as one of the leading export industries. The textile craft has been vital in Iceland for centuries, and in recent years a great deal of energy has been directed toward tapestry and textile weaving in the studio and in fashion design for the garment industry. The younger textile designers are also beginning to work with printed textiles, although at present this new field is limited to studio production. For several years, the Textile Association has participated in the Nordic Textile Triennale. This cooperation with other Scandinavian countries has contributed to the distinguished reputation of Icelandic textiles today, and the works of leading figures such as Asgerdur Buadottir are known internationally.

Like textiles, metalwork has a long and honored tradition in Iceland. That the craft survived until the present century is due largely to the design of the Icelandic woman's national costume, which is richly decorated with silver and gold filigree ornaments. Icelandic metalsmiths today have preserved the highly developed manual skills required for the fashioning of these ornaments, but they have departed from traditional forms and techniques. Sculptural or ab-

stract forms are dominant in Icelandic metalwork, as is evident in the work of Jens Gudhjonsson, who today must be considered the Nestor of Icelandic silversmiths. His work reflects the ease with which only the true master of materials and techniques is able to work.

Iceland now has its first studio glass artist in the person of Sigrun Olöf Einarsdottir. This development indicates that the applied arts and design are becoming an important aspect of Icelandic culture. Furthermore, it is evident that young designers in Iceland are using the nature and heritage of this country in the attainment of their creative goals, and, needless to say, are willing to work hard to develop their own particular art or craft.

The most important task now facing Icelandic artists and designers is to consolidate their efforts to establish wider national and international contacts and to foster cooperation with the manufacturing industries in order that their talents may be exercised. The end result—influencing positively the design of objects and environments—is well worth the effort.

GLIMPSES OF RECENT NORWEGIAN DESIGN HISTORY
Rolf Himberg-Larsen
Director, Landsforbundet Norsk Brukskunst

From 1918, when the Norwegian arts and crafts organization was officially founded, until 1970, the nation's combined forces of art and craft cooperated in a mutually beneficial relationship. Artisans and industrial and interior designers worked jointly under an umbrella organization, the Foreningen Brukskunst, later known as the Landsforbundet Norsk Brukskunst (LNB; Norwegian Society of Arts and Crafts and Industrial Design). It was customary for many of the artisans who belonged to this organization to work independently in the creation of unique studio works and also to design for production in industry; both roles were seen as aspects of the same process of design. Interior designers cooperated with artisans and industrial designers to create better everyday products and improved living environments; in these efforts, the comprehensive approach toward design issues fostered an increased understanding and respect for quality in design and production and a vital aesthetic sensibility. Aesthetics, in fact, became a key word in the language of design. Throughout the decades prior to the 1970s, the LNB arranged a great number of arts and crafts exhibitions which featured examples of industrial designs for everyday use as well as studio craft, and these exhibitions had a great impact in generating public interest in the various fields of design. The LNB was the recipient of regular appropriations from the Ministry of Industry as a free and independent organization that could serve as a connecting link between the producers and the consumers of domestic products.

However, developments during the decade of the 1970s disrupted this cooperative pattern. Specialization entered the picture in the fields of the fine arts, crafts, and design, as it did in many others. Almost simultaneously in all the Nordic countries, changes took place focusing on the restructuring of the educational system that provided training for craftsmen and designers. As a result, design activity was demarcated into a group of separate, highly independent specialties, each of which maintained its own profile, standards, and goals. These developments brought the craftspeople nearer to the realm of the fine arts and away from industry, and moved the designers into a closer alignment with the engineering fields that are such an important part of industry.

In the opinion of many people this has been a necessary process that has produced notable results. For artisans in particular, the "breaking away" process has led to an important change in role and status that has positive indications for the future. A new Norwegian cultural policy, formulated during this critical decade, now classifies artisans and those in the "fine" arts as one entity, and both groups benefit from the supportive legislation of the Ministry of Cultural and Scientific Affairs, which aids the arts. This new Norwegian cultural policy is unique and extremely progressive.

The industrial designers have likewise made progress during the past decade, both in their education and training and in their enhanced relationship with industrial institutions. The results of this new relationship cannot be fully evaluated at this point, but future plans for the field are more consistently directed than ever before, and a new commitment to the progress of design can certainly be recognized.

The segregation of design activities may be partially due to a generational change: it is the younger generation of artists and designers that has brought about this "revolution." The older generation has not been fully in agreement with this separation of the fields, and many have remained dedicated to the concept of "brukskunst," since they feel that it is more important now than ever to stand together in interdisciplinary cooperation. There are also critics who assert that an inordinate amount of politics and self-promotion in the arts and crafts is detrimental to the quality of the work.

LNB has followed these developments with great attention and concern—sometimes with skepticism, sometimes with admiration. We have accepted the changes that have taken place and will work toward creating a new climate of cooperation in which the partners can be encouraged to participate in joint efforts.

LNB is now establishing a comprehensive design center in Oslo where artisans, industrial designers, interior designers, and textile, clothing, and graphic designers can maintain their own offices. In this center there will also be meeting space, which may encourage cooperative efforts in a number of important projects as well as facilitating the independent endeavors of each group.

There are many signs indicating that a new cooperation in the arts, crafts, and design is developing and that shared expertise will again become an important aspect of design history. Perhaps more than ever before, we need creative forces within Norwegian industry today—not only the industrial designer who will be furnishing our environments during the eighties and nineties, but also the artisan who can create industrial products with "soul" and not simply technological content. As our Finnish colleague Tapio Periäinen has eloquently stated "handicraft and design are one and the same thing."

BETTER EVERYDAY GOODS AND A NEW SENSUALITY: SOME THOUGHTS ON SWEDISH DESIGN

Lennart Lindkvist
Director, Föreningen Svensk Form

When the Boilerhouse Project opened in London in 1981, with an exhibition entitled "Art and Industry," the Swedish pioneers of design were given a prominent place. In Sweden, however, many people were asking "Has Swedish industrial design really played such an important role in the history of design?"

Through our work at the Föreningen Svensk Form (Swedish Society of Crafts and Design), we receive ample proof of the enormous international impact of Swedish design—not only in the past, but also in the present. After all the triumphs of Swedish design in exhibitions abroad, one can see that we are maintaining our position in the field of design and that the design situation in Sweden is indeed healthy and flourishing. In contrast to this point of view is another, expressed in the mass media in Sweden: "Swedish design has lost its world reputation. Where have the 'better everyday goods' gone? How can crafts survive?"

The advantage of working within an organization which, since 1845, has been an active proponent of good-quality Swedish products is that one does not lack a rich and vital sense of history. Sometimes, in fact, this venerable and distinguished history of design success can become somewhat burdensome, and there occurs a reaction against tradition. The "revolution" in the universities during the late 1960s had repercussions in the field of design and in the education and training of new designers. One result was that both crafts and industrial design were challenged and the authority of tradition viewed with suspicion. As one industrialist noted, "Sweden lost a whole generation of designers in the 1970s."

At the same time there was an unmistakable renaissance in the crafts, involving a renewed interest in handmade, one-of-a-kind objects, both functional and nonfunctional. Those who left the crafts and design schools in Sweden often started their own workshops. Within a short time, many of this new generation of craftspeople and designers faced severe economic difficulties, but they continued to be highly suspicious of industry as an employer. The schools of crafts and design widened this gulf between design students and industry, since their instruction was primarily concerned with individual creativity in the crafts and the pursuit of "free" art, liberated from the demands of industrial or production design. During the late 1970s, the split within the fields of design affected industrial designers who, with their technical background, were further separated from the independent craftsmen. The differences between these two groups have become even more distinct in the past few years.

Parallel with these developments within the field of design were changes within industry itself. Sweden's industrial arts—including glass, porcelain, textiles, and furniture—have grappled with major problems of their own, both economic and structural. The number of Swedish industrial companies has declined dramatically in the recent past, and the number of designers employed by them has fallen accordingly.

I feel that when we reach the mid-1980s, we will go through a period of transition, full of potential and promise for the future but characterized by many conflicting trends.

For instance, craftsmen have been forming joint sales organizations and exhibition facilities in order to survive, and many of these ventures have proven highly successful. They have also organized within their own ranks and become active lobbyists for state and local government support; their demands have included not only special grants-in-aid for individuals but also support to establish crafts centers and to mount crafts exhibitions that will tour throughout the country.

It seems as if changes are noticeable within the schools of crafts and design as well. It is true that the old belief still persists that crafts and industrial design are mutually enriching fields. In contrast to this view is that taken, for example, by the School of Crafts and Design at the University of Göteborg, which for several years has maintained separate departments for design and crafts. The Swedish School of Fine Arts, Crafts, and Design in Stockholm has also established a new department of industrial design. In addition, 259 this institution is planning a postgraduate product research and development facility, which will provide a necessary channel for contact between the schools, the designers, and industry.

The economic slump in Swedish industry has forced companies to analyze and reevaluate their products. We at the Föreningen Svensk Form have seen how product analysis has in many cases revitalized belief in the importance of good design, and this has indirectly encouraged us in the pursuit of our goals. We often hear that only through good design and high standards of technical quality can Swedish industry maintain itself amidst international competition, and such sentiments are pertinent to the Föreningen Svensk Form's own reasons for existence.

This renewed belief in the importance of design, apparent in the schools and among craftsmen and designers, appears as well within industrial organizations and even in the National Industrial Board, which recently organized a committee to consider the needs for state aid to industrial design.

The Föreningen Svensk Form has also witnessed a new interest in reopening our design center in Stockholm, one whose activities and services will be comparable to those already provided at the innovative design center operated by the Society in Malmö. We have received support and encouragement in this plan from numerous professional design and crafts organizations and from many manufacturers and consumer groups.

For some years, the Föreningen Svensk Form has been working on a research project with the National Board for Consumer Policies. We wish to reaffirm in this project the philosophy of design expressed in the landmark 1917 exhibition sponsored by the Society and in its keynote phrase *Vackrare vardagsvara* (more beautiful everyday goods). At the same time we are trying to enrich the understanding of the concept of "good design" and to expand the traditional idea of quality to include issues that go well beyond function and form. This comprehensive view means that products are well made in a humane and pleasant working environment, produced without wasting valuable and irreplaceable natural and human resources, and sold at reasonable prices to satisfy real needs.

While this is being written, at the beginning of 1982, a major exhibition entitled "Design and Tradition in Sweden" is about to open at the Röhss Museum of Arts and Crafts in Göteborg. The exhibition traces developments in the crafts and industrial design since the 1890s and also, importantly, gives students in the schools of crafts and design an opportunity to illustrate how they view today's design situation and what they envision for the future. Two major categories of intention are used in the exhibition: *Poetic Functionalism* and *Visions of the New Sensuality*. Might these be the mottoes of design in the 1980s? There does seem to be a dream of enriching functional industrial design with a new artistic sensibility. In Sweden, which has firm roots in functionalism and socio-esthetic ideals, we may find in the coming decade that designers are able to impart a new poetic and sensual dimension to necessary everyday goods.

It is certainly exciting to observe and participate in all the current design developments in Sweden.

BIOGRAPHICAL NOTES

Note: Country of birth is included within the parentheses. If the artist worked in a different country, its name appears outside the parentheses. Full details of exhibition catalogues are given in the Bibliography.

The following abbreviations are used:

ART SCHOOLS AND COLLEGES

Denmark AA, Copenhagen: Academy of Architecture (Kunstakademiets Arkitektskole)

IT, Copenhagen: Institute of Technology (Teknologisk Institut)

RDA, Copenhagen: Royal Danish Academy of Fine Arts (Det Kongelige Danske Kunstakademi)

SAA, Copenhagen: School of Applied Arts (Skolen for Brugskunst, formerly Det Tekniske Selskabs Skoler)

SAC, Copenhagen: School of Arts and Crafts (Kunsthåndværkerskolen)

TU, Copenhagen: Technical University of Denmark (Danmarks Tekniske Højskole)

Finland CSI, Helsinki: Central School of Industrial Design (Taideteollinen Korkeakoulu)

HUT, Helsinki: Helsinki University of Technology (Helsingin Teknillinen Korkeakoulu)

Iceland CAC, Reykjavik: Icelandic College of Arts and Crafts (Myndlista -og Handidaskoli Islands)

Norway CAD, Bergen: Bergen College of Art and Design (Bergens Kunsthåndverksskole)

NAFA, Oslo: National Academy of Fine Art (Statens Kunstakademi)

NCAD, Oslo: National College of Art and Design (Statens Håndverks -og Kunstindustriskole)

Sweden RAAS, Stockholm: Royal Academy Art School (Kungliga Konsthögskolan)

RIT, Stockholm: Royal Institute of Technology (Kungliga Tekniska Högskolan)

SAC, Göteborg: School of Arts and Crafts, now School of Industrial Design (Konstindustriskolan)

SACD, Stockholm: Swedish State School of Arts, Crafts and Design (Konstfackskolan)

EXHIBITIONS

DS: "Design in Scandinavia," U.S., 1954–57
H 55: Hälsingborg, 1955
FE: "Finnish Exhibition," West Germany, 1956–57
NF: "Neue Form aus Dänemark," Germany, 1956–59
FS: "Formes Scandinaves," Paris, 1958
AD: "The Arts of Denmark," U.S., 1960–61
Fi: "Finlandia," Zurich, Amsterdam, London, 1961
GJ: "Georg Jensen Silversmithy 77 Artists 75 Years," Washington, D.C., 1980
MT: Milan Triennale

The following are international exhibitions, indicated by city and year:

Barcelona 1929
Brussels 1910, 1935, 1958
Chicago 1893 (World's Columbian)
Montreal 1967
New York 1939
Paris 1889, 1900, 1925 (Arts Décoratifs et Industriels Modernes), 1937 (Arts et Techniques), 1938
St. Louis 1904 (Louisiana Purchase)
San Francisco 1915 (Panama-Pacific), 1939 (Golden Gate)
Stockholm 1897 (Art and Industry), 1930

AABERG, GUNHILD *(b. 1939, Denmark)*. *Ceramics*. Graduated SAC, Copenhagen, 1964. Formed workshop, Strandstraede Keramik, with Jane Reumert and Beate Andersen in Copenhagen. Also designs for Royal Copenhagen Porcelain Manufactory and Dansk Designs. Exhibited "Dansk Kunsthaandvaerk," Stockholm and Hälsingborg, 1975; "Dansk Miljø," Eastern Europe, 1975–77; Det Danske Kunstindustrimuseum, Copenhagen, 1976, 1977; Nordenfjeldske Kunstindustrimuseum, Trondheim, 1981; "Danish Ceramic Design," University Park, Pa., 1981.

AALTO, ALVAR *(1898–1976, Finland)*. *Architecture, interior design, furniture*. Graduated HUT, Helsinki, 1921 (architecture). Own architecture office from 1923. Founded Artek, Helsinki, along with Aino Aalto, Nils-Gustaf Hahl, and Maire Gullichsen 1933. Professor at Massachusetts Institute of Technology (MIT) 1940–49. Extensive architectural commissions. Also designed lighting fixtures, textiles, and glass. Received numerous awards including honorary doctorate Princeton University, 1947; Royal Gold Medal of Architecture, Great Britain, 1957; first, second, and third prizes Finnish Pavilion Competition, New York 1939; first and second prizes (shared with A. Ervi and V. Rewell) Finnish Pavilion Competition, Paris 1937. Numerous exhibitions include Museum of Modern Art, New York, 1938; DS; H 55; FS; Fi. Member of the Finnish Academy. See Bibliography for monographs.

ACKE, JOHAN AXEL GUSTAF *(1859–1924, Sweden). Furniture.* Educated RAAS, Stockholm, 1876–81 (painting); studied in Paris and Italy. Although primarily a painter all of his life, he also designed furniture in the Art Nouveau mode about the turn of the century.

ACKING, CARL-AXEL *(b. 1910, Sweden). Architecture, furniture.* Educated SACD, Stockholm, and RIT, Stockholm. Has maintained his own design studio since 1939. Taught at SACD, Stockholm, and the Lund Institute of Technology (Tekniska Högskolan i Lund). One of designers of H 55. Designer of Swedish Embassy, Tokyo, and interior designer for ships of the North Star Line. Has designed furniture for Kooperativa Förbundet, Stockholm; Nordiska Kompaniet, Stockholm; and Svenska Möbelfabrikerna, Bodafors. Also designs wallpaper, textiles, and lighting fixtures. Awarded Lunning Prize 1952. Exhibited MTs, Paris 1937, New York 1939, "Lunning Prize Winners Exhibition," New York, 1956.

ADLERCREUTZ, MARIA *(b. 1936, Sweden). Textiles.* Established own workshop 1971–72, weaving textiles, many of which document political events.

ANDERSEN, HANS MUNCK *(b. 1943, Denmark). Ceramics.* Educated SAC, Copenhagen, 1968, and AA, Copenhagen, 1972–73. Designer for Royal Copenhagen Porcelain Manufactory 1968–71. Own workshop at Rø, Bornholm, since 1973. One-man shows at Royal Copenhagen Porcelain 1968, 1971. Exhibitions include Hetjen Museum, Düsseldorf, 1970; "Concorso Internazionale della Ceramica," Faenza, 1971, 1976; Bornholms Museum 1975, 1981; Galerie Inart, Amsterdam, 1979; "Danish Design Cavalcade," Det Danske Kunstindustrimuseum, Copenhagen, 1980; "Danish Ceramic Design," University Park, Pa., 1981.

ÄNGMAN, JACOB *(1876–1942, Sweden). Metalwork.* Educated RIT, Stockholm, 1893 and part time 1896–1903. Worked at Otto Meyer Bronze Casters 1896–98; Stockholm bronze foundry of C. G. Hallberg 1899; and with Otto Bommer, a metal sculptor in Berlin, 1903–4. Managed the engraving, casting, and metalwork department of Elmquist of Stockholm 1904–7. Joined Guldsmedsaktiebolaget, Stockholm, in 1907, became its artistic director and remained with them until 1942. Worked with Gunnar Asplund on St. Peter's Church, Malmö, 1919–20. Exhibitions include the Baltic Exhibition, Malmö, 1914; Metropolitan Museum of Art, New York, 1927; memorial exhibition Nationalmuseum, Stockholm, 1942.

ÅSE, ARNE *(b. 1940, Norway). Ceramics.* Educated CAD, Bergen. Teacher at NCAD, Oslo, from 1965, presently head of ceramic department. Own workshop from 1965, working with porcelain and stoneware.

ASPLUND, (ERIK) GUNNAR *(1885–1940, Sweden). Architecture, furniture.* Educated RAAS, Stockholm. Started own architecture firm 1909, working mainly on small houses. Chief architect, Stockholm 1930. Also designed furniture for Nordiska Kompaniet, Stockholm. Exhibitions include Liljevalchs Art Gallery, Stockholm, 1917; Paris 1925.

AURDAL, SYNNØVE ANKER *(b. 1908, Norway). Textiles.* Independent studio artist. Has worked with appliqué and designed her own weavings since the early 1940s, employing traditional techniques to create abstract patterns.

AXELSSON, ÅKE *(b. 1932, Sweden). Furniture.* Furniture designer for AB Herbert Andersson, Gärsnäs, and teacher.

AXÉN, GUNILA *(b. 1941, Sweden). Textiles.* Designed printed fabrics for Kooperativa Förbundet, Stockholm. Member of 10-Gruppen (Group of Ten Designers) since 1971.

BÄCKSTRÖM, OLOF *(b. 1922, Finland). Metalwork.* Studied independently. Cutlery designer for Oy Fiskars, Helsinki, since 1958. Also designs utility goods and metal tools. Awarded silver medals MT 1957, 1960. Exhibited FS; Fi.

BANG, JACOB E. *(1899–1965, Denmark). Architecture, glass, metalwork, ceramics.* Studied sculpture. Educated RDA, Copenhagen (architecture). Industrial designer at Holmegaard glassworks 1925–42, artistic director there in 1928. From 1957 artistic director of Kastrup glassworks. Free-lance designer for Nymølle

faience factory, Pan Aluminium, and F. Hingelberg, silversmith. Exhibited MTs; DS; NF; FS; AD.

BAUER, LISA *(b. 1920, Sweden). Glass, graphics.* Educated SAC, Göteborg, and SACD, Stockholm, 1937–42. Free-lance designer for Kosta Boda since 1969, specializing in engraved designs for Sigurd Persson's glass. Exhibitions include "Adventure in Swedish Glass," Australia, 1975.

BENKTZON, MARIA *(b. 1946, Sweden). Industrial design.* Specializes in designs for the handicapped. Since 1971 works for the Ergonomi Design Group, Stockholm.

BERGH, ELIS *(1881–1954, Sweden). Glass, metalwork.* Designer of unique and utility glass for Kosta from 1929, artistic director there until 1950.

BERGSLIEN, GRO (SOMMERFELDT) *(b. 1940, Norway). Textiles, glass.* Educated NCAD, Oslo. Studied weaving and printing in Amsterdam. Textile designer at Plus, Fredrikstad. Glass designer at Hadeland glassworks since 1964.

BERGSTEN, CARL *(1879–1935, Sweden). Architecture, furniture.* Educated RASA, Stockholm, 1901–3 (architecture). Architect and furniture designer for buildings at the Norrköping Exhibition, 1906. Director of Nordiska Kompaniet furniture department, Stockholm.

BERNADOTTE, SIGVARD *(b. 1907, Sweden). Metalwork, industrial design.* Son of King Gustavus VI Adolphus of Sweden, and brother of Ingrid, queen mother of Denmark. Educated RAAS, Stockholm, from 1929. Designed for Georg Jensen, Copenhagen, from 1930. Partner with Acton Bjørn of industrial design firm Bernadotte & Bjørn, Copenhagen and Stockholm, since 1939. Member of Board of Directors of Georg Jensen Sølvsmedie. Exhibited GJ.

BINDESBØLL, THORVALD *(1846–1908, Denmark). Ceramics, furniture, metalwork, textiles.* Educated as an architect. Became leading designer in many fields around the turn of the century. Employed at Københavns Lervarefabrik ceramics factory during the 1890s. Developed a highly personal expressionistic style that permeated all of his work.

BJÖRQUIST, KARIN *(b. 1927, Sweden). Ceramics.* Educated SACD, Stockholm. Assistant to Wilhelm Kåge at Gustavsberg. Designer there from 1950, artistic director since 1978. Inherited Kåge's studio at Gustavsberg after his death in 1960. Awarded gold medal MT 1954, Lunning Prize 1963.

BLOCK-HELLUM, CHARLOTTE *(b. 1911, Germany). Norway. Ceramics, metalwork, enamel.* Educated at the applied art academies of Dresden and Berlin (pottery). Own workshop in Oslo since 1946. In recent decades has specialized in enameling.

BOBERG, ANNA KATARINA *(1864–1935, Sweden). Ceramics, glass, textiles.* Designed ceramics for Rörstrand, Lidköping, and multicolored art glass for Reijmyre glassworks, Rejmyra, 1900–1902. Textile designer for Handarbetets Vännar. Wife of architect and designer Ferdinand Boberg.

BOJESEN, KAY *(1886–1958, Denmark). Metalwork, wood.* Trained at Georg Jensen, Copenhagen, 1907–10, and Royal Craft School of Precious Metals, Württemberg, 1911. Worked as craftsman in Paris and Copenhagen. Own workshop in Copenhagen since 1913. Art consultant for Bing & Grøndahl, Copenhagen, 1930–31. Designed stainless steel for Motala Verkstad, Sweden, and Universal Steel Co. In 1952 awarded appointment as silversmith to the king. Also internationally recognized as designer of children's toys. Awarded Grand Prix MT 1951, gold medal and *diplôme d'honneur* 1954. One-man show Det Danske Kunstindustrimuseum, Copenhagen, 1938. Exhibitions include Paris 1925; New York 1939; MT 1941; DS; NF; FS; AD.

BONDERUP, CLAUS *(b. 1943, Denmark). Lighting fixtures.* Has designed lighting fixtures for Focus Belysning, Holte.

BORG, OLLI *(1921–1979, Finland). Interior design, furniture.* Educated CSI, Helsinki, and abroad. Interior designer for Te-Ma Ltd. 1947–50, Viljo Rewell 1950–54, and Askon Tehtaat Oy, Lahtis, 1954–57, 1964–67. Head of industrial design department CSI, Helsinki, 1956. Maintained own design studio. Exhibited MT 1954; DS; FS.

BRANDT, ÅSA (b. 1940, Sweden). Glass. Educated SACD, Stockholm, 1962–67; Gerrit Rietveld Akademie, Amsterdam, 1967; and Royal College of Art, London, 1967. Own workshop in Torshälla since 1968. Along with Ulla Forsell, Eva Ullberg, and Anders Wingård started independent studio cooperative called Freeblowers. One-woman exhibitions include Varbergs Museum, Sweden, 1970; Konsthantverkarna, Stockholm, 1972, 1978, 1981. Group exhibitions include Swedish Design Center, Malmö, 1969; "International Studio Glass," traveling exhibition in Europe, 1975–79; National Museum of Modern Art, Tokyo, Kyoto, Japan, 1980; "Scandinavian Glass," Habatat Galleries, U.S., 1980; Haaretz Museum, Tel Aviv, Israel, 1982. Member of Konsthantverkarna, Stockholm.

BREIDFJORD, LEIFUR (b.1945, Iceland). Stained glass, textiles. Stained- and flat-glass artist. Also designs textiles in collaboration with his wife, Sigridur Johannsdottir.

BRØRBY, SEVERIN (b. 1932, Norway). Glass. Educated NCAD, Oslo. Trained as engraver. Designer at Hadeland glassworks, Jevnaker, since 1956.

BRUMMER, ARTTU (1891–1951, Finland). Interior design, glass. Teacher of composition, furniture design, and heraldry at CSI, Helsinki, director there 1944–51. Curator of Museum of Crafts and Design, Helsinki. Own interior design office from 1913. Designer for Riihimäki glassworks. Awarded diplôme d'honneur Paris 1937. Editor of Domus magazine during the 1930s. Chairman of ORNAMO (Finnish Association of Designers); member of Administrative Board of Finnish Industrial Design Association; member of the Board of Directors of Friends of Finnish Handicraft.

BRYK, RUT (b. 1916, Finland). Ceramics. Educated CSI, Helsinki. Engaged by Arabia, Helsinki, since 1942. Awarded Grand Prix MT 1951, diplôme d'honneur 1954. First Finnish woman to receive the order of Commandeur dans l'Ordre des Arts et des Lettres from the French Ministry of Culture and Communication 1980. Exhibited MT 1957, 1960; DS; FS; H 55; FE.

BUADOTTIR, ASGERDUR ESTER (b. 1920, Iceland). Textiles. Icelandic textile artist. Participated in numerous international exhibitions and received many awards.

BÜLOW-HÜBE, TORUN (b. 1927, Sweden). Metalwork. Educated SACD, Stockholm. Designer for Georg Jensen, Copenhagen, since 1967. Own workshop in Stockholm 1951–60; Paris and Germany from 1960; and Indonesia since 1978. Awarded gold medal MT 1960 and Lunning Prize 1960. Exhibited GJ.

CARLSSON, DANIEL JOHAN (1853–1922, Sweden). Furniture, ceramics. Designed Viking revival style of decoration for Gustavsberg, working with August Malmström and Magnus Isaeus.

CHRISTENSEN, KARI (b. 1938, Norway). Ceramics. Educated NCAD, Oslo (ceramics). Engaged by Royal Copenhagen Porcelain Manufactory 1961–66. Own workshop in Oslo since 1966.

CYRÉN, GUNNAR (b. 1931, Sweden). Glass, metalwork. Trained as silversmith in Gävle. Educated SACD, Stockholm, and Kölner Werkschule, Cologne. At Orrefors since 1959. Independent silversmith. Awarded Society for Industrial Design's Medal for Proficiency and Industry 1956, Lunning Prize 1966.

DAHL, BIRGER (b. 1916, Norway). Interior decoration, lighting fixtures. Educated NCAD, Oslo. Designer of lighting fixtures at Sønnico Fabrikker, Oslo, 1944–59. Also designs wallpaper. Consultant for Vallø wallpaper factory. Senior faculty member at NCAD since 1947.

DAHL, EMIL FERDINAND (1819–1879, Denmark). Metalwork. Designed jewelry in the Viking revival style.

DAVID-ANDERSEN, ARTHUR (1875–1970, Norway). Metalwork. Son of David Andersen, founder of David Andersen, Oslo. Artistic director of family firm 1901–52. Designed mainly in earlier and later part of career. Awarded gold medal MT 1954.

DAVID-ANDERSEN, IVAR (b. 1903, Norway). Metalwork. Apprentice in family goldsmith workshop. Educated NCAD, Oslo. Studied sculpture with Ossip Zadkine, Paris. Began designing in the late 1920s; from the late 1930s, was occupied mainly with management of family firm, whose artistic development he

strongly influenced, especially when he became its sole director in 1952.

DITZEL, NANNA (b. 1923, Denmark). Metalwork, furniture, textiles, ceramics. Educated SAC, Copenhagen. Established with her husband, Jørgen Ditzel (1921–1961), own design firm 1946. Engaged by Georg Jensen, Copenhagen, since 1954. Own design office and showroom in London since 1970. Awarded first prize Goldsmiths' Guild Competition 1950, Lunning Prize 1956, gold medal MT 1960. Exhibited GJ.

DYSTHE, SVEN IVAR (b. 1931, Norway). Interior design, furniture. Trained as cabinetmaker. Educated Royal College of Art, London (industrial design). Chief designer for Sønnico Fabrikker, Oslo, 1944–60. Awarded International Design Award of American Institute of Designers.

ECKHOFF, TIAS (b. 1926, Norway). Ceramics, metalwork. Educated NCAD, Oslo (ceramics). Studied ceramics with Nathalie Krebs at Saxbo, Copenhagen. Designer at Porsgrund porcelain factory from 1949, artistic director there from 1953. Designer in metal for Georg Jensen, Copenhagen, and Norsk Stålpress, Bergen. Awarded two prizes for decorative and utility glass Hadelands competition 1951; first prize for silver cutlery in Georg Jensen's inter-Scandinavian competition 1953; Lunning Prize 1953; two gold medals MT 1954, two gold medals 1957, gold medal 1960; Norwegian ID Prize 1962, 1965, 1966. Exhibited "Lunning Prize Winner Exhibition," New York, 1956; GJ.

EINARSDOTTIR, SIGRUN (b. 1952, Iceland). Glass. Trained in Denmark. Has recently established the first glass workshop in Iceland. As independent artist produces unique works, and has designed production glassware.

EINARSSON, GUDHMUNDUR (1895–1963, Iceland). Ceramics. Studied in Munich 1921–26. Established, in Reykjavik, first ceramic workshop in Iceland, 1927. Exhibited New York 1939. Leading figure in the development of native Icelandic ceramic tradition.

EKHOLM, KURT (1907–1975, Finland). Ceramics. Artistic director of Arabia, Helsinki, 1932–48. Organized Arabia Museum from factory collection in 1943. Engaged by Rörstrand, Lidköping, 1949–50. After 1950 taught ceramics in Göteborg.

ENGBERG, GABRIEL (1872–1953, Finland). Textiles. Studied with Akseli Gallen-Kallela. Designed textiles for the Friends of Finnish Handicraft, notably those for Paris 1900.

ENGELHARDT, VALDEMAR (1869–1915, Denmark). Ceramics. Chemical engineer. Engaged as technical manager in 1891 by Royal Copenhagen Porcelain Manufactory, where he developed an important series of crystalline glazes that became a standard feature of the factory's art production.

ENGLUND, EVA (b. 1937, Sweden). Glass, ceramics. Began designing glass 1964. Worked for Pukeberg. Engaged by Orrefors since 1974, where she is particularly known for her use of the graal technique. Also works in ceramics. Exhibitions include "Adventure in Swedish Glass," Australia, 1975.

ENGØ, BJØRN (1920–1981, Norway). Interior design, enamel, furniture, textiles. Educated NCAD, Oslo. Worked independently from 1948 and on a free-lance basis for production. Designed furniture, lighting fixtures, textiles, and domestic wares in aluminum, but mostly known for works in enameled copper.

ERIKSSON, ALGOT (1868–1930, Sweden). Ceramics. Educated technical school, Stockholm, 1882–89, and in Denmark, Germany, and France. At Rörstrand, Lidköping, from the 1880s to 1920. Specialized in underglaze painting and relief decoration.

ESKOLIN-NURMESNIEMI, VUOKKO (b. 1930, Finland). Textiles. Educated CSI, Helsinki (ceramics). At first worked in ceramics and glass. Designed prints and woven textiles for Marimekko, Helsinki. Established her own firm, Vuokko, in Helsinki in 1964. Awarded gold metal MT 1957 and Lunning Prize 1964.

FINCH, ALFRED WILLIAM (1854–1930, Brussels). Finland. Ceramics. Studied painting at Academy of Art in Brussels, 1878–80, and ceramics at Boch Frères at La Louviéres, Belgium. Among the founders of Belgian avant-garde group Les Vingt, 1884. Settled in Finland in late 1890s. Head of ceramic department at Iris Factory, Porvoo, 1897. After Iris closed in the early 1900s, he taught ceramics at CSI, Helsinki.

FISKER, KAY (1893–1965, Denmark). *Architecture, furniture, metalwork.* Graduated AA, Copenhagen, 1920; professor there 1936–63. Designed in metal for A. Michelsen, Copenhagen. Also designed furniture and book covers. Awards include gold medal Ghent 1921, Eckersberg Medal 1928, C. F. Hansen Medal 1947. One-man shows Charlottenborg 1934; Paris 1949; London 1950; Charlottenborg and Århus 1953. Exhibitions include Paris 1925.

FORSELL, ULLA (b. 1944, Sweden). *Glass.* Educated SACD, Stockholm, and Gerrit Rietveld Akademie, Amsterdam. Worked at Orrefors. Own workshop in Stockholm since 1975. Along with Åsa Brandt, Eva Ullberg, and Anders Wingård started independent studio called Freeblowers. Numerous exhibitions in Sweden and abroad.

FRANCK, KAJ (b. 1911, Finland). *Textiles, ceramics, glass.* Educated CSI, Helsinki. Teacher there since 1945 and art director since 1960. Textile designer for Te-Ma Ltd. 1933–37, United Woollens 1937–39. Since 1945 designer at Arabia, Helsinki, and Nuutajärvi-Notsjö, artistic director of latter in 1950. Engaged by Iittala 1946–49. Design executive of Wärtsilä, Helsinki, from 1950. MT awards: gold medal 1951, *diplôme d'honneur* 1954, Grand Prix 1957. Awarded Lunning Prize 1955, Fulbright Scholarship 1955, Compasso d'Oro 1957, Prince Eugen Medal 1964. Exhibitions include Göteborg 1955; Copenhagen 1956; DS; H 55; FS; FE; Fi.

FRANK, JOSEF (1885–1967, Austria). *Sweden. Architecture, interior design, furniture, textiles.* Educated in Vienna. Professor at Kunstgewerbeschule, Vienna, 1919–27. Own interior design firm, Haus und Garten, 1925–34. Settled in Sweden 1932. Designed furniture, prints, and interior decoration for Svensk Tenn, Stockholm, from 1932. Teacher at New School for Social Research, New York, 1941–43. Awarded Litteris et Artibus Medal. Exhibited Paris 1925; "Die Wohnung," Stuttgart, 1928; Paris 1937; New York 1939. Author of *Architectur als Symbol* (1930), *Accidentism* (1958).

FREIJ, EDLA (b. 1944, Norway). *Glass, ceramics.* Educated NCAD, Oslo. At Hadeland glassworks, Jevnaker, 1968–70 and since 1976, primarily designing glass with cut or etched decoration.

FRIBERG, BERNDT (1899–1981, Sweden). *Ceramics.* Trained at Höganäsbolaget stoneware factory, Höganäs. Educated technical school and studied at various workshops in Denmark and Sweden. Worked at Gustavsberg from 1934. Awarded gold medals MT 1948, 1951, 1954; Gregor Paulsson trophy 1960. One-man shows at Nordiska Kompaniet, Stockholm, 1954, 1956, 1959, 1964. Exhibited Nordiska Kompaniet, Stockholm, 1946; Nationalmuseum, Stockholm, 1949; "Vi Tre," Göteborg and Karlstad, 1954–55; "Stengods av Skånelera," Höganäs, 1956; Malmö Museum, 1957; Smålands Museum, Växjö, 1958. Monograph by Ulf Hård af Segerstad, *Berndt Friberg Keramiker,* Nordisk Rotogravyr, Stockholm (1964).

FRISTEDT, SVEN (b. 1940, Sweden). *Textiles.* Textile designer for Borås Wäfveri since the 1960s.

GABRIELSEN, BENT (b. 1928, Denmark). *Metalwork.* Educated Danish College of Jewelry, Silversmithing and Commercial Design, 1950–53. Designed for Hans Hansen, Kolding, 1953–69, and Georg Jensen, Copenhagen. Special projects include designing communion silver and altarpieces for Braendkjaer Church, Kolding. Own workshop since 1969. Awarded gold medal MT 1960, Lunning Prize 1964. Exhibited NF; AD; "Modern Scandinavian Jewelry," New York, 1964; "Lunning Prize Winners," Den Permanente, Copenhagen, 1967; "Two Centuries of Danish Design," London, 1968; "Modern Danish Design," Moscow, 1969; "Jewelry Arts Exhibition," Tokyo, 1973, 1976, 1979; GJ.

GALLEN-KALLELA, AKSELI (AXEL GALLÉN) (1865–1931, Finland). *Furniture, interior design, graphics, textiles.* Studied painting at School of Fine Arts Society (Taideyhdistyksen Piirustuskoulu), Helsinki, 1881–84; Académie Julian and Atelier Fernand Cormon, Paris, 1884–90. Awarded gold medal Paris 1900 for furnishings of Iris room. Also executed frescoes for Finnish pavilion.

Changed name from Axel Gallén 1905. Traveled in U.S., including Chicago and New Mexico, 1923–26. Executed ceiling frescoes of Suomen Kansallismuseo (Finnish National Museum), Helsinki, 1928. Prime force in Finnish national romantic movement. Exhibitions include major retrospective, Hungary, 1906–8; own section at Venice Biennale 1914 and at San Francisco 1915.

GARDBERG, BERTEL (b. 1916, Finland). *Metalwork.* Educated CSI and the Goldsmith School, Helsinki. Taught at CSI 1951–53. Has maintained own studio in Helsinki since 1949. Awarded gold medals MT 1954, 1957, and four silver medals 1960; Lunning Prize 1961. Exhibited Göteborg 1955; Copenhagen 1956; GJ.

GATE, SIMON (1883–1945, Sweden). *Glass.* Educated SACD, Stockholm, and RAAS, Stockholm. At Orrefors from 1916. During 1920s designed for Sandvik glassworks, Hofmantorp. With Edward Hald, one of the leaders of modernism in Swedish design. Developed the *graal* technique. Exhibited Society for Industrial Design, 1917; Paris 1925.

GAUDERNACK, GUSTAV (1865–1914, Bohemia). *Norway. Metalwork, enamel.* Educated Vocational School for Glass and Metal Industry 1880–81 (industrial design); Ceramics Vocational School, Tetschen, 1885–87; School of Art and Craft, Vienna, 1888–91. Emigrated to Norway 1891. Designed glass for Christiania (Oslo) Glasmagasin 1891; metalwork for David Andersen, Oslo, 1892–1910. Established own workshop in Oslo for silver, filigree, and enamel 1910. First principal instructor for goldsmiths at NCAD, Oslo, 1912. Awarded silver medal Paris 1900, shared Grand Prize with David Andersen, St. Louis 1904; gold medal Centenary Exhibition at Frogner, Oslo, 1914. Exhibited Bergen Exhibition 1898, Paris Salon 1907. Monograph, *Gustav Gaudernack en europeer i norsk jugend,* with text in Norwegian and English, Utgitt av Kunstindustrimuseet Oslo (1979).

GILLGREN, SVEN ARNE (b. 1913, Sweden). *Metalwork.* Trained as engraver with C. G. Hallberg 1933. Educated SACD, Stockholm, 1936. Principal teacher in department of metalworking and industrial design at SACD, Stockholm, 1955–70. Designer at Guldsmedsaktiebolaget, Stockholm, from 1937, art director 1942–75. Engaged at G. Dahlgren & Co., goldsmiths, Malmö, from 1944. Own studio since 1975. Awarded first prize Stockholm Handicraft Society competition 1958; first prize "The International Design Competition for Sterling Silver Flatware," Museum of Contemporary Crafts, New York, 1960; Prize of Honor, Swedish Design Center, 1963; Prince Eugen Medal 1964; Eligius Prize 1966.

GJERDRUM, REIDUN SISSEL (b. 1954, Norway). *Ceramics.* Educated Art School, Trondheim (ceramics). Worked at Trondheim Municipal Workshop for Arts & Crafts from 1979; own workshop since 1981.

GUDHJONSSON, JENS (b. 1920, Iceland). *Metalwork.* Leading Icelandic metalsmith, producing primarily jewelry and hollow ware in gold and silver. Maintains own studio and showroom in Reykjavik. Numerous international awards.

GUDHNADOTTIR, JONINA (b. 1943, Iceland). *Ceramics.* Educated Reykjavik School of Art; CAC, Reykjavik; SACD, Stockholm. Maintains own studio. One-woman shows at Unuhus Gallery, Reykjavik, 1968; the Nordic House, Reykjavik, 1975; Solon Islandus Gallery, Reykjavik, 1977. Exhibitions include the Nordic Centre of Culture, Stockholm; Kjarvalsstadhir, Reykjavik, 1980; traveling exhibition in Denmark, 1981.

GUDJONSDOTTIR (RUNA), SIGRUN (b. 1926, Iceland). *Ceramics.* Icelandic ceramist and illustrator. Instructor at CAC, Reykjavik. Designer for Bing & Grøndahl, Copenhagen. Maintains private studio with her husband, Gestur Thorgrimsson, who creates the ceramics that she decorates.

GUDME-LETH, MARIE (b. 1910, Denmark). *Textiles.* Educated Industrial Art School for Women, Copenhagen; RDA, Copenhagen; Kunstgewerbeschule, Frankfort. Headed textile department at SAC, Copenhagen, 1931–48. Cofounder of Dansk Kattuntrykkeri, Copenhagen, 1935, director there until 1940. Own silkscreen workshop since 1940. Awarded gold medal Paris 1937, gold medal MT 1951. Exhibited DS; NF; FS; AD.

GULBRANDSEN, NORA *(1894–1978, Norway). Ceramics, metalwork.* Artistic director of Porsgrund porcelain factory 1928–48. Own studio in Oslo 1948–57. During the 1960s designed enamel and silver for David-Andersen, Oslo. Also produced designs for textiles, wallpaper, glass, and bookbindings.

GUSRUD, SVEINN *(b. 1944, Norway). Furniture.* Furniture designer in collaboration with Hans Christian Mengshoel in designs for chairs in the *Balans* series.

HAGLUND, BIRGER *(b. 1918, Sweden). Metalwork.* Independent silversmith. Own workshop since 1964.

HALD, EDWARD *(1883–1980, Sweden). Glass, ceramics.* Studied painting at Artists' Studio School, Copenhagen; at Artists' League school, Stockholm; with Henri Matisse. Engaged at Orrefors from 1917, managing director there 1933–44. Worked for Rörstrand, Lidköping, 1917–27 and Karlskrona porcelain works 1924–33. With Simon Gate, one of the leaders of modernism in Swedish design. Awarded Grand Prix Paris 1925, Prince Eugen Medal 1945. Elected honorary member Royal Designers for Industry, London, 1939; honorary fellow Society of Glass Technology, Sheffield; honorary member of Swedish Society of Industrial Design.

HANSEN, FRIDA *(1855–1931, Norway). Textiles.* Studied painting 1871. Started own embroidery shop in Stavanger 1882; established own studio 1890. Moved to Oslo 1892. Director of weaving workshop Det Norske Billedvæveri (DNB), Oslo. Collaborated with Gerhard Munthe on a series of tapestries. Awarded gold medals for individual work and for DNB Paris 1900. Exhibited Chicago 1893. Major retrospective "Frida Hansen europeeren i Norsk Vevkunst," Oslo, 1973. Author of *Husflid og Kunstindustri i Norge,* Oslo (1899).

HANSEN, KARL GUSTAV *(b. 1914, Denmark). Metalwork.* Son of Hans Hansen. Designed for his father's silversmithy in Kolding, artistic director there 1940–62, since 1962 its artistic consultant and designer. Has also worked for Rosenthal, Germany.

HEGERMANN-LINDENCRONE, EFFIE *(1869–1945, Denmark). Ceramics.* Designer for Bing & Grøndahl, Copenhagen, from 1886, specializing in fully pierced porcelain vessels.

HEIKKILÄ, SIMO *(b. 1943, Finland). Furniture, exhibition design, interior design.* Furniture designer for Asko Oy, Haimi Oy, Nupponen Oy, and Vivero Oy, Helsinki. Maintains own studio. Has collaborated with Yrjö Wiherheimo on furniture in the 1970s and 1980s.

HELLMAN, ÅSA *(b. 1947, Finland). Ceramics.* Works in a collective workshop called Pot Viapori in Suomenlinna near Helsinki, producing utility and unique ceramics.

HELLSTEN, LARS *(b. 1933, Sweden). Glass.* Worked for Skruf glassworks 1964–72. Since then engaged by Orrefors. His designs for glass include numerous sculptural works. Exhibitions include "Adventure in Swedish Glass," Australia, 1975.

HENNING, GERHARD *(1880–1967, Sweden). Denmark. Ceramics, textiles.* Studied sculpture. Designed figurines at Royal Copenhagen Porcelain Manufactory 1908–25. Also designed patterns for textiles woven by his wife, Gerda Henning.

HENNINGSEN, POUL *(1894–1967, Denmark). Architecture, lighting fixtures.* Educated technical school and TU, Copenhagen. Independent architect, Copenhagen, from 1920. Designed series of "PH" lamps for Louis Poulsen & Co., Copenhagen. Exhibited Paris 1925. Editor of periodical *Kritisk Revy* 1926–28.

HERNMARCK, HELENA *(b. 1941, Sweden). Textiles.* Independent textile artist who has produced many large tapestries for public buildings. In the mid-1960s moved to Montreal, then to London, and finally to New York, where she maintains a studio. Tapestries in Sweden House, Stockholm, and the Federal Reserve Bank of Boston.

HILLFON, HERTHA *(b. 1921, Sweden). Ceramics.* Educated SACD, Stockholm. Own studio in Stockholm since 1959. Awarded Society for Industrial Design's Medal for Proficiency and Industry 1957, Lunning Prize 1962. Exhibited MT 1960.

HÖGLUND, ERIK *(b. 1932, Sweden). Glass, metalwork.* Educated SACD, Stockholm (sculpture). Designer at Kosta Boda 1953–73. Awarded Lunning Prize 1957. Numerous exhibitions in Sweden and abroad.

HOLMBOE, THOROLF *(1866–1935, Norway). Ceramics, textiles.* Studied painting in Berlin and at Atelier Fernand Cormon in Paris 1889–90. Educated NCAD, Oslo (sculpture). Joined Symbolist *fin-de-siècle* group of Scandinavian artists. Designed underglaze porcelain decoration at Porsgrund porcelain factory 1908–11. Also designed and illustrated books. Exhibited Paris 1900; Venice, Rome, and Vienna 1909; Vienna 1912; San Francisco 1915.

HOLZER-KJELLBERG, FRIEDL *(b. 1905, Austria). Finland. Ceramics.* Designer for Arabia, Helsinki, 1924–70, artistic director there from 1948. Specialized in "rice" pattern porcelain bowls and unique stoneware pieces.

HONGELL, GÖRAN *(1902–1973, Finland). Glass.* Educated CSI, Helsinki (decorative art). Taught decorative painting at CSI. Engaged by Iittala in 1932. At Karhula glassworks from 1940. Known primarily for production designs.

HOPEA, SAARA *(b. 1925, Finland). Ceramics, metalwork, enamel, glass, interior design, furniture, lighting fixtures.* Educated CSI, Helsinki (interior design). Free-lance interior designer 1946–49. Designed lighting fixtures for Taito. Assistant to Kaj Franck at Wärtsilä/Arabia, Helsinki, 1952–59; designed in silver for Ossian Hopea firm in Porvoo. Emigrated to U.S. 1960, working there as free-lance silver designer; now lives in Finland. Awarded silver medals MT 1954, 1957. Exhibited Helsinki 1953; DS; Brussels 1954; H 55; FE; Fi.

HVIDT, PETER *(b. 1916, Denmark). Architecture, furniture.* Trained as cabinetmaker. Educated SAC, Copenhagen (furniture design). In partnership with Orla Mølgaard-Nielsen since 1944. Designed furniture for France & Son, Ltd., Fritz Hansens Eftf., Allerød, and Søborg Møbelfabrik. Awarded *diplôme d'honneur* MT 1951, 1954.

HYDMAN-VALLIEN, ULRICA *(b. 1938, Germany). Sweden. Ceramics, glass.* Own workshop in Åfors, Sweden. Designer for Kosta Boda since 1970. Has made a specialty of ceramic sculpture. Exhibitions include "Adventure in Swedish Glass," Australia, 1975.

ILVESSALO, KIRSTI *(b. 1920, Finland). Textiles.* Educated CSI, Helsinki. Designed for Friends of Finnish Handicraft 1947–52. Own workshop in Helsinki since 1952. At Barker-Littoinen Ltd. since 1958. Also designs silver. Worked with Alvar Aalto on the interiors of some of his buildings, including National Pensions Office, Helsinki, Cultural Center, Helsinki, and Teachers' Training College, Jyväskylä. Awarded gold metals MT 1951, 1960; Grand Prix 1954; gold medal at international textile exhibition, California, 1960. One-woman show Copenhagen 1959. Exhibited DS, FS, Fi.

ISOLA, MAIJA *(b. 1927, Finland). Textiles.* Educated CSI, Helsinki. Designer for Marimekko, Helsinki, since the 1950s. Numerous exhibitions include DS; FS; Fi; MT 1957.

JACOBSEN, ARNE *(1902–1971, Denmark). Architecture, furniture, metalwork, lighting fixtures, textiles.* Graduated SAA, Copenhagen, 1924 (bricklaying), and RDA, Copenhagen, 1927 (architecture), where he studied with Kay Fisker. Professor at RDA, Copenhagen. Architect of many public and private buildings. Designed furniture for Fritz Hansens Eftf., Allerød, from 1932. Designed silver and stainless steel for A. Michelsen, Copenhagen; lighting fixtures for Louis Poulsen & Co., Copenhagen; and textiles for Grautex, Aug. Millech, and C. Olesen. Awarded silver medal Paris 1925, Grand Prix MT 1957. Professor Emeritus RDA, Copenhagen, 1956.

JACOBSEN, JAC. *(b. 1901, Norway). Lighting fixtures.* Director of Jac. Jacobsen, Oslo, which manufactures the *Luxo* lamp and other lighting fixtures.

JENSEN, (ARTHUR) GEORG *(1866–1935, Denmark). Metalwork.* Apprenticed as goldsmith 1884. Educated RDA, Copenhagen, 1887–92 (sculpture). Worked in ceramics workshop with Christian Joachim from about 1895–1901, and as potter with Aluminia and Bing & Grøndahl, Copenhagen. Founded own silversmith workshop 1904, which became a limited company in 1916. Awarded honorable mention Paris 1900, gold medal Brussels 1910, first prize San Francisco 1915, Grand Prix Paris 1925, Grand Prix Barcelona 1929. Exhibitions include Århus 1909; Museé des Arts Décoratifs, Paris, 1909. Monograph, *Georg Jensen Silversmithy*, Smithsonian Institution Press, Washington, D.C. (1980).

JERNDAHL, ARON *(1858–1936, Sweden). Metalwork.* Sculptor. Many of his designs were intended to be made in pewter by such Stockholm firms as Fabriks Herkules.

JEZORSKI, GUDBRANDUR J. *(b. 1943, Iceland). Metalwork.* Metalsmith working primarily in gold, with a specialization in jewelry. Maintains own studio and sales gallery in Reykjavik.

JOACHIM, CHRISTIAN *(1870–1943, Denmark). Ceramics.* Educated RDA, Copenhagen, 1893. Engaged by Royal Copenhagen Porcelain Manufactory 1901. Director of Aluminia, Copenhagen.

JOBS, GOCKEN *(b. 1914, Sweden). Textiles, ceramics.* Works in family studio in Leksand producing ceramics and handprinted textiles. The Jobs family firm has remained active since the mid-1940s.

JOBS-SÖDERLUND, LISBET *(1909–1961, Sweden). Ceramics, textiles.* Worked along with her sister Gocken in the family studio in Leksand.

JOHANNSDOTTIR, SIGRIDUR *(b. 1948, Iceland). Textiles.* Independent textile artist in Reykjavik. Maintains own studio and often executes the textile designs of her husband, Leifur Breidfjord.

JOHANSSON, WILLY *(b. 1921, Norway). Glass.* Educated NCAD, Oslo. Trained at Hadeland glassworks, Jevnaker; head of design team there since 1947. MT awards: *diplôme d'honneur* 1954, gold medal 1957, silver medal 1960. Has designed production and art wares.

JOHANSSON-PAPE, LISA *(b. 1907, Finland). Furniture, textiles, lighting fixtures.* Educated CSI, Helsinki. Designed furniture for Kylmäkoski Ltd. 1928–30 and Stockmann, Helsinki, 1937–49; lighting fixtures for Stockmann from 1942. Textile designer for Friends of Finnish Handicraft 1928–37 and artistic director there from 1952. Also designed ceramics and glass. Awarded first and second prize and *diplôme d'honneur* Paris 1937; silver medals MT 1951, 1960 and gold medal 1954.

JUHL, FINN *(b. 1912, Denmark). Architecture, interior design, furniture.* Educated RDA, Copenhagen (architecture). Director of School of Interior Design, Frederiksberg, 1945–55. Furniture designer for Nils Vodder, Allerød; France & Son, Ltd. Also designer of turned wooden bowls. Designer for Bing & Grøndahl, Copenhagen. Awarded Eckersberg Medal 1947. Exhibited DS; NF; FS; AD.

JUHLEN, SVEN-ERIC *(b. 1940, Sweden). Ceramics, utility goods.* Worked for Gustavsberg during the 1960s. Since 1976 designer for the Ergonomi Design Group, Stockholm. Has contributed numerous designs for the handicapped and for children.

JUNG, DORA *(1906–1980, Finland). Textiles.* Educated CSI, Helsinki. Fabric designer for Tampella linen works, Tampere. Own studio in Helsinki from 1932. Awarded Grand Prix MT 1951, 1954, 1957; gold medal Paris 1937. Elected honorary member Royal Designers for Industry, London, 1979, and Royal Academy of Art, London, 1980. Exhibited independently and in group shows, including Göteborg 1955 and Copenhagen 1956.

JUTREM, ARNE JON *(b. 1929, Norway). Glass, textiles, metalwork, ceramics.* Educated NCAD, Oslo (lithography) and the Léger Academy, Paris (painting). Designer with Hadeland glassworks, Jevnaker, since 1950. Awarded gold medal MT 1954 and Lunning Prize 1959. Exhibited Montreal 1967.

KÅGE, WILHELM *(1889–1960, Sweden). Ceramics.* Studied painting at Valand Art School, Göteborg; with Carl Wilhelmsson, Stockholm; with Johan Rohde, Copenhagen; at Plakatschule, Munich. Gained recognition as poster designer. At Gustavsberg 1917–60, art director until 1947. Kåge's distinctive work includes innovative tableware and unique sculptural pieces. Awarded Grand Prix Paris 1925. Exhibited Liljevalchs Art Gallery, Stockholm, 1917, and had contributed designs to all major

exhibitions in Sweden and abroad.

KÄHLER, HERMAN AUGUST *(1846–1917, Denmark). Ceramics.* Trained in studio of sculptor H. V. Biesen and at ceramic factories in Berlin and Zurich. Took over father's pottery studio at Næstved 1872. Produced designs by Thorvald Bindesbøll, O. Eckmann, and Karl Hansen Reistrup. Exhibited Paris 1889; Chicago 1893; Munich Sezession 1899; Paris 1900.

KAIPIAINEN, BIRGER *(b. 1915, Finland). Ceramics.* Educated CSI, Helsinki. Designer for Arabia, Helsinki, 1934–54 and since 1958; for Rörstrand, Lidköping, 1954–58. Awarded *diplôme d'honneur* MT 1951, Grand Prix 1960. One-man shows in Helsinki, Milan, Malmö, New York, Göteborg. Exhibited DS; Fi.

KALLIO, HEIKKI *(b. 1948, Finland). Glass.* Produces unique and utility glassware in own workshop.

KANSANEN-STØRSETH, MAIJA *(1889–1957, Finland). Textiles.* Textile designer also active in Norway.

KAYSER, FREDRIK A. *(1924–1968, Norway). Furniture, interior design.* Educated NCAD, Oslo. Designed furniture for Rastad & Relling; free-lance designer from 1956. Recipient of numerous awards.

KIELLAND, GABRIEL *(1871–1960, Norway). Architecture, glass, furniture.* Studied painting in Munich, 1891–92; Weimar, 1892–94; and Paris, 1894. Worked as painter and architect in Trondheim from 1890s. Director of private art school in Trondheim. Designed furniture and posters for Nordenfjeldske Kunstindustrimuseum, Trondheim.

KITTELSEN, GRETE PRYTZ *(b. 1917, Norway). Metalwork, enamel.* Educated NCAD, Oslo; in France; and the School of the Art Institute of Chicago. Designer of jewelry and enameled silver for J. Tostrup, Oslo, since 1945. Also designs enameled stainless steel. Awarded Lunning Prize 1952; Grand Prix MT 1954, gold medals 1957, 1960.

KITTELSEN, THEODOR *(1857–1914, Norway). Ceramics, book illustration.* Studied painting in Munich 1884–87. Illustrated editions of folk tales (particularly renowned for his trolls and fairies) and children's stories. Designer for Porsgrund porcelain factory in the early 1900s.

KJÆRHOLM, POUL *(1929–1980, Denmark). Furniture, interior design.* Educated SAC, Copenhagen (cabinetmaking and furniture), and RDA, Copenhagen. Lecturer at SAC, Copenhagen, 1952–56; at RDA, Copenhagen, in furniture and interior design department since 1955. Designer for E. Kold Christensen, Copenhagen. Designer for several Danish applied-arts exhibitions including MT 1960, where he was awarded gold medal. Awarded Grand Prix MT 1957, Lunning Prize 1958, Eckersberg Medal 1960. Exhibitions include NF; FS; AD.

KJARVAL, SVEINN *(1919–1981, Iceland). Furniture, interior design.* Educated SAC, Copenhagen. Influenced Icelandic furniture design during the 1950s and 1960s.

KLINT, KAARE *(1888–1954, Denmark). Architecture, furniture.* Trained as architect and designer by his father, P. V. Jensen Klint, and Carl Petersen. Founded department of furniture at RDA, Copenhagen, 1924; professor of architecture there from 1944. Designed furniture and fittings for Fåborg Museum 1914–15, Thorvaldsens Museum, Copenhagen, 1922–25, and Det Danske Kunstindustrimuseum, Copenhagen, 1924–54. Worked with master cabinetmakers N. M. Rasmussen, Copenhagen; Holbaek; and N. C. Jensen Kjaer. Awarded Eckersberg Medal 1954. Exhibited DS; NF; FS; AD. Comprehensive memorial exhibition Det Danske Kunstindustrimuseum, Copenhagen, 1956. Elected honorary member of the Royal Designers for Industry, London, 1949.

KLINT, VIBEKE *(b. 1927, Denmark). Textiles.* Educated SAC, Copenhagen, where she studied with Gerda Henning; studied with master-weaver Jean Lurçat at Aubusson in France. Own studio since 1951. Industrial fabric designer for C. Olesen's Cotil. Awarded Lunning Prize 1960. Exhibited NF; FS; AD.

KNAG, CHRISTIAN (CHRISTOPHER) *(1855–1942, Norway). Furniture.* Cabinetmaker and furniture designer. Established own workshop and salesroom in Bergen in 1878. Specialized in inlay work. Awarded gold medal Paris 1900, Grand Prize St. Louis 1904. Exhibitions include Oslo Kunstindustrimuseet, 1909.

KNOBLICH, F. W. *(1808–1879, Denmark). Metalwork.* Designed jewelry in the Viking revival style for A. Michelsen, Copenhagen.

KOCH, MOGENS *(b. 1898, Denmark). Architecture, furniture, textiles.* Educated RDA, Copenhagen (architecture). Study-tours throughout Europe, U.S., and Mexico. Professor at RDA from 1950. Established own design office 1934. Furniture designer for Rud. Rasmussens Snedkerier, Copenhagen, Danish C.W.S., and Interna, Frederikssund. Designed fittings, silver, and fabrics for church restorations in Denmark. Awarded Eckersberg Medal 1938. Exhibited MTs; FS; AD. Author of *Modern Danish Art—Craftsmanship* (1948).

KOPPEL, HENNING *(1918–1981, Denmark). Metalwork, ceramics, glass.* Educated RDA, Copenhagen, and Académie Ranson, Paris. Designer for Georg Jensen, Copenhagen, from 1945; associated with Bing & Grøndahl from 1961; free-lance designer for Orrefors from 1971. Awarded gold medals MT 1951, 1954, 1957; Lunning Prize 1953; and International Design Award of the American Institute of Designers 1963. In 1966 Georg Jensen awarded ID Prize from Danish Society of Industrial Design for tableware designed by Koppel. Exhibited DS; NF; FS; AD; "Adventure in Swedish Glass," Australia, 1975; GJ.

KORSMO, ARNE *(1900–1968, Norway). Architecture, metalwork, exhibition design.* Educated Technical University of Norway (Norges Tekniskne Høgskole), Trondheim. Director of NCAD, Oslo, 1936–56. Professor at Technical University of Norway, Trondheim, from 1956. Own design office from 1929. Designed in metal for J. Tostrup, Oslo. Designed Norwegian section Paris 1937, MT 1954. Awarded Grand Prix and gold medal MT 1954.

KREBS, NATHALIE *(1895–1978, Denmark). Ceramics.* Educated TU, Copenhagen (civil engineering). Engaged by Bing & Grøndahl, Copenhagen, 1919–29. Set up stoneware pottery studio in Copenhagen with Gunnar Nylund in 1929; in 1930 took it over and named it Saxbo, where she worked in collaboration with Eva Stæhr-Nielsen. Awarded gold medal MT 1957. Exhibited DS; NF; FS; AD.

KRISTIANSEN, BO *(b. 1944, Denmark). Ceramics.* Educated SAC, Copenhagen, 1965. Own studio in Gudhjem from 1968, in Copenhagen since 1979. Engaged by Royal Copenhagen Porcelain Manufactory since 1974. One-man shows at Galerie Inart, Amsterdam, 1980; Galerie der Kunsthandverk, Hamburg, 1981. Exhibited Bornholms Museum, Copenhagen, 1969, 1973, 1980; Det Danske Kunstindustrimuseum, Copenhagen, 1973; "International Ceramics," London, 1971; "Dansk Miljø," Eastern Europe, 1975–77; "Danish Ceramic Design," University Park, Pa., 1981.

KROG, ARNOLD *(1856–1931, Denmark). Ceramics.* Graduated RFA, Copenhagen, 1880. Worked on the interior decoration of Frederiksborg Palace while a student. Employed at the design office of architect Henrik Hagemann 1883. At Royal Copenhagen Porcelain Manufactory from 1884, artistic director there 1891–1916; while there, he developed a special style of underglaze decoration. Exhibited "Scandinavian Exhibition of Industry, Agriculture and Art," Copenhagen, 1888; Paris 1889; Paris 1900.

KROGH, HENRIK *(1886–1927, Sweden). Textiles, ceramics, metalwork.* Studied painting. In addition to his work in ceramics and metalwork, Krogh supplied designs for woven tapestries, some of which were executed by Märta Måås-Fjetterström, Båstad.

KROHN, PIETRO *(1840–1905, Denmark). Ceramics.* Artistic director of Bing & Grøndahl, Copenhagen, 1885–97. First director of Det Danske Kunstindustrimuseum, Copenhagen. Also painter, illustrator, costume designer.

LANDBERG, NILS *(b. 1907, Sweden). Glass.* Educated SAC, Göteborg. Trained at Orrefors engraving school. At Orrefors 1925–72. Awarded gold medal MT 1954. Exhibited Paris 1937; New York 1939; Zurich 1948, 1957; DS; FS; Amsterdam 1959; California State Fair 1956, 1957, 1959, 1960.

LAVONEN, MAIJA *(b. 1931, Finland). Textiles.* Designs both industrial and unique textiles in a variety of techniques including *ryijy* and double weaves.

LIE-JØRGENSEN, THORBJØRN *(1900–1961, Norway). Metalwork.* Educated NCAD, Oslo (trained as goldsmith under Henrik Lund) and NAFA, Oslo (painting). Received goldsmith journeyman diploma 1918. Department head at NCAD 1939–61. Designed silver, jewelry, and enamel for David Andersen, Oslo, from 1927. Awarded gold medal MT 1954, Munich 1955. Winner of competition for table silver for Oslo town hall.

LIISBERG, CARL FREDERICK *(1860–1909, Denmark). Ceramics.* Sculptor and underglaze painter for Royal Copenhagen Porcelain Manufactory 1885–1909.

LILJEDAHL, BENGT *(b. 1932, Sweden). Metalcraft.* Graduated SACD, Stockholm, 1953. Studied at École Nationale Supérieure des Arts Décoratifs, Paris, 1958. Has worked independently in own workshop in Stockholm since 1964.

LILJEFORS, ANDERS *(1923–1970, Sweden). Ceramics.* Studied sculpture and painting 1942–43. Educated RDA, Copenhagen, 1945–47. Worked for Gustavsberg 1947–53 and 1955–57. Own workshop during the 1960s near Karlskrona. One-man shows include Nordiska Kompaniet, Stockholm, 1952; Stockholm 1957; Göteborg 1957. Numerous group exhibitions.

LINDAU, BÖRGE *(b. 1932, Sweden). Furniture, interior design.* Furniture and interior designer working with Bo Lindekrantz for Lammhults Mekaniska, Lammhult. Awarded Lunning Prize 1969.

LINDBERG, STIG *(1916–1982, Sweden). Ceramics, textiles.* Educated technical school and SACD, Stockholm, 1935–37. Studied with Wilhelm Kåge and in Paris. Joined Gustavsberg 1937, artistic director there 1949–57 and 1970–77. Designer for Målerås glassworks 1945–47. Designer of hand-printed textiles for Nordiska Kompaniet, Stockholm, from 1947. Senior lecturer at SACD, Stockholm, from 1957. MT awards: gold medals 1948, 1957; Grand Prix 1951, 1954. Awarded Cannes gold medal 1955; gold medal California State Fair 1958, 1959; Gregor Paulsson trophy 1957; Prince Eugen Medal 1968. One-man shows in Europe, Japan, and U.S. Exhibitions include New York 1939; DS; FS; H 55. Monograph, *Stig Lindberg—Swedish Artist and Designer*, Rabén & Sjögren, Stockholm (1963).

LINDEKRANTZ, BO *(b. 1932, Sweden). Furniture, interior design.* See Lindau, Börge.

LINDH, RICHARD *(b. 1929, Finland). Ceramics.* Educated CSI, Helsinki. Engaged by Arabia, Helsinki, 1955, head of industrial art department from 1960, artistic director since 1973. Awarded first prize in competition at Museum of Contemporary Crafts, New York. Exhibitions include H 55; Fi; MT 1957, 1960.

LINDSTRAND, VICKE *(b. 1904, Sweden). Glass.* Educated SAC, Göteborg. Designer at Orrefors 1928–40. Art director of Upsala-Ekeby 1940–49; also worked at Kosta glassworks. Designed windows for Swedish pavilion Paris 1937, fountain for pavilion New York 1939. Exhibitions include MTs since 1933; Stockholm 1930; Paris 1937, 1954; New York 1939; H 55; Amsterdam 1959.

LIPPE, JENS VON DER *(b. 1911, Norway). Ceramics.* Educated NCAD, Oslo, Staatliche Keramische Fachschule, Schlesien, Istituto statale d'Arte per la Ceramica, Faenza. Teacher at NCAD, Oslo, 1939–75, head of ceramics department since 1956. Own pottery workshop in Oslo with his wife, Margrethe, since 1933.

LOHMANN, JAN *(b. 1944, Denmark). Metalwork.* Earned certificate of apprenticeship 1964. Studied in workshop in Switzerland 1966–68. Completed courses in gemology and cutting of gems 1970. Own workshop in Copenhagen since 1968. Study-tours including Peru, Ecuador, Guatemala, Mexico, and New York 1976. Awarded silver medal Goldsmiths Guild 1966; Goldsmiths Guild Scandinavian Design Award 1972, 1976, 1978. Numerous exhibitions include Det Danske Kunstindustrimuseum, Copenhagen, 1974; "Dansk Miljø," Eastern Europe, 1975–77; Gallery for Contemporary Silver and Goldsmiths Art, Copenhagen, 1978, 1980.

LUKANDER, MINNI *(b. 1930, Finland). Ceramics.* Free-lance ceramist since 1950. One of the founders of Pot Viapori studio at Suomenlinna near Helsinki.

LUNDIN, INGEBORG *(b. 1921, Sweden). Glass.* Educated SACD, Stockholm. Designer at Orrefors 1947–71. Awarded Lunning Prize 1954. One-woman show Stockholm 1959. Exhibited MT 1957, 1960; Orrefors exhibitions since 1948, including traveling U.S. exhibition 1958; DS; H 55; FS; Zurich 1957; Amsterdam 1959.

LUTHERSSON, PETUR B. *(b. 1936, Iceland). Furniture, interior design, lighting fixtures.* Interior designer of public buildings and private homes and furniture designer in wood and metal including office furniture. Developed extensive range of lighting fixtures in spun aluminum.

LÜTKEN, PER *(b. 1916, Denmark). Glass.* Educated SAC, Copenhagen (painting, mechanical drawing). At Holmegaard glassworks since 1942. Participated in Holmegaard exhibitions; MTs since 1951; DS; NF; FS; AD; "Creative Craft in Denmark Today," New York, 1962.

LYNGGAARD, FINN *(b. 1930, Denmark). Ceramics, glass.* Educated SAC, Copenhagen (painting and ceramics). Own workshop since 1958. Pioneer in Danish studio glass. Exhibited MT 1960; AD.

MÅÅS-FJETTERSTRÖM, MÄRTA *(1873–1941, Sweden). Textiles.* Leading textile artist who established influential workshop in Båstad 1919. Was responsible for the execution of many designs contributed by distinguished artists. After her death, workshop directed by Barbro Nilsson, and it is still active today.

MAGNUSSEN, ERIK *(1884–1961, Denmark). Metalwork.* Studied independently. Educated Kunstgewerbeschule, Berlin, 1907–9. Own jewelry workshop from 1909. Worked in U.S. 1925–39 as director of Gorham Silver Co., R.I. Maintained own workshop in Chicago and Los Angeles. Exhibitions include Det Danske Kunstindustrimuseum, Copenhagen, 1901, 1904, 1907; Salon d'Automne, Paris, 1922; Metropolitan Museum of Art, New York, 1926, 1927, 1937; Brooklyn Museum, New York, 1931, 1937.

MAGNUSSEN, ERIK *(b. 1940, Denmark). Metalwork, ceramics, furniture.* Graduated SAC, Copenhagen, 1960 (pottery). Has taught at RDA, Copenhagen. Designer at Bing & Grøndahl, Copenhagen, since 1962. Hollow ware designer for Georg Jensen, Copenhagen, since 1978. Also maintains his own workshop, where he produces stoneware, glass, cutlery, and furniture. Awarded Lunning Prize 1967; twice awarded ID Prize from Danish Society of Industrial Design. Exhibited GJ.

MAGNUSSON, GUNNAR *(b. 1933, Iceland). Furniture, interior design.* Leading Icelandic furniture and interior designer. His works include furnishings for public buildings, banks, and offices. Also an instructor.

MALINOWSKI, ARNO *(1899–1976, Denmark). Ceramics, metalwork.* Educated RDA, Copenhagen. Engaged at Royal Copenhagen Porcelain Manufactory. Designed for Georg Jensen, Copenhagen, 1936–65. Awarded silver medal Paris 1925 and Eckersberg Medal 1933. Exhibited GJ.

MALINOWSKI, RUTH *(b. 1928, Austria). Denmark, Sweden. Textiles.* Educated SAC, Copenhagen. Own workshop in Reftele, Sweden, since 1958. Her simple, geometric, flat-woven patterns reflect a painterly approach. Exhibitions include one-woman shows at Nationalmuseum, Stockholm, 1968, and Röhsska Konstslöjdmuseet, Göteborg, 1969; Det Danske Kunstindustrimuseum, Copenhagen, 1977.

MALMSTEN, CARL *(1888–1972, Sweden). Furniture, textiles.* Trained by cabinetmaker Per Jönsson, then studied independently. Founded Olof School, Stockholm, 1928, director there until 1941; Nyckelvik School for handicrafts and folk art, Stockholm, 1945; and Capellagården School for creative work in Vickelby. Awarded first prize 1916 for furniture design, Stockholm Town Hall, where he worked until 1923. Designed Stockholm Concert Hall 1924–25. Awarded Litteris et Artibus Medal 1926; Prince Eugen Medal 1945. Exhibitions include Stockholm 1917;

Göteborg 1923, 1956; Paris 1927; New York 1939. Author of *Beauty and Comfort in the Home* (1923), *A Central Domain* (1944), and *Live in Peace* (1958).

MALMSTRÖM, AUGUST *(1829–1901, Sweden). Ceramics.* Educated RAAS, Stockholm, 1849–56 (painting). In Paris 1857–58, Italy 1859–60. Professor at RAAS, Stockholm, from 1867, later director. Designer at Gustavsberg 1868–74, where he was particularly noted for his Viking revival designs.

MARKELIUS, SVEN *(1889–1972, Sweden). Architecture, town-planning, textiles.* Educated RIT and RAAS, Stockholm. Designed for Nordiska Kompaniet, Stockholm, and Knoll Textiles Inc. during the 1950s. Building Administration member 1938–44; Stockholm town-planning director 1944–54. Architect of Hälsingborg Concert Hall and contributed to the planning of the UN Building, New York. Assisted with Stockholm 1930 and designed Swedish pavilion, New York 1939. Co-author of publication *Accept* (1931).

MARSIO-AALTO, AINO *(1894–1949, Finland). Architecture, glass, ceramics, textiles.* Educated HUT, Helsinki. Founded Artek along with her husband, Alvar Aalto, Nils-Gustaf Hahl, and Maire Gullichsen 1933, supervising director there 1941–48. Designed glass for Karhula glassworks.

MARTEINSDOTTIR, STEINUNN *(b. 1936, Iceland). Ceramics.* Internationally recognized Icelandic ceramist. Maintains own studio near Reykjavik. Numerous exhibitions and international awards, including Vallauris, France, 1976.

MATHSSON, BRUNO *(b. 1907, Sweden). Furniture.* Trained by father, Karl Mathsson, in Värnamo as furniture designer and maker. Designed for Firma Karl Mathsson, Värnamo, and later for Dux Company. Awarded Gregor Paulsson trophy 1955. One-man and group exhibitions include Paris 1937; San Francisco and New York 1939; Svensk Form, Copenhagen, 1946; H 55; DS; "Interbau," Berlin, 1957; FS; Amsterdam 1959; Zurich and Munich 1960.

MENGSHOEL, HANS CHRISTIAN *(b. 1946, Norway). Furniture.* Collaborated in design of chairs in the *Balans* series.

MEYER, GRETHE *(b. 1918, Denmark). Architecture, furniture, glass, ceramics.* Educated RDA, Copenhagen, 1947 (architecture). Designed glassware with Ibi Trier Mørch for Kastrup glassworks 1959. Designed tableware for Royal Copenhagen Porcelain Manufactory since 1960. In conjunction with Børge Mogensen designed cabinet system *Boligens Byggeskabe* 1957. Worked with State Institute for Building Research 1955–60; specialized in projects for National Institute for Building Research; collaborated with Poul Kjærgaard and Bent Salicath on research for housing requirements and standard sizes for consumer goods. Private architecture practice since 1960. Awarded silver medal, International Exhibition of Ceramics, Vicenza, 1965; Scandinavian Industrial Art and Design Award, 1973. Exhibited Society of Danish Arts and Crafts and Industrial Design, Copenhagen; MTs; AD.

MEYER, JENNY *(1866–1927, Denmark). Ceramics.* Painter. Engaged by Royal Copenhagen Porcelain Manufactory 1892–1927, where she developed a distinctive style of underglaze painting in the Art Nouveau manner.

MOGENSEN, BØRGE *(1914–1972, Denmark). Architecture, furniture.* Apprentice cabinetmaker 1934. Educated SAC, Copenhagen, 1936–38; RFA, Copenhagen, 1938–41 (furniture). Assistant to Kaare Klint at RFA, Copenhagen, 1945–47. Worked with Hans Wegner 1945–46. Chairman of furniture design department of the Association of Danish Cooperative Societies, 1942–50. Collaborated with furniture manufacturers Søborg Møbelfabrik; Fredericia Stolefabrik; Karl Andersson & Söner, Huskvarna, Sweden. Designed furnishing fabrics with Lis Ahlmann for C. Olesen. Awarded Bissens Legacy 1945; Eckersberg Medal 1950; silver medal Dansk Købestaevne 1953; Copenhagen Cabinetmakers Guild award of honor 1958.

MØLGAARD-NIELSEN, ORLA *(b. 1907, Denmark). Furniture.* Trained as cabinetmaker. Educated SAC and RDA, Copenhagen. In partnership with Peter Hvidt since 1944. Designer for France &

Son, Ltd.; Fritz Hansens Eftf., Allerød; and Søborg Møbelfabrik. Awarded *diplôme d'honneur* MT 1951, 1954. Exhibited DS; NF; FS; AD.

MOTZFELDT, BENNY (*b. 1909, Norway*). *Glass.* Educated NCAD, Oslo. Designer at Hadeland glassworks 1955–67, then at Randsfjords glassworks. Designer of studio glass at Plus, Fredrickstad, from 1970. Exhibitions include one-woman show Germany, 1977; Smithsonian Institution Traveling Exhibition Service, U.S., 1979–81.

MUNTHE, GERHARD (*1849–1929, Norway*). *Textiles, interior design, furniture.* Studied painting with J. F. Eckersberg, Knud Bergslien, and Julius Middlethun, Oslo, prior to study in Düsseldorf, 1874. Lived in Munich 1877–82. Designed tapestries and book illustrations using Norwegian folk art and poetry as his subject matter. Designed tapestries for Det Norske Billedvæveri (DNB), Oslo. Awarded gold medal Paris 1900. Exhibitions include Oslo 1893. Monographs by Hilmar Bakken, *Gerhard Munthes dekorative kunst,* Oslo (1946) and *Gerhard Munthe,* Oslo (1952).

MUNTHE-KAAS, HERMAN (*1890-1977, Norway*). *Architecture, furniture.* Early functionalist architect and furniture designer. Established partnership with Gudolf Blakstad in the 1920s. One of the early exponents of tubular steel furniture in Norway.

MUONA, TOINI (*b. 1904, Finland*). *Ceramics.* Educated CSI, Helsinki; studied ceramics with Alfred William Finch. Engaged at Arabia, Helsinki, 1931–70. Awards include Barcelona 1929; MT 1933, 1951, 1954, 1957; Brussels 1935; Paris 1937; Cannes 1955. Exhibited DS; H 55; FE; FS; Fi.

MYRDAM, LEIF HEIBERG (*b. 1938, Norway*). *Ceramics.* Educated NCAD, Oslo. Served apprenticeship with Erik Pløen. Independent designer since 1967. Established own studio near Oslo 1970.

NIELSEN, ERIK (*1857–1947, Denmark*). *Ceramics.* At Royal Copenhagen Porcelain Manufactory about 1890. Collaborated with Arnold Krog in production of unique ceramics.

NILSSON, BARBRO (*b. 1899, Sweden*). *Textiles.* Studied weaving at school founded by Johanna Brunsson; instructor there 1918–20. Educated SACD, Stockholm; teacher there 1931–57, head of textile department after 1947. Taught at Nordenfeldt School, Göteborg, 1925–27. Own workshop in Stockholm from 1927. Art director of AB Märta Måås-Fjetterström, Båstad, 1942–71. Awarded Litteris et Artibus Medal 1948, Prince Eugen Medal 1954. Exhibited H 55; DS; FS; Amsterdam 1960.

NILSSON, WIWEN (KARL EDVIN WIWEN-NILSSON) (*1897–1974, Sweden*). *Metalwork.* Trained by his father, Anders Nilsson. Educated Hanau Zeichenakademie 1913–14 and 1920–21. Studied at the Paris studio of Georg Jensen while at the Académie de la Grande Chaumière and Académie Colarossi, Paris. Designed for his father's business in Lund from 1923, took it over in 1928. Awarded gold medal Paris 1925, Gregor Paulsson trophy 1955, Swedish Goldsmiths' and Jewellers' Guild gold medal 1956, Prince Eugen Medal 1958. Exhibited New York 1939; H 55; DS; FS; GJ.

NORDSTRÖM, PATRICK (*1870–1929, Sweden*). *Denmark. Ceramics.* Educated Svenska Slöjdföreningens Skola, Göteborg, 1889–90, and Tekniska Yrkesskolan, Lund, 1894–95. At Royal Copenhagen Porcelain Manufactory 1911–23, then established own workshop in Islev. Pioneer of Danish stoneware that emphasized unusual glazes. Exhibited Paris 1900; Baltic Exhibition, Malmö, 1914; retrospective at Det Danske Kunstindustrimuseum, Copenhagen, 1956.

NUMMI, YKI (*b. 1925, Finland*). *Interior design, lighting fixtures.* Educated CSI, Helsinki (painting). Designed lighting fixtures for Stockmann, Helsinki, since 1950. Headed color-design department Schildt & Hallberg since 1950. Collaborated with Lisa Johansson-Pape as color specialist for Stockmann/Orno, Kerava. Independent designer of lighting fixtures, functional furnishings, and utility goods. Awarded gold medals MT 1954, 1957. Exhibited DS; FS; H 55; FE; Fi. Author of a variety of essays and articles on lighting and color and the philos-ophic principles of design.

NURMESNIEMI, ANTTI (*b. 1927, Finland*). *Interior design, furniture, domestic wares.* Educated CSI, Helsinki (interior design). Freelance designer of furniture, goods, and installations, Helsinki. Awarded silver medal MT 1957, Grand Prix 1960; Lunning Prize 1959. Designed exhibitions in Sweden 1956, Germany 1956–57, Athens 1958, MT 1960, MT 1963 (with Vuokko Eskolin-Nurmesniemi). One-man shows Helsinki 1957, Oslo 1960. Exhibited DS; FE; Fi.

NYMAN, GUNNEL (*1909–1948, Finland*). *Furniture, glass, textiles, lighting fixtures.* Graduated CSI, Helsinki, 1932 (furniture design). Designer of furniture, textiles, and lighting fixtures. Designer for Riihimäki, Iittala, Nuutajärvi-Notsjö, and Karhula glassworks.

OHLSSON, OLLE (*b. 1927, Sweden*). *Metalwork.* Apprentice to Hallberg jewelers 1949. Worked at Atelier Borgila with Erik Fleming. Educated SACD, Stockholm, 1954–59. Designer at Gekå Jewels. Free-lance artist with own workshop since 1963. Awarded second prize and diploma at World Silver Fair, Mexico City, 1974. One-man show at Nordiska Kompaniet, Stockholm, 1966.

OLLERS, EDVIN (*1888–1959, Sweden*). *Glass.* Worked for Kosta in 1917 and 1931–32 and for Reijmyre glassworks, Rejmyra, 1918–20. Also designed ceramics, pewter, and silver.

OLLESTAD, ANDREAS (*1857–1936, Norway*). *Ceramics.* Worked at Egersund ceramic factory 1886–1936, production manager there from 1905. Responsible for introducing Art Nouveau style at Egersund, based on his knowledge of Continental developments.

OLSEN, HARALD (*1851–1910, Norway*). *Architecture, furniture, glass, metalwork, enamel.* Architect in Oslo in the 1880s. Designer at Hadeland glassworks, Jevnaker. Designed silver and enamel for J. Tostrup, Oslo, and David Andersen, Oslo.

OPSVIK, PETER (*b. 1939, Norway*). *Furniture.* Educated design schools in Bergen and Oslo. During the 1970s studied in England and at the Volkwangschule für Kunstgewerbe in Essen, Germany, where he became interested in ergonomy. Designer at Tandberg Radio Factory 1965–70. Has collaborated with Hans Christian Mengshoel in the development of innovative seating devices as part of the *Balans* series.

OSIPOW, ANNA MARIA (*b. 1935, Finland*). *Ceramics.* Maintains own studio where she produces utility ceramics and sculptural works.

OSSLUND, HELMER (*1866–1938, Sweden*). *Ceramics.* Studied painting. Worked at Gustavsberg 1889–94 and at Höganäs Stenkohlsverk 1897.

ØSTERN, BJØRN SIGURD (*b. 1935, Norway*). *Metalwork.* Educated CAD, Bergen, 1955–56, and NCAD, Oslo, 1956–61. Designer at David-Andersen, Oslo, since 1961.

PALMQVIST, SVEN (*b. 1906, Sweden*). *Glass.* Educated SACD and RAAS, Stockholm; Académie Ranson, Paris. Designer at Orrefors from 1936. Awarded Grand Prix MT 1957. Exhibited Paris 1937; New York 1939; FS; Orrefors traveling exhibitions in U.S. 1958.

PANTON, VERNER (*b. 1926, Denmark*). *Architecture, interior design, furniture, lighting fixtures.* Educated technical school, Odense; graduated AA, Copenhagen, 1951. Designed exhibitions. Designed lighting fixtures for Louis Poulsen & Co., Copenhagen. Awarded International Design Award from the American Institute of Designers 1963, 1968; Rosenthal Studio Prize 1967. Numerous exhibitions in Denmark and abroad.

PEHRSON, ANDERS (*b. 1912, Sweden*). *Lighting fixtures.* Designs and produces lamps and lighting fixtures. Director of Ateljé Lyktan, Åhus.

PERCY, ARTHUR CARLSSON (*1886–1976, Sweden*). *Ceramics, glass, textiles.* Educated Artists' Union School (Konstnärsförbundets Skola), Stockholm; studied with Henri Matisse, Paris, 1908. Designer with Gefle porcelain works, Gävle, 1922–59 and at Karlskrona porcelain works from 1943. Designed printed fabrics for Elsa Gullberg Ltd. from 1936. With Gullaskruf glassworks in 1952. Awarded *diplôme d'honneur* Paris 1925 and Prince Eugen medal 1957. One-man shows Stockholm 1957, Gävle 1971.

Exhibited Paris 1925; Barcelona 1929; Stockholm 1930; Paris 1937; New York 1939; H 55. Monograph, *Arthur Percy*, Nordiska Museet (1980).

PERSSON (BIP), BRITT-INGRID *(b.1938,Sweden).Ceramics*. Independent studio ceramist since 1966. Own workshop in Stockholm where she produces primarily sculptural works.

PERSSON, SIGURD *(b. 1914, Sweden). Metalwork, glass*. Trained as silversmith with his father, Fritiof Persson, Hälsingborg. Educated Academy of Applied Art, Munich, and SACD, Stockholm, 1942. Own workshop in Sweden since 1942 producing cutlery and jewelry. Also designs for industry. Awarded medals at MT 1951, 1954, 1957, and 1960; Prince Eugen Medal 1970; Swedish Prize for Artists 1967; and Gregor Paulsson trophy. Exhibited Stockholm 1950; DS; Sydney 1954; Pforzheim 1955; H 55; Havana 1956. Author of *Modern Swedish Silver* (1951), *Sigurd Persson Silver* (1979), and *Sigurd Persson Smycken* (1980).

PERSSON-MELIN, SIGNE *(b. 1925, Sweden). Ceramics, glass*. Trained at Andersson & Johansson, Höganäs; studied ceramics with Nathalie Krebs, Copenhagen. Educated SACD, Stockholm (ceramics and sculpture) and SAC, Copenhagen (ceramics). Engaged by Kosta Boda from 1967 and recently at Rörstrand, Lidköping. Own ceramic workshop in Malmö since 1950. Awarded Lunning Prize 1958. One-woman shows Stockholm 1953; Göteborg and Malmö 1954. Exhibited MTs; DS; Amsterdam 1959; "Adventure in Swedish Glass," Australia, 1975.

PETERSEN, OLE BENT *(b. 1938, Denmark). Metalwork*. Educated SAC, Copenhagen, 1957–59, and RDA, Copenhagen, 1959–60. Own workshop since 1960, making jewelry and small sculptures. With Georg Jensen, Copenhagen, since 1978. Numerous exhibitions include GJ.

PETTERSEN, SVERRE *(1884–1958, Norway). Glass*. Educated NCAD, Oslo. Later became its director. Art director at Hadeland glassworks, Jevnaker, 1928–49. Also designed ceramics, textiles, and books.

PLØEN, ERIK *(b. 1925, Norway). Ceramics*. Trained in ceramics at Schneider & Knutzen Workshop near Oslo. Own pottery workshop in Ljan from 1946. Visiting professor at University of Chicago 1963–64. Awarded Lunning Prize 1961. Numerous exhibitions in Norway and abroad.

PROCOPÉ, ULLA *(1921–1968, Finland). Ceramics*. Educated CSI, Helsinki. Designer for Arabia, Helsinki, 1948–67. Awarded *diplôme d'honneur* MT 1957. Exhibited FS; FE; Fi.

PRYTZ, JACOB *(1886–1962, Norway). Metalwork*. Son of Torolf Prytz (1856–1938). Educated NCAD, Oslo, and in Paris. Head of NCAD 1914, rector 1945. Art director and proprietor of J. Tostrup, Oslo. Cofounder of Applied Art Association 1918, chairman 1920–39. Chairman of National Applied Art Federation 1946–48. Exhibited Paris 1938.

PRYTZ, TOROLF *(1856–1938, Norway). Metalwork*. Architect in Oslo in 1881. Associated with J. Tostrup, Oslo, from 1885, manager from 1890.

RANTANEN, KIRSTI *(b. 1930, Finland). Textiles*. Independent textile designer. Maintains own studio and teaches.

RASMUSSEN, JØRGEN *(b. 1931, Denmark). Industrial design, furniture*. Graduated AA, Copenhagen, 1955. Designer of office furniture and industrial products for Kevi, Glastrup. Exhibited "Knoll au Musée," Paris, 1972.

RATIA, ARMI *(1912–1979, Finland). Textiles*. Founded Marimekko Oy, Helsinki, in 1951, where she brought together numerous artists and designers including Maija Isola and Vuokko Eskolin-Nurmesniemi.

RELLING, INGMAR *(b. 1920, Norway). Furniture, interior design*. Educated NCAD, Oslo. Designs have been produced by Vestlandske Møbelfabrikk, Ørsta.

REUMERT, JANE *(b. 1942, Denmark). Ceramics*. Educated SAC, Copenhagen, 1964. Established workshop, Strandstraede Keramik, with Beate Andersen and Gunhild Aaberg in Copenhagen 1964. Engaged by Dansk Designs Ltd. and Kosta Boda. One-woman shows include Den Permanente, Copenhagen, 1970, and Röhsska Konstslöjdmuseet, Göteborg, 1977. Exhibited

"Kunst und Kunsthandwerk aus Dänemark," Wiesbaden, 1971; "Exempla," Munich, 1974; Hälsingborg Stadsmuseum, 1975; "Danish Ceramic Design," University Park, Pa., 1981.

ROHDE, JOHAN *(1856–1935, Denmark). Metalwork*. Studied medicine. Educated RDA, Copenhagen, 1881–82 (painting and graphics). Founded Artists' Studio School (Kunstnernes Studieskole) in 1882, where he taught anatomy; head of school 1908–12. Designer for Georg Jensen, Copenhagen, 1903. Also designed textiles and furniture. Awarded bronze medal Paris 1900, Grand Prix Paris 1925, Thorvaldsens Medal 1934. One-man shows include Det Danske Kunstindustrimusem, Copenhagen, 1908; Stockholm 1917. Exhibitions include Berlin 1891; Chicago 1893; Århus 1909; Brooklyn 1927; Helsinki 1928, 1931; GJ. Monograph by Sigurd Schultz, *Johan Rohde Sølv*, Copenhagen (1951).

ROSENBERG, WALLE (GUSTAV VALDEMAR) *(1891–1919, Finland). Metalwork*. Studied painting in Helsinki, Paris, and Rome. Influenced by Post-Impressionists, especially by the work of Henri Matisse. Also designed silver produced by Alm Oy, Porvoo.

RYGGEN, HANNAH *(1894–1970, Sweden). Norway. Textiles*. Swedish textile artist and teacher. Settled in Ørlandet, Norway, in 1924, where she set up her own studio, spinning and dying the yarn for her textiles herself. Many of her tapestries depict strong political sentiments based on current world events.

SAARINEN, ELIEL *(1873–1950, Finland). Architecture, interior design, furniture*. Educated HUT, Helsinki. Architectural partnership with Herman Gesellius and Armas Lindgren 1896–1907. Designed Finnish pavilion at Paris 1900. One of the leaders of national romantic movement in Finland. Emigrated to U.S. 1923. Awarded second place Chicago Tribune Tower competition 1922. Designed buildings for Cranbrook Foundation, Mich., from 1925, where he also taught. In partnership with his son Eero 1937. U.S. works include Kleinhans Music Hall, Buffalo, N.Y., 1938, Tanglewood Opera Shed, Stockbridge, Mass., and Tabernacle Church of Christ, Columbus, Ind., 1941–42. Author of *The City* (1943), *Search for Form* (1948).

SALMENHAARA, KYLLIKKI *(1915–1981, Finland). Ceramics*. Educated CSI, Helsinki, 1943. At Arabia, Helsinki, 1947–63. MT awards: silver medal 1951, *diplôme d'honneur* 1954, Grand Prix 1957, gold medal 1960. Exhibited DS; H 55; FE; Fi.

SALTO, AXEL *(1889–1961, Denmark). Ceramics*. Educated RDA, Copenhagen (painting). Engaged with Bing & Grøndahl, Copenhagen, 1922–25; with Nathalie Krebs; at Royal Copenhagen Porcelain Manufactory from 1933. Designed patterns for bookbinding paper 1934 and printed fabric for L. F. Foght 1944. Headed restoration of Jørgen Sonne's frieze of 1846 on Thorvaldsens Museum, Copenhagen. Awarded Grand Prix MT 1951. Numerous exhibitions in Denmark and abroad. Cofounder of periodical *Klingen* in 1917.

SAMPE, ASTRID *(b. 1909, Sweden). Textiles*. Educated SACD, Stockholm, and Royal College of Art, London. At Nordiska Kompaniet, Stockholm, from 1936, head of textile department from 1937. Worked with architect Sven Markelius on Swedish pavilion for New York 1939. Designed for Donald Bros., Dundee; Knoll International, New York; Svängsta Klädesfabrik; Almedahl-Dalsjöfors. Awarded Grand Prix MT 1954 and Gregor Paulsson trophy 1956. Exhibited Paris 1937. Elected honorary member Royal Designers for Industry, London, 1949. Published *Textiles Illustrated* with Vera Diurson (1948).

SANDNES, EYSTEIN *(b. 1924, Norway). Glass, ceramics*. Educated NCAD, Oslo. At Magnor glassworks, Stavangerflint stoneware factory, and Porsgrund porcelain factory, where he was art director from 1959. Awarded silver medal MT 1960. Numerous exhibitions in Norway and abroad.

SARPANEVA, TIMO *(b. 1926, Finland). Glass, ceramics, textiles, metalwork*. Graduated CSI, Helsinki, 1948 (graphics). Teacher of textile design and cloth printing CSI, Helsinki, 1953–57. Engaged with Iittala glassworks from 1950; art director of Pori Cotton 1955. MT awards: silver medal 1951, Grand Prix 1954, two Grand Prix 1957, silver and gold medals 1960. Three first-place awards in "American Young Scandinavian Exhibition," U.S., 1956; Lunning Prize 1956; Eurostar Prize. Designed several Finnish home exhibitions, H 55, Finnish section of MT 1957, Fi, and Finnish section Montreal 1967. Numerous exhibitions in Finland and abroad. Elected honorary member of the Royal Designers for Industry, London, 1963.

SCHARFF, ALLAN *(b. 1945, Denmark). Metalwork.* Educated the Goldsmith School. Artistic consultant and designer for Hans Hansen Sølvsmedie, Kolding, from 1978. Independent designer and silversmith since 1979 at own workshop. One-man show Det Danske Kunstindustrimuseum, Copenhagen, 1980. Recipient of many grants and awards. Numerous exhibitions in Denmark and abroad.

SCHNEIDER, ANDREAS *(1867–1931, Norway). Ceramics.* Painter. Studied ceramics in Copenhagen, 1894. Own workshop from 1895 near Oslo. Engaged by Egersund ceramics factory from 1910. Also designed furniture and textiles.

SCHUMACHER-PERCY, ULLA *(b. 1918, Sweden). Textiles.* Studied painting at School of Otte Sköld 1936–37. Educated SACD, Stockholm, 1938–41. Artistic director of Stockholm Domestic Crafts Association from 1947. Produces embroideries and rugs in own workshop in Stockholm since 1949. One-woman shows in Stockholm 1957, 1960. Exhibitions include FS.

SEENAT GROUP POTTERY *(est. 1977, Finland). Ceramics.* Collaborative workshop in which Terhi Juurinen, Lea Klemola, and Riitta Pensanen design and fabricate utility goods in limited production. All objects made at the workshop are signed with a workshop symbol rather than with an individual potter's name.

SIIMES, AUNE *(1909–1964, Finland). Ceramics.* Educated CSI, Helsinki. At Arabia, Helsinki, from 1932, working in stoneware and porcelain. Awarded silver medal Paris 1937; gold medal MT 1951, silver medal 1954. Exhibited DS; H 55; FE; Fi.

SIMBERG-EHRSTRÖM, UHRA-BEATA *(1914–1979, Finland). Textiles.* Educated CSI, Helsinki. Designed rugs for Friends of Finnish Handicraft from 1935. Industrial designer for Inhemsk Ull (Native Woollens) from 1938 and Finlayson-Forssa from 1958. Art consultant for Norna Domestic Crafts 1950–58. Awarded diploma Paris 1937; *diplôme d'honneur* MT 1954, Grand Prix 1957, gold medal 1960. Exhibited DS; H 55; Fi.

SKOGSTER-LEHTINEN, GRETA *(b. 1900, Finland). Textiles.* Own studio from 1921–75, producing textiles, carpets, and tapestries. Her textiles have been used as furniture coverings.

SLANG, GERD *(b. 1925, Norway). Glass.* Educated NCAD, Oslo. Designer at Hadeland glassworks, Jevnaker, 1948–52 and 1963–72. Free-lance designer 1952–63. Exhibitions include "Craftsmen from Norway," New York, 1970.

SLOTT-MØLLER, HARALD *(1864–1937, Denmark). Metalwork, ceramics.* Studied painting. Designed silver for A. Michelsen, Copenhagen, and ceramics for Aluminia, Copenhagen.

SØRENSEN, JOHNNY *(b. 1944, Denmark). Furniture.* Graduated SAC, Copenhagen, 1967. In partnership with Rud Thygesen since 1966. Awards include first prize in the Society of Cabinetmakers Jubilee Exhibition 1966; first prize in the Society of Cabinetmakers Furniture Competition 1968; the Central Bank's Jubilee Award 1969, 1975; the Society of Furniture Makers Award 1971; third prize in Scandinavian Idea Competition, 1973; Alex. Foss's Industrifond-Award 1976. Exhibited with Rud Thygesen and separately at Den Permanente, Copenhagen, 1972; Det Danske Kunstindustrimuseum, Copenhagen, 1976; Chicago 1977.

SØRENSEN, OSKAR *(b. 1898, Norway). Metalwork.* Goldsmith, designer, and teacher. Worked with J. Tostrup, Oslo, and Nordisk Aluminiumindustri.

SOTAVALTA, IMPI *(1885–1943, Finland). Textiles.* Designer for the Friends of Finnish Handicraft 1917–43. Specialized in rug design.

SPARRE, LOUIS *(1863–1964, Italy). Finland. Furniture, ceramics.* Studied painting at Académie Julian, Paris, 1886–90. Settled in Finland 1891–1911, then in Stockholm. Founder of Iris factory in Porvoo in 1897. Also designed and illustrated books. With Akseli Gallen-Kallela, pioneer of modern Finnish design.

Awarded first prize in competition by Friends of Finnish Handicraft for furniture 1894.

STÆHR-NIELSEN, EVA *(1911–1976, Denmark). Ceramics.* Educated SAC, Copenhagen, 1930–33. Joined Saxbo, Copenhagen, where she worked with Nathalie Krebs, 1932–68. At Royal Copenhagen Porcelain Manufactory 1968–76. Awarded gold medal Paris 1937; gold medals MT 1954, 1957. Numerous exhibitions of Saxbo, with whom she exhibited, include Det Danske Kunstindustrimuseum, Copenhagen, 1954, 1957; DS; NF: Malmö Museum, 1957; FS; "Dansk Form og Miljø," Stockholm, 1959; AD; "Two Centuries of Danish Design," London, 1968; Åborg Kunstmuseum, 1975.

STÅLHANE, CARL-HARRY *(b. 1920, Sweden). Ceramics.* Studied painting with Isaac Grünewald, Stockholm, and sculpture with Ossip Zadkine at Académie Colarossi, Paris. Teacher of ceramics at SAC, Göteborg. At Rörstrand, Lidköping, since 1939. Own workshop in Lidköping since 1973. Awarded gold medal MT 1951, *diplôme d'honneur* 1954; International Design Award of American Institute of Decorators 1960. Participated in Rörstrand exhibitions in Stockholm 1948, Copenhagen 1954, and London 1957. One-man shows in Stockholm 1951, 1957, 1960; Göteborg 1946; Malmö 1950; New York 1960.

STEPHENSEN, MAGNUS *(b. 1903, Denmark). Architecture, metalwork, ceramics, furniture.* Educated RDA, Copenhagen (architecture). At Kay Bojesen, Copenhagen, 1938–52; at Georg Jensen, Copenhagen, from 1950. During the 1960s also designed for Royal Copenhagen Porcelain Manufactory and Aluminia, Copenhagen. Awarded Eckersberg Medal 1948. MT awards: three gold medals 1951, two Grand Prix 1954, three gold medals 1957, silver medal 1960. Exhibited DS; NF; FS; AD; GJ. Author of *Bogen om Japans Brugsting* (1968).

STURE, ALF *(b. 1915, Norway). Interior design, furniture.* Educated NCAD, Oslo. Apprentice cabinetmaker and designer with Hiorth & Østlyngen, Oslo, 1940–50. Independent design studio from 1950. Numerous exhibitions in Norway and abroad.

SVEINSDOTTIR, JULIANA *(1889–1966, Iceland). Textiles.* Educated RDA, Copenhagen, 1912–17. Leading Icelandic nonfigurative textile artist whose first work, interior textiles, appeared in 1921. Major tapestry work in chambers of Supreme Court, Denmark. Awarded Eckersberg Medal 1947, gold medal MT 1951. Numerous exhibitions include MTs; DS; FS; retrospective exhibition in Copenhagen, 1963.

SVENSSON, INEZ *(b. 1923, Sweden). Textiles.* Artistic director of Borås Wäfveri from 1957. Worked on design projects for UNESCO, including in Afghanistan. Member of 10-Gruppen, Stockholm, from the early 1970s. Also a journalist.

TAPIOVAARA, ILMARI *(b. 1914, Finland). Interior design, furniture.* Graduated CSI, Helsinki, 1937 (interior design). Apprenticed with Le Corbusier in Paris. Professor at School of the Art Institute of Chicago; visiting professor of product design, Illinois Institute of Technology, Chicago, 1952–54; chairman of the interior design department CSI, Helsinki, 1951–52, 1953–56. Artistic director of Askon Tehtaat, Lahtis, 1938–41, and of Keravan Puusepänteollisuus, Kerava, 1941–51. Awarded gold medals MT 1951, 1954, 1957, and 1960. Exhibited FS; DS; Fi; Museum of Modern Art traveling exhibition 1949–51. Elected honorary member of the Royal Designers for Industry, London, 1964.

THORDARDOTTIR, THORBJÖRG *(b. 1949, Iceland). Textiles.* Educated CAC, Reykjavik, 1968–72, and SACD, Stockholm, 1975. Teacher at CAC since 1975. Member of Gallery Langbrok Collective, Reykjavik. Exhibited "Icelandic Women's Art," 1975; "Icelandic Crafts," 1976; Nordisk Textiltriennale 1976–77, 1979–80. Group exhibitions Solon Islandus Gallery, Reykjavik, 1976–77; Icelandic Textile Federation 1978, 1981; Gallery Langbrok's Summer Show, Reykjavik, 1979.

THORGRIMSSON, GESTUR *(b. 1920, Iceland). Ceramics.* Assistant professor in visual arts at CAC, Reykjavik. His ceramic work is done in collaboration with his wife, Sigrun Gudjonsdottir (Runa).

THORUP, TORSTEN *(b. 1944, Denmark). Lighting fixtures.* Has designed lighting fixtures for Focus Belysning, Holte.

THYGESEN, RUD (b. 1932, Denmark). Furniture. Graduated SAC, Copenhagen, 1966. In partnership with Johnny Sørensen since 1966. Awards include first prize in the Society of Cabinetmakers Jubilee Exhibition 1966; first prize in the Society of Cabinetmakers Furniture Competition 1968; the Central Bank's Jubilee Award 1969, 1975; the Society of Furniture Makers Award 1971; third prize in Scandinavian Idea Competition, 1973; Alex. Foss's Industrifond-Award 1976. Exhibited with Johnny Sørensen and separately at Den Permanente, Copenhagen, 1972; Det Danske Kunstindustrimuseum, Copenhagen, 1976; Chicago 1977.

TOIKKA, OIVA (b. 1931, Finland). Ceramics, glass. Designed for Arabia, Helsinki, 1956–59. Artistic director of Nuutajärvi-Notsjö glassworks since 1963. Awarded Lunning Prize 1970.

TYNELL, HELENA (b. 1918, Finland). Glass, ceramics. Graduated CSI, Helsinki, 1943. Designed ceramics for Arabia, Helsinki, 1943–46, lighting fixtures for Taito Oy 1943–53, and glass for Riihimäki since 1946. Worked with Nord, New York, from 1957. Exhibited MT 1954–60; H 55; Fi.

VALLGREN, CARL WILHELM (VILLE) (1855–1940, Finland). Sculpture, metalwork, ceramics. Studied with C. E. Sjöstrand in Helsinki. In 1902 became a French citizen, but returned to Finland in 1913. Produced many sculptural works, but also designed small metalwork objects and ceramics. Awarded gold medal Paris 1889, Chevalier de la Légion d'Honneur, 1894, Grand Prix Paris 1900, Officier de la Légion d'Honneur 1901.

VALLIEN, BERTIL (b. 1938, Sweden). Glass, ceramics. Educated SACD, Stockholm, 1956–61. Studied and worked in U.S. in 1961–63 on Royal Scholarship. Teacher at SACD, Stockholm, since 1967. At Kosta Boda from 1963 and in own ceramics workshop in Åfors. Awarded Illum Prize and Swedish Prize for Artists. Numerous exhibitions in Sweden and abroad.

VANGSGAARD, ERIK INGOMAR (b. 1938, Denmark). Metalwork. Became silversmith 1958. Educated SAC, Copenhagen, 1962–64. Industrial designer 1964–72. Established own workshop in Skevinge 1974. Several exhibitions in Denmark and abroad.

VASEGAARD, GERTRUD (b. 1913, Denmark). Ceramics. Educated SAC, Copenhagen, 1930–32. Worked with Axel Salto and Bode Willumsen and in 1933 set up studio in Gudhjem with her sister Lisbeth Munch-Petersen until 1935. Own studio there 1936–48. Associated with Bing & Grøndahl, Copenhagen, from 1945–59. Since 1959 has maintained a studio in Copenhagen with her daughter Myre Vasegaard. Designed for Royal Copenhagen Porcelain Manufactory 1960–75. Awarded gold medal MT 1957. Numerous one-woman shows in Denmark. Exhibited DS; FS; "XX Ceramic International," Syracuse Museum of Fine Arts (now the Everson Museum of Art), 1958; AD; "Creative Craft in Denmark Today," New York, 1962; "Two Centuries of Danish Design," London, 1968; "Acht Deense Ceramisten," Rotterdam, 1976; "Danish Ceramic Design," University Park, Pa., 1981.

VASEGAARD, MYRE (b. 1936, Denmark). Ceramics. Educated SAC, Copenhagen, 1955–59. Trained at Herman A. Kähler, Næstved, and in the Inger & Clement Workshop. Artist-in-residence with Bing & Grøndahl, Copenhagen, 1955–59. Since then has maintained her own studio with her mother, Gertrud Vasegaard. Exhibitions include "Dansk Form og Miljø," Stockholm, 1959; AD; "Creative Craft in Denmark Today," New York, 1962; "Two Centuries of Danish Design," London, 1968; "Acht Deense Ceramisten," Rotterdam, 1976; "Danish Ceramic Design," University Park, Pa., 1981.

VIGELAND, TONE (b. 1938, Norway). Metalwork. Educated NCAD, Oslo. Journeyman diploma conferred 1960, Master diploma 1962. Designer at Plus, Fredrikstad, 1958–61. At Norway Silver Designs, Ltd. Has maintained own workshop in Oslo since 1961. Awarded four prizes in Goldsmiths' Guild competition. Exhibited "Craftsmen from Norway," New York, 1970.

WALLANDER, ALF (1862–1914, Sweden). Ceramics, glass, textiles, metalwork, furniture. Educated SACD, Stockholm, 1878–85.

Artistic director Rörstrand, Lidköping, 1895. Designed furniture and textiles for Svensk Konstslöjdsutställning Selma Giöbel; director there from 1899. Designed for Kosta 1907–11 and Reijmyre glassworks, Rejmyra, 1908–14. Exhibitions include Stockholm 1897, Paris 1900.

WANSCHER, OLE (b. 1903, Denmark). Architecture, furniture. Educated RDA, Copenhagen (architecture). Professor of architecture RDA 1953–73. One of original founders of Copenhagen's Cabinetmakers Guild. Has designed for many Copenhagen furniture firms. Awarded gold medal MT 1960. Exhibitions include DS; NF; FS; AD; GJ. Author of Furniture Types (1932), Outline History of Furniture (1941), English Furniture c. 1680–1800 (1944), History of the Art of Furniture (1946–56).

WÄRFF, ANN (b. 1937, Germany). Sweden. Glass. Studied graphic arts in Hamburg, Ulm, and Zurich. At Kosta Boda from 1964–79. Works in own studio in Stenskyta, Sweden. Awarded with her husband, Göran Wärff, Swedish State traveling scholarship 1967, Lunning Prize 1968. Numerous exhibitions in Sweden and abroad including "Adventure in Swedish Glass," Australia, 1975.

WÄRFF, GÖRAN (b. 1933, Sweden). Glass. Studied architecture and industrial design in Brunswick and Ulm. At Pukeberg glassworks 1959–64; free-lance designer for Kosta Boda since 1964. Awarded with his wife, Ann Wärff, Swedish State traveling scholarship 1967 and Lunning Prize 1968. Emigrated to Sydney, Australia, in 1974. Numerous exhibitions in Sweden and abroad, including "Adventure in Swedish Glass," Australia, 1975.

WECKSTRÖM, BJÖRN (b. 1935, Finland). Metalwork, glass. Graduated the Goldsmith School of Helsinki, 1956. Free-lance designer 1956–63. At Hopeakontu Oy 1957, Lapponia Jewelry Oy, Helsinki, from 1963, Kruunukoru, 1964. Is a sculptor in various materials and has also designed furniture. Awards include MT 1960; Lunning Prize 1968; Illum Prize 1972; second prize Finnish Jewelry Society 1962, medal for merit 1967; Pro Finlandia medal 1971. Numerous one-man shows in Finland and abroad. Monograph published in 1980 by Kustannusosakeyhtiö Otavan.

WEGNER, HANS J. (b. 1914, Denmark). Furniture. Apprenticed cabinetmaker. Educated AA, Copenhagen, 1936–38; SAC, Copenhagen. Employed by Arne Jacobsen and Erik Møller until 1943. Designs primarily for Johannes Hansen, Copenhagen. Participated in all exhibitions of Cabinetmakers Guild, Copenhagen, and supervised and arranged Danish art and handcraft exhibitions 1949–52. Awarded Lunning Prize 1951, 1954; Grand Prix MT 1951, diplôme d'honneur and gold medal MT 1954, silver medal MT 1957; Eckersberg Medal 1956; Copenhagen Cabinetmakers Guild prize 1959, 1965; International Design Award of the American Institute of Designers 1961, 1968; Prince Eugen Medal 1961. One-man shows include Zurich 1958; Georg Jensen, New York, 1959, 1965; Oslo Kunstindustrimuseet 1966; Röhsska Konstslöjdmuseet, Göteborg, 1967. Exhibitions include DS; NF; FS; "Dansk Form og Miljø," Stockholm, 1959; "Creative Craft in Denmark Today," New York, 1962; "Two Centuries of Danish Design," London, 1968; "Dansk Miljø," Eastern Europe, 1975–77; "Danish Design," Dublin, 1978. Elected honorary member of the Royal Designers for Industry, London, 1959. Monograph by Henrik Sten Møller, Tema med Variationer, Sønderjyllands Kunstmuseum, Tønder (1979).

WEISS, IVAN (b. 1946, Denmark). Ceramics. Employed as painter at Royal Copenhagen Porcelain Manufactory 1962–66, as designer 1966–70. Study-tour in Japan 1970–72. Returned to Royal Copenhagen Porcelain as artist-in-residence. Has taught at College of Arts and Crafts, Kolding. One-man shows at Royal Copenhagen Porcelain 1973; Kyushu, Japan, 1977; Dordrecht Museum, the Netherlands, 1979; Sopot, Poland, 1970; Det Danske Kunstindustrimuseum, Copenhagen, 1979. Exhibitions include "Danish Ceramic Design," University Park, Pa., 1981.

WENNERBERG, GUNNAR (1863–1914, Sweden). Ceramics, glass, textiles. Studied in Uppsala; studied painting in Paris, 1886–95, and at Sèvres. Artistic director of Gustavsberg 1895–1908. Designed for Kosta 1898–1909. Made cartoons for tapestries woven by Handarbetets Vännar. Numerous exhibitions in Sweden and abroad including retrospective exhibition at Waldemarsudde, Stockholm, 1981.

WESTMAN, CARL (1866–1936, Sweden). *Architecture, interior design, furniture.* Studied in England 1900. Highly influenced by English designers such as Voysey and Baillie Scott. His furniture is generally of simplified, expressive form.

WIHERHEIMO, YRJÖ (b. 1941, Finland). *Furniture, industrial design.* Furniture designer for Haimi Oy, Asko Oy, and Vivero Oy, Helsinki. Also industrial designer in plastics for Nokia Oy. Collaborated with Simo Heikkilä on furniture in the late 1970s and 1980s.

WIINBLAD, BJØRN (b. 1918, Denmark). *Ceramics, graphics, glass, textiles.* Educated RDA, Copenhagen (illustration), and studied ceramics with Lars Syberg. Designer for Nymølle faience factory 1946–56 and for Rosenthal, Germany, since 1956. Stage designer for Dallas Theater Center 1965 and the Pantomime Theatre in Tivoli Gardens, Copenhagen. Hotel and restaurant decorator in Japan, England, and U.S. Produced silver sculpture with Hans Hansen Sølvsmedie, Kolding. Also designed metalwork and furniture. Numerous awards and exhibitions in Denmark and abroad. Monograph published by Det Danske Kunstindustrimuseum, Copenhagen (1981).

WILLUMSEN, JENS FERDINAND (1863–1958, Denmark). *Ceramics.* Educated technical school and RDA, Copenhagen, 1881–85. Artistic director of Bing & Grøndahl, Copenhagen, 1897–1900. Awarded honorable mention Paris 1889, Thorvaldsens Medal 1947. Exhibited Paris 1900. Monograph by V. Jastrau, *J. F. Willumsen,* Copenhagen (1929).

WINCKLER, IDA (b. 1930, Denmark). *Textiles.* Textile artist for the Danish Handicraft Guild, specializing in patterns for cross-stitch embroideries.

WIRKKALA, TAPIO (b. 1915, Finland). *Glass, exhibition design, metalwork, graphics.* Graduated CSI, Helsinki 1936 (sculpture). At Iittala glassworks since 1947. Artistic director of CSI 1951–55. Headed design department of A. Ahlström Oy 1957–65. Worked with design firm Raymond Loewy, New York, 1955–56, and German firm of Rosenthal since 1956. Designed several Finnish industrial design exhibitions including the Finnish pavilion at MT in 1951 and 1954 and the Finnish pavilion at Brussels 1958. Numerous awards include seven Grand Prix and one gold and one silver medal at MT, Lunning Prize 1951. Numerous exhibitions in Finland and abroad including "Contemporary Finnish Design," Smithsonian Institution traveling exhibition, U.S., 1970–72 and major retrospective worldwide traveling exhibition 1981–82. Elected honorary member of Royal Society of Arts, London, 1961, named Academician 1972. Holds honorary doctorate from the Royal College of Art, London.

SELECTED BIBLIOGRAPHY

GENERAL

Anker, Peter. *The Art of Scandinavia.* London, New York, P. Hamlyn, 1970.

Beer, Eileene Harrison. *Scandinavian Design; Objects of a Life Style.* New York, Farrar, Straus and Giroux; The American-Scandinavian Foundation, 1975.

Design in Scandinavia; an exhibition of objects for the home from Denmark, Finland, Norway, Sweden. Richmond, Virginia, Virginia Museum of Fine Arts, 1954.

Hård af Segerstad, Ulf. *Design in Scandinavia: Denmark, Finland, Norway, Sweden.* Exhibition catalogue. State Galleries of Australia in Perth, Adelaide, Brisbane, Sydney, Canberra, Melbourne, Hobart. Stockholm, Victoria Pettersons Bokindustri, 1968.

————. *Modern Scandinavian Design.* Oslo, Gyldendal Norsk Forlag, 1961.

————. *Modern Scandinavian Furniture.* Stockholm, Nordisk Rotogravyr, 1963.

————. *Scandinavian Design.* Eng. trans. by Nancy and Edward Maze. Stockholm, Nordisk Rotogravyr, 1961.

Hatje, Gerd and Ursula. *Design for Modern Living: A Practical Guide to Home Furnishings and Interior Design.* New York, Harry N. Abrams, 1962.

Hayward, Helena, ed. *World Furniture, an Illustrated History.* New York and Toronto, McGraw Hill, 1965.

Hughes, Graham. *The Art of Jewelry.* New York, Viking Press; London, Studio Vista, 1972.

————. *Modern Jewelry, an international survey, 1890–1963.* London, Studio Books; New York, Crown Publishers, 1963.

————. *Modern Silver Throughout the World, 1880–1967.* London, Studio Vista; New York, Crown Publishers, 1967.

Jensen, Georg. *The Lunning Prize Designers' Exhibition.* Copenhagen, Georg Jensen, 1957.

Møller, Viggo Sten. *Funktionalisme og brugskunst siden 1920 erne.* Copenhagen, Rhodos, 1978.

Nordisk Industridesign. Exhibition catalogue; text in Swedish, English, and Finnish, by Alf Bøe. Göteborg, Röhsska Konstslöjdmuseet, 1971.

Rabén, Hans. *Det Moderne Hemmet; inredningskonst i Sverige och andra landen.* Stockholm, Bokförlaget Natur och Kultur, 1937.

Scandinavian Design. Exhibition catalogue. Jerusalem, Israel Museum, 1974.

Scandinavian Viewpoint. New York, Georg Jensen, Inc., 1964.

Zahle, Erik, ed. *Scandinavian Domestic Design.* Copenhagen, Hassings Forlag, 1961. Eng. ed. London, 1963.

————. *A Treasury of Scandinavian Design.* New York, Golden Press, 1961.

DENMARK

Andersen, Rigmor. *Kaare Klint Møbler.* Copenhagen, Kunstakademiet, 1979.

The Arts of Denmark, Viking to Modern. Copenhagen, Det Berlingske Bogtrykkeri, 1960.

Bengtsson, Gerda. *Gerda Bengtsson's Book of Danish Stitchery.* New York, Van Nostrand Reinhold, 1972.

Bjørn Wiinblad; Arbejder Gennem 40 År/Forty Years' Creativity. Copenhagen, Det Danske Kunstindustrimuseum, 1981.

Danish Ceramic Design. Exhibition catalogue; selection and catalogue by William Hull. University Park, Pa., Pennsylvania State University, 1981.

Det Danske Hjem. Copenhagen, A. Busck, 1934.

Dansk 50-tal. Exhibition catalogue. Stockholm, Nationalmuseum, 1981.

Dansk Kunsthåndværker Leksikon (Danish Craftsman's Dictionary). 2 vols. Copenhagen, Rhodos, 1979.

Dansk Sølv, 1550–1950. Copenhagen, Det Danske Kunstindustrimuseum, 1953.

Dansk Sølvkorpus '78. Exhibition catalogue. Copenhagen, Det Danske Kunstindustrimuseum, 1978.

Dansk Silver 1900–1950. Exhibition catalogue. Stockholm, Nationalmuseum, 1950.

Ditzel, Nanna and Jørgen, eds. *Danske Stole—Danish Chairs.* Copenhagen, Høst, 1954; New York, G. Wittenborn, 1954.

Enevoldsen, Birgit, and Enevoldsen, Christian. *Brugskunst: Møbler, Textiler, Lamper.* Copenhagen, Arkitektens Forlag, 1958.

Faber, Tobias. *Arne Jacobsen.* New York, Frederick A. Praeger, 1964; London, Alex Tiranti, 1964.

Georg Jensen: Centenary Exhibition, 1866–1966. Exhibition catalogue. London, Goldsmiths' Hall, [1966].

Georg Jensen Silversmithy: 77 Artists, 75 Years. Exhibition catalogue. Washington, D.C., Smithsonian Institution Press, 1980.

Hayden, Arthur. *Royal Copenhagen Porcelain: its history and development from the 18th century to the present day.* London, 1911.

Hiort, Esbjørn. *Modern Danish Silver.* New York, Museum Books; London, Zwemmer, 1954.

———. *Modern Dansk Keramik.* Copenhagen, Jul Gjellerups Forlag, 1955.

Johansson, Gotthard, and Reventlow, Christian Ditlev. *Sigvard Bernadotte Sølvarbejder, 1930–1955.* Copenhagen, Georg Jensen Sølv, 1955.

Karlsen, Arne; Salicath, Bent; and Utzon-Frank, Mogens, eds. *Contemporary Danish Design.* Copenhagen, Danish Society of Arts and Crafts and Industrial Design, 1960.

Karlsen, Arne, and Tiedemann, Anker. *Dansk Brugskunst.* Copenhagen, 1960.

———. *Made in Denmark.* Trans. by Eve Wendt. Copenhagen, Jul Gjellerups Forlag, 1960; New York, Reinhold Publishing Co., [1960].

Kastholm, Jørgen. *Arne Jacobsen.* Copenhagen, 1968.

Kaufmann, Edgar, Jr.; Lassen, Erik; and Reventlow, Christian D. *Fifty Years of Danish Silver in the Georg Jensen Tradition.* Copenhagen, Det Schønbergske Forlag, 1954.

Koppel, Henning, et al. *Landsforeningen Dansk Brugskunst og Design.* Copenhagen, 1972.

Larsen, Alfred; Riismøller, Peter; and Schlüter, Mogens. *Dansk Glas 1825–1925.* Copenhagen, Nyt Nordisk Forlag, 1963.

Lassen, Erik. *En københavnsk porcelænsfabriks historie; Bing & Grøndahl 1853–1978.* Copenhagen, 1978.

Lassen, Erik, ed. *The Arts of Denmark.* Copenhagen, Danish Society of Arts and Crafts and Industrial Design, 1960.

Lassen, Erik, and Schlüter, Mogens. *Dansk Glas 1925–1975.* Copenhagen, Nyt Nordisk Forlag Arnold Busck, 1975.

Lübecker, Pierre. *Applied Art by Kay Bojesen.* Copenhagen, National Association of Danish Handicrafts, 1955.

Madsen, Karl Johan Vilhelm. *Thorvald Bindesbøll.* Copenhagen, Det Danske Kunstindustrimuseum, 1943.

Møller, Henrik Sten. *Danish Design.* Trans. by Douglas Holmes. Copenhagen, Rhodos, 1975.

———. *Rud Thygesen-Johnny Sørensen Industri & Design.* Copenhagen, Rhodos, 1976.

———. *Tema med variationer: Hans J. Wegner's møbler.* Tønder, Sønderjyllands Kunstmuseum, 1979.

Møller, Svend Erik. *34 Designers.* Copenhagen, Høst og Søns Forlag, 1967.

Møller, Svend Erik, ed. *Danish Design.* Trans. by Mogens Kay-Larsen. Copenhagen, Det Danske Selskab, 1974.

Møller, Viggo Sten. *Dansk Kunstindustri, 1850–1950.* 2 vols; with English summary. Copenhagen, Rhodos, 1969–70.

———. *Henning Koppel.* Trans. into English by Ellen Branth, into German by Albrecht Leonhardt. Copenhagen, Rhodos, 1965.

Møller Nielsen, Johan. *Wegner; En Dansk Møbelkunstner.* Copenhagen, Gyldendalske Boghandel, 1965.

Nielsen, Laurits Christian. *En dansk kunstner virksomhed; Georg Jensen sølvet gennem 25 aar.* Copenhagen, C. C. Petersen, 1929.

———. *Georg Jensen; an artist's biography.* Copenhagen, Fr. Bagge, 1921.

Porcelænsfabrikken Bing & Grøndahl, 1853–1928. Copenhagen, 1928.

Rasmussen, Steen Eiler. *Danish Textiles.* Leigh-on-Sea, England, F. Lewis, 1956.

Reventlow, Christian Ditlev. *Georg Jensen sølvsmedie gennem fyrretyve, 1904–1944.* Copenhagen, Nordlund, 1944.

The Royal Copenhagen Porcelain Manufactory 1775–1975. Eng. trans. by David Hohnen. Copenhagen, Royal Copenhagen, Ltd., 1975.

Salicath, Bent, ed. *Lunning Prize Designers Exhibition: Denmark, Finland, Norway, Sweden.* Exhibition catalogue. New York, Georg Jensen, Inc., 1967.

Salicath, Bent, and Karlsen, Arne, eds. *Modern Danish Textiles.* Copenhagen, Danish Society of Arts and Crafts and Industrial Design, 1959.

Salto, Axel. *Salto's Keramik.* Copenhagen, 1930.

Schultz, Sigurd. *Johan Rohde Sølv.* Copenhagen, Fischers, 1951.

Schwartz, Walter. *Georg Jensen, en Kunstner, hans tid og slægt.* Copenhagen, Georg Jensen & Wendel, 1958.

Stavenow, Åke, and Reventlow, Christian Ditlev. *Harald Nielsen, et tilbageblik på en kunstners arbejder ved 60-arsdagen.* Copenhagen, Georg Jensen & Wendel, 1952.

"Tre danske brukskunstnere om sitt fag; Helga Foght, Finn Juhl, Nathalie Krebs." In *Nordenfjeldske Kunstindustrimuseum Årbok, 1950.*

Zahle, Erik. *Bing & Grøndahl 1853–1953.* Copenhagen, 1953.

———. *Hjemmets Brugskunst; Kunsthåndværk og Kunstindustri i Norden.* Copenhagen, Hassings, 1961.

FINLAND

Alvar Aalto. Zurich, Verlag für Architektur, 1965.

Annala, Vilho. *Nuutajärven lasitehdas 1873–1943.* Helsinki, 1943.

———. *Suomen Lasiteollisuus.* 2 vols. Helsinki, 1931, 1948.

Aro, P. *Arabia Design.* Helsinki, 1958.

Björn Weckström. Keuruu, Kustannusosakeyhtiö Otava Painolaitokset, 1980.

Bruun, Erik; Sarpaneva, Timo; and Thiel, Osmo. *Finnish Design 1875–1975; 100 Years of Finnish Industrial Design.* Helsinki, 1975.

Carring, Holger, ed. *Keramiikka ja Lasi* (Ceramics and Glass). Helsinki, Wärtsilä Arabia Oy, 1961–67.

Christ-Janer, A. *Eliel Saarinen.* Chicago, 1948.

Designed in Finland. Annual. Helsinki, Finnish Foreign Trade Association, 1961–.

Fields, Jack, and Moore, David, eds. *Finland Creates.* Jyväskylä, Gummerus, 1980.

A. W. Finch, 1854–1930. Exhibition catalogue. In Swedish. Stockholm, Prins Eugens Waldemarsudde, 1981.

Finlandia; moderne finnische Gebrauchskunst. Exhibition catalogue. Hamburg, Museum für Kunst und Gewerbe, 1963.

Finland 1900: Schilderkunst; Architectuur; Kunstnijverheid. Exhibition catalogue. Brussels, Paleis voor Schone Kunsten, 1974.

Finnish Art Industry. Helsinki, Ornamo, 1962.

Finnish Design at Jensen's. New York, Georg Jensen, Inc., 1964.

Finskt 1900. Exhibition catalogue; in Swedish and Finnish. Stockholm, Nationalmuseum, 1971.

Form Function Finland. Periodical. Helsinki, 1980–.

Form und Struktur; Konstruktivismus in der modernen Kunst, Architektur und Formgebung Finlands. Exhibition catalogue. Vienna, Österreichisches Museum für Angewandte Kunst, 1980.

Funkis; Suomi Nykyaikaa Etsimässä Modernismens intåg i Finland. Exhibition catalogue by Kirmo Mikkola et al. Helsinki, Suomen Rakennustaiteen Museo, 1980.

Gleaming Glass from K-I. Helsinki, Karhula-Iittala Glassworks, 1961.

Gutheim, Frederick Albert. *Alvar Aalto.* New York, George Braziller, 1960.

Hård af Segerstad, Ulf. *Modern Finnish Design.* Denmark, F. E. Bording, 1968; England, Weidenfeld and Nicholson, 1969; New York, Frederick A. Praeger, 1969.

Haycraft, John. *Finnish Jewellery and silverware: an introduction to contemporary work and design.* Helsinki, 1962.

Johansson-Pape, Lisa, et al., eds. *Sata vuotta. Suomen Käsityön Ystävät 1879–1979.* Helsinki, 1979.

Kallas, H., and Nickels, S., eds. *Finland: Creation and Construction.* New York, Helsinki, 1968.

Karhula-Iittala Finnish Glass. Helsinki, Karhula-Iittala Glassworks, 1962.

Keinanen, Timo. *Funktionalismin läpimurto Suomen lasiteollisuudessa.* Helsinki, Suomen Taideteollisuusyhdistys, 1981.

Klemola, Marketta. *Juodaan kunnes Iittala näkyy; Iittalan lasitehtaan Juomalasit 1881–1981.* Hämeenlinna, 1981.

Kopisto, Sirkka. *Lasia; Suomen kansallismuseon kokoelmista.* With English summary. Helsinki, 1978.

Korpikaivo-Tamminen, Laura. *Ryijy-Rugs.* Helsinki: Taidekutomo Textile Studio, 1961.

Krohn, A., ed. *Art in Finland. Survey of a Century.* Helsinki, 1953.

Laitinen, Kai. *Vision.* Helsinki, 1966.

Louhio, Anja. *Taideryijyjä* (Modern Finnish Rugs). Helsinki, 1970.

Louis Sparre 1863–1964. Exhibition catalogue; summary in English. Stockholm, Prins Eugens Waldemarsudde, 1981.

Mäki, Oili, ed. *Taide Ja Työ. Finnish Designers of Today*. Helsinki, Werner Söderström Osakeyhtiö, 1954.

The Marimekko Story. Helsinki, Marimekko-Printex Oy, 1964.

Métamorphoses finlandaises; architecture et design. Catalogue of exhibition at Centre Georges Pompidou, Paris. Helsinki, 1978.

Niilonen, Kerttu. *Finnish Glass*. Helsinki, Kustannusosakeyhtiö Tammi, 1966.

Okkonen, O. *Akseli Gallen-Kallelan Taidetta*. Helsinki, 1936.

"One Hundred Great Finnish Designs," *Mobilia*, no. 284 (1979).

ORNAMO. *L'art Décoratif de Finlande*. Helsinki, 1962.

———. *The Ornamo Book of Finnish Design*. Helsinki, Finnish Society of Crafts and Design, 1962.

Pearson, Paul David. *Alvar Aalto and the International Style*. New York, Watson-Guptill Publications, Whitney Library of Design, 1978.

Riihimäen Lasi 1910–1960. Riihimäki, 1960.

Röneholm, H.; West, W.; and Wahlroos, W., eds. *Applied Art in Finland*. Published by the Finnish Section of New York World's Fair, 1939. Helsinki, 1939.

Runeberg, Tutta and Christian. *Jugend*. In Finnish. Helsinki, 1974.

Saarikivi, S.; Niilonen, K.; and Ekelund, H. *Art in Finland*. 5th ed. Helsinki, 1964.

Sirelius, U. T. *The Ryijy Rugs of Finland, A Historical Study*. Helsinki, Otava Publishing, 1926.

Smith, John Boulton. *The Golden Age of Finnish Art—Art Nouveau and the National Spirit*. Keuruu, Kustannusosakeyhtiö Otavan Painolaitokset, 1976.

Toikka-Karvonen, A., ed. *Gallen-Kallelan, Tarvaspää*. Museum guide; text in Swedish, Finnish, and English. Espoo, Akseli Gallen-Kallelan Museosäätiö, [n.d.].

Tuomi, Ritva. "On the search for a new national style," *Abacus, Museum of Finnish Architecture*. Yearbook 1979. Helsinki, 1979.

Willcox, Donald J. *Suomalaisen muotoilun kuviot*. Porvoo, 1973.

Wohnumwelt in Finnland; Architektur und Kunstgewerbe. Exhibition catalogue. Weimar, Kunsthalle, 1979.

Zilliacus, Benedict. *Decorative Arts in Finland*. Helsinki, Werner Söderström, 1963.

Zilliacus, Benedict, ed. *Finnish Designers*. Helsinki, Suomen Taideteollisuusyhdistys.

ICELAND

Gardner, Ralph R., ed. *Icelandic Arts and Crafts*. New York, Icelandic Arts and Crafts Shop, 1964.

Møller, Svend Erik. "Iceland Observed," *Mobilia*, no. 294 (1980), pp. 46–49.

Rothery, Agnes. *Iceland—New World Outpost*. New York, Viking Press, 1948.

Note: Articles in English on Icelandic crafts and design are also to be found in *Atlantica and Icelandic Review*, published quarterly in Reykjavik. Articles in Icelandic are to be found in *Hugur og Hönd*, published annually by Rit Heimilisidhnadharfélags Islands. Also in Icelandic is *Idhnadharmál*, published bimonthly by The Industrial Development Institute.

NORWAY

Aars, Ferdinand. *Arts and Crafts, Industrial design in Norway*. Oslo, Royal Norwegian Ministry of Foreign Affairs, Office of Cultural Relations, 1953.

Anker, Peter. *Norsk Brukskunst*. Oslo, 1969.

Applied Art in Norway. Oslo, Royal Ministry of Foreign Affairs, 1966.

The Art of Norway, 1750–1914. Exhibition catalogue, Louise Lincoln, ed. Madison, Wisc., University of Wisconsin; Minneapolis, The Minneapolis Institute of Arts; Seattle, Seattle Art Museum, 1978.

Benny Motzfeldt; A Norwegian Pathfinder in Glass. Catalogue of an exhibition sponsored by the Royal Norwegian Ministry of Foreign Affairs and circulated in the United States by the Smithsonian Institution Traveling Exhibition Service, 1979–81.

Bøe, Alf. "Gustav Gaudernack, Tegninger og utførte arbeider." In *Kunstindustrimuseet i Oslo Årbok*, 1959–62, pp. 41–72. With English summary.

———. "Industridesigneren Tias Eckhoff; Produksjons-og designproblemer i lys av hans verk." In *Kunstindustrimuseet i Oslo Årbok*, 1965, pp. 50–93. With English summary.

———. *Den Norske Designpris de syv første år*. Oslo, 1969.

———. *Porsgrunds Porselænsfabrik, Bedrift og Produksjon gjennoma 80 år*. Oslo, Porsgrunds Porselænsfabrik, in commission with Johan Grundt Tanums Forlag, 1967.

Bøhn, Tora. "Billedveversken Hannah Ryggen." In *Nordenfjeldske Kunstindustrimuseum Årbok, 1946*, pp. 58–107.

Brukskunstneren Sverre Pettersen. Oslo, Kunstindustrimuseet, 1954.

Clayhills, Harriet. *33 Brukskunstnere*. Oslo, [1959].

Craftsmen from Norway. Exhibition catalogue. New York, American Federation of Arts, 1970.

David-Andersen 1876–1951. Oslo, David-Andersen, 1951.

Engelstad, Helen. *Porselen og paramenter; Brukskunstneren Nora Gulbrandsens arbeider*. Oslo, 1944.

Frida Hansen (1855–1931); Europeeren i norsk vevkunst. Exhibition catalogue, ed. by Anniken Tue; with English summary. Oslo, Kunstindustrimuseet, 1973.

"Gerhard Munthe om inspirasjonen til 'c'est ainsi.'" In *Kunstindustrimuseet i Oslo Årbok, 1965*, pp. 94–97.

Glasskunstneren Benny Motzfeldt. With English summary. Oslo, Kunstindustrimuseet, 1973.

Grieg, Sigurd. *Industriredet; Vallø tapetfabrik A/S 1891–1966*. Vallø, 1966.

Hadelands Glassworks. *Glass Is Our Material (Glas Er Vart Material)*. Oslo, 1961.

———. *Hadeland Crystal*. Oslo, 1960.

———. *Hadeland of Norway*. Oslo, 1961–62.

———. *Hadeland's Art Glass*. Oslo, 1962.

———. *Hadeland Tradition*. Oslo, 1961.

Hannah Ryggen. Oslo, Office of Cultural Relations; Norwegian Ministry of Foreign Affairs, 1964.

Hannah Ryggen. Trondheim, Nordenfjeldske Kunstindustrimuseum, [1965?].

Hidle, Jonas. *Lys i nye og gamle rom*. Oslo, 1969.

Hoffman, Marta. "1880-årenes nye billedvev i Norge og litt om utviklingen senere." In *Vestlandske Kunstindustrimuseum Årbok, 1963–68*, pp. 66–106. With English summary.

Hofgaard, Conrad. *Norway Arts and Crafts*. Oslo, Norwegian Export Council, 1950.

Huldt, Åke H. "Industrial Design." In *Nordenfjeldske Kunstindustrimuseum Årbok, 1951*, pp. 44–58.

Jutrem, Arne Jon. "Glass og glassformere på Hadeland." In *Nordenfjeldske Kunstindustrimuseum Årbok, 1958*, pp. 53–74.

En Kavalkade av aktuell kunstindustri gjennom hundre år. With English captions. Oslo, 1976.

Kavli, Guthorm. "Norwegian Enamel," *American-Scandinavian Review*, vol. 48 (1960), pp. 335–42.

Kielland, Thor B. *Om Gullsmedkunst i hundre år: J. Tostrup, 1832–1932*. Oslo, Grøndahl, 1932.

Kjellberg, Reidar. *Thorbjørn Lie-Jørgensen*. Oslo, Kirstes Boktrykkeri, 1961.

Kloster, Robert. *Fra snekkermøbler til fabrikmøbler; en kort oversikt over møbelhistorien*. Oslo, 1942.

Korsmo, Arne and Grete. "La Boutique esthétique et technique." In *Nordenfjeldske Kunstindustrimuseum Årbok, 1957*, pp. 85–119.

Kristoffersen, K., ed. *Norwegian Textile Times (Norsk Tekstil Tidende)*. Special history for 150th textile trade anniversary. Bergen, Norsk Tekstil Teknisk Forbund, 1963.

Lieberman, Sima. *The Industrialization of Norway 1880–1920*. Oslo, Universitetsforlaget, 1970.

Lorentzen, Olaf, and Kielland, Thor B. *A/S Egersunds Fayancefabriks Co., 1847–1947*. Stavanger, Tryky i Dreyers Grafiske Anstalt, 1947.

Møbler (Norwegian Furniture). Tormod Alnaes, picture ed. Oslo, 1957.

Modern Homes (Moderne Hjem). Oslo, A. M. Hancke Forlag, 1963.

Møller, Viggo Sten. "Tendenser i nordisk kunsthaandvaerk." In *Nordenfjeldske Kunstindustrimuseum Årbok, 1959–60*, pp. 94–109.

Norsk Konsthantverk. Exhibition catalogue. Stockholm, Nordiskt Kulturcentrum, 1976.

Norsk Kunsthåndverk; Landsforbundet Norsk Brukskunst ved 50-års-jubileet 1968. Liv Schjødt, ed. Oslo, Landsforbundet Norsk Brukskunst, 1968.

Norwegian Craftsmen Today. Oslo, Landsforbundet Norsk Brukskunst, 1973.

Norwegian Tapestries. Exhibition catalogue. Washington, D.C., Smithsonian Institution, 1959.

Opstad, Jan-Lauritz. *David-Andersen 100 år i norsk gullsmedkunst*. With English summary and captions. Oslo, 1976.

———. *Gustav Gaudernack, en europeer i norsk jugend*. Oslo, Kunstindustrimuseet, 1979.

———. *Norsk Art Nouveau*. Oslo, C. Huitfeldt Forlag, 1979.

Østby, Leif; Alsvik, H.; and Revold, R. *Norges billedkunst i det mittende og tyvende arhundre*. 2 vols. Oslo, Tyldendal, 1951, 1953.

Polak, Ada Buch. *Norwegian Silver*. Oslo, 1972.

———. *Old Norwegian Glass (Gammelt Norsk Glas)*. Oslo, Tyldendal Norsk Forlag, 1953.

Remlov, Arne. "The Art of Norway: contemporary applied art," *The Studio*, vol. 146 (1953:2), pp. 124–27.

Schjødt, Liv, ed. *Norwegian Applied Art*. Oslo, 1964.

Silver and Enamel (Sølv og Emalje). Oslo, David-Andersen Sølvsmed, 1964.

Tschudi Madsen, Stephan. "Dragestilen; Honnør til en hånet stil." In *Vestlandske Kunstindustrimuseum Årbok, 1949–50*, pp. 19–62.

———. "Uedle metaller i edlere form." In *Nordenfjeldske Kunstindustrimuseum Årbok, 1957*, pp. 38–84. With English summary.

Vriem, Halvor. *Norwegian Decorative Arts Today*. Oslo, Fabritius and Sons, 1937.

SWEDEN

Adventure in Swedish Glass; 16 artists from Kosta-Boda and Orrefors. Exhibition catalogue; text by Helena Lutteman; trans. by Claude Stephenson. Stockholm, Swedish Institute and the Crafts Board of the Australian Council for the Arts, 1975.

Andrèn, Erik. *Swedish Silver*. Translated from Swedish by Lillian Ollén. New York, Barrows, 1950.

Contemporary Swedish Silver. Exhibition catalogue. Zurich, Museum Bellerive, 1975.

Danielson, Sofia. *Om Handarbetets Vänner*. Stockholm, Liljevalchs Konsthall, 1974.

Decorative Arts from Sweden. Exhibition catalogue. New York, Metropolitan Museum of Art, 1927.

Eklund, Hans. *Den nya bygglådan. Början av en tidsalder*. Exhibition catalogue. Stockholm, Stadsmuseet/Kulturhuset, 1980.

Ericsson, Anne-Marie. *Arthur Percy: Konstnär och Formgivare*. Stockholm, Nordiska Museet, 1980.

Föreningen Handarbetets Vänner 1874–1949; Jubileumsutställning. Stockholm, Nationalmuseum, 1949.

Frick, Gunilla. *Svenska Slöjdföreningen och Konstindustrin före 1905*. Stockholm, 1978.

Funder, Lise, et al., eds. *Form og funktion*. Sophienholm, Lyngby-Taarbæk Kommune, 1980.

Graverade glas i nationalmusei samlingar. Stockholm, 1946.

Gunnar G:son Wennerberg. Exhibition catalogue. Stockholm, Prins Eugens Waldemarsudde, 1981.

Gustavsberg 150 ar. Exhibition catalogue; with English summary. Stockholm, Nationalmuseum, 1975.

Hald, Arthur. *Swedish Design*. Stockholm, The Swedish Institute, 1958.

Hald, Arthur, ed. *Simon Gate, Edward Hald en Skildring av människorna och konstnärliga*. Stockholm, Norstedt, 1948.

Hald, Arthur, and Skawonius, Sven Erik. *Nyttokonst*. Stockholm, 1951.

Hård af Segerstad, Ulf. *Berndt Friberg, Keramiker*. Stockholm, Nordisk Rotogravyr, 1964.

———. *Modern Svensk Textilkonst*. Stockholm, 1963.

Hård af Segerstad, Ulf, and Granath, Karl-Eric. *Keramik: Sekelskifte till sjuttiotal*. Stockholm, 1976.

Hedstrand, Björn. *Servisgods från Gustavsberg av Wilhelm Kåge 1917–45*. Motala, Borgströms Tryckeri Aktiebolag, 1975.

Henscher, Angvar, ed. *Den Svenska hemslöjden* (Handcraft in Sweden). Stockholm, 1951.

Huldt, Åke H., ed. *Konsthandverk och hemslöjd i Sverige, 1930–40*. Göteborg, 1941.

Huldt, Åke H., and Benedicks, Eva, eds. *Design in Sweden Today*. New York, A. Bonnier, [1948].

Industridesign under 200 år. Exhibition catalogue. Stockholm, Nationalmuseum, 1978.

Josef Frank; tjugo år i Svenskt Tenn. Exhibition catalogue. Stockholm, Nationalmuseum, 1952.

Karin Björquist of Gustavsberg. New York, Georg Jensen, Inc., 1965.

Klyvare, Berndt, and Widman, Dag. *Stig Lindberg—Swedish Artist and Designer*. Trans. by P. A. Burke. Stockholm, Rabén & Sjögren, 1963.

KONTUR (Swedish Design Annual). Stockholm, The Swedish Society for Industrial Design, 1950–66.

Kosta Glasbruk 1742–1942; jubileumsskrift utgiven av Kosta glasbruk 200 år ije verkamhet. Stockholm, 1942.

Lagerqvist, Marshall. *Svenska stolar efter holländsk engelska förebilder*. Göteborg, Röhsska Konstslöjdmuseet, 1946.

Larsson, Carl. *Ett Hem*. Stockholm, 1899.

Lindkvist, Lennart, ed. *Design in Sweden*. Trans. by Claude Stephenson. Stockholm, The Swedish Institute in collaboration with the Swedish Society for Industrial Design, 1972.

Lundgren, Tyra. *Märta Måås-Fjetterström och vävverkstaden i Båstad*. With English summary. Stockholm, Bonniers, 1968.

Markfelt, Barbro. *Swedish Handcraft Times (Svensk Slöjdtidning)*. Stockholm, Sveriges Textillärares Riksforening, 1964.

Mellan funkis och framtid; Svensk Form 1930/80. Catalogue of an exhibition sponsored by Svensk Form. Stockholm, 1980.

Møller, Viggo Sten, and Nilsson, Pål-Nils. *En bok om Barbro Nilsson*. Stockholm, 1977.

Nylén, Anna-Maja. *Swedish Handicraft*. Lund, Håkan Olssons, 1976.

Nystrom, Bengt. "Alf Wallander och Rörstrand; nagot om svensk jugendkeramik." In *Fataburen* (Yearbook of the Nordiska Museet). Stockholm, 1967.

———. *Konsten till industria; Trå formgivare från sekelskiftet, Alf Wallander och Gunnar G:son Wennerberg*. Lund, 1982.

150 år Gustavsberg. Stockholm, Nationalmuseum, 1975–76.

Orreforsglas. Göteborg, Röhsska Konstslöjdmuseet, 1970.

Palme, Per, and Nordenson, Eva. *Svensk keramik*. Stockholm, 1967.

Palmgren, Nils. *Wilhelm Kåge; Könstnar och Hantverkare*. Stockholm, Nordisk Rotogravyr, 1953.

Paulsson, Gregor, ed. *Modernt svenskt glas*. Stockholm, 1943.

———. *Vackrare vardagsvara*. Stockholm, 1919.

Paulsson, Gregor, and Paulsson, Nils. *Tingens bruk och prägel*. Stockholm, 1956.

Persson, Sigurd. *Modern Swedish Silver*. Stockholm, Lindqvist, 1951.

Selander, Malin. *Swedish Handweaving.* Göteborg, Wezäta Förlag, 1959.

Stavenow, Åke. *Silversmeden Jacob Ångman 1876–1942.* Stockholm, Nordisk Rotogravyr, 1955.

Stavenow, Åke, et al., eds. *Swedish Arts and Crafts/Swedish Modern—A movement toward sanity in design.* Exhibition catalogue; trans. by Gösta A. Sandström. Published by the Royal Swedish Commission, New York World's Fair, 1939.

Stavenow, Åke, and Huldt, Åke. *Design in Sweden.* Stockholm, Bokförlaget Gothia, 1961; Stockholm, AB Åetåtryck Åhlen & Akerlunds Tryckerier, 1964.

Stavenow-Hidemark, Elisabet. *Svensk Jugend.* With English summary. Stockholm: Nordiska Museet, 1964.

Steenberg, Elisa. *Svenskt glas.* Stockholm, 1953. Trans. as *Swedish Glass.* New York, Barrows, 1960.

The Story of Boda and Erik Höglund. Boda, Boda Glassworks, 1965.

Svenskt Jugendglas; överfångsglas 1898–1918. Exhibition catalogue. Stockholm, Nationalmuseum, 1980.

The Swedish Institute. *Design in Sweden.* Malmö, AB Tryckeri-gruppen, 1977.

Swedish Textile Art—Five Temperaments. Exhibition catalogue; text in English and Spanish by Beate Sydhoff. Malmö, The Swedish Institute, 1976.

Swedish Textiles Today. Catalogue of an exhibition organized by the Royal Ministry of Cultural Affairs, the Swedish Institute for Cultural Development, and the Swedish Society for Industrial Design; circulated by the Smithsonian Institution. Stockholm, Stellan Stais Boktryckeri, 1958.

Verkstad Måås-Fjetterström. Exhibition catalogue. Stockholm, Nationalmuseum, 1967.

Walterstorff, Emelie von, ed. *Swedish Textiles.* Stockholm, Nordiska Museet, 1925.

Wennerholm, Eric. *Carl Malmsten hel och hållen.* Stockholm, 1969.

Wettergren, Erik. *The Modern Decorative Arts of Sweden.* Eng. trans. by Tage Palm. Malmö, Malmö Museum, 1926.

Widman, Dag. *Konsthantverk, konstindustri, design, 1895–1975.* Stockholm, 1975.

Widman, Dag, ed. *Svensk konsthantverk från sekelskifte till sextiotal* (Yearbook of the Swedish National Museum of Fine Arts). With English summary. Stockholm, Rabén & Sjögren, 1967.

Widman, Dag, and Klyvare, Berndt. *Stig Lindberg—Swedish Artist and Designer.* Stockholm, Nordisk Rotogravyr, 1963.

Wilhelm Kåge Gustavsberg. Exhibition catalogue. Stockholm, Nationalmuseum, 1953.

Wollin, Nils G. *Nutida svensk konstslöjd i bild.* Stockholm, 1931.

Zahle, Erik, ed. *Konsthandverk och konstindustri i Norden.* Malmö, 1961.

ACKNOWLEDGMENTS

Three years ago, when the opportunity of organizing an exhibition as part of the SCANDINAVIA TODAY program was presented, my immediate enthusiasm emanated from a variety of sources. Probably my first experience with Scandinavian design of the most traditional nature was watching with fascination as my Norwegian-descended mother skilfully created delightful pastry confections for our family at Christmastime. Years later, while a student at the University of Minnesota, I became cognizant of a different sort of Scandinavian design, an interest sparked by Dr. Marion Nelson of the Art History Department, whose appreciation of Scandinavian art history—fine art, folk art, and modern design—was transmitted to all who studied with him.

Transforming an ambitious idea into the reality of "Scandinavian Modern: 1880–1980" demanded a truly international effort among colleagues in the fields of decorative arts and design as well as close cooperation among cultural and governmental institutions and organizations both in the United States and abroad. The enormous contributions of individuals and organizations in accomplishing this exhibition and publication can only be summarily acknowledged here, but to all who have played a role in the arduous and satisfying work of the past years, I extend my sincere gratitude.

To coordinate the exhibition and publication activities within Scandinavia, and to serve as expert advisors in the selection of material to be included, a Curatorial Committee was formed. Dr. Helena Dählbeck Lutteman, Curator of Applied Art at the Nationalmuseum in Stockholm, graciously served as Head of the Committee; for her knowledge, efficiency, and encouragement in all aspects of the project I shall remain indebted. Marianne Uggla of the Nationalmuseum served as the most competent coordinator one could have hoped for, and her skill and patience deserve a special acknowledgment. To the other Committee members: Erik Lassen, Director of Det Danske Kunstindustrimuseum in Copenhagen; Jarno Peltonen, Director of Taideteollisuusmuseo, Helsinki; Jan-Lauritz Opstad, Director of Nordenfjeldske Kunstindustrimuseum, Trondheim; and Stefán Snæbjörnsson of Iceland, I offer my gratitude for their unfailing guidance and judgment and for their incisive essays.

The day-to-day activities surrounding the planning and implementation of both the exhibition and its accompanying volume, and the overall coordination of this exhibition within the broader program of SCANDINAVIA TODAY, could not have occurred without the expertise and support of The American-Scandinavian Foundation of New York, under the leadership of Dr. Patricia McFate. To Brooke Lappin, National Coordinator of SCANDINAVIA TODAY, a special accolade must be given, not only for his administrative talents and diplomatic finesse, but also for his unshakeable commitment to quality in the accomplishment of SCANDINAVIA TODAY. To Bruce Kellerhouse, whose good counsel and coordination forged a strong bond between the program and this Museum, to Albina De Meio, Exhibition Coordinator for SCANDINAVIA TODAY, for her ready and able advice in the negotiation and documentation of loans, and to Kathleen Madden and Larry Clark, I likewise acknowledge my debt.

To Carl Tomas Edam, Secretary General, SCANDINAVIA TODAY, Nordic Council of Ministers, for his ability to facilitate the complex international relationships that are a part of this program, and to Ms. Bente Noyons of his staff, I include a special note of gratitude. Martha Gaber-Abramsen is also acknowledged for her facile translations of essays included in this publication.

Colleagues and institutions within each of the five Scandinavian countries also deserve a distinctive recognition for their continuous spirit of generous assistance, advice, and encouragement. In Denmark, Jens Bernsen, Director of the Danish Design Council, contributed to the catalogue, and John Vedel-Rieper served as an invaluable friend and contact with the craftspeople active in that country.

In Finland, I should like to specially thank Marianne Aav of the Taideteollisuusmuseo for her efficient handling of requests for information and photographs, and Dr. Tapio Periäinen, Director of the Finnish Society of Crafts and Design, for his advice and contribution to the publication.

In Iceland, our efforts were greatly aided by several scholars and government officials whose hospitable welcomes to that country were always appreciated.

In Norway, the knowledge of Lauritz Opstad, Director of the Oslo Kunstindustrimuseet, was essential to the project, as was the close cooperation of Dr. Peter Anker, Director of Vestlandske Kunstindustrimuseum in Bergen, who also contributed a major essay to this publication. Rolf Himberg-Larsen made the facilities and resources of the Landsforbundet Norsk Brukskunst available to me and wrote an essay as well.

In Sweden, Dr. Per Bjurström offered every courtesy at the Nationalmuseum for research and for loans. At the Nordiska Museet, Sune Zachrisson, Director, assured the cooperation of the museum, and Dr. Elisabet Stavenow-Hidemark, Curator, shared her expertise with admirable enthusiasm, securing loans and contributing an important essay to the catalogue. Lennart Lindkvist, Director of Föreningen Svensk Form, has been a guide in the selection of contemporary design materials and has contributed to the publication, for which I am grateful. At the Svenska Institutet, a special acknowledgment goes to Göran Löfdahl, Director, and to Sonja Martinsson, without whose intelligent advice and friendship the project could not have succeeded as smoothly. To Jan Brunius, Director of Röhsska Konstslöjdmuseet in Göteborg, I am grateful for important loans. To other friends and advisors in Sweden, I extend my thanks, with a special salute to Astrid Sampe, whose dedication to the field of design served as an inspiration. To Ulf Hård af Segerstad, whose perceptive and keen intelligence has enriched this publication, I reiterate my gratitude.

In the United States, I am indebted to Samuel C. Miller, Director of The Newark Museum, and Ulysses G. Dietz, the museum's Curator of Decorative Arts, for their willingness to make loans available, and to Dr. Sherman E. Lee, Director of The Cleveland Museum of Art, and Henry Hawley, Chief Curator, Later Western Art, for additional American loan material. Of the private collectors in the United States who have shared in this exhibition, special thanks goes to Robert and Sherry Schreiber and to Leo Kaplan. Dean Swanson, Director of The Minnesota Museum of Art in Saint Paul, and Lloyd Herman, Director of The Renwick Gallery of The National Museum of American Art, Smithsonian Institution, have given invaluable aid in the organization and circulation of this exhibition in the United States.

At Cooper-Hewitt Museum, the support received in this entire project from our Director, Lisa Taylor, and from Christian Rohlfing, Assistant Director, was inestimable in value. In the Department of Decorative Arts, I wish to thank Barbara A. L. Woytowicz for her constant and much-needed assistance and for her compilation of biographical information on the artists and designers; Deborah Shinn for her research assistance, along with Liesl Feitelberg; and Piera Maria Watkins, whose support and aid assured the continuity and progress of both the publication and the exhibition. Dorothy Twining Globus, Coordinator of Exhibitions, and Robin Parkinson, Designer, have shared their talents in the design and installation of the exhibition, and Cordelia Rose, Registrar, with her staff, has played a key role in the organization of the exhibition and its subsequent tour. To Kurt Struver and Libby McKirdie, a sincere thank you for administrative assistance.

The production of this publication, which accompanies the exhibition, brought together many talents from Harry N. Abrams, Inc. Paul Gottlieb and Margaret Kaplan indicated their enthusiasm for the project in its early stages, and that spirit continued throughout the compilation of this extensive volume. Pat Cunningham and Steven Schoenfelder provided the book's provocative and handsome design. Margaret Donovan, Senior Editor, was a source of continual insight and sound advice, and this volume reflects her intelligent and sensitive editing. Lory Frankel has proven her editorial mettle in the midst of translations and rewritings, lending grace and wit to the language. To both, I offer a special salute for patience, expertise, and good humor under the pressure of deadlines.

Finally, I wish to thank Helsingin Sanomat, Finland; Wartsila/Arabia, Finland; Kansallis-Osake-Pankki Bank, Finland; Union Bank of Finland, Ltd.; Pohjola Group of Insurance Companies, Finland; CITIBANK/CITICORP; and the New York Chapter of The American-Scandinavian Foundation for their support of this project, and the public, private, and corporate lenders whose names follow: Ahlström, Iittala Glassworks; Timo Arjas; Oy Artek AB; Ateljé Lyktan AB; Åke Axelsson; Bing & Grøndahl; Åsa Brandt; Rut Bryk; Asgerdur Buadottir; E. Kold Christensen A/S; Collection of the Ministry of Education, Finland; The Danish State Art Foundation; David-Andersen; Sigrun Einarsdottir; Lydia Palsdottir Einarsson; The Finnish Glass Museum; Firma Svenskt Tenn; Focus Belysning; Ulla Forsell; Bent Gabrielsen; Mr. and Mrs. Rolf Gaudernack; Asmundsson Gisli; Gestur and Sigrun Gudjonsdottir; Jens Gudjonsson; Jonina Gudnadottir; AB Gustavsberg; Håg USA, Inc.; Birger Haglund; Hans Hansen Silver, Ltd.; Charlotte Block-Hellum; Höganäs Museum; Peter Hvidt & O. Mølgaard-Nielsen, m.a.a.; Jac. Jacobsen A/S; Georg Jensen Sølvsmedie A/S; Gudbrandur J. Jezorski; Sigridur Johannsdottir and Leifur Breidfjord; Kevi A/S; Le Klint; Kooperativa Förbundet; Kosta Boda AB; Kustannusosakeyhtiö Otava; Lammhults Mekaniska AB; Lapponia Jewelry Oy; Library of The Royal Academy of Fine Arts, Copenhagen; Jan Lohmann; Martin Lundgren; Malmsteypa A. Sigurdhsson; Marimekko Oy; Steinunn Marteinsdottir; A. Michelsen A/S; Ministry for Foreign Affairs of Finland; Lennart Nisser; Nuutajärvi-Notsjö; Nyvirki, Ltd.; AB Orrefors Glasbruk; Anna-Maria Osipow; Palace Hotel, Helsinki; Ole Bent Petersen; Eva Polland; Louis Poulsen & Co. A/S; Prins Eugens Waldemarsudde; Kirsti Rantanen; Rud. Rasmussens Snedkerier Aps; Jane Reumert; RFSU Rehab; Riihimäen Lasi Glassworks; Rörstrand AB; The Royal Copenhagen Porcelain Manufactory Ltd.; Tuoko Saari; Smålands Museum; Carl-Harry Stålhane; Stelton A/S; Leifur Sveinsson; 10-Gruppen; Thorbjörg Thordardottir; Erik Ingomar Vangsgaard; Vivero Oy; Vuokko Oy; Oy Wärtsilä Ab Arabia; Westnofa USA, Inc.; Gerda and Salomo Wuorio Foundation, Hvitträsk; and all the anonymous lenders and those whose names were not available at the time of publication.

David Revere McFadden
Curator of Decorative Arts, Cooper-Hewitt Museum

INDEX

Page numbers are in roman type, illustration numbers in italic type. See "Biographical Notes" section for further information on designers.

Aaberg, Gunhild, 261; *no. 284*
Aalto, Aino, 18, 20, 108, 115, 116, 122, 124; *no. 115*
Aalto, Alvar, 20, 26, 44, 105, 108, 113, 115, 116, 119, 124, 127, 144, 179, 182, 245; *nos. 97, 101, 128, 148, 211, 221*
Aarne, glassware pattern (Hongell), 136; *no. 138*
About Identities, stoneware sculpture (Persson, B.), 227; *no. 307*
Abstract Constructivism, 108
Acke, J. A. G., 78, 81; *no. 59*
Acking, Carl-Axel, 134, 146; *no. 151*
Adlercreutz, Maria, 192, 238; *no. 328*
Adventure (Eventyr), porcelain figural group (Henning, Gerhard), 88; *no. 72*
A 805, floor lamp (Aalto, Alvar), 179; *no. 211*
Ahlmann, Lis, 105, 127, 161
Åhlström, Betzy, 84
Aino, table service (Ekholm), 121
Airam, Ltd., Helsinki, *no. 199*
AJ pattern, stainless steel cutlery (Jacobsen, A.), 169; *no. 191*
Alm metalworks, Porvoo, Finland, *no. 53*
Alnæs, Tormod, 177
Andersen, David, 74, 77
Andersen, David, metalworks, Oslo, 50, 77, 78, 101, 105; *nos. 5, 23, 50, 91.* See also David-Andersen metalworks
Andersen, Hans Munck, 227; *no. 309*
Andersen, Valdemar, 91
Anderson, Beate, 216
Andersson, Herbert, Gärsnäs, Sweden, *no. 268*
Anglepoise, English lamp, 113
Ångman, Jacob, 98, 120, 128; *nos. 87, 124*
Animal and Man, earthenware sculpture (Hydman-Vallien), 227; *no. 306*
Ant, chair (Jacobsen, A.), 179; *no. 209*
Apple, glass vase (Lundin), 157; *no. 170*
Arabia ceramics, Helsinki, 34, 71, 73, 108, 121, 151, 154, 157, 159, 164, 186; *nos. 28, 42, 105, 131, 159, 166, 168, 183, 184, 231, 240, 320*
Argenta, stoneware (Kåge), 108, 121; *no. 102*

Århus Exhibition, Denmark, 17, 91
Art Deco style, 38, 45, 105
Artek furniture, Helsinki, 116; *nos. 148, 211*
Artists' Movement, Norway, 240, 244
Art Marketing Center, Norway, 240
Art Nouveau style: Belgium, 55, 58, 62, 73; England, 81; France, 55, 62, 78; Scandinavia, 15, 16, 17, 43, 55, 58, 62, 65, 67, 68, 73, 77, 78, 81, 88, 91, 148, 244; Scotland, 62; Vienna, 58, 62, 65
Arts and Crafts movement, 58, 73, 77, 81, 88
"Arts of Denmark, The," traveling exhibition, United States, 22
Åse, Arne, 213; *no. 274*
Asplund, Gunnar, 18–19, 26, 94, 102; *no. 96*
Atelier (AB) Märta Måås-Fjetterström, Båstad, Sweden, 101; *nos. 90, 150*
Ateljé Lyktan, Åhus, Sweden, *no. 344*
Aurdal, Synnøve Anker, 177, 201; *no. 258*
Austria, 33; *see also* Vienna, Austria
Ax, chair (Hvidt and Mølgaard-Nielsen), 180; *no. 217*
Axelsson, Åke, 207; *no. 268*
Axén, Gunila, *no. 253*

Bäckström, Olof, *no. 255*
Bærtling, Olle, 148
Balans Activ, chair (Gusrud and Mengshoel), 247; *no. 342*
Balans Variable, chair (Opsvik and Mengshoel), 247; *no. 343*
Baltic Exhibition, Malmö, Sweden, 17, 67, 91, 94
Bang, Jacob E., 99, 105, 115, 124; *no. 116*
Baroque, glass vase (Nyman), 136; *no. 140*
Bauer, Lisa, 231; *no. 310*
Bauhaus School, the, 20, 34, 38, 102, 105, 108, 111, 121, 122, 124, 127
Beauty for All/Skönhet för alla (Key, E.), 58
Behrens, Peter, 20
Belgium, 55, 58, 62, 73, 84
Bengtson, Hertha, 166
Benktzon, Maria, *no. 345*
Bergh, Elis, 115, 124; *no. 114*
Bergslien, Gro (Sommerfeldt), 177, 218; *no. 290*

Bergsten, Carl, 17, 78, 83; *no. 66*
Bernadotte, Sigvard, 119, 128, 171; *nos. 121, 195*
Bindesbøll, Johanne, 83
Bindesbøll, Thorvald, 16, 67, 68, 74, 78, 83, 88; *nos. 31, 38, 47, 57, 65*
Bing & Grøndahl ceramics, Copenhagen, 47, 67–68, 94, 99, 102, 105, 121, 161, 169; *nos. 1, 14, 22, 189*
BIP, *see* Persson, Britt-Ingrid
Björquist, Karin, 166, 210; *no. 272*
Block-Hellum, Charlotte, 238; *no. 327*
Blomberg, David, Stockholm, *no. 96*
Bloomingdale Brothers department store, New York, 22
Blue Line, earthenware pattern (Meyer, G.), 184; *no. 225*
Boberg, Anna, 62, 84; *no. 27*
Boberg, Ferdinand, 14, 62, 78
Boda Glasbruk, Sweden, 159, 166; *nos. 176, 177*
Bøe, Alf, 224
Bojesen, Kay, 21, 102, 105, 113, 128, 133; *no. 112*
Bojesen, Kay, Copenhagen, 169; *no. 158*
Boman furniture, Turku, Finland, *no. 29*
Bomann, Carl Johan, 151
Bonderup, Claus, 245; *no. 338*
Bongard, Hermann, 177
Bonytt (Interior News), Norwegian periodical, 131
Borg, Olli, 171; *no. 198*
Brandt, Åsa, 221; *no. 291*
Breidfjord, Leifur, 242; *no. 334*
Breuer, Marcel, 105
Bride in My Mind, tapestry (Rantanen), 247; *no. 341*
Broken Bridge, The, glass plate (Hald), 96; *no. 85*
Brørby, Severin, 177, 192; *no. 241*
Brummer, Arttu, 101–2, 124, 136; *no. 136*
Bryk, Rut, 235; *no. 320*
Buadottir, Asgerdur Ester, 201; *no. 256*
Bülow-Hübe, Torun, 172, 194; *no. 243*
Busch-Jensen, H. O., 99
BV, porcelain pattern (Björquist), 210; *no. 272*

"Cabinetmaker Borgersen," Oslo, *no. 8*
Cabinetmakers Guild, Copenhagen, 116, 154
Canton pattern, stainless steel cooking pan

(Gardberg), 171; *no. 197*
Carlsson, Daniel J., 48; *no. 2*
ceramic design, *see under* Denmark; Finland; Iceland; Norway; Scandinavian design; Sweden
"Chair, The" (Wegner), 43, 148, 154; *no. 156*
Chanterelles, glass vases (Wirkkala), 141; *no. 143*
Christensen, Augusta, 50
Christensen, E. Kold, Copenhagen, *nos. 206, 265*
Christensen, Kari, 232; *no. 314*
Christiania Haandværks og Industriforening, Norway, *no. 67*
Christiania Jernsengfabrikk, Oslo, *no. 99*
Clément, Adolphe, 73
Constructivist art, 151
Contemporary Swedish Silver (Nutida Svensk Silver Association), 172
Continental, silver pattern (Jensen), 77; *no. 52*
Cooperative Society of Sweden, The (Kooperativa Förbundet), Stockholm, *no. 188*
Cooper-Hewitt Museum, New York, 17
"Creative Craft in Denmark," exhibition, Cooper Union Museum, New York, 22
Cubism, 108
Curman, Carl, 48
Cylinda series, stainless steel domestic wares (Jacobsen, A.), 195; *no. 248*
Cyrén, Gunnar, 192, 224; *nos. 239, 302*

Dahl, Birger, 179; *no. 208*
Dahl, E. F., 50, 52
Dance, The, pewter bowl (Jerndahl), 74; *no. 48*
Danish Handcraft Guild, 105, 242
Danish Museum of Decorative Art (Det Danske Kunstindustrimuseum), Copenhagen, 57, 105, 113
Dansk Kattuntrykkeri, Copenhagen, 119; *no. 119*
David-Andersen, Arthur, 77, 101; *no. 50*
David-Andersen, Ivar, 101; *no. 91*
David-Andersen metalworks, Oslo, 141; *nos. 120, 142, 249. See also* Andersen, David, metalworks
Davis, J. Lionberger, 17
Denmark, 28, 101; architecture in, 26, 42, 67, 91; Art Nouveau in, 16, 43, 65, 67; ceramic design in, 16, 19, 26, 30, 43, 67–68, 88, 92, 94, 99, 102, 105, 121, 122, 133, 161, *nos. 1, 14, 18, 22, 31, 32, 37–39, 43, 45, 71, 72, 76, 133, 160, 162, 189, 225, 271, 276, 283, 284, 287, 309, 315;* design aesthetics of, 42; design development in, 12, 27, 32–33, 34, 35, 37–38, 41–43, 44, 65, 87, 88, 91, 94, 133, 134, 148, 154, 189, 210, 218, 235; English influence on, 30, 34; functionalism in, 105, 113, 116, 121, 124, 154; furniture design in, 16, 18, 20, 21, 42, 43, 67, 74, 88, 99, 102, 105, 113, 116, 133, 146, 148, 154, 161, 166, 177, 181, *nos. 65, 93, 94, 98, 122, 126, 152, 154–56, 202–4, 206, 209, 215, 217–19, 260, 265, 266, 337, 338, 340;* geography of, 30, 31; glass design in, 99, 105, 122, 124, 159, 161, 221, *nos. 116, 172, 292;* historical background of, 31, 47, 87, 107, 131; map of, 29; metalwork in, 16, 18, 21, 43, 50, 52, 62, 74, 87, 88, 99, 102, 105, 128, 133, 154, 159, 161, 172, 235, *nos. 7, 25, 26, 47, 51, 52, 69, 70, 88, 89, 92, 112, 121, 181, 182, 185, 186, 190–92, 195, 248, 254, 297, 298, 300, 318, 319, 331, 332;* oriental influence in, 16, 58, 65, 67, 68, 169, 213, 216; textile design in, 16, 67, 105, 127, 148, 161, 242, *nos. 57, 119, 152, 207, 296, 333;* Viking revival in, 50, 52; woodwork in, *no. 158*
"Design in Scandinavia," traveling exhibition, United States and Canada, 21, 22, 25, 134, 141, 142
Dessau, Ingrid, 161
Dietrichson, Lorentz, 48, 50
Digre, P. A. O., 48
Ditzel, Jørgen, 166
Ditzel, Nanna, 161, 166, 198; *nos. 186, 254*

Dokka Møbler, Norway, *no. 223*
Domus, armchair (Tapiovaara), 151; *no. 157*
Dragonfly, brooch (Jensen), 62; *no. 25*
Dragonfly (Trollslända), printed fabric (Jobs), 142; *no. 146*
dragon style, *see* Viking revival style
Dutch Delft school, 119
Dysthe, Sven Ivar, 177, 182; *no. 223*

Eames, Charles, 151
Eat and Drink, tableware (Ergonomi Design Group), 18, 251; *no. 346*
Eckhoff, Tias, 148, 172, 177, 186, 194–95; *nos. 230, 245*
Egersunds Fayancefabrik, Norway, 60, 99; *no. 19*
Egg, chair (Jacobsen, A.), 180; *no. 215*
Einarsdottir, Sigrun, 224; *nos. 303, 304*
Einarsson, Gudhmundur, 108, 122; *no. 106*
Ekholm, Kurt, 108, 121; *no. 105*
Eklund, Jarl, 55
Engberg, Gabriel, 55; *no. 9*
Engelhardt, Knud V., 91
Engelhardt, Valdemar, 16–17, 73; *no. 45*
England, 30, 32, 33, 34, 58, 78, 81, 84
Englund, Eva, 96, 231; *no. 311*
Engø, Bjørn, 148, 177, 195; *no. 247*
Ergonomi Design Group, Stockholm, 18, 251; *nos. 345, 346*
Eriksen, Sigurd Alf, 177
Eriksson, Algot, *no. 13*
Eskolin, Vuokko, *see* Eskolin-Nurmesniemi, Vuokko
Eskolin-Nurmesniemi, Vuokko, 154, 179, 198; *no. 252*
Esplanade des Invalides, Paris Exposition (1925), furniture for, 102
Eva, chair (Mathsson), 119, 124; *no. 127*
Eventyr (Adventure), porcelain figural group (Henning, Gerhard), 88; *no. 72*
Exhibition of Art and Industry, Stockholm (1897), 15–16
Expectation of Mary, The, earthenware sculpture (Hillfon), 214; *no. 282*
"Exposition des Arts Décoratifs et Industriels Modernes," exhibition, Paris (1925), 18, 19, 42, 92, 96, 101–2, 105
Exposition Universelle, Paris (1889), 58; (1900), 11, 14, 15, 16, 32, 33, 48, 50, 55, 58, 62, 65, 67, 88

Fåborg Museum, Denmark, furniture for archives room of (Klint, K., and Petersen, C.), 99, 102; *nos. 93, 94*
Farsta, stoneware (Kåge), 152; *no. 161*
Fennia series, earthenware vase from (Arabia), 65, 73; *no. 28*
Finch, Alfred William, 71, 73; *no. 40*
Finland, 91, 101; architecture in, 11, 15, 26, 32, 33, 44, 52, 58, 62, 65, 73, 91, 108; Art Nouveau style in, 16, 55, 58, 62, 73, 81; ceramic design in, 26, 34, 73, 81, 121, 151, *nos. 28, 40–42, 105, 131, 159, 166, 168, 183, 184, 240, 273, 275, 285, 286, 320;* design aesthetics of, 45; design development in, 12, 16, 33, 34, 35, 37–38, 44–45, 52, 55, 58, 62, 65, 87, 101, 127, 133, 134, 151, 154, 189, 235; functionalism in, 33, 113, 116, 119, 121, 122, 124; furniture design in, 20, 23, 44, 58, 65, 73, 81, 101, 113, 116, 119, 151, 247, *nos. 29, 61, 97, 128, 129, 157, 198, 211, 216, 221, 261, 339;* geography of, 30–31; German influence on, 73; glass design in, 21, 44, 101, 122, 124, 136, 148, 151, 162, *nos. 101, 115, 136–40, 143, 171, 173, 178, 179, 199, 229, 231, 232, 234, 236, 237, 294, 312;* historical background of, 31, 47, 52, 87, 101, 107, 131; Karelian revival style in, 15, 52, 55, 65, 73; map of,

29; metalwork in, 58, 77, 78, 128, 172, *nos. 53, 54, 193, 196, 197, 244, 255, 299, 321, 329;* national romanticism in, 88, 91, 101; oriental influence in, 133; Swedish influence in, 88; textile design in, 21, 44, 52, 55, 58, 65, 81, 101–2, 111, 127, 131, 148, 151, 154, 172, 196, 221, 238, *nos. 9, 30, 107, 129, 148, 149, 201, 210, 213, 214, 250, 252, 259, 326, 341;* woodwork in, 151, *no. 222*
"Finlandia," exhibition, Zurich, 22
Finlandia, glass vase (Brummer), 136; *no. 136*
Finnish Association of Designers (ORNAMO), 91
Finnish Society of Crafts and Design, exhibitions organized by, 22
Firma Karl Mathsson, Värnamo, Sweden, *no. 127*
Fiskars scissors (Bäckström), 198; *no. 255*
Fisker, Kay, 98; *no. 89*
flambé glazing technique, 88
Flame, rug (Gallen-Kallela), 55, 65
Fleming, Erik, 172
Flora, glassware pattern (Toikka), 189; *no. 234*
Flower Bowl, glass vase (Englund), 231; *no. 311*
Flower Pot series, lamps (Panton), 207; *no. 266*
Flying Bird, porcelain plate (Christensen, K.), 232; *no. 314*
Focus Belysning, Holte, Denmark, *no. 338*
Fog-Fishes, tapestry (Ryggen), 111; *no. 109*
Folcker, Erik, 91
Foreningen Brukskunst (Society of Applied Arts), Norway, 91
Föreningen Svensk Form (Swedish Society of Crafts and Design), Stockholm, 40, 91
Föreningen Svensk Hemslöjd (Swedish Handicraft Society), 55, 58
"Formes Scandinaves," exhibition, Paris, 22
Forsell, Ulla, 209; *no. 270*
Four Colors, rug (Simberg-Ehrström), 172; *no. 201*
France, 55, 62, 78, 84
Franck, Kaj, 151, 154, 159, 171, 191; *nos. 166, 171, 196, 236*
Frank, Josef, 21, 119, 127–28, 131, 134; *no. 130*
Franck, Kaj, 151, 154, 159, 171, 191; *nos. 166, 171, 196, 236*
Freij, Edla, 218; *no. 289*
Friberg, Berndt, 16, 20, 162, 166; *no. 180*
Friends of Finnish Handicraft (Suomen Käsityön Ystävät), Finland, 52, 65, 127; *nos. 9, 30, 107, 201*
Friends of Textile Art Association (Handarbetets Vänner), Sweden, 52, 55, 81
Fristedt, Sven, 201; *no. 257*
Frosterus, Sigurd, 58
Frugtlygte, lanterns (Klint, K.), 148; *no. 154*
Fuga series, glass bowls from (Palmqvist), 166; *no. 187*
Fuglevaag, Britt, 177
furniture design, *see under* Denmark; Finland; Iceland; Norway; Scandinavian design; Sweden

Gabrielsen, Bent, 164; *nos. 181, 182*
Gallé, Émile, 57, 58, 83, 84
Gallén, Axel, *see* Gallen-Kallela, Akseli
Gallen-Kallela, Akseli, 16, 52, 55, 65, 71, 73, 81, 101; *no. 30*
Gardberg, Bertel, 171; *no. 197*
Gate, Simon, 19, 92, 94, 96, 115, 124; *nos. 78–80, 82*
Gaudernack, Christian, 177
Gaudernack, Gustav, 16, 52, 60, 78; *nos. 5, 20, 21, 23*
Gauguin, Jean, 102
Gefle Porslinsfabrik, Gävle, Sweden, 94, 122; *no. 108*
Germany, 33, 47, 48, 73, 84–85, 105, 122, 131
Gesellius, Herman, 11, 52, 58, 65
Gillgren, Sven Arne, 142, 172; *no. 147*
Gjerdrum, Reidun Sissel, 213; *no. 278*
glass design, *see under* Denmark; Finland; Iceland;

Norway; Scandinavian design; Sweden
graal technique, 96, 192, 231
Grand Prix, cutlery pattern (Bojesen), 113; *no. 112*
Grasshopper, brooch (Magnussen), 62; *no. 26*
Gråsten, Viola, 26
Gray Lines, ceramic pattern (Kåge), 133; *no. 134*
Gropius, Walter, 20
Gudhjonsson, Jens, 237; *nos. 322, 323*
Gudhnadottir, Jonina, 214; *no. 280*
Gudjonsdottir, Sigrun (Runa), 227; *no. 308*
Gudme-Leth, Marie, 119; *no. 119*
Gulbrandsen, Nora, 91, 105, 121; *no. 75*
Guldsmedsaktiebolaget, Stockholm, *nos. 87, 124, 147*
Gullichsen, Maire, 116
Gusrud, Svein, *no. 342*
Gustavsberg ceramics, Gustavsberg, Sweden, 16, 17, 19, 20, 67, 68, 73, 94, 111, 121, 162, 166, 210; *nos. 2, 35, 36, 73, 74, 102, 104, 132, 134, 135, 161, 164, 165, 180, 227, 272, 345*
Gustavus VI Adolphus, king of Sweden, 119

Haavardsholm, Frøidis, 101
Hackman & Sorsakoski, Sorsakoski, Finland, *no. 197*
Hadelands Glassverk, Jevnaker, Norway, 94, 99, 122, 159, 177, 189, 192, 218; *nos. 81, 83, 174, 175, 238, 241, 289, 290*
Håg, Oslo, *nos. 342, 343*
Haglund, Birger, 195; *no. 246*
Hahl, Nils-Gustaf, 116, 119
Håkon Hall, Bergen, Norway, decoration of (Munthe, G.), 91, 99
Hald, Edward, 19, 92, 94, 96, 115, 231; *nos. 77, 85, 86*
Halvorsen, Arne, 177
Handarbetets Vännar (Friends of Textile Art Association), Sweden, 52, 55, 81
Hansen, Frida, 81; *no. 58*
Hansen, Hans, Sølvsmedie, Kolding, Denmark, 241; *no. 332*
Hansen, Johannes, Copenhagen, *nos. 155, 156*
Hansen, Karl Gustav, 241; *no. 332*
Hansens Eftf., Allerød, Denmark, *nos. 209, 215, 217*
Hård af Segerstad, Ulf, 154
Hausen, Marika, 172
Hegermann-Lindencrone, Effie, 60, 68; *no. 22*
Heikkilä, Simo, 36, 247; *no. 339*
Hellman, Åsa, 210; *no. 273*
Hellsten, Lars, 189; *no. 233*
"Hemutställningen" ("Home Exhibition"), Liljevalchs Art Gallery, Stockholm, 17, 88, 94
Henning, Gerda, 105
Henning, Gerhard, 88, 94, 99; *no. 72*
Henningsen, Poul, 10, 18, 42, 102, 105, 133, 174; *nos. 100, 202–4*
Hernmarck, Helena, 192, 196; *no. 251*
Heron, porcelain service (Krohn), 57, 68; *no. 14*
"H 55," exhibition, Hälsingborg pier, Sweden, 22, 40, 45, 141, 161
"High Tech" style, 244
Hillfon, Hertha, 166, 214; *no. 282*
Hiorth & Østlyngen, Oslo, *no. 153*
Hoffmann, Josef, 78
Höganäsbolaget, Höganäs, Sweden, *no. 16*
Höglund, Erik, 159, 166; *nos. 176, 177*
Holmboe, Thorolf, 58, 68; *no. 17*
Holmegaards Glasverk, Holmegaard, Denmark, 99, 105, 115; *nos. 116, 172*
Holmenkollen Turisthotell, Oslo, furniture for "Fairy Tale Room" of (Munthe, G.), 50, 55; *no. 8*
Holzer-Kjellberg, Friedl, 133; *no. 131*
"Home Exhibition" ("Hemutställningen"), Liljevalchs Art Gallery, Stockholm, 17, 88, 94
Hongell, Göran, 124, 136; *no. 138*
Hopea, Saara, 151, 159, 238; *nos. 173, 329*

House of Parliament, Helsinki, furniture for (Brummer), 91, 101, 113
Hvidt, Peter, 180; *no. 217*
Hvitträsk castle, Karelia, Finland (Gesellius, Lindgren, Saarinen), 52, 65
Hydman-Vallien, Ulrica, 227; *no. 306*

Iceland, 21, 26–27, 101; ceramic design in, 108, 122, 184, *nos. 106, 279, 280, 308;* Danish influence on, 184; design development in, 12, 33, 35, 43, 88, 134, 184, 235, 244; furniture design in, 184, *nos. 220, 263, 269;* geography of, 30; glass design in, 184, 224, *nos. 303, 304;* historical background of, 87; map of, 29; metalwork in, 184, 237, *nos. 322–25;* national romanticism in, 122; textile design in, 21, 184, 245, *nos. 200, 256, 334, 336*
Icelandic School of Applied Art, 134
Iittala Lasitehdas, Iittala, Finland, 136, 141, 151, 159; *nos. 101, 138, 143, 178, 179, 229, 232, 237, 312*
Ilvessalo, Kirsti, 196; *no. 250*
Inca, armchair (Magnusson), 207; *no. 269*
Industrial Design (ID) award, 241
Informalism, 189
In Her Eyes the Light of the People Is Reflected, tapestry (Adlercreutz), 238; *no. 328*
Interior News (Bonytt), Norwegian periodical, 131, 133
Interna, Frederikssund, Denmark, *no. 126*
Iris factory, Porvoo, Finland, 71, 73, 81; *nos. 40, 41, 61*
Iris Room (Gallen-Kallela), Finnish Pavilion, Paris Exposition (1925), 16, 65
Isaeus, Magnus, 48
Isola, Maija, 151, 154, 179, 203; *no. 259*
Italy, 22, 210
Iversen, A. J., Copenhagen, *no. 219*

Jacobsen, Arne, 20, 133, 151, 154, 161, 169, 179, 180, 195; *nos. 191, 209, 215, 248*
Jacobsen, Jac., 105, 113; *no. 111*
Jensen, Georg, 74, 77, 88, 98, 99, 102, 105; *nos. 25, 51, 52, 88, 92*
Jensen, Georg, New York, 141
Jensen, Georg, Sølvsmedie, Copenhagen, 62, 98, 128, 164, 166, 169, 194; *nos. 25, 51, 52, 70, 88, 92, 121, 181, 185, 186, 190, 192, 195, 254*
Jerndahl, Aron, *no. 48*
Jezorski, Gudbrandur J., 237; *nos. 324, 325*
Joachim, Christian, 92; *no. 76*
Jobs, Gocken, 142; *no. 146*
Jobs Keramik, Västanik, Sweden, *no. 145*
Jobs-Söderlund, Lisbet, 142; *no. 145*
Johannsdottir, Sigridur, 242; *no. 334*
Johannson-Pape, Lisa, 128, 151; *no. 129*
Johansson, Willy, 159, 177; *no. 175*
Jubileum, porcelain pattern (Sandnes), 157; *no. 167*
Jugend style, 16, 17, 55, 58, 62, 67, 68, 74, 78, 81. *See also* Art Nouveau style
Juhl, Finn, 146, 148, 151, 154; *nos. 152, 158*
Juhlin, Sven-Eric, *no. 345*
Jung, Dora, 21, 131, 148, 180; *nos. 213, 214*
Jung, Gunilla, 128
Jutrem, Arne Jon, 159, 177; *no. 174*

Kadmium, earthenware pattern (Kåge), 121
Kåge, Wilhelm, 17, 88, 94, 96, 108, 111, 121, 122, 133, 134, 152; *nos. 73, 74, 102–4, 132, 134, 161*
Kähler, H. C., 68
Kähler, Herman A., ceramics workshop, Næstved, Denmark, 68; *no. 39*
Kaipiainen, Birger, 192; *no. 240*

Kalela, studio home (Gallen-Kallela), 52
Kalevala, Finnish national epic, 52, 88
Kallio, Heikki, 221; *no. 294*
Kansanen-Størseth, Maija, 120, 127; *no. 123*
Käppi, Aino, *no. 341*
Karelian revival style, 15, 52, 55, 65, 73; *see also* Viking revival style
Karhula glassworks, Finland, 115, 122, 124; *no. 115*
Karttunen, Laila, 127
Kastrup Glassworks, Denmark, 184
Kayser, Fredrik A., 177, 207; *no. 267*
Keravan Puusepänteollisuus, Kerava, Finland, *no. 198*
Kevi, Glostrup, Denmark, *no. 340*
Key, Alex, 48
Key, Ellen, 42, 58
KF Interiör, Stockholm, *no. 253*
Kielland, Gabriel, 78, 81, 83; *no. 64*
Kilimantšaro, pendant (Weckström), 222; *no. 299*
Kilta, earthenware pattern (Franck), 151, 154; *no. 166*
Kittelsen, Grete Prytz, 78, 172, 174, 177; *no. 205*
Kittelsen, Theodor, 69, 73; *no. 46*
Kjærholm, Poul, 42, 154, 177, 203, 204; *nos. 206, 265*
Kjarval, Sveinn, 181, 184; *no. 220*
Klint, Kaare, 18, 42, 99, 102, 105, 113, 116, 120, 133, 148, 154, 203; *nos. 93, 94, 98, 122, 154*
Klint, Vibeke, 148, 177; *nos. 152, 207*
Knag, Christian, 83; *no. 63*
Knoblich, F. W., *no. 7*
Knoll International, 179, 247
Knudsen, Jan Lunde, 177
Københavns Lervarefabrik, Copenhagen, *no. 31*
Koch, Mogens, 203; *no. 126*
Konstantin-Hansen, Elise, 83; *no. 57*
Kooperativa Förbundet (The Cooperative Society of Sweden), Stockholm, *no. 188*
Koppel, Henning, 24, 133, 148, 161, 164, 169; *nos. 185, 192*
Korhonen furniture, Turku, Finland, *nos. 128, 221*
Korsmo, Arne, 141, 148, 172; *no. 144*
Kosta Boda glassworks, Kosta, Sweden, 221, 232; *no. 293*
Kosta Glasbruk, Kosta, Sweden, 57, 84, 94, 115, 124, 191; *nos. 10, 24, 84, 114, 235, 310, 330*
Krebs, Nathalie, 26, 105, 152, 184; *no. 162*
Krenchel, Herbert, 161
Kristiansen, Bo, 232; *no. 315*
Krog, Arnold, 58, 67, 68, 73; *nos. 18, 37, 45*
Krogh, Henrik, 78; *no. 56*
Krohn, Pietro, 57, 67, 68; *no. 14*
Kukkapuro, Yrjö, 151
Kunst, Die, German periodical, 58
Kyhn, Knud, 102

Lalique, René, 78
Lammhults Mekaniska, Lammhult, Sweden, *no. 262*
Landberg, Nils, 6, 157; *no. 169*
Landsbyen (Village), printed fabric (Gudme-Leth), 119; *no. 119*
Landsforbundet Norsk Brukskunst (Norwegian Society of Arts and Crafts and Industrial Design), Norway, 43–44, 91, 218
Landsforeningen Dansk Brugskunst og Design (Danish Society of Applied Art and Industrial Design), Denmark, 91, 210, 218
Lapponia Jewelry, Helsinki, *no. 299*
Larsson, Axel, 21, 119
Larsson, Carl, 62, 88
Lavonen, Maija, 238; *no. 326*
Le Corbusier (Charles-Édouard Jeanneret), 20, 42, 154
Le Klint, Copenhagen, *no. 154*

Lie-Jørgensen, Thorbjørn, 119, 128, 141, 172, 177; nos. 120, 142
Liekki, stoneware pattern (Procopé), 157; no. 168
Liisberg, C. F., 67; no. 32
Liljeblå, earthenware pattern (Kåge), 17, 88, 94, 96; no. 74
Liljedahl, Bengt, 172, 194; no. 242
Liljefors, Anders, 154, 166; no. 164
Liljevalchs Art Gallery, Stockholm, 17, 39, 88, 94
Lindaas, Arne, 172
Lindau, Börge, 203; no. 262
Lindberg, Stig, 20, 134, 148, 154, 166, 184; nos. 135, 165, 227
Lindekrantz, Bo, 203; no. 262
Lindgren, Armas, 11, 52, 58, 65, 73
Lindh, Richard, 186; no. 231
Lindlof, flintware pattern (Wennerberg), 67; no. 35
Lindstrand, Vicke, 115, 124; no. 113
Line Play, textile pattern, napkin from (Jung, D.), 180; no. 214
Linqvist, Martti, no. 222
Lippe, Jens von der, 184; no. 226
Listvinahusid Ltd., Reykjavik, no. 106
Ljungberg, Erik, textiles, Floda, Sweden, nos. 194, 212
Ljungbergs Textiltryck, Dala-Floda, Sweden, no. 146
Lohmann, Jan, 235; no. 318
Lönngren, Frida, no. 62
Louisiana Purchase Exposition, St. Louis, Missouri, 16–17, 65
Lukander, Minni, 216; no. 285
Lukki Chair (Tapiovaara), 23
Lundin, Ingeborg, 157, 166; no. 170
Lunning, Frederik, 141
Lunning, Frederik, Inc., New York, 21
Lunning Prize, 141, 174, 177, 186, 194
Luthersson, Petur B., 204; no. 263
Lütken, Per, 159, 161; no. 172
Luxo, lamp (Jacobsen, J.), 105, 113; no. 111
Lynggaard, Finn, 161, 221; no. 292

Maaru, glassware pattern (Wirkkala), 231; no. 312
Måås-Fjetterström, Märta, 17, 101; nos. 90, 150
Magnussen, Erik, 74, 203, 241; nos. 26, 260, 331
Magnusson, Gunnar, 207; no. 269
Malinowski, Arno, 92; no. 76
Malinowski, Ruth, 221; no. 296
Malmsten, Carl, 94, 96, 102; no. 95
Malmström, August, 48; no. 2
Marimekko textiles, Helsinki, 44, 154, 179; nos. 210, 259
Markelius, Sven, 119, 166, 169; no. 194
Marsh Pond, stoneware wall relief (Bryk), 235; no. 320
Marsio-Aalto, Aino, see Aalto, Aino
Marteinsdottir, Steinunn, 213; no. 279
Marx, Roger, 58
Mathsson, Bruno, 119, 124, 166, 245; no. 127
Mathsson, Karl, Firma, Värnamo, Sweden, no. 127
Matisse, Henri, 96
Maya, cutlery pattern (Eckhoff), 194–95; no. 245
Mengshoel, Hans Christian, nos. 342, 343
metalwork, see under Denmark; Finland; Iceland; Norway; Scandinavian design; Sweden
Metropolitan Museum of Art, New York, 19
Metsovaara, Marjatta, 151, 154
Meyer, Grethe, 161, 184; no. 225
Meyer, Jenny, 73; no. 43
Michelsen, A., metalworks, Copenhagen, nos. 7, 47, 69, 89, 191
Michelsen, Anton, 52, 102
Mies van der Rohe, Ludwig, 20, 154
Milan Triennale, see Triennale exhibitions, Milan

Möbleringsaffär, Carl Johanssons, Stockholm, no. 59
Modern Art, lamp (Nummi), 180; no. 216
Moderne Bauformen, German periodical, 58
Mogensen, Børge, 154, 180; no. 218
Mølgaard-Nielsen, Orla, 180; no. 217
Monsen, Magne, no. 158
More Beautiful Things for Everyday Use/Vackrare vardagsvara (Paulsson), 18, 94, 96
Morris, William, 32, 58
Motzfeldt, Benny, 177, 189, 218; no. 288
Motzfeldt, Benny, Plus, Fredrikstad, Norway, no. 288
Munthe, Alf, 26
Munthe, Gerhard, 11, 14–15, 26, 50, 84, 91, 99; nos. 4, 8
Munthe-Kaas, Herman, 20, 105; no. 99
Muona, Toini, 152; no. 159
Muthesius, Hermann, 91
Myrdam, Leif Heiberg, 214; no. 281
My Soil, tapestry (Rantanen), 247; no. 341

national romanticism, 77, 87, 88, 91, 99, 101, 122; see also Karelian revival style; Viking revival style
Newark Museum, Newark, New Jersey, 19
Nielsen, Erik, 68; no. 37
Nielsen, Evald, 102
Nielsen, Jais, 102
Nielsen, Kai, 94, 99, 102
Night, tapestry (Aurdal), 201; no. 258
Nilsson, A., Lund, Sweden, nos. 117, 118
Nilsson, Barbro, 127, 134, 146; no. 150
Nilsson, Wiwen, 116, 128, 172; nos. 117, 118
NK, see Nordiska Kompaniet, Stockholm
Nordenfjeldske Kunstindustrimuseum Carpenter Workshop, Trondheim, Norway, no. 64
Nordenfjeldske Kunstindustrimuseum Tapestry Studio, Trondheim, Norway, no. 4
Nordic Cultural Commission, 224
"Nordic Industrial Design—What, Why, How," exhibition, Oslo Museum of Applied Art, 227
Nordiska Kompaniet (NK), Stockholm, 148, 166, 179; nos. 194, 212
Nordiska Museet, Sweden, 55
Nordström, Patrick, 16, 26, 88; no. 71
Norrköping, Sweden, exhibition at, 17, 78, 83
Norske Billedvæveri, Det (Norwegian Tapestry Weaving School), Oslo, 81; no. 58
Norske Træskjærerkunst, Den/The Norwegian Art of Carving (Dietrichson), 50
Norsk Stålpress, Bergen, Norway, no. 245
Norway, 91, 101; Art Nouveau in, 16, 55, 78, 81; ceramic design in, 68, 73, 99, 105, 121, 172, 213, nos. 17, 19, 44, 46, 75, 167, 226, 230, 274, 277, 278, 281, 314; Danish influence in, 172; design development in, 12, 33, 34, 35, 43–44, 50, 87, 131, 133, 134, 148, 172, 177, 189, 218, 235, 240, 244; English influence in, 81; functionalism in, 105, 119, 121, 122, 124, 172; furniture design in, 20, 78, 81, 105, 119, 166, 172, 177, 182, nos. 8, 63, 64, 67, 68, 99, 111, 153, 208, 223, 264, 267, 342, 343; geography of, 30, 31; glass design in, 99, 101, 122, 124, 172, 177, nos. 81, 83, 174, 175, 238, 288–90; historical background of, 31, 47, 87, 107, 131; map of, 29; metalwork in, 15, 16, 44, 48, 50, 52, 55, 60, 74, 75, 78, 99, 101, 105, 128, 136, 141, 172, 177, nos. 3, 5, 20, 21, 23, 50, 55, 91, 110, 120, 125, 142, 144, 205, 245, 247, 249, 316, 317, 327; national romanticism in, 88, 91, 99; oriental influence in, 68, 213; textile design in, 11, 14, 26, 44, 50, 55, 81, 84, 91, 99, 148, 177, nos. 4, 58, 109, 123, 258; Viking revival in, 50, 52; woodwork in, 101
Norwegian Art of Carving, The/Den Norske Træskjærerkunst (Dietrichson), 50

Norwegian Society of Arts and Crafts and Industrial Design (Landsforbundet Norsk Brukskunst), Norway, 43–44, 91, 218
Norwegian Tapestry Weaving School (Det Norske Billedvæveri), Oslo, 81
Nummi, Yki, 180; no. 216
Nurmesniemi, Antti, 151, 169; nos. 193, 261
"Nursery, The" (Larsson, C.), from Ett hem (A Home), 62
Nutida Svensk Silver (Contemporary Swedish Silver), 172
Nuutajärvi-Notsjö Glass, Nuutajärvi, Finland, 136, 151, 159, 189, nos. 139, 171, 173, 234, 236
Nyhavn, embroidered panel (Winckler), 242; no. 333
Nylund, Gunnar, 26, 105
Nyman, Gunnel, 124, 136; nos. 139, 140
Nyvirki Ltd., Reykjavik, nos. 220, 269

Ohlsson, Olle, 172, 227; no. 305
Öhrström, Edvin, 124
Oktav, glassware pattern (Vallien), 221; no. 293
Old Nordic style, see Viking revival style
Olesen, C., textiles, Denmark, no. 152
Olesen, Magnus, Durup, Denmark, no. 337
Ollers, Edvin, 94, 96; no. 84
Ollestad, Andreas, 60; no. 19
Olsen, Harald, 78, 83, 84; nos. 67, 68
Opa metalworks, Finland, no. 321
Oppo, printed fabric (Fristedt), 201; no. 257
Opsvik, Peter, no. 343
Orfeus, tapestry (Schumacher-Percy), 242; no. 335
ORNAMO (Finnish Association of Designers), 91
Orrefors Glasbruk, Orrefors, Sweden, 19, 20, 92, 94, 96, 99, 101, 115, 124, 136, 157, 166, 192, 231; nos. 80, 85, 86, 113, 141, 169, 170, 187, 239, 311
Ørskov, Torben, and Co., Copenhagen, no. 260
Oscar II, king of Sweden, furniture for (Boberg), 14, 62
Osipow, Anna Maria, 213; no. 275
Oslo Museum of Applied Art, 227
Osslund, Helmer, 58; no. 16
Østern, Bjørn Sigurd, 196; no. 249
"Our National Character" (Stenstadvold), article in Interior News, 133

Paadar's Ice, glass pattern (Wirkkala), 191; no. 237
Pacific Overseas, Inc., San Francisco, 22
Paimio Sanatorium, Finland (Aalto, Alvar), 108, 113
Palmqvist, Sven, 166, 136; nos. 141, 187
Panton, Verner, 207; no. 266
Pariersølv, cutlery pattern (Prytz, J.), 122; no. 125
Paris exhibitions, see "Exposition des Arts Décoratifs et Industriels Modernes," Paris; Exposition Universelle, Paris; Paris Exposition; World's Fair, Paris
Paris Exposition (1937), 108
Paulsson, Gregor, 18, 94, 96
Peach, glass pattern (Johansson), 159; no. 175
Pearl Fishers, The, glass sculpture (Lindstrand), 115; no. 113
Pehrson, Anders, 249; no. 344
Pehrson, Karl Axel, 148
Percy, Arthur, 94, 111, 122; no. 108
Permanente, Den, Denmark, exhibition and sales facility, 105
Persson, Britt-Ingrid (BIP), 166, 227; no. 307
Persson, Sigurd, 166, 172, 222, 231; nos. 188, 301, 310
Persson-Melin, Signe, 166, 184, 232; nos. 228, 313
Perugia, wall hanging (Måås-Fjetterström), 101; no. 90

Petersen, Carl, 99, 102; *nos. 93, 94*
Petersen, Ole Bent, 222; *nos. 297, 298*
Pettersen, Sverre, 94, 99, 122, 124; *nos. 81, 83*
PH Artichoke, lamp (Henningsen), 174; *nos. 202, 203*
PH 5, lamp (Henningsen), 174; *no. 204*
"PH" lamps (Henningsen), 10, 42, 102, 105, 174; *nos. 100, 202–4*
plique à jour technique, 60, 74
Pløen, Erik, 213; *no. 277*
Pony, chair (Alnæs), 177
Pop, glassware (Cyrén), 192; *no. 239*
Porsgrunds Porselænsfabrik, Porsgrunn, Norway, 58, 68, 91, 99, 105, 121, 172, 177; *nos. 17, 46, 75, 167, 230*
Portrait of a Bottle series, bottle from (Brandt), 221; *no. 291*
Poulsen, Louis, & Co., Copenhagen, 102; *nos. 202, 204, 266*
Praktika, earthenware pattern (Kåge), 108, 121; *no. 104*
Prickstone, printed fabric (Ratia), 179; *no. 210*
Primeur, porcelain pattern (Persson-Melin), 232; *no. 313*
Printex, Helsinki, 179
Procopé, Ulla, 157; *no. 168*
Prytz, Grete, *see* Kittelsen, Grete Prytz
Prytz, Jacob, 78, 122, 128; *nos. 55, 125*
Prytz, Torolf, 48; *no. 3*
Pyörre, printed fabric (Eskolin-Nurmesniemi), 198; *no. 252*
Pythagoras, printed fabric (Markelius), 169; *no. 194*

raku (low-fired) technique, 213
Rantanen, Kirsti, 247; *no. 341*
Rasmussen, Jørgen, 247; *no. 340*
Rasmussen, N. M., Copenhagen, *no. 94*
Rasmussen, R. P., 83
Rasmussens Snedkerier, Copenhagen, *no. 122*
Rastad, Rolf, 177
Ratia, Armi, 154, 179; *no. 210*
Ravenna series, glass bowl from (Palmqvist), 136; *no. 141*
Red Chair (Klint, K.), 42, 113
Red Madonna, The, tapestry (Kansanen-Størseth), 120; *no. 123*
Red Square, The, glass sculpture (Hellsten), 189; *no. 233*
Regent, porcelain pattern (Eckhoff), 186; *no. 230*
Reijmyre Glasbruk, Rejmyra, Sweden, 84; *no. 27*
Reistrup, K. Hansen, 68
Relling, Ingmar, 177, 204; *no. 264*
Renaissance revival style, 47, 48, 50
Reumert, Jane, 216; *no. 283*
RFSU Rehab, Stockholm, *no. 346*
Riihimäen Lasi glassworks, Riihimäki, Finland, 136; *nos. 136, 137, 140*
Ripple, glassware pattern (Sarpaneva), 186; *no. 229*
Rococo revival style, 47, 88
Rohde, Johan, 74, 87, 88, 99; *no. 70*
Romantica, glass pattern (Wirkkala), 161; *no. 178*
Rörstrand ceramics, Lidköping, Sweden, 11, 16, 34, 57, 68, 71, 73, 94, 152, 166, 232; *nos. 11–13, 15, 77, 163, 313*
Rosen, Anton, 91
Rosenberg, Walle, 78; *no. 53*
Rosenholm, cutlery pattern (Ängman), 120; *no. 124*
Rosenlew & Co., Porin Konepaja, Finland, *no. 244*
Royal Copenhagen Porcelain Manufactory Ltd., Denmark, 16, 19, 43, 58, 67, 73, 88, 94, 102, 161, 184; *nos. 18, 32, 37, 43, 45, 71, 72, 76, 133, 225, 276*
Royal Hotel, Copenhagen, furniture for (Jacob-

sen, A.), 180
Runa, *see* Gudjonsdottir, Sigrun
Ruskin, John, 32
Russia, 47, 131
Ryggen, Hannah, 26, 111, 177, 192; *no. 109*
ryijy (rya) technique, 44, 55, 65, 102, 111, 127, 172, 196, 238

Saarinen, Eliel, 11, 52, 58, 65, 73, 101; *no. 29*
Sadolin, Ebbe, 121
Safaristol, chair (Klint, K.), 116, 120; *no. 122*
Salmenhaara, Kyllikki, 164; *no. 184*
Salto, Axel, 16, 102, 121, 122, 133; *no. 133*
Sammenhæng I, tapestry (Malinowski, R.), 221; *no. 296*
Sampe, Astrid, 127, 148, 166, 179; *no. 212*
Samvirkende Fagforeninger, De, Norway, *no. 68*
Sandnes, Eystein, 157, 172; *no. 167*
Sandvik Glasbruk, Hofmanstorp, Sweden, 94, 96, 99; *no. 82*
Sarpaneva, Timo, 22, 151, 186, 194, 235; *nos. 229, 232, 244, 321*
Savoy vase (Aalto, Alvar), 107
Saxbo, Copenhagen, 43, 105, 152; *no. 162*
Scandinavian design: aesthetics of, 13, 17–18, 22, 23, 25–26, 45, 84; architecture, 108, 142; centers of, 26–27; ceramics, 11, 12, 19, 21, 119, 121, 122, 148, 161, 189, 216, 249; characteristics of, 12, 13–14, 39, 142; classicism and, 38; climatic influence on, 31–32, 37; development of, 15, 32–35, 37–45, 47, 87–88, 107–8, 111, 113, 134, 141–42, 148, 151, 184, 189, 192, 209–10, 218, 224, 227, 235, 240, 244, 249; economic influence on, 34, 38–39, 209; English influence on, 30, 32, 33, 34, 58, 78, 81; exhibitions of, 11–23, 25, 26, 32, 33, 34, 37, 40, 43, 65, 67, 78, 91, 94, 101, 108, 111, 113, 133, 134, 141, 154, 166, 224, 227, 240; folk tradition and, 14, 15, 48, 50, 52, 55, 65, 73, 74, 88, 92, 108, 119, 142, 184; functionalism and, 19, 20, 21, 28, 33, 38, 40, 102, 105, 108, 111, 113, 116, 119, 121, 122, 124, 127–28, 141, 142, 146, 148, 154, 171, 172, 174, 177, 184; furniture, 11, 12, 19, 21, 38, 83, 102, 108, 111, 113, 119, 124, 148; geographic influence on, 26, 28, 30–31, 37; German influence on, 48, 73, 84–85, 105, 122; glass, 12, 18, 19, 21, 38, 122, 161, 244; industrialization and, 28, 34, 38–39, 40, 41, 84–85, 87, 94, 107, 141, 172; materials, importance of, 32, 38, 39, 41, 44, 81, 102, 108, 113, 116, 119, 128, 131, 144, 148, 151, 154, 161, 171, 184; metalwork, 11, 18, 21, 120; motifs of, 50, 62, 67, 68, 81, 128, 148; neoclassicism and, 15, 18, 19; organizations of, 17, 43–44, 91, 94, 134, 141, 172, 210, 218; oriental influence on, 16, 58, 65, 67, 68, 88, 133, 162, 169, 213, 216; social responsibility and, 18, 27, 28, 33, 40, 41, 45, 58, 84, 88, 94, 96, 107, 119, 161, 192, 210, 218, 227, 235, 238, 251; techniques, 52, 60, 67, 74, 81, 88, 96, 102, 111, 133, 166, 213, 227, 231, 238; textiles, 11, 12, 19, 21, 38, 122, 127, 148, 221, 247, 249; urbanization and, 17, 107, 111, 141, 172; *see also* Denmark; Finland; Iceland; Norway; Sweden
"Scandinavian Design Cavalcades," annual exhibitions, 40, 141
Scharff, Allan, 222; *no. 300*
Schauman, Wilhelm, furniture, Jyväskylä, Finland, *no. 157*
Schneider, Andreas, 68, 73; *no. 44*
Schneider workshop, Christiania (Oslo), *no. 44*
School of Applied Art, Helsinki, 136
Schreuder & Olsson, Stockholm, *no. 49*
Schumacher-Percy, Ulla, 242; *no. 335*
Scott, Baillie, 58
Seenat Group Pottery, 216; *no. 286*
Servus, cutlery pattern, stainless steel (Persson,

S.), 166; *no. 188*
Sèvres porcelain factory, France, 73
Shadows in the Snow, rug (Ilvessalo), 196; *no. 250*
Shand, Morton, 19, 96
Shells, tapestry (Nilsson, B.), 134, 146; *no. 150*
Shells IV, weaving (Jung, D.), 180; *no. 213*
Siena, printed fabric (Aalto, Alvar), 144; *no. 148*
Siesta, chair and footstool (Relling), 204; *no. 264*
Sigurdhsson, Amundi, Ltd., Reykjavik, Iceland, *no. 263*
Siimes, Aune, 164; *no. 183*
Silkkikuikka, printed fabric (Isola), 203; *no. 259*
Simberg-Ehrström, Uhra-Beata, 172; *no. 201*
Sinivalko, earthenware pattern (Ekholm), 108, 121; *no. 105*
Skansen Museum, Stockholm, 58
Skogster-Lehtinen, Greta, 127, 128, 131, 144; *nos. 129, 149*
Skönhet för alla/Beauty for All (Key, E.), 58
Skønvirke, Danish design periodical, 65, 91
Skrufs Glassworks, Skruf, Sweden, *no. 233*
Slang, Gerd, 177, 192; *no. 238*
Slott-Møller, Harald, 85; *no. 69*
Snake, The, tapestry (Sveinsdottir), 172; *no. 200*
Snedkerlauget furniture, Copenhagen, 26, 43
Snødroppe, ceramic pattern (Wennerberg), 67; *no. 36*
Society of Applied Art and Industrial Design (Landsforeningen Dansk Brugskunst og Design), Denmark, 91, 210, 218
Society of Applied Arts (Foreningen Brukskunst), Norway, 91
Soft Forms, stoneware table service (Kåge), 134
Soinne et Kni, Helsinki, *no. 222*
Sønnico Fabrikker, Oslo, *no. 208*
Sørensen, Johnny, 245; *no. 337*
Sørensen, Oskar, 111, 128, 177; *no. 110*
Sotavalta, Impi, 111; *no. 107*
Sparre, Louis, 52, 71, 73, 81, 101; *no. 61*
Spisa Ribb, stoneware dishes (Lindberg), 154; *no. 165*
Split Peas, embroidered cushion cover (Bindesbøll, T.), 78; *no. 57*
Spring in the Air, stoneware wall relief (Gudhnadottir), 214; *no. 280*
S 70-3, stool (Lindau and Lindekrantz), 203; *no. 262*
Stæhr-Nielsen, Eva, 133, 152; *no. 162*
Stålhane, Carl-Harry, 152, 166; *no. 163*
Stelton, Gentofte, Denmark, *nos. 248, 331*
Stenstadvold, Håkon, 133
Stephensen, Magnus, 133, 161, 169; *no. 190*
Still Life, porcelain pattern (Hald), 92; *no. 77*
Still-McKinney, Nanny, 151
Stockholm Exhibition (1897), 58, 67; (1899), 78; (1909), 67, 91; (1930), 19–20, 26, 33, 40, 105, 108, 111, 113, 119, 121, 124, 169
Stockmann/Keravan Puusepantehdas, Kerava, Finland, *no. 129*
Stockmann/Orno, Kerava, Finland, *no. 216*
Stolefabrik, Fredericia, Denmark, *no. 218*
Strandstraede Keramik, Copenhagen, 216; *nos. 283, 284*
Studio, The, English periodical, 11, 14, 55
Sture, Alf, 119, 172, 177; *no. 153*
Suomen Käsityön Ystävät (Friends of Finnish Handicraft), Finland, 52, 65, 127; *nos. 9, 30, 107, 201*
Supertube, lighting system (Pehrson, A.), 249; *no. 344*
Surrea, ceramic series (Kåge), 133, 134; *no. 132*
Suur Merijoki, hall at (Gesellius, Lindgren, Saarinen), 52
Suvanto, Liisa, 151, 154
Sveinsdottir, Juliana, 21, 172; *no. 200*
Svenska Möbelfabrikerna, Bodafors, Sweden, *no. 151*
Svenska Slöjdföreningen (Swedish Society of

Industrial Design), Stockholm, 17, 91, 94, 218
Svensk Konstslöjdsutställning Selma Giöbel, Sweden, 81; *no. 62*
Svensk Tenn, Stockholm, *no. 130*
Svensson, Inez, 221; *no. 295*
Sverige (Sweden), tapestry (Hernmark), 196; *no. 251*
Swan, chair (Jacobsen, A.), 180
Sweden, 26, 28; architecture in, 48, 62; Arts and Crafts movement in, 58; ceramic design in, 11, 16, 17, 19, 20, 26, 34, 40, 41, 48, 62, 67, 68, 73, 92, 94, 96, 121, 122, 134, 148, 162, 166, *nos. 2, 11–13, 15, 16, 33–36, 73, 74, 77, 102–4, 108, 132, 134, 135, 145, 161, 163–65, 180, 227, 228, 270, 272, 282, 306, 307, 313;* Danish influence in, 166; design development in, 12, 27, 33, 34, 35, 37–38, 39–41, 43, 48, 55, 58, 62, 67, 87, 91, 94, 96, 101, 133–34, 148, 161, 172, 189, 218, 235; English influence in, 33, 58, 78; functionalism in, 33, 40, 105, 119, 121, 124, 134; furniture design in, 17–19, 21, 26, 34, 40, 48, 62, 78, 81, 94, 96, 119, 134, 166, *nos. 59, 60, 66, 95, 96, 127, 151, 262, 268, 344–46;* geography of, 31; glass design in, 19, 20, 34, 40, 41, 42, 62, 84, 94, 96, 99, 101, 124, 162, 166, *nos. 10, 24, 27, 78–80, 82, 84–86, 113, 114, 141, 169, 170, 176, 177, 187, 233, 235, 239, 246, 270, 291, 293, 310, 311, 330;* historical background of, 31, 47, 87, 107, 131, 142; Jugend style in, 16, 17, 55, 58, 62, 67, 68, 74, 78, 81; map of, 29; metalwork in, 41, 62, 128, 166, 172, 194, *nos. 48, 49, 87, 117, 118, 124, 147, 188, 242, 243, 246, 301, 302, 305;* national romanticism in, 87, 88; oriental influence in, 16, 68, 88, 162; textile design in, 17, 26, 34, 39, 40, 41, 55, 62, 67, 81, 91, 101, 127–28, 134, 142, 148, 166, 192, 221, *nos. 56, 62, 90, 130, 146, 150, 194, 212, 251, 253, 257, 295, 328, 335;* Viennese influence in, 83; Viking revival in, 48
Sweden (Sverige), tapestry (Hernmarck), 196; *no. 251*
"Swedish Contemporary Decorative Arts," exhibition, Metropolitan Museum of Art, New York, 19
Swedish Handicraft Society (Föreningen Svensk Hemslöjd), 55, 58
Swedish Society of Crafts and Design (Föreningen Svensk Form), Stockholm, 40, 91
Swedish Society of Industrial Design (Svenska Slöjdföreningen), Stockholm, 17, 91, 94, 218

Tachism, 189
Tampella textiles, Tampere, Finland, *no. 214*
Tanier, George, Inc., New York, 21
Tapiovaara, Ilmari, 23, 151; *no. 157*
10-Gruppen, Stockholm, 221; *no. 295*
Terma, stoneware cooking pan (Lindberg), 154; *no. 165*
Textile design, *see under* Denmark; Finland; Iceland; Norway; Scandinavian design; Sweden
Thordardottir, Thorbjörg, 245; *no. 336*
Thorgrimsson, Gestur, 227; *no. 308*
Thorup, Torsten, 245; *no. 338*
Three Suitors, The, tapestry (Munthe, G.), 50; *no. 4*
Thygesen, Rud, 245; *no. 337*
Tivoli Gardens, Copenhagen, 42
Toikka, Oiva, 151, 189; *no. 234*
Tostrup, J., 74
Tostrup, J., Oslo, 50, 105; *nos. 3, 55, 110, 125, 144, 205*
Triad, rug (Lavonen), 238; *no. 326*
Triennale exhibitions, Milan, 44, 164; (1951), 20–21, 22, 133, 134, 151, 172, 182; (1954), 134, 141, 142, 159, 171, 172, 174, 179, 186; (1957), 171, 177, 180, 186; (1960), 12, 157, 164, 171, 186, 194; (1973), 227
Trollslända (Dragonfly), printed fabric (Jobs), 142; *no. 146*
Tulip series, glasses from (Landberg), 6, 157; *no. 169*
Tynell, Helena, 136; *no. 137*

United States, 210, 244

Vackrare vardagsvara/More Beautiful Things for Everyday Use (Paulsson), 18, 94, 96
Vallgren, Carl Wilhelm, 77, 78; *no. 54*
Vallien, Bertil, 221, 238; *nos. 293, 330*
Vangsgaard, Erik Ingomar, 235; *no. 319*
Vasegaard, Gertrud, 43, 133, 161, 169, 210, 216; *nos. 189, 271*
Vasegaard, Myre, 216; *no. 287*
Vatne Lenestolfabrikk, Norway, *no. 267*
Vegetable Tree, printed fabric (Frank), 131, 134; *no. 130*
Velde, Henri van de, 58, 65, 73
Vestlandske Mobelfabrikk, Ørsta, Norway, *no. 264*
Vienna, Austria, 58, 62, 65, 84
Vigeland, Emmanuel, 101
Vigeland, Gustav, 99, 101
Vigeland, Tone, 177, 232; *nos. 316, 317*

Viking revival style, 15, 48, 50, 52, 55
Village (Landsbyen), printed fabric (Gudme-Leth), 119; *no. 119*
Villa Maire, Finland, interiors for (Aalto, Alvar), 116, 119
Vivero, Helsinki, *no. 339*
Vodder, Nils, furniture, Allerød, Denmark, *no. 152*
Vuokko, Helsinki, 44; *nos. 252, 261*
Vuorelma, Helmi, *no. 341*

Wäfveri, Borås, *nos. 253, 257*
Wagner, Otto, 58, 65
Wallander, Alf, 16, 17, 57, 58, 68, 73, 74, 81, 84, 94; *nos. 11, 12, 15, 49, 62*
Wanscher, Ole, 133, 154, 181; *no. 219*
Wärff, Ann, 191; *no. 235*
Wärff, Göran, 191; *no. 235*
Wärtsilä, Helsinki, *nos. 193, 196*
Weaving 1, tapestry (Buadottir), 201; *no. 256*
Weckström, Björn, 151, 222; *no. 299*
Weekend, earthenware pattern (Kåge), 108
Wegner, Hans, 21, 43, 133, 148, 154; *nos. 155, 156*
Weiss, Ivan, 213; *no. 276*
Wennerberg, Gunnar, 16, 17, 57, 62, 67, 68, 73, 84, 94; *nos. 10, 24, 33–36*
Werenskiold, Dagfin, 101
Westman, Carl, 78, 81; *no. 60*
Wettergren, Erik, 94
Widman, Dag, 134
Wiherheimo, Yrjö, 36, 247; *no. 339*
Wiinblad, Bjørn, 152; *no. 160*
Willumsen, Jens Ferdinand, 47, 68, 74; *no. 1*
Winckler, Ida, 242; *no. 333*
Windy Way, printed fabric (Sampe), 179; *no. 212*
Wirkkala, Tapio, 21, 133, 141, 148, 151, 161, 162, 171, 182, 191, 231; *nos. 143, 178, 179, 199, 222, 237, 312*
"Wohnung, Die," exhibition, Stuttgart, 20
Wold-Torne, Oluf, 99
Woodland Scene, tapestry (Krogh), *no. 56*
World Craft Council, 244
World's Fair, New York (1939), 21, 108, 169
World's Fair, Paris (1938), 122

Y 61, stool (Aalto, Alvar), 182; *no. 221*

Z, folding chair (Magnussen), 203; *no. 260*

PHOTO CREDITS

Unless otherwise indicated, references are to caption numbers.

Arabia Museum, Helsinki: 28, 131, 240. *Art News,* vol. 53, no. 1 (March, 1954), page 31: page 22. Atelje o Foto, Åhus, Sweden, C. Bernhardsson: 344; page 249. *Ateneum Internationell, illustrered tidskrift för literatur kunst och spörsmål af allmänt intresse,* Treaje årgången 1900, Helsingfors, 1900: page 65. Svend Bessing Fotografi ApS, Denmark: 202, 204. Bing & Grøndahl Museum, Copenhagen: 14, 22, 189; Ole Woldbye: 1. Bengt Carlen, Stockholm: 305. E. Kold Christensen A/S, Copenhagen: 265. Poul Christiansen, Copenhagen: 154. The Cleveland Museum of Art, Cleveland, Ohio: 54. Cooper-Hewitt Museum, New York, Tom Rose: 176, 177, 312; Scott Hyde: 213, 214. Danish Design Council, Fotograf Aasmul: 341. Det Danske Kunstindustrimuseum, Copenhagen: 126, 155, 162, 190, 207, 219, page 42; Ole Woldbye: 6, 7, 25, 26, 31, 38, 51, 57, 65, 69, 70, 89, 94, 112, 116, 119, 152, 160, 172, 185, 206, 215, 218, 260, 271, 283, 284, 296, 297, 298, 300, 309, 315, 333. D. James Dee, New York: 11, 12, 13, 15. Fåborg Museum, Denmark: 93. Fotograferne Lotzbeck & Graae, Copenhagen: 92. Gustavsberg Museum/AB Gustavsberg, Sweden: 33, 34, 35, 36, 103, 132, 227, 272, 345; Enzo Poire: 102, 104, 135. Cabinetmaker Johannes Hansen, Architect Hans J. Wegner: 156. Hans Hansens Sølvsmedie A/S, Copenhagen: 332. Höganäs Museum, Sweden: 16. Iittala Museum/Iittala Lasitehdas, Iittala: 138, 143, 178 (left), 179, 229, 237. Georg Jensen Sølvsmedie A/S, Copenhagen: 52, 88, 121, 181, 186, 192, 195, 254; page 98 (below). Martti Kapanen, Finland: 128 (left), 221. Kooperativa Förbundet Fotoatelje, Stockholm: 188. Kunstakademiets Bibliotek, Copenhagen: 98. Nationalmuseum, Stockholm: pages 17, 26, 33, 39, 52, 62; Sven Nilsson and Alexis Daflos: frontispiece, 10, 24, 48, 49, 58, 59, 62, 72, 73, 74, 77, 82, 84, 90, 95, 108, 113, 114, 118, 124, 127, 134, 145, 146, 147, 150, 151, 164, 165, 180, 194, 228, 233, 235, 242, 243, 251, 253, 257, 282, 293, 301, 306, 307, 310, 328, 335. The Newark Museum, Newark, New Jersey, Armen: 85, 140. Nordenfjeldske Kunstindustrimuseum, Trondheim: 44, 46, 64, 123, 174, 175, 223, 238, 241, 245, 249, 277, 278, 289, 317. Nordiska Museet, Stockholm: 2, 60, 66, 96; pages 14, 18, 48 (below). Norsk Folkemuseum, Oslo, A. Lindahl: page 50. *L'Oeil:*

page 12. Lennart Olsen, Sweden: 212. Orrefors Glasbruk Museum/AB Orrefors Glasbruk, Sweden: 78, 79; Björn Lindberg: 141, 169, 170, 187, 239, 311; page 6. Oslo Kunstindustrimuseet: 19, 99, 110, 153, 208, 264 (above), 316, 343. Max Petrelius, Finland: 252 (below). PF-Studio, Helsinki: 97, 128 (right), 198, 224, 261; page 23. Louis Poulsen & Co., A/S, Copenhagen: 100, 203, 266. Prins Eugens Waldemarsudde, Stockholm: 27. Private Collections: 5, 23, 29, 106, 111, 122, 163, 182, 200, 201, 220, 246, 256, 263, 269, 270, 279, 280, 295, 299, 303, 304, 308, 318, 319, 320, 322, 323, 324, 325, 326, 334, 336, 346; page 10. *Progressive Architecture,* vol. 37, no. 4 (April, 1956): Swedish National Travel Office, 40 (above); Danish National Travel Office, 40 (below); Finnish Society of Arts and Crafts and Design, 41 (above); Norwegian Travel Office, 41 (below). Rabén, Hans, *Det Moderna Hemmet,* Stockholm, 1937: 19, 20 (above and below), 21 (below). Röhsska Konstslöjdmuseet, Göteborg, Sweden: 39, 56, 87, 117, 161, 292, 302. Rörstrand AB, Lidköping: 313. Royal Copenhagen Porcelain Manufactory Ltd.: 276; Royal Copenhagen Porcelain Museum: 37; Strüwing Reklamefoto: 225; Ole Woldbye: 18, 32, 43, 45, 71, 76, 133. Saksisarja: 255. Rolf Salomonsson AB/Fotograf, Sweden: 262, 268. SFF/Europhot, Teddy Aarni, Eskilstuna, Sweden: 291. Sixten Sandell, Göteborg, Sweden: 330. Smålands Museum, Växjö, Owe Hedman: 80, 86. Statens Kunstfond, Copenhagen: 287. Stelton A/S, Gentofte, Denmark: 248, 331. Strüwing Reklamefoto, Denmark: 191, 209, 217, 338. AB Svensk Tenn, Stockholm: 130. *Swedish Arts and Crafts: Swedish Modern— A Movement Towards Sanity in Design,* published by the Royal Swedish Commission, New York World's Fair, 1939, page 69: page 21 (above). Taideteollisuusmuseo, Helsinki: 9, 101, 107, 178 (right), 183, 193, 196, 259, 329; page 116; Jan Alanco: 166; Aimo Hyvärinen: 30, 40, 41, 42, 53, 61, 136, 137, 139, 148, 149, 157, 159, 168, 171, 173, 184, 197, 199, 210, 211, 216, 222, 231, 232, 234, 236, 244, 250, 252 (above), 273, 285, 286, 321, 340; Kari Parviainen: 105. Teigens Fotoatelier A/S, Oslo: 3, 17, 20, 21, 50, 63, 67, 68, 75, 81, 83, 91, 109, 120, 142, 226, 281, 288, 314, 327, 342; page 48 (above). Rauno Träskelin, Helsinki: 115, 129, 275, 294. Seppo Hilpo Valokuvaaja Fotograf, Helsinki: 339. Vestlandske Kunstindustrimuseum, Bergen: 4, 8, 55, 125, 144, 167, 205, 230, 247, 258, 267, 274, 290. ·